To our friend, Tom, who turned our dream dining room into a reality!!

Jim and Millie
1968

The American Heritage History of Colonial Antiques

The American Heritage History of Colonial Antiques

By the Editors of
AMERICAN HERITAGE
The Magazine of History

Author and Editor in Charge
Marshall B. Davidson

Published by
American Heritage Publishing Co., Inc.

Book Trade Distribution by
Simon and Schuster, Inc.

Staff for this Book

EDITOR
Marshall B. Davidson

ART DIRECTOR
Barbara Asch

ASSOCIATE EDITOR
Mary B. Durant

COPY EDITOR
Beverley Hilowitz

PICTURE EDITOR
Robert Bishop

ASSISTANT EDITOR
Audrey N. Catuzzi

ASSISTANT COPY EDITOR
Carol Kerr

ASSISTANT PICTURE EDITOR
Deborah Aronsohn

ART ASSISTANTS
Ruth Ohlhausen
Marlene Rothkin

EDITORIAL ASSISTANT
Anne Palmbaum

 Printed In The United States of America. Library of Congress Catalog Card Number: 67–23439.

Table of Contents

Preface	6
Our Medieval Heritage The Puritan Century (1607–1685)	8
Fashions from Abroad The William and Mary Style (1685–1720)	60
The Triumph of the Curve The Queen Anne Style (1720–1750)	120
Patterns of Elegance The Chippendale Period (1750–1785)	182
The Colonial House at Work Functioning Forms in the Home	260
From the Rhine to the Susquehanna The Pennsylvania Germans	298
Glossary of Terms	353
Style Charts	364
Acknowledgments and Index	372

Preface

Americans were slow to realize the interest and the importance of their colonial heritage. For about a century following the Declaration of Independence the new nation was concerned with crucial and absorbing developments; developments that led the people of the country to think of the present and to look toward the future rather than to reflect upon the past. First, there were the immediate and critical problems involved in founding a strong, stable republic in a warring world. More than a generation passed before those problems seemed finally settled with the conclusion of the War of 1812 (sometimes called our "second war of independence"). Then came the social and political turbulence attending the advent of Jacksonian democracy, the headlong surge of people to the West, and the tragic conflict of interests and feelings that resulted in the agony and the carnage of the Civil War.

As the century advanced Americans remained convinced that they were creating a new order and a model for the world, and that they were following a "manifest destiny" prepared for them by Providence. Their longing was not so much for what had once been as for what was going to be. The vast wilderness, which was the nation's birthright, could only be possessed by those who saw it, not as it was and had been for countless millenniums, but as it would be some day in the future. Indeed, for many of the scores of thousands who spread out over that wilderness during the nineteenth century, to discard the past altogether was to affirm their faith in an illimitable tomorrow.

In 1876 the nation paused to celebrate the first century of its independence, and to look back with pride and wonder on all that had been achieved in those hundred years. Great numbers of Americans who learned to sing of this "Land where our fathers died! Land of the Pilgrims' pride," had come to this country in cramped immigrant ships generations after the *Mayflower*, and their own fathers had died in places far from Bunker Hill or Saratoga. But the typical newcomer was eager to identify himself with the American experience and to share the nation's pride in its accomplishments.

Out of the thought given to the Centennial celebration emerged a new and suddenly poignant longing to recover an image of the colonial past that had been so long neglected. "As the one hundredth anniversary of our national independence draws near," reported *Harper's New Monthly Magazine* in 1874, "the thoughts of our people are eagerly turned...to a more familiar observation of the men and women who were actors in that great event...to take note of their appearance, manners, and customs; to cross their thresholds and see...what entered into their domestic appointments and belongings." To illustrate that point the article reproduced a variety of colonial furniture and other "domestic appointments." Two years later the exhibits at the Philadelphia Centennial Exposition included a "New England Kitchen of 1776," with beamed ceiling, leaded casement windows, a great fireplace, and a complement of colonial furnishings, all attended by a group of ladies dressed in colonial costume. The display was a great popular success.

The fresh interest in early American antiques generated by such articles and demonstrations developed into a craze in the years that followed. "Early American" became a fashionable style in architecture as well as in furnishings. Public interest in the antiques themselves was, and long remained, largely sentimental —and largely uninformed. As it referred to furniture, the word "colonial" was loosely applied to whatever was old and picturesque and presumably of American origin. Historians and art critics paid little heed to such matters; it was left for private collectors and antiquarians to explore fields that professional scholars considered too remote or too humble to bother with. When a broad cross section of the findings of those early explorers was presented in 1924, with the opening of the American Wing of the Metropolitan Museum of Art, nothing in the history books or books on art had prepared either the press or the general public for what they saw there. For those whose image of the colonial world was formed by the somber tales of Nathaniel Hawthorne and the gloomy pictures drawn from them by popular illustrators, the grace, sophistication, and colorful nature of the material on display came as a startling revelation.

The astonishment with which the newspaper and magazine reporters and critics greeted that occasion seems naïve today. "American Art Really Exists," one paper proclaimed in its headline; here, it continued, was the refutation of critics of American culture. Why, exclaimed *The New York World*, casting aside the rules of grammar in its enthusiasm, "those ancestors of ours had taste equally if not surpassing ours!" And, striking a quieter note, *The New York Times* asked, for essential knowledge of the past "where can we look with more assurance of true guidance than to the homes of men?" Today, less than fifty years later, most of us are keenly aware that the artifacts fashioned and used by our ancestors represent history in its most intimate and expressive form, and we are satisfied that those early forefathers were endowed with a full measure of good taste. And we pay them the tribute of faithfully reproducing those colonial artifacts, finding that in their design and structure they not only delight the eye but also satisfy the needs of comfort and convenience in our own day.

We may perhaps find in the products of colonial craftsmanship meaning and beauty that our forefathers were not aware of. But unless we give these objects understanding attention, we may also fail to see much of interest that was commonplace to past generations. To see these artifacts, so far as we are able, as the craftsman and their patrons saw them when they were made would acquaint us with ideas that are a neglected part of our heritage. One of the major purposes of this book is to place the eight hundred or more objects illustrated on the following pages in historical and social context. A large proportion of these pieces represent thoroughly skilled craftsmanship and a sensitive understanding of design. Even the least pretentious examples combine the utilitarian and the decorative in a way that reflects a long tradition of sound workmanship and an intimate knowledge of the materials that were used.

The commonly accepted terms for the styles that succeeded one another during the colonial period have been kept as convenient guides that give the stranger to the past his bearings, and that aid the collector in his studies, although to the contemporaries of this art such terms would have been almost meaningless. The dates ascribed to the successive periods are also given as convenient references, although they are more or less arbitrary. Styles have never started or stopped at given dates; they form and fade as the years drift by, and often coexist over a long period of time.

In the end, we have included here a comprehensive and fair sampling of the finest and the most typical of colonial antiques in virtually all mediums and forms. They are presented in a manner that suggests their relation to one another as well as to the way of life they served. The selection was made from the collections of museums, individuals, and dealers, all of whom have co-operated in this undertaking with a generous interest in its success. Their help is specifically and gratefully acknowledged on pages 372 to 375.

M.B.D.

Our Medieval Heritage

The Puritan Century (1607-1685)

Colonists to new lands always try to re-create the world they leave behind them—especially those aspects of it that they best remember and most highly value. So it was with the Englishmen who settled along the Atlantic seaboard of America in the seventeenth century. Whatever their motives in crossing the ocean, however different their opinions and beliefs from those that prevailed in England, they hoped in good time to reproduce in the New World the familiar and cherished amenities of life as they had known them at home.

In the face of a strange and hostile—or indifferent—wilderness this was not the work of a season. Indeed, at the beginnings of most of the colonies, it seemed an all but hopeless prospect. "Wanting houses and other comforts," half the members of the Plymouth community died during the first bitter winter. A few years later, at the Massachusetts Bay colony, the earliest arrivals were forced to "burrow themselves in the Earth for their first shelter under some Hill-side, casting the Earth aloft upon Timber," and for comfort to sing psalms, pray, and praise the Lord beside the smoky fires of such "poore Wigwames." Even that most steadfast Puritan John Winthrop revealed in his diary more than a decade after the founding of the colony that, had he foreseen the circumstances of those years, he would never have left England. At Jamestown, New Netherland, and other colonies the first settlers fared little better. It was at the start a rough life that called for a great deal of fortitude and a good measure of luck. As Governor William Bradford sarcastically observed of the faint of heart, "They are too delicate and unfitte to begine new plantations and collonies that cannot enduer the biting of a muskeeto. . . ."

The earliest arrivals in the New World brought little enough with them. All the treasured heirlooms that allegedly came over on the *Mayflower* would have had to hang from the yardarms to be accommodated on that epic voyage. Nevertheless, a number of even the first generation of settlers who survived at Plymouth and other early outposts left adequate if not abundant estates—including chests, chairs, tables, and the like—upon their death. Some of these furnishings were no doubt imported, although letters advising prospective emigrants what "conveniences" they should bring to the New World listed tools, bedding, glass for windows, and metal housewares, with little mention of furniture. "Before you come," wrote the Reverend Francis Higginson, first minister at Salem, "be careful to be strongly instructed what things are fittest to bring with you for your more comfortable passage at sea, as also for your husbandry occasions when you come to the land. For when you are once parted with England you shall meete neither markets nor fayres to buy what you want. Therefore be sure to furnish

Opposite: An arrangement of furnishings, largely 17th century; for descriptions see p. 373

Pewter platter and iron pot brought to Plymouth colony by Miles Standish

An adjustable, hanging candleholder

yourselves with things fittest to be had before you come: as meale for bread, malt for drinke, woolen and linnen cloath, and leather for shoes, and all manner of carpenters tools, and a great deale of iron and steele to make nails, and locks for houses, and furniture for ploughs and carts, and glasse for windows, and many other things which were better for you to think of there than to want them here." That same year, in 1630, John Winthrop asked his wife to bring over pewter, leather bottles, drinking horns, soap, and axes, among other supplies.

Higginson also advised prospective colonists to bring with them complete armor, with a "long piece," a sword bandoleer, and ammunition. For weapons and armor were considered essential equipment for able-bodied emigrants. When John Smith left Jamestown in 1609, he noted that there were more helmets and cuirasses, or breastplates, in the colony than there were men; and sixteen years later it was reported that Virginians could muster 342 "complete armors" and 260 "coats of mail and head pieces" among a lot of other military gear. Settlers of both the Plymouth and the Massachusetts Bay colonies brought plate armor with them. Some was actually manufactured in Hartford, Connecticut, but as the century waned all such heavy protection was found to be impractical in wilderness warfare against Indian adversaries who fought like savage guerrillas rather than European soldiers.

What was sorely needed in Massachusetts, wrote William Wood in 1634, were men skilled in the crafts—"an ingenious Carpenter, a cunning Joyner, a handie Cooper, such a one as can make strong ware for the use of the countrie." During this decade, roughly between 1630 and 1640 and known as the period of the Great Migration, about sixty thousand discontented Englishmen left their homes for a new life overseas. A ballad "Summons to New England" was sung on the streets of English towns and a "great giddiness" to emigrate swept the land. Approximately one third of this mass of people sailed for New England and ended up in Massachusetts, Rhode Island, and Connecticut. Among them, obviously, were men skilled in a variety of crafts, for remarkably soon after the first strains of settlement had eased, they were raising permanent structures and fashioning furniture, silverware, and other household equipment that in quality and character differed little from English models. The workmanship may have been modest in pretension, but it was by no means crude—in those examples of it, at least, which have survived.

If those settlers transported little paraphernalia to the "howling Desart" that received them, they did bring habits and customs that were deeply rooted in past experience. Most of them came from small towns and rural villages that lingered in the fading glow of the Middle Ages, districts that were barely touched by the transforming influence of the Renaissance. The latter introduced

Goldsmiths at work in the 17th century

not only new styles in architecture and all the other arts but also new ideas about the organization of life, more deliberate efforts to achieve convenience and comfort, privacy and efficiency in the home than had ever been considered in medieval times. These filtered down the social scale only slowly from the courtly circles where they were first adopted.

It is hard to realize, for instance, that when Elder William Brewster of the Plymouth Plantation was a lad in England, even such elementary devices as chimneys, solid and permanent bedsteads, glass windows, wooden floors, and pewter tableware (instead of wood, leather, and horn) were relatively novel features of the ordinary English home. Chairs were not widely used. As in the Middle Ages they were generally reserved for persons of importance, the others sat on stools or benches. At a time when tables often consisted of removable boards set upon trestles, he who occupied the principal seat had that distinction we recall in the phrase "chairman of the board." Coffee and tea and all the pots, kettles, bowls, spoons, and other gear that were later developed to serve and drink them with were unheard of. Even forks were unknown. When they were introduced from Italy in the first half of the seventeenth century, they were considered by some to be foppish innovations, unnecessary for people who washed their hands before eating. Ben Jonson thought their use was a laudable new custom, since it spared the napkins. As one of the niceties of life he hoped to enjoy in his new home, Governor Winthrop brought over one fork in its case when he came to America in 1630; but evidence suggests that in the years to come the early generations of Harvard students still ate their meat with their fingers, or at best with knives, from wooden trenchers, then cleaned their hands by rinsing them with rose water.

It was such a domestic world, in transition from the simple arrangements of ages-old tradition to the more specialized accommodations of modern life, that was first re-created in the American colonies. The world newly founded was for a while and in some ways less new than the one that had been quitted. Cut off from immediate and frequent contact with developments abroad, and eager to preserve a familiar way of life, the early colonists perpetuated styles and customs long after they had been damned as unfashionable in the courts and capitals of Europe. As late as 1689 one English merchant observed that New Englanders, at least, were "a very home-bred people," and in addition they were "exceeding wedded to their own way."

The most picturesque reminder of that archaic strain in colonial life is in Virginia rather than New England. St. Luke's Church, built in Isle of Wight County, in 1632, twenty-five years after the founding of Jamestown, with its pointed-arch windows and brick tracery, its buttressed walls, and its steeply

Cast-iron 17th-century fireback similar to those used in the Dutch colonies

A halberd discovered at Plymouth

A "chairman" leading family worship in 1563

pitched roof, is a small, remote, but direct descendant of the great Gothic cathedrals of England. Although it was built almost fifty years later, in 1681, the First Parish Church of Hingham, Massachusetts, remains another example—more impressive in its scale—of the survival of late Gothic techniques and styles in the colonies. Here, as in the great manorial halls of old England, the huge beams, rafters, and trusses of the interior were left exposed in a handsome, functional arrangement of angles and curves rising in a lofty pointed arch. Actually, these trusses span a hall, forty-five feet across, which is wider than the nave of any English Gothic cathedral. Because of the resemblance of this structural woodwork to an inverted ship's hull, the church is commonly known as the "Old Ship" meetinghouse—which brings to mind, in passing, that the colonists had long since built ships that were far larger than the *Mayflower*. About 1650 Edward Johnson recalled that "Many a fair ship had her framing and finishing here [in Massachusetts], besides lesser vessels, barques and ketches. . . ." Shipbuilding was in fact a vital and a major industry in all the seaports of New England virtually from their beginnings. The stories, often repeated, that certain early houses and pieces of furniture were constructed by ship carpenters could well be true, as it would be just as true to say that many early ships were built by carpenters or joiners who also built houses and made furniture. As later explained in more detail, there was little or no specialization in woodworking, or in any other craft, during the seventeenth century.

And in the graveyards that were soon a feature of every community the grim effigies, the scythe-bearing skeletons, and the fire-and-brimstone skulls that adorned the tombstones—the earliest examples of our native sculpture—reflected a preoccupation with the drama of death that was no less typical of the late Middle Ages. That, to us, somewhat morbid interest in the grave was by no means limited to the Puritans of New England, nor did it soon decline. In January, 1710 (six years after the death of his father), William Byrd II of Virginia noted in his diary, "I had my father's grave opened to see him but he was so wasted there was not anything to be distinguished." And he added, "I ate fish for dinner."

The typical seventeenth-century dwelling in America was also built in accordance with traditions that were centuries old. Most of the permanent houses that replaced the first temporary structures were made of stout timbers securely joined by mortise and tenon and raised with spirited ceremony about a massive chimney pile. They were all but identical with earlier English models. (There were no log cabins in the first English colonies. They were introduced by the Swedes who settled along the Delaware River in the late 1630's.) Until late in the century, at least, Boston and other New England villages, with their casement-windowed, unpainted buildings with upper stories overhanging the streets, must have borne a close resemblance to the towns of Elizabethan England. For, even in this land of vast distances and open spaces, it was reported of Boston in 1663 that "the houses were for the most part . . . close together on each side of the streets as in London."

At best these early homes lacked most of the comforts that have long since become commonplace. They were poorly heated and ventilated. As Benjamin Franklin remarked of those who sat before the roaring fire in the principal room of a winter night, they scorched before and froze behind and never hoped to warm the room throughout, no less the whole house. For the current of air required to feed such a large flame was, when doors and windows were closed, a contraband that whistled through every crack and cranny of the structure. In the winter of 1697 Cotton Mather, shivering before such "a great Fire," noted that "the Juices forced out at the end of short billets of wood by the heat of the flame on which they were laid, yett froze into Ice on their coming out." The ceilings were low, and the skeleton of the structure was exposed on the inside (as it often is, to save space, in modern apartments). Even a man of average height must duck in some of these rooms to avoid cracking his skull on the central, summer beam. (Young Ben Franklin hit his head on such a beam in Cotton Mather's house, and thereupon was given a maxim that he never forgot—"When you come to a low place, stoop!") Small casement windows with diamond-shaped panes of irregular glass (or simply oiled paper) admitted little light by day, and adequate lamps for night were still in the future.

John Smith in his breastplate

Throughout most of the century domestic life centered in the principal room, known as the "hall," a room that recalled in its function the "great hall" of early English manors—and anticipated the all-purpose living area of some modern homes. It was in this area that most of the vital activity of the household took place. Here the cooking was done (before separate kitchens were added), and here the family often ate, sometimes slept, and usually stored a variety of household gear, firearms, tools, and some farm equipment. At a time when, as in Plymouth and other seventeenth-century communities, the average household consisted of nine or ten people, the hall must have often presented a cluttered and untidy appearance hard to imagine from the decoratively arranged examples of such interiors as they are shown in most museums and other historical restorations. Under the circumstances, privacy was of course rarely possible within the house. In the winter of 1631 Thomas Dudley, trying to write by the fireside of such a living room, explained that his whole family was congregated there to keep warm, "though they break good manners, and make mee many times forget what I would say, and say what I would not."

In all but the simplest and meanest homes there were other rooms of somewhat more special and often more refined character—the parlor, or "best" room as it was often called, and the chambers upstairs; but in cold weather these functioned comfortably only as sleeping quarters. However, in more clement seasons they were used for polite entertainment and formal ceremonies. In 1688 Samuel Sewall of Boston noted in his now-famous diary that "Mr. James Sherman Married Richard Fifield and Mary Thirston . . . in our Bed-Chamber, about 9. at night." And a few years later he wrote that he entertained eleven guests at dinner "in my wives Chamber at the great Oval Table."

There were some houses built in seventeenth-century America that were larger and more elaborate than any that have survived. Of those that have survived few have retained their original appearance. From time to time, as families grew, changes and additions—lean-tos and ells—were made to old structures until, as in the case of the House of the Seven Gables, the result was a picturesque agglomeration of different elements.

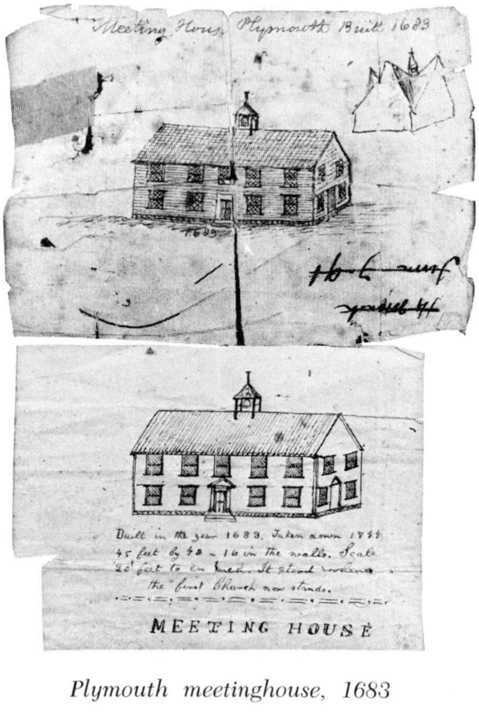

Plymouth meetinghouse, 1683

By the 1670's American colonies had long since grown from mere outposts in the wilderness into communities that enjoyed most of the advantages of civilized life. William Harris, a visiting Englishman, wrote from Boston that "the merchants seem to be rich men, and their houses [are] as handsomely furnished as most in England." This was probably an exaggeration; yet it was reported to the Lords of Trade the next year that in Massachusetts alone there were about thirty merchants worth from £10,000 to £20,000, very substantial sums for the

St. Luke's Church, in Smithfield, Va. (above)
Timbers of the Old Ship meetinghouse (below)

time. That same year one champion of the older order published a lament that the good old days of austerity and simplicity had been all too "quickly sin'd away for love of gold." That olden time of happy memory, the plaint continued was

> . . . ere the Islands sent their Presents in,
> Which but to use was counted next to sin.
> Twas ere a Barge had made so rich a fraight
> As Chocholatte, dust-gold and bitts of eight.
> Ere wines from France and *Moscovadoe* too
> Without the which the drink will scarsly doe,
> From western Isles; ere fruits and dilicacies,
> Did rot maids teeth and spoil their hansome faces.

It was true enough that with the rising tide of trade, forward-looking colonists were spending proportionately more time at their ledgers and perhaps less with their Bibles. To facilitate business the General Court of Massachusetts as early as 1652, in defiance of restrictions laid down in England, established a mint and hired the local goldsmith John Hull to serve as master, directing him to coin "bullion, plate, or Spanish coine" into shillings, sixpences, and threepenny bits. Among these mintings were the pine-tree, oak-tree, willow-tree shillings, and fractions thereof, which are so coveted by collectors today. ("Goldsmith" and "silversmith" are interchangeable terms; the colonial smith worked with either metal as occasion required.)

Coins from far parts of the world found their way to the colonies—gold and silver doubloons from Spain, johannes and moidores from Portugal, crowns from France, pistoles, ducats, and pieces of eight. Sometimes worn or clipped or otherwise of dubious value, these miscellaneous coins caused problems of exchange that only a goldsmith could resolve. In a day before there were banks as we know them, the goldsmith in fact played banker to his community. For those who wished to conserve the profits of their trade or to hoard their wealth safely, a most sensible practice was to call upon the smith to melt the coin down and hammer gold or silver of certified purity into such handsome and useful objects as tankards, porringers, spoons, and beakers. Bearing the maker's mark and usually the engraved initials of the owner, these could be identified in case of theft, as coins could not be; they could always be melted and fashioned back into coinage if need be; and they made a handsome display in the home, to be passed along to later generations if all went well. As Lieutenant Colonel William Fitzhugh of Virginia wrote his London agent in 1688: "I esteem it as well politic as reputable, to furnish my self with an handsom Cupboard of plate which gives myself the present use & Credit, is a sure friend at a dead lift, without much loss, or is a certain portion for a Child after my decease. . . ."

During the middle years of the seventeenth century, particularly during Cromwell's protectorate, the various colonies had largely grown in their own ways without serious interference from official England. Because of inherent differences in backgrounds and circumstances these ways developed into a variety of regional cultures that was reflected in the work of craftsmen. The colonists, craftsmen among them, came from different counties of England and different areas of the Continent, and they brought with them different traditions of style and form from those separate localities. In America new conditions and materials brought about gradual modification of such inherited and imported patterns. So long as overland travel remained difficult and tedious, as it did for many years to come, the waterways provided the principal means of communication—carriers of culture as well as of men and cargoes. Thus it was about the shores of Chesapeake Bay, the Hudson and Connecticut rivers, Narragansett Bay, and Massachusetts Bay that regional patterns of design and craftsmanship tended increasingly to develop into native styles in architecture, woodwork, and metalwork that are often clearly distinguishable one from the other. Collectors and students find such regional characteristics, especially in furniture and silverwork, a strong lure to their interest.

These developments took time and were not always immediately apparent in this early period. However, the circumstances that were to shape them were already established. The Virginia Company enlisted skilled craftsmen of various nationalities—Dutch, French, Italians, Germans, Poles, and even one "John Martin, the Persian"—to practice at Jamestown. However, because of its rural, plantation economy and the absence of towns of any consequence, once Virginia established its vital tobacco trade with England, that southern area turned to the mother country for much of its household equipment—as Fitzhugh did for his silverware and other furnishings. In 1681, for example, he wrote to London requesting a "feather bed & furniture, curtains & vallens. The furniture, Curtains & Vallens," he explained, "I would have new, but the bed at second hand, because I am informed new ones are very full of dust." In letter after letter, like his fellow aristocrats in the colony, Fitzhugh ordered other furnishings from abroad for his home until he had, as he advised one correspondent, "all accomodations for a comfortable & gentile living."

In Virginia, as in all the colonies, it was initiative and industry, rather than

Rubbings of three 18th-century gravestones from the Connecticut colony

the dead hand of custom, that marked a man for distinction and preferment. Despite those abiding legends of Virginia Cavaliers with ancestries dating to the Battle of Hastings, the wealthy aristocrats whose influence was so powerful in the development of that colony owed their prominence more to their capabilities and opportunities than to their pedigrees. "It is known," wrote John Hammond in 1656, "such preferment hath this country rewarded the industrious with, that some, from being wool-hoppers and of as mean and meaner employment in England, have there grown great merchants and attained to the most eminent advancements the country afforded." The F.F.V.'s became the first families *in* Virginia, to a great extent by their own efforts and their own good judgments.

In 1664, although Peter Stuyvesant stamped his wooden leg in protest, England took over New Netherland from the Dutch "without a blow or a tear" and added a colony that, in spite of constant infiltration of Englishmen, long retained its Dutch flavor. Early visitors from other colonies described the plastered walls of its brick houses, the woodwork "kept very white scowr'd," the enclosed beds, and the "stair cases laid all with white tile which is ever clean" as though they were in a strangely different world. It was a world that mirrored the scenes depicted in the luminous paintings of the Dutch Little Masters, some of which undoubtedly hung on the walls of those tidy homes.

Woodcut portrait of Richard Mather

New Amsterdam attracted a growing stream of New England traders as well as merchants from every island in the West Indies and from most of the Atlantic ports of Europe. It was decidedly a polyglot world. "Our chiefest unhappyness here," complained an early resident, "is too great a mixture [of peoples]." But in New York, as the colony was renamed, Dutch, Huguenot, Flemish, and English craftsmen worked side by side in a variety of traditional styles that in time tended to fuse into an attractive and highly distinctive local expression, as will be shown on later pages.

The population of New England, in its wide scattering of separate colonies and towns, remained far more homogeneous than that of New Netherland ever was, although it was by no means 100 per cent Puritan stock. (One of the earliest Boston silversmiths, William Rouse, was a Dutchman who emigrated from Wesel in the Rhineland.) A large proportion of the seventeenth-century antiques that have come down to us were fashioned in that area and reflects the continuous traditions of the English past that lived on so lustily in the New World. In their design and construction the chests and cupboards, chairs and tables, tankards and other silverware for a while yet show little impress of an American environment, unless it be a tendency toward simplification that was to become more pronounced in years to come. Conditions in the early colonies—and for long afterward in America—did not encourage the time-consuming virtuosity that characterized workmanship for wealthy patrons in the capitals of Europe.

Nevertheless, much of the furniture was handsomely carved and far more of it than has survived in that condition was brightly painted with decorative motifs. Neither Puritanism nor the demanding problems of pioneering blighted the creative side of human nature. The most earnest Puritans were not indifferent to beauty, although they eschewed extravagance. The novels of Nathaniel Hawthorne and other romantics of the last century have led us to think of our early New England forefathers as rather forbidding effigies, everlastingly somber in thought and drab in dress. Their morals were high, no doubt, but they were not arbitrary, and these hardy men and women had their share of human weakness. "Drinking and fighting occur there [in New England] not less than elsewhere," observed one early visitor—a statement that gets some support from the relatively large number of capacious drinking vessels that have survived from

Thomas Savage of Boston, with lace-trimmed coat and gold-fringed sash

the time. (The cargo of the *Mayflower* included a precious supply of "hot waters" and beer; John Alden, the cooper, was charged with maintaining the barrels these were stored in.) In 1675 Cotton Mather complained that every other house in Boston was an alehouse—a statement that was repeated a century later by another reputable observer. And the wardrobes, like the homes, of these people were more colorful than legends have indicated. Elder William Brewster, most venerable of the Pilgrims, owned red and white caps, a violet-colored coat, a blue suit, a green waistcoat, black silk stockings, and green drawers. Governor Richard Bellingham of the Bay colony owned a scarlet coat as a mantle of respectability and authority, and the records tell of violet-colored petticoats, red breeches, blue aprons, silver buttons, and other colorful bits of finery. Only ministers followed the ancient sacerdotal custom of wearing black. Conformity in such matters is hardly apparent in the historical evidence. There is a strangely topical ring in John Endecott's protest against Harvard boys "Wearing long hair after the manner of Ruffians."

A typical Dutch interior, about 1660

Little if any of the furnishings that remain from the period considered in this chapter can be dated before 1650. Much of it was made in the last quarter of the century and some from the early years of the eighteenth, beyond the dates given at the chapter head. Styles changed only slowly, and furniture, for example, continued to be made in the earlier manner for years after the century had closed. Broadly speaking this style is known as Jacobean, after *Jacobus*, the Latin word for James. (It was James I who reigned in England when Jamestown and Plymouth were settled.) In construction the style is based on straight elements joined together at right angles, in contrast to the curved and twisted structural forms that were later to appear and that were to dominate design for most of the following century. The carving is in low relief, moldings are simple, but the turnings, at their best, are bold and vigorous. In our own day, with its strong emphasis on planned obsolescence, these stout and solid objects may seem uncompromisingly massive, even severe at times, but they have virtues of design and decoration that reveal a decided and unwavering sense of form and beauty. They are, as well, abiding testimonials to sound, proficient craftsmanship. And, it is also true, they speak to us about intimate aspects of American experience when formal histories remain dumb.

Coins made at the Massachusetts mint by the goldsmiths Hull and Sanderson

Detailed view of 16th-century London

1. A Brewster-type chair with eight banks of turned spindles

2. The date 1678 and the owner's initials appear on this painted chest of drawers.

3. Like both of the other pieces here illustrated, this paneled chest was made in New England.

Turner, Carver, Joiner & Painter

"The Lord hath been pleased to turn all the wigwams, huts, and hovels the English dwelt in at their first coming, into orderly, fair, and well-built houses, well furnished many of them. . . ." In 1642 Edward Johnson, a trained joiner, thus described the industry and ingenuity of his fellow colonists. Generally speaking, every man was his own carpenter on the wild shores of the New World; but in the furniture that has survived we see the handiwork of craftsmen who brought to America the jealously prized skills of Old World trade guilds. Rounded legs of tables and stools, the supporting columns of large cupboards, and the spindles of chairs were turned on a lathe. Elder Brewster is said to have had such a chair as the one shown here (1). A similar type called a Carver chair, after an example owned by the first governor of Plymouth, had a single row of back spindles and none under arms and seat. Joinery, an art "whereby several Pieces of Wood are so fitted . . . they shall seem one intire Piece," utilized mortise and tenon—an ancient method of all-wood construction. Solid surfaces were embellished with shallow carvings in traditional designs and often heightened with vivid colors (3). All four techniques were used to produce this chest of drawers (2). It is joined in the strict rectilinear form of the period, adorned with turned and split spindles, and both carved and painted. The tendrils painted on the drawers appear to be an imitation of marquetry, an elaborate inlay of vari-colored woods and other materials then popular in England.

4. This elaborate press cupboard, made in Massachusetts late in the 17th century, is in the style of Thomas Dennis of Ipswich, but it may have been made by one of his contemporaries working in that area. Native woods, painted black to simulate ebony, were used for the heavy balusters and for the split spindles and other applied ornaments.

The chest, oldest of known furniture forms, was the most important single item in early colonial households. It could serve as a chair or table; since it was portable, it could also serve as luggage. But above all, a chest provided storage space, a vital necessity before there were closets. Seventeenth-century craftsmen enlarged upon the basic structure (a box with a hinged lid) and added one or more drawers below, thereby creating a more convenient receptacle for clothing and other fabrics.

Textiles, homespun or imported, were highly valued and preserved with great care. Precisely listed in inventories—"one Cotten table Cloath, one cradle rugg, 1 pr. of cloth drawers, 1 silke Neckcloth"—woolens, linens, cottons, and silks were passed on as heirlooms.

Spices, often treasured under lock and key, were stored in small chests that stood on a table or cupboard. This spice chest (6), dated 1679 and bearing the initials of its original owner, is attributed to Thomas Dennis of Ipswich, Massachusetts, one of the few seventeenth-century joiners and carvers whose name is known to us today.

The press cupboard (4), one of the most ambitious and characteristic of Jacobean designs, gave further storage space—as well as solid evidence of colonial affluence. Such strapwork and "jewelwork" (applied ornamental shapes), as appear on the doors and panels of this ornate example, had been popular in England since the Elizabethan Age, not only for furniture but for plasterwork, wall panels, and silver and gold plate. Bulbous turnings were another Elizabethan feature that originated with the Renaissance and reached England by way of Flanders.

In addition to the Brewster and Carver types, colonists made slat-back chairs (7), a traditional provincial style, and solid-back or wainscot chairs (5), majestic reminders of the Middle Ages when such massive structures were reserved for nobility and high-ranking clergy. The carved figures, or "grotesques," on the back of this chair were frequently used on European furniture of the time, but they are exceptional in colonial design.

5. This wainscot chair epitomizes the traditions of Gothic design.

6. A series of little drawers line the interior of this small spice chest.

7. A slat-back armchair, of pine and ash, with a velvet seat cushion

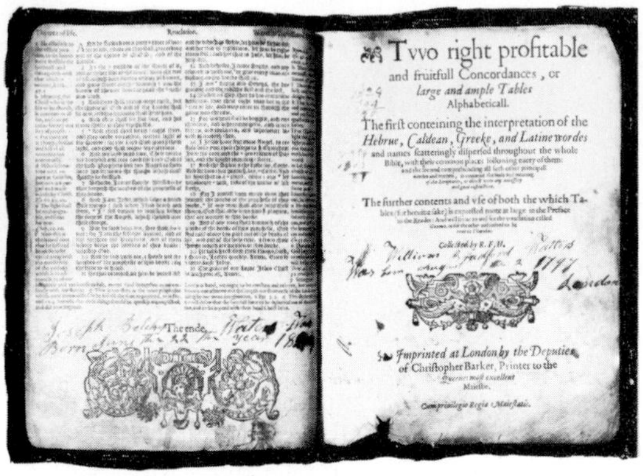

Tvvo right profitable
and fruitfull Concordances, or
large and ample Tables
Alphabeticall.

The first conteining the interpretation of the
Hebrue, Caldean, Greeke, and Latine wordes
and names scatteringly dispersed throughout the whole
Bible, with their common places following euery of them:

The further contents and vse of both the which Ta-

Collected by R. F. H.

Imprinted at London by the Deputies
of Christopher Barker, Printer to the
Queenes most excellent
Maiestie.

Cum priuilegio Regiæ Maiestatis.

8. A title page from Governor Bradford's Bible

9. A half-octagon box, of oak and pine, with lunette carvings

10. A book box with tulip pattern and the owner's initials

11. A small box, with Dutch carving, from New Amsterdam

12. Benches, like stools, often had splayed legs for extra strength and better balance.

Among the most useful and decorative items of a seventeenth-century colonial house were handsomely carved wooden boxes (9, 10, 11), comparable to the caskets and coffers of the Middle Ages and designed for the safekeeping of small objects, important documents, coins, jewelry, and certainly for the bits of finery so cherished in the wilderness. Even in rock-ribbed, Puritan New England the colonists owned a good number of frivolities. A Boston merchant in 1651 included among his stock: "silk breast buttons, silk and bone lace," and ear "wiers" (for earrings); and the Bay colony's ban on "wicked apparel" proves the prevalence of such forbidden pleasures as "knots of ryban, double ruffles and cuffs," gold and silver thread, embroideries, and false curls.

Some boxes were fitted with pigeonholes to create a portable desk, like the medieval scholar's box. Others, of course, held the great leather-bound Bibles brought from England, as was this one owned by Governor Bradford (8); hence, the descriptive term Bible boxes. Governor Winthrop's *Journal*, that amazing account of theocracy in Massachusetts, may have been kept in a Bible box. And it is in this *Journal* we find one of the earliest mentions of a "form" (12), the term used at that time to describe a long, backless bench. "Captain Underhill," wrote Winthrop, "standing upon a form, he did, with many deep sighs and abundance of tears, lay open his wicked course. . . ." This event took place in 1640 in the First Church in Boston, evidently furnished with benches in Puritan fashion. Benches, or forms, and stools were also the customary seating at the dining table. The head of the household may have sat in a wainscot chair (13), as befitted his position, with a cushion to ease the discomfort of the hard oak seat.

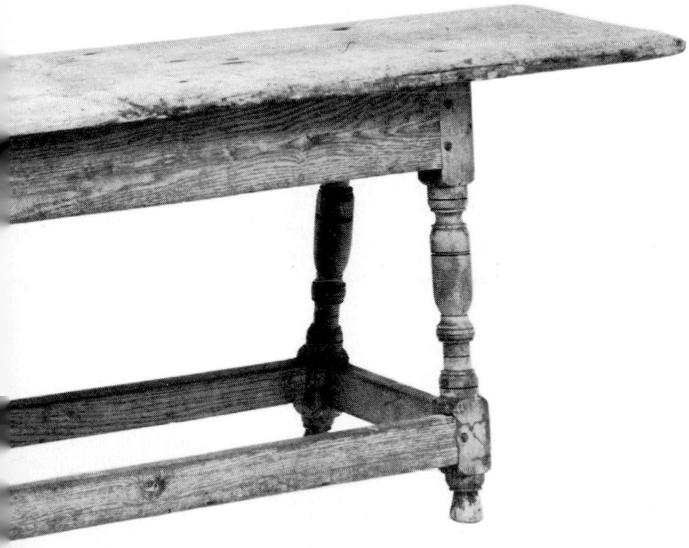

13. The carving on this oak wainscot chair includes a guilloche motif and rosettes.

14. A joint stool, exceptional for the delicacy of its turnings

Most Gothic furniture was made of oak, and it remained the wood favored in Jacobean England and seventeenth-century America. Native pine was at first employed in the colonies largely as a secondary wood for shelves and backings. It was also used for lids of chests and for tops of tables, wherever the strength of oak was not needed. A stretcher table (15) made in this fashion has an oak base and a pine top. The bulbous-leg table with pendants (17) is entirely oak, but the top is detachable, presumably to simplify moving.

Maple lent itself to turning better than oak. Red cedar or walnut was found suitable for applied moldings and jewelwork. Ash was tough and elastic and easily shaped into slats and spindles. Both pine and maple, so often considered the classic colonial woods, did not come into their own until the end of the century. This joint—or "joyned" —stool (14), which can be dated about 1680 to 1700, is a rare, early example of all-maple furniture.

The ingredients of American Jacobean forms, therefore, differed from their English counterparts in only a few details: the presence of native woods, drawer pulls of wood rather than wrought iron, and hinges in plain functional patterns rather than decorative ones.

15. A stretcher table with lunette, or half-moon, carving on the drawer

Despite a report given Charles II in 1682 that described South Carolina as "cloathed with odoriferous and fragrant woods . . . the lofty Pine, the sweet-smelling Cedar and Cypress trees, of both of which are composed goodly Boxes, Chests, Tables, Scrittores, and Cabinets. . ." relatively little furniture was made in the seventeenth-century southern colonies. And less has survived. New England was the center of the furniture crafts. The oak and pine court cupboard shown here (16), thoroughly Jacobean in all its aspects, is unique because it is of Virginian origin. The doors are carved with rosettes, a Tudor symbol, and tulips in the round. The center panel also carries a tulip, an age-old motif that has been found in Mesopotamian pictographs.

Court cupboards, from the French *court*, or short, were a mark of wealth, as were press cupboards (4), and they have been called the "most Jacobean of colonial Jacobean styles." Whereas the press cupboard was primarily used to store clothing, the court cupboard with its open shelf was used as a sideboard. The tops of both were commonly covered with bright cloths of velvet, needlework, wool, or damask; and the family's best plate, pewter, pottery, or porcelain were set out on display. The term court cupboard first appears in inventories during Elizabeth I's reign.

16. An oak court cupboard, a distinctive Jacobean design

17. "Bun" feet, as shown above, came into style late in the century.

Salt, treasured since the beginnings of history as a condiment and preservative, was "sett in the myddys of the tabull" during the Middle Ages in sumptuous standing receptacles, extravagantly wrought in precious metals. Guests of honor sat "above the salt" near the host and hostess, children and other lesser folk "below the salt." This standing salt of English pottery (18) is a modest expression of the medieval tradition. The little reservoir of precious salt was often covered with a napkin or a small dish, as illustrated here (19) in a still life by the Dutch

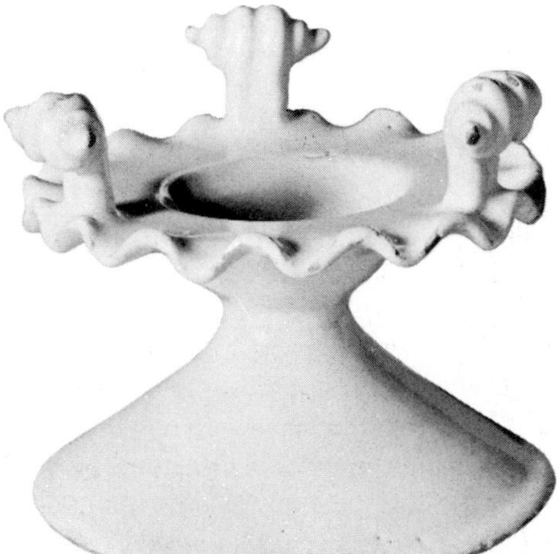

18. A standing salt of English delftware. At least four of similar design are known to have been made by early colonial silversmiths.

19

painter Pieter Claesz, which explains the function of the knobs on seventeenth-century salts of this type. Throughout the remainder of the century almost all the pottery, glassware, pewter, and much of the other metalwork used in the colonies was imported from abroad. Salt, too, was a commodity brought from other lands, despite efforts by the junior John Winthrop and others to produce sufficient quantities from evaporated sea water.

Many of the wealthy settlers also ordered large amounts of furniture from abroad, but the northern colonies continued to supply the local demand. This Massachusetts chest-on-frame (20), with hinged top and a drawer, is a rare survivor of a charming but short-lived Jacobean style designed to eliminate the inconvenience of bending down to reach into a low chest. Later, the highboy would create a new inconvenience with the necessity "of getting on to chairs to place anything in the upper drawers."

20. The chest-on-frame was a Jacobean innovation, best described as an intermediary step between the low chest and the lofty highboy. This one is made of oak and pine and still has its original coat of black paint. The brass candlesticks and the delft puzzle jug (49) set on display are typical of the items imported to the colonies at this time.

The Children's Corner

Among surviving colonial toys are silver or gold, bell-trimmed whistles with "teethers"—usually of coral. These rich baubles, both imported and American made, were given to children of the well to do, probably as christening gifts. The gold and rock crystal De Peyster whistle (23) is held by Jacques de Peyster (21) in his portrait. John Hancock had a "wissel and bells," as did John Quincy Adams' family, and Martha Washington ordered one from Philadelphia in the 1790's, presumably for her first great-grandchild. The wood and wax doll (22), an enchanting survivor of the 1640's, may not have been a child's plaything, but a "fashion baby"—an imported model of the latest European styles.

21. Jacques de Peyster with his gold whistle, a 1633 Dutch painting. 22. Wax dolls were imported to America from England and Europe.

25. This colonial "walker" is similar to the one shown below. Its four casters gave the small toddler free-wheeling support.

23. The De Peyster whistle, brought to America from Holland. 24. A Flemish child, with whistle and padded headgear, in his "walker"

26. A 17th-century Dutch interior showing a wicker cradle. *27. The wicker cradle that was brought to Plymouth on the* Mayflower

For the majority of colonial boys and girls, toys were homemade—rag dolls, or cornhusk dolls, like those Indian children played with; rattles of pebbles, shells, or dried seeds; boats, tops, and blocks whittled from scraps of wood. The world of children also included furniture scaled to their size, such as the diminutive rocking chair (30), and the high chair (29). Wicker was sometimes used for children's furniture, as it was in Holland and England, and was mentioned in early inventories. In Virginia, Captain Adam Thoroughgood's will, 1639–40, specified "One chair of wicker for a child." A wicker cradle (27), brought from Europe, was used for Peregrine White, born on the *Mayflower* in Provincetown harbor in 1620. The wooden cradle (28) was fitted with knobs at the side, to which an outer coverlet could be fastened, and rocking posts at bottom and on the open hood.

Childhood in seventeenth-century America was not easy. Families were large, infant mortality high, and medicine medieval. One recommended cure for infantile diseases was a tonic consisting largely of snails, earthworms, and "The Strongest Ale." Discipline was severe. In many households children were not allowed to sit while eating, as did their elders, but stood at the table during meals—in silence. School days were long. Lessons were shrouded in somber theology and warnings of impending doom. *The New-England Primer*, first published in 1683, was liberally illustrated with symbols of the grave and carried such rhymed couplets as "Xerxes did die, And so must I" and "While Youth do cheer, Death may be near."

28. A walnut cradle from New York

29. *A many-spindled, Brewster-type high chair from New England, made of maple and elm.* 30. *A New Amsterdam setting with a child's rocker. (A linen press is in the background.)*

John Hull of Boston, Goldsmith

In 1635, when he was a lad of ten, John Hull was taken from his school in Leicestershire, England, to emigrate with his family to the New World. The Great Migration was in full course and, along with thousands of other Puritans fleeing the "many popish Injunctions" that threatened their consciences at home, the Hulls headed for the new little village of Boston in the Massachusetts Bay colony. There the youngster went back to school for a time and helped his father in the fields. Eight or nine years later he wrote in his diary, "I fell to Learning (by the help of my Brother) and to practising the trade of A gold smith; and through gods help obtained that abilitye in it, as I was able to get my living by it." For the next forty years "John Hull of Boston, goldsmith," as he continued to refer to himself in spite of the other distinctions that came his way, pursued a God-fearing career that touched on almost every aspect of New England life and won him worldly success and the reputation of a "saint upon earth."

There was nothing incompatible about being a Puritan saint and accumulating earthly rewards. Like the governing fathers of the Massachusetts colony, who, he observed, were "no babes nor windyheaded men," Hull recognized that this new society had to be founded on a solid economic base. "The heavinly King," he said, "knoweth Easily how to make all worke for our best good."

As a goldsmith Hull functioned from the beginning as a banker for the community. This was not only a matter of converting the miscellaneous coins and bullion of his neighbors into handsome vessels of guaranteed purity. He also kept the coins of his fellow New Englanders in safe custody, presumably paying interest on the deposit, until he made the coins up into plate or refunded them. In 1667, for example, Richard Garraway's inventory noted that he had "In money at John Hull's £68–08–2."

The first generation of colonists perforce did their business largely by barter. Enough reliable currency simply was not available for use in daily transactions. Taxes were paid in kind and small change was made by "muskett bulletts of a full boare," each representing a farthing, and by white wampum. Hull returned to his home greatly annoyed on one occasion, when he was serving as the colony's treasurer, because a delinquent taxpayer paid up with a load of oats instead of money.

In 1652 the colony established a mint to alleviate this cumbersome procedure and to provide a standardized currency. Hull was named mintmaster and he chose as his partner, his friend Robert Sanderson. Their partnership extended to the fashioning of silver objects as well and lasted until Hull's death. The earliest silver surviving from the colonial period bears the marks of these two master smiths, either individually or together. In his *Grandfather's Chair*, Nathaniel Hawthorne repeated or created the colorful legend that to calculate her dowry upon her marriage to young Samuel Sewall, Hull's daughter Hannah was set on one side of the mint's scales while the other was heaped with pine-tree shillings until her weight was balanced. (Actually the dowry of five hundred pounds was paid on the installment plan.)

In 1659 Hull noted in his diary, "I received into my house Jerimie Dumer & Samuell Paddy to serve me as Apprentices eight yeares. the lord make me faithfull in discharge of this new trust Comitted to me & let his blessing be to me & them." Sam dropped out of the program. Years later Hull wrote to him, "Had you abode here and followed your Calling you might have bene worth many hundred pounds of cleare estate and you might have enjoyed many more helpes for your sole. Mr. Dummer lives in good fashion hath a wife and three children and a good Estate is a member of the church and like to be very useful in his Generation."

It seems likely that Sanderson hammered up most of the silverwork undertaken by the partnership. In any case,

Hull was very soon occupied with other affairs that grew out of and added to his prominence in the colony and that must have distracted him from his metal-work. As a young man he started to develop a many-sided business with the help of his uncle, a haberdasher, and his "loveing cozen" Edward Hull at the "Hatt-in-Hand" within Aldegate, London. Apparently these relatives made a practice of sending to the colonies all the imported hats they could not sell in England. As a consequence, at one point Hull found himself stuck with "severall hundred poundes of [French] hatts that are out of fashion." He complained but he resigned himself to a loss with true Christian forbearance.

However, this was but one other facet of his enterprise and, for the most part, the mintmaster's affairs flourished. One way or another he acquired a fleet of vessels, and in these and other ships he freighted trade goods in picturesque variety to numerous ports throughout the Atlantic world—always with injunctions to his skippers "to see to the worship of God every day . . . and suppression of all prophaines" aboard ship. In 1671, for example, he instructed John Alden (son of *the* John Alden) to sail the ketch *Friendship* to Virginia with the first fair wind, trade his cargo for tobacco, take that to Ireland for sale, invest the proceeds in serge cloth and "some lead and shott," and return home—unless en route he found he could make better deals on the spot, including selling the ketch itself at a good price.

Once Hull sent a sloop manned by a crew of cutthroats (piously enjoined, as usual, not to swear) to the West Indies to salvage treasure from a sunken wreck, which they did. Again, he shipped a brace of black slaves to Madeira in exchange for red wine. At Barbados and at Jamaica, his shipmasters or agents swapped salt fish and meat, firkins of butter, and other homely New England products for logwood, sugar, indigo, and bullion. In England he exchanged Caribbean products as well as beaver and moose skins from the North American hinterland for assorted cargoes of textiles and other European manufactures. In spite of his scruples, Hull invested in privateering voyages when England was at war with foreign powers; this was not an uncommon form of speculation among Puritan venturers. On two occasions he contributed to the ransom of New England sailors who had been taken in slavery by the Barbary pirates. To insure his reputation on the London exchange, he made several trips to the home country. And he prospered.

Hull also owned timberland and part of a sawmill in New Hampshire. In the latter enterprise, for the good of everyone concerned, he implored the managing agent not to "imploye drunken sottes nor tipplinge fellowes." With several Rhode Island merchants Hull acquired from the Narraganset Indians the Pettaquamscutt Purchase, a tract which included some of the richest land in Rhode

Island. Here he raised kine and swine to provide him with salt meat and tallow for his expanding market. And here, in fenced-off pastures, he attempted to breed horses for coach, saddle, and draft—some for shipment to the West Indies, others for the fashionable folk of Boston. From Cape Cod, where he kept herds that ran wild, Hull asked for "a good fair Ambling beast or a couple of fair Trotters that was much of a hight color and likeness." It may be that from Hull's experiments in horse breeding, the famous Narragansett pacers of a later day were developed.

Before he was twenty-four years old, John Hull had been promoted to corporal in the local militia, a reward of merit that greatly pleased and impressed him as a young man. The Puritans revived the principle of universal military training, and Hull, provided at his own expense with the prescribed arms and armor, no doubt participated in the monthly drills and annual musters. In 1660 he joined the Ancient and Honorable Artillery Company, and in good time he became its captain—and thus was one of the most esteemed men in the colony.

Hull was over fifty when King Philip's War broke out in 1675, over the age for active service in that very bloody and crucial conflict—in proportion to the population, probably the bloodiest war in American history. (Town after New England town was devastated or abandoned, its inhabitants massacred, captured, or routed.) However, as one of the committee for the war and also treasurer for the war and then treasurer of the colony, Hull played a heroic role commandeering the resources, under the most vexatious of circumstances, necessary to prosecute the war. In the end he had to draw heavily upon his own credit to keep the soldiers supplied.

When he died on October 1, 1683, the colony still owed him over twenty-one hundred pounds for his loans and services. His death caused general lamentation, especially among the congregation of the Old South Church of which he had been a founding member. As a prototype of the Puritan merchant, he had struggled as a champion of God in daily battle with Mammon. Few of the New England businessmen who followed him were keener traders; but few, either, looked to such a strict conscience in managing their affairs and dealings.

Hull was also the progenitor of a noble line of craftsmen, some of whom he trained directly. His mute and enduring legacy is not alone in the forthright, handsome forms that he fashioned but also in the work of those who followed him in successive generations. It seems likely that John Coney (1655–1722), one of the most accomplished of all colonial goldsmiths, was an apprentice in Hull and Sanderson's shop. To Coney's shop, in turn, when he had become a master smith in his own right, came one Apollos De Revoire or Rivoire from the isle of Guernsey, whither his Huguenot family had fled from France following the revocation of the Edict of Nantes. Apollos became another brilliant goldsmith but, after he had Americanized his name to Paul Revere, he fathered a son and namesake who forever eclipsed his fame.

32. A standing cup by Hull and Sanderson

31. The earliest-known American porringer, made by Hull and Sanderson for Arthur and Johanna Mason, who were married in 1655

33. A standing salt by Jacobus Vanderspiegel

Men of Metal

During the late Middle Ages and the Renaissance goldsmithing was considered a major art. To some degree that traditional prestige accompanied the craft to America. Long before the colonies produced a portrait painter or a landscapist of any consequence, they supported scores of master craftsmen whose work in silver, and occasionally in gold, was simple in design but handsomely proportioned and scrupulously wrought.

Boston and New York were the earliest centers of this highly practical art, and almost all surviving examples from the seventeenth century were made in those two areas. Before refinements in the table service were introduced, the forms were relatively few—mostly drinking vessels for use in church or home and simple tools for eating. In 1655 the partners John Hull and Robert Sanderson of Boston made the earliest-known American porringer (31) and, about the same time, the earliest-known slip-end spoon (35). Porringers and spoons were two of the commonest forms in colonial silver. The former were apparently used for almost anything potable or semi-potable. The same smiths made the graceful communion cup (32) with a bequest of five pounds from Thomas Willet, first English-speaking mayor of New York, to the church at Rehoboth, Massachusetts, in 1674. A Dutch Bostonian, William Rouse (1639–1704/5), made the sucket fork shown below (34), a very handy double-ended device for eating fruits, both dried and preserved in syrup.

Silver fashioned in New York shows strong Dutch influences. A standing salt (33), made about 1690 by Jacobus Vanderspiegel (1668–1708), whose name clearly reveals his Dutch descent, recalls the one shown in the painting reproduced on page 26. The ceremonial spoon below (36), with its shank cast in the form of an animal's hoof, almost duplicates examples made in seventeenth-century Holland.

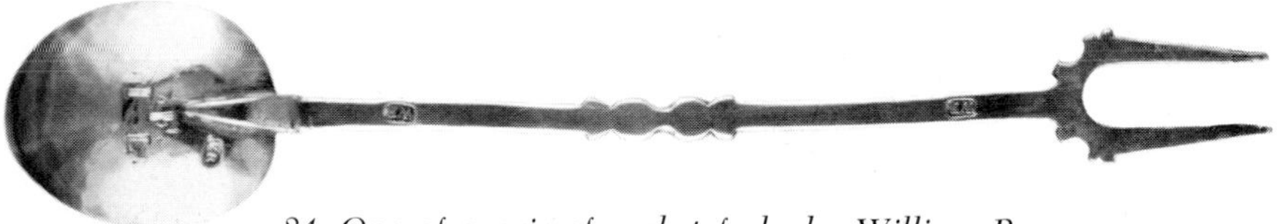

34. One of a pair of sucket forks by William Rouse

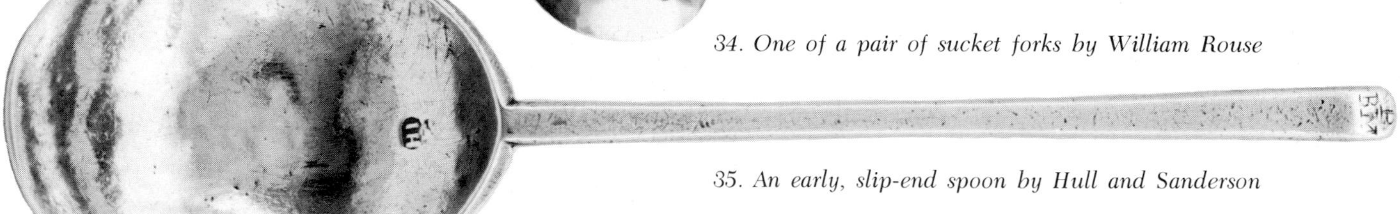

35. An early, slip-end spoon by Hull and Sanderson

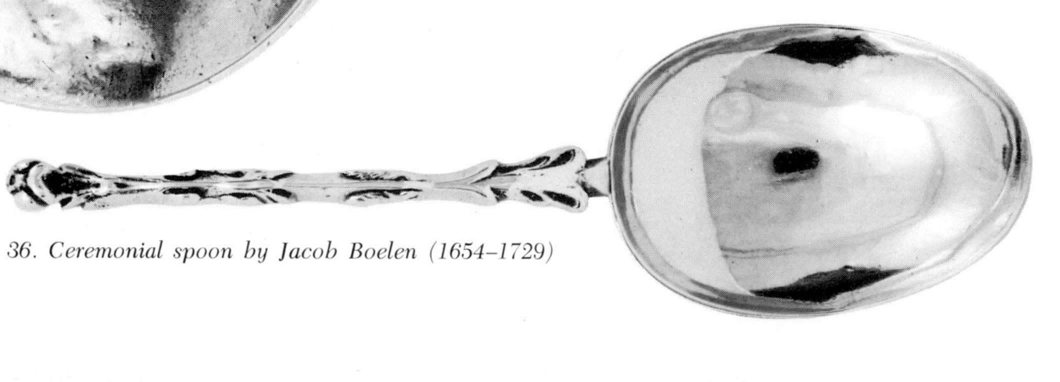

36. Ceremonial spoon by Jacob Boelen (1654–1729)

In 1651 Hull and Sanderson made the earliest-known piece of colonial silver, a little dram cup (it is less than three inches in diameter) with twisted wire handles and floral decorations (39). "Dram" was a common seventeenth-century term for distilled spirits. At the other end of the scale is a huge, two-quart tankard (37) with Sanderson's mark alone and made about 1668. It would take a strong and steady hand to lift such a piece when it was filled with cider or ale. Sanderson also fashioned a two-handled cup decorated with the figure of a native American turkey amid flowers and foliage (40). Such gourd-shaped vessels were used for drinking caudle, a warm mixture of gruel with spiced wine and sweetening—a concoction apparently indispensable at baptisms, weddings, funerals, and feasts.

With its engaged shaft of eight clustered columns, vaguely reminiscent of cathedral architecture, a candlestick (38) wrought by Jeremiah Dummer (1645–1718), Hull's onetime apprentice and now a man of importance, is another reminder of the Gothic strain that lingered in colonial design. This stick is one of a unique pair.

37. Robert Sanderson's mark appears alone on this exceptionally large tankard.

38. One of two candlesticks, by Jeremiah Dummer, commemorating the marriage of David and Elizabeth Jeffries in 1686

39. Hull and Sanderson fashioned this small dram cup in 1651, before Hull was appointed master of the Massachusetts mint.

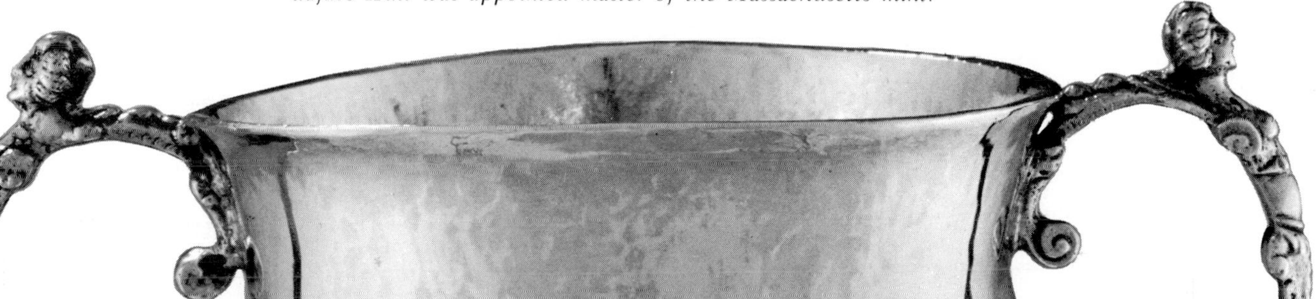

40. This caudle cup, another of the few pieces by Sanderson alone, was made for Thomas and Ann Shepherd, married in 1656.

Cornelius Vanderburgh, the first native-born New York goldsmith, was born in 1653 when the city was still in Dutch hands. In 1693, after a generation of English rule, the city fathers commissioned him to fashion a gold cup for the royal governor, Benjamin Fletcher, which suggests that by then he enjoyed a high reputation among the community's craftsmen. The cup has long since disappeared, but a beaker he made some years earlier remains one of the most unusual surviving examples of early New York silverwork. This ceremonial piece was made in 1685 for Robert Livingston to present to Robbert Sandersen. Sandersen was well liked and trusted by the Indians and served as interpreter (and strong persuader, probably) when Livingston, long a commissioner for Indian affairs, negotiated the purchase of a huge tract of land, six hundred acres known as Tachkanick (Taconic), from the local tribe. Livingston was a canny Scot who by a fortunate marriage, good social and political connections, and very adroit "deals," such as the one mentioned, parlayed his landholdings into a princely domain.

To embellish the beaker, Vanderburgh copied illustrations, engraved by Adriaen van der Venne, from the works of Jacobus Cats, a Dutch moralist. The allegorical fables of "Father Cats," as he was called, were almost as popular as the Bible among Dutchmen on both sides of the Atlantic. To allegorize the human virtue of integrity (b), he tells of the ermine who, surrounded by mud, prefers to starve rather than to soil his handsome pelt. Faithfulness (d) is represented by death astride a crocodile; even with such a burden the crocodile continues to grow, as does true love. Forgetting humility (e), the tortoise considers himself an honored cosmopolite when the eagle bears him aloft to view the world; but the eagle drops his prey to crack the shell and to devour the flesh.

41. The beaker, a form probably derived from a section of a drinking horn, was especially popular in New York where it often served for communion vessels as well as domestic drinking cups. The former were often engraved, like imported Dutch examples, with figures symbolizing Faith, Hope, and Charity and, like the one above, adorned with engraved strapwork panels beneath the lip and applied designs about the base.

41a

41b

41c

41d

41e

Two of the scenes above only incompletely illustrate the allegories. In one concerning magnanimity (c) a spider eats a fly, a lizard eats the spider, a stork seizes the lizard, and a snake coils about the stork; beyond that in the original engraving a dragon gobbles up the snake and a peasant kills the dragon. In the other (a) a lazy fox starves keeping his feet dry while geese feed busily and happily in a swamp. The geese are rewarded for their industry by having full bellies.

The Art and Mystery of a Goldsmith

The colonial silversmith fashioned his wares by practices and techniques that were ages old; methods that account in good measure for the special character of antique silver, quite aside from the interest and the merit of its design.

British America produced virtually no silver or gold and the craftsman was obliged to use coins and miscellaneous pieces of metal, often of questionable fineness. These he melted down and refined, with reference to a touchstone, to an acceptable standard of purity. Pure silver is relatively soft and for practical use it must be toughened with other metals, chiefly copper, as an alloy. Long before the first American colonies were founded, England had established a standard of quality, known as sterling, that required all silverwork, including coin of the realm, to contain 92.5 per cent pure silver. (To this day the hallmarks on English silver guarantee, among other things, that the standard has been maintained.) Such regulations did not extend to colonial work; the only pledge of quality in early America was the mark of the individual maker and, to be sure, his reputation. Many colonial smiths actually warranted their wares "as good as Sterling."

Almost all the hollow ware produced in the colonies—the bulk of production—was hammered up on anvils from solid, seamless sheets of metal, a process called "raising." First, the silversmith cast his refined, molten metal into a solid form. This, in turn, was hammered into a flat, smooth sheet of the required gauge—generally thicker than that of most modern silverware. On this, with a pair of compasses, he measured a series of concentric circles which he cut out of the sheet with saws or shears. (The centering mark left by the point of the compass can be seen on the base of an old tankard or bowl.) Since the metal spread in the making, the diameter of this disk was somewhat less than the combined base and height of the piece to be finished.

As a start to the raising process, the disk was placed over one of various-sized, shallow hollows in a wooden sinking block and repeatedly struck with blows of a mallet or hammer in a continuous spiral toward the perimeter,

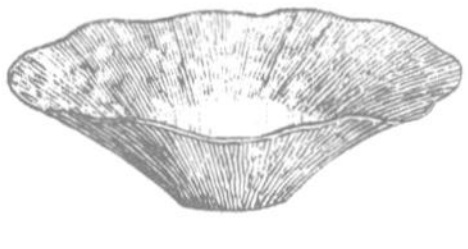

leaving the central area for the base of the form. The piece was then transferred to the first of a series of raising anvils, of different sizes and shapes, and on these hammered into its final form. As one can still witness at Colonial Williamsburg and other places where the craft has been revived, or where it has survived, this hammering procedure calls for muscle, skill, and patience.

To complete the raising it was often necessary to resort to a fluted T-shaped anvil, crimping the piece in order to

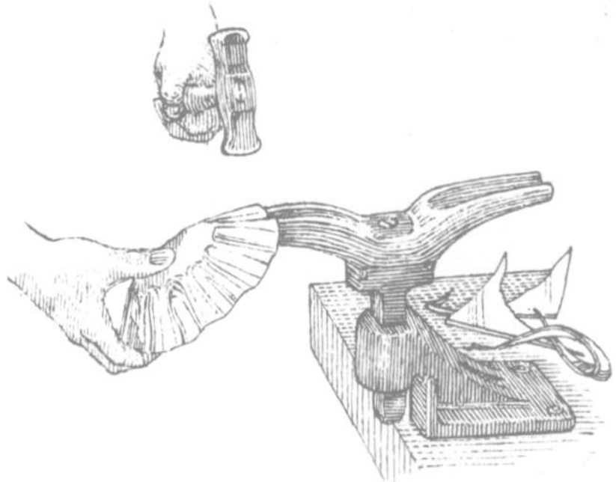

equalize the stresses set up in the metal by repeated hammering and to prevent it from splitting. Then, changing both anvil and hammer, the smith carefully

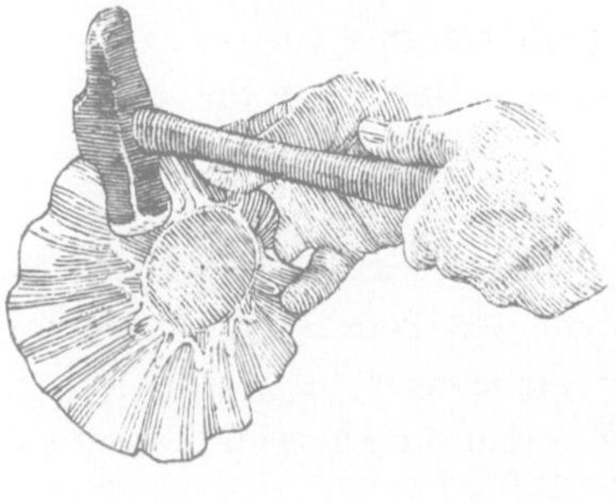

smoothed out those creases, always working from bottom to top to bring the piece gradually closer to its final shape. By successive maneuvers of this sort, the use of hammers of different sorts and anvils—or stakes, held in a vise—of different contours that could reach inside the vessel, almost any curved or straight surface could be contrived. To

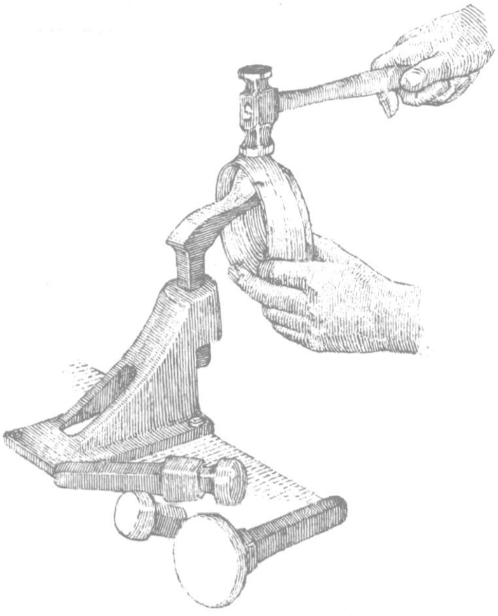

reach far inside a deep vessel in order to create a raised pattern on the exterior, a snarling iron was used—a Z-shaped iron, one end of which could be inserted inside the form. By striking the outside

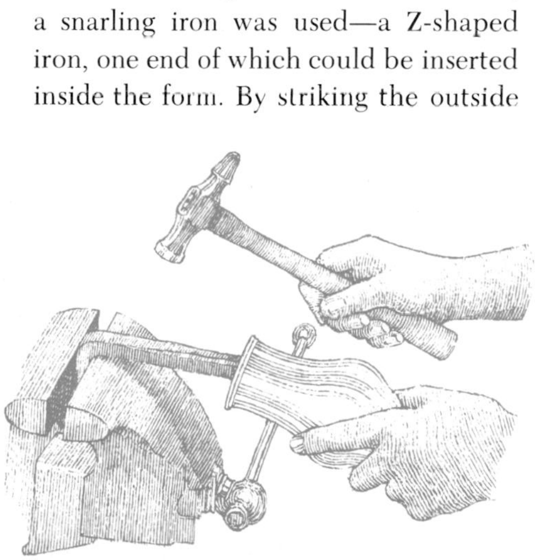

of the iron with a hammer, the smith could transmit the percussion by reciprocal action along the bar to the inside and create an embossed, or *repoussé*, pattern on the surface. The patterns were given greater definition by being indented from the outside with chasing punches that did not cut into the metal but that did sharpen the outlines of the

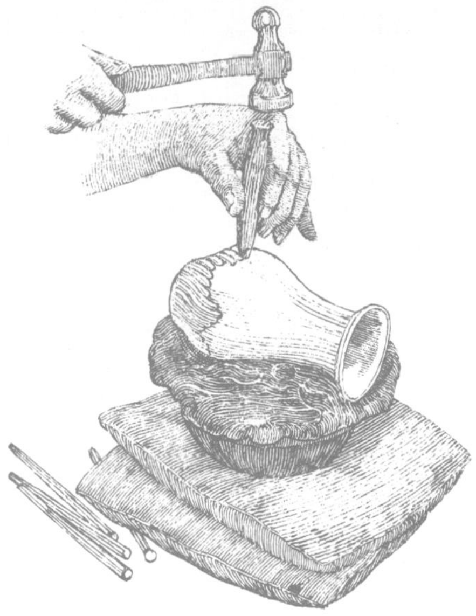

various ornamental elements—(the piece was filled with pitch so that its shape would not be distorted in the process). For other kinds of decoration, such as coats of arms, initials, and inscriptions, a graver was used; this actually cut away the surface of the silver and produced a thin, sharp-edged channel. Many colonial silversmiths were accomplished engravers.

To provide a piece of hollow ware with moldings at the lip or base, a strip of metal was drawn a number of times through the opening between two dies

on a drawing bench. The opening provided the profile of the molding, and with each drawing it was narrowed until the desired thickness was achieved. These finished moldings often faithfully reproduced, on a tiny scale, the contours of those used in monumental architecture.

The uneven marks left by the raising hammers were smoothed out by further blows from a planishing hammer, and at

the end of these procedures, by being rubbed with a pumice stone, and finally by being polished with a burnishing tool. From time to time, throughout the various steps in its making, the piece had to be annealed, or reheated, over a charcoal fire to keep it malleable. In the course of this operation, oxygen in the air united with the copper of the alloy to form a thin film of gray or bluish oxide. Neither this so-called fire skin nor all the evidences of hammering were eliminated in the polishing of the metal. The unevenness of the surface and its warm color are two attractive qualities of old silverwork that has not been buffed down by modern methods.

OVERLEAF: *A composite view of the operations in a London silversmith's shop, 1707*

Space Savers

In the Middle Ages kings and nobility traveled with their own beds, tables, chairs, silver plate, and tapestries when a royal retinue was on the move. As a consequence, furniture was often collapsible and portable. Trussing beds, for example, designed to be packed and transported, were frequently listed in early wills and inventories. They were owned by such personages as John of Gaunt, Catherine of Aragon, and Cardinal Wolsey, who had one trussing bed "partly gilte and paynted" and a second one made of alabaster. Furthermore, in medieval and Tudor times the concept of privacy was hardly developed, and the life of the household—eating, sleeping, and working—centered in the "hall," a room of all purposes. Thus, removable or folding furniture was also desirable for saving space—a housekeeping problem that carried over to seventeenth-century America.

Most early settlers were of modest means and from modest backgrounds. The first houses they built often included only one or two rooms with an attic or loft above. To save space in such close quarters, they also resorted to portable and folding furniture and pieces with dual functions. Chair-tables (42), which first appeared at the end of the Middle Ages, were common in the seventeenth century—both in England and in America.

42. With the top open, a New England chair-table served as a high-backed seat (above); with the top closed, the chair became a table.

43. An early folding bed, such as this one with trestle feet, was a useful space saver in the crowded rooms of the early colonial homes.

44. A round oak chair-table, which originally had a drawer underneath the seat

In the opening act of *Romeo and Juliet*, a servingman cries, "Away with the joint stools, remove the court cupboard"; and as the dancing begins, Capulet orders his servants then to "turn the tables up." These would have been the long trestle tables made of massive boards resting on a series of supports, a medieval form that still survives as picnic and similar informal gear. They were originally designed to be set up or stored out of the way, as the occasion demanded, and were built in varying degrees of simplicity or ornateness. In 1444 a Yorkshire merchant bequeathed to his son "a long table with three carved trestles." Two centuries later a colonial craftsman, working in the Jacobean tradition, made the long table with three trestles under a removable board illustrated above (45). This is considered to be one of the earliest-known American tables.

45. *A Jacobean trestle table, more than 12 feet in length*

46. *Bulbous legs and split spindles decorate a Massachusetts folding-top table.*

The gate-leg table, also a useful space saver and still manufactured to the present day, can be traced to the Tudor period; one John Coote of Bury St. Edmunds, for example, in 1502 bequeathed "the best faldyn table" in his hall. In 1641 a London household inventory speaks of "an ovall Table of wanscote with falling sides." The earliest folding tables were, indeed, "ovall" or semi-circular, with a single leaf supported by one pivoting gate. The colonial example shown here (46) was made in the Elizabethan tradition with baluster columns and applied ornaments, like those found on court and press cupboards, and was painted to simulate marble. The familiar structure for a gate-leg table (47)—a fixed center section and two hinged leaves—evolved in England early in the 1600's and was produced in a wide variety of forms in colonial America.

47. *A maple and pine gate-leg table (opposite), made about 1680, with trestle base; the same table with leaves down*

Pottery from Far Places

Although some coarse pottery was made in America in the seventeenth century, by far the greatest amount of the earthenware used in colonial households came from abroad. Excavations at the sites of early colonial settlements, as well as records of the time, reveal that pottery made in such various places as Portugal, Spain, Holland, England, and the Rhineland found its way to the colonies—not to mention some porcelain from the distant Orient.

Chinaware, as porcelain from the Far East was commonly called, was transported to Europe in growing quantities during the seventeenth century, and the gleaming white surface with characteristically blue decorations of the Ming ware gave a sharp stimulus to potters on the Continent and in England. By using a glaze made white and opaque with ashes of tin, painted with various shades of blue made from cobalt (some other colors were also used), they achieved a superficial resemblance to Ming examples many years before the secret of making true porcelain was learned in the Occident. The town of Delft in Holland has given its name to such "blue-and-white earthenware," as it was often referred to in colonial inventories and wills, although wares of this general type were produced earlier in England. (The term for the English ware is not capitalized.)

Occasionally European products (55) seem at a glance almost undistinguishable from the Oriental (52). At times purely western forms are painted with fanciful depictions of Chinese people (48), a type of decoration that became immensely popular in the next century. Among a variety of typical native forms England developed such whimsies as the puzzle jug (49), a pitcher with a perforated neck that made a jest of pouring from it. "Here Gentlemen come try your skill," reads the inscription on one of them, "I'll hold a wager if you will, That you can't drink this liquor all, Without you spill or let some fall." Another entertaining form was the so-called fuddling cup (56), with three or more receptacles intricately entwined as a single piece to fuddle a drinker.

"Neat Square Dutch Tiles to be set in Chimnies," as one Boston merchant advertised this attractive kind of Delftware in 1725, were already growing in popularity as a bordering for fireplaces in the seventeenth century. The colonies were also provided with other types of pottery, as already remarked. From the kilns of Devonshire came jugs and other shapes. One jug (50), which has survived intact, was enlivened by sgraffito decorations and sprightly verses. Stoneware bottles from the Rhineland, so-called bellarmines, with bearded masks molded at the neck, were originally designed as wine containers, but went on to serve as durable containers for any liquid. After a long popularity these were generally replaced, for table use, by the graceful delft wine bottles (51). The latter are usually dated, possibly to record when they were filled from the barrels in which the wine was imported. Around the middle of the seventeenth century inexpensive glass bottles became popular. These, with their tight-fitting corks, made it possible for the first time to mature wine in glass.

48. A 17th-century English delft shaving bowl

49. An English delft puzzle jug (opposite), 1689

50. *Harvest jug from Devonshire, dated 1698*

51. *An English delft bottle for white wine*

52. *A porcelain plate made in China for the western market in the 17th century. Compare this one with the similar plate opposite (55).*

53. *Delft fireplace tiles of the 17th century*

54. *Stoneware bellarmine from the Rhineland*

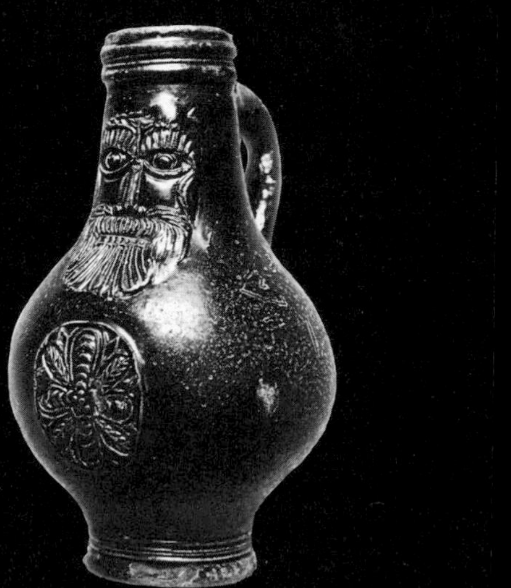

55. *A Delft plate made in the 17th century*

56. *A five-lobed English delft fuddling cup*

57. *A Cromwell side chair with "Turkey work" used as the upholstery fabric*

58. *A spiral-turned walnut side chair*

59. An upholstered settee is a rare colonial example in the Cromwell style.

60. A leather-covered beech armchair

Built-in Ease

Late in the 1500's, Sir John Harrington wrote that every merchant's hall in England had "easye quilted and lyned formes and stooles." Sir John suggested that with voluminous, balloon-shaped breeches passing out of fashion, "men can scant endewr to sitt upon" hard plank benches and wainscot stools. Although upholstered furniture had been known in court circles since Henry VIII's reign, it was not until the middle of the seventeenth century that in England, and somewhat later in America, built-in comfort would become commonplace. However, loose cushions had long been in use for added ease, and chairs were occasionally made with dished seats to accommodate cushions, as in this example (58) from New Jersey. The upholstered side chair (57) evolved from an earlier form originally intended for the dining table and called a "back stool," since it was, in effect, a padded stool to which a padded back had been added.

In the colonies upholstered chairs of the seventeenth century were usually covered in leather or in "Turkey work," a coarse needlework done in imitation of Turkish carpets that was held in place with brass-headed nails. Chairs of this type were profusely listed in colonial inventories at the close of the 1600's. In 1692 Captain Kidd's New York household included "one dozen Turkey work chairs [and] One dozen double-nailed leather chairs." Because leather-upholstered side chairs with ball turnings on legs and stretchers had been introduced into England under the Commonwealth, they became known as Cromwell chairs. This term has come into use for all upholstered chairs and settees of this period with similar turnings (57, 59). Spiral turnings (58) were of Dutch origin. In England walnut and beech became preferred woods for chairs, and this fashion was copied in the colonies. The side chair (58) is made of walnut.

The eastern shore line of North America abounds in navigable waterways, inevitable routes of exploration, trade, and expansion. And in each of the great river valleys, distinctive customs and styles tended to persist and develop according to the cultural backgrounds of the colonists who settled along those routes. The Dutch, from their first outpost on Manhattan Island around 1613 (four rude houses and a handful of fur traders), spread out along the length of the Hudson River, which rises in the Adirondacks three hundred and fifteen miles from the sea. The Hudson River valley, shown here in a 1675 map, became an extension of the thriving commercial world of the Netherlands with trade as the first concern of the majority of early Dutch settlers. They brought with them a taste for luxury and comfort. Early inventories list precious jewels, gold and silver trinkets, porcelains, furniture, and fabrics apparently far in excess of those owned by their Puritan neighbors.

A dramatic example of Dutch taste is the *kas*, or *kast*, a great cupboard. The proportions of such a piece were indicated by the account of Margharita Van Varick's "great Dutch *kas*" that was too massive to be moved from Flatbush by her heirs and sold, therefore, for twenty-five pounds. The finest Dutch and German *kasten* were heavily carved with fruits and flowers. Those made in the Hudson River valley were frequently painted in imitation of the traditional carving. (These decorations might well have been the first still-life paintings done in America.) The *kas* shown here (63) typifies the Dutch colonial cupboards. The decoration was painted in *grisaille*, tints of gray, a technique that became popular in Europe in the late seventeenth century and was designed to simulate figures in relief.

The early bench (62) is decorated with a verse written in Dutch script, which reads:

God's judgment is now ready
There is still time to leave folly
Good Sheep will be separated from Bad Goats
God's wisdom encircles the universe.

The scene of the Last Judgment is typical of colorful Dutch painting on furniture.

Rivers of Style

61. *A turned chair from early New York*

62. *A bench, or stool, made in 1702, might be one of the "church seats" that were carried to services.*

63. A Dutch colonial kas *made of oak and gumwood and painted in a monochrome of fruits and flowers*

The Connecticut River, rising in northern New Hampshire and flowing three hundred and forty-five miles to the sea, was first claimed by the Dutch who later sailed upstream to the present site of Hartford and there founded Fort Good Hope in 1633. Within a few years settlers from Plymouth and Massachusetts overwhelmed the Dutch claims and established along the Connecticut Valley, shown here in a detail from a 1675 map, a flourishing English colony. Traditional furniture forms gradually developed local characteristics until, as the seventeenth century neared its close, the Connecticut River towns had created distinctive regional styles of their own.

Some typical Connecticut chests, such as the one illustrated below (64), stem from the Hartford area, and their design is attributed to Peter Blin, active as a joiner and carver in Wethersfield from about 1675 to 1725. The split spindles and applied ornaments are Jacobean; the carving on the panels, commonly described as tulips and sunflowers, or asters, is found only on Connecticut Valley chests. These flower motifs, however, have been linked with the Tudor rose and the Scotch thistle.

Around Hadley, Massachusetts, another style of chest appeared (66), decorated with over-all flat carving in vine, leaf, and flower patterns, and painted red, black, brown, or sometimes green. Most of these chests, usually bearing a date and the initials of the original owner, appear to have been used as dower chests. Over one hundred and twenty have survived, evidence they were a very popular local product from about 1675 to 1740.

At the close of the seventeenth century another style developed (67), particularly in Guilford, Connecticut. In lieu of carving, chests were painted in designs drawn from Tudor and Dutch sources, the formal patterns of wooden inlay used in Europe.

64. A two-drawer Connecticut Valley chest with the sunflower design on the center panel and applied Jacobean ornaments stained black to simulate ebony

65a. The detail opposite is from the Connecticut chest illustrated on page 58.

65. *The painted landscapes on this chest of drawers recall a 1357 account of an English coffer painted with "various figures moving like life . . . beasts and birds flying to and fro."*

66. A Hadley chest made for Mary Pease about 1714, probably by her father, John Pease, a joiner in Enfield, Connecticut

67. A pine chest with the painted decorations that became popular around Guilford, Connecticut, at the end of the 1600's

ST OMER

Fashions from Abroad

The William and Mary Style (1685-1720)

Throughout the colonial period visitors from abroad frequently remarked on the similarities of colonial and English life, usually with considerable surprise. It seemed improbable that a people perched on the edge of a remote wilderness could so closely approximate the sophisticated ways of European civilization. "A Gentleman from *London* would almost think himself at home at *Boston*," wrote one of them about 1700, "when he observes the Numbers of People, their Houses, their Furniture, their Tables, their Dress and Conversation, which perhaps is as splendid and showy, as that of the most considerable Tradesman in *London*. . . . There is no Fashion in *London*, but in three or four Months is to be seen at *Boston*." To others, some colonists among them, it seemed that America was indeed too far from "home" to enjoy fully the benefits of civilization. (One Virginian, very touchingly, left directions in his will that upon his death his heart should be removed from his corpse, embalmed, and sent "home" to England, there to be interred with the remains of his friends and relatives.) Generally speaking, however, what went on in England was carefully noted in the colonies, and the affairs of the British Empire had an influence on even the details of colonial life.

As the seventeenth century waned and the new century dawned, the affairs of empire were marked by upheavals that radically changed the course of English history and redirected the future of colonists as well as of Englishmen. The first of these was the overthrow of Cromwell's Puritan protectorate in 1660 and the restoration of the Stuart monarchy under Charles II, the voluptuary "merry monarch," who had spent a dozen unemployed years on the Continent waiting for this moment of vindication and glory. Charles took as his queen Catherine of Braganza, who brought from her native Portugal the richest dowry in Europe and, in her train, hundreds of Portuguese artisans. (As part of the matrimonial agreement English ships were to enjoy free trading rights in Brazil and the Portuguese East Indies, and the Portuguese possessions of Tangier and Bombay were to be ceded to the English, a concession that widely opened the door to the East for England.) After the drab years of Cromwell's authority, Charles' extravagant and pleasure-loving habits combined with Catherine's rich and varied resources worked remarkable changes in the life of the court and in those who aped it—changes that, among other things, marked the beginning of the end of England's insular traditions and a growing appreciation of continental taste, design, and custom.

In this new dispensation furniture was desired to be something more than useful; it was required to serve new and special purposes. The heavy oak forms of earlier days were swept out of fashion; and in their place proliferated a novel

Opposite: objects of the late 17th and early 18th centuries; for descriptions see p. 373

A Chinese lacquer cabinet on an elaborately carved 17th-century English stand

variety of chairs, tables, cabinets, and other pieces made of walnut, other fine woods, and veneers better suited to "the politer way of living" that was introduced with the Restoration. "The King do mind nothing but pleasures," Samuel Pepys discovered soon after Charles donned his crown. To serve those pleasures and to ease the fatigues of the beau monde, gaming tables, tea tables, special tables for private dining, upholstered easy chairs, day beds and chairs with resilient, East-India-style, caned seats and backs, and other effete contraptions were either introduced for the first time or, at least, were given new importance. The diarist John Evelyn, himself a Royalist and a man of many parts, deplored the popularity of these foreign modes and the "luxury (more than Asiatick . . .)" that was "corrupting [the] ancient simplicity" of English life.

The Glorious Revolution of 1688 ended the reign of James II, brother and successor of Charles II, and summoned the Dutchman William of Orange across the Channel to rule the empire with his English wife, Mary Stuart. Their reign in turn brought the island into even closer relationships with the Continent. Dutch and Flemish craftsmen, architects and cabinetmakers among them, came to England to practice their skills and to transplant their own traditions on British soil. Following the revocation of the Edict of Nantes in 1685, which deprived French Protestants of the right to practice their religion, Huguenot craftsmen, seeking refuge in England, gave fresh popularity to French styles. (More than a few Huguenots found their way to America, among them skilled craftsmen and seasoned men of affairs.) William's own court designer and architect, Daniel Marot, was a Paris-born refugee. Both Portugal and Holland, as the principal traders with the Far East, had an old familiarity with the exotic wares of the Orient—with porcelains and lacquers, tea and caned furniture, and other "India and Chinese curiosities." Standing as they did at the crossroads of world trade, they also had developed traditions of art in which designs, materials, and customs of divers origins, eastern and western, had been blended into fresh amalgams that were strange and exciting to sensitive Englishmen. In English furniture there now appeared such features as Flemish scrolls, Spanish feet, Dutch turnings, and similar borrowings from continental sources.

Modern England began with Charles' accession to the throne. One relatively minor point in favor of that statement is that tea, coffee, and chocolate, those three non-alcoholic drinks which have ever since played such a pleasant part in English—and American—social life, first became popular during the Restoration. Tea had long been known in England, but its merits were disputed and its peculiar delights barely savored. Some thought of it as a medicinal drink (or as an herb to be chewed) good for, among other ailments, a "cold and defluxions" and "the Headache giddiness and heaviness thereof." Others considered it a "damned weed," a "rank poison far-fetched and dear bought." At first it was indeed a costly drink. As late as 1664 the East India Company presented Charles with slightly over two pounds of tea valued at forty shillings a pound. Nevertheless, as Catherine demonstrated to the ladies of her court, tea could be drunk from dainty porcelain cups for sheer pleasure. The vogue caught on, and it was not many years before Daniel Defoe complained that the shops and warehouses that sprang up to meet the demands of the tea-drinking public transformed the character of London streets. The thirst for coffee and chocolate and the invention of pots and other apparatus for their service developed about the same time and in much the same way. By the early eighteenth century there were some five hundred coffeehouses in London alone, where all these drinks could be ordered.

In the decades following the Restoration the vogue for other Oriental products —porcelain, lacquer, painted fabrics and wallpapers—developed into a virtual mania. Such wares, like tea, had long before been known in England; but with their own collections and enthusiasms first Catherine and then Mary gave new glamour to these exotic fancies. The comic dramatists and the poets of the time had great sport with the new vogues, as when John Gay in *To a Lady on her Passion for Old China* playfully reproved his mistress for diverting her infatuation from him to her porcelains. The passion for lacquer was so great that even little girls at school were anxious to learn how to produce such "japanned" ware, as English imitations of lacquer were termed. "Everybody is mad about japan work," wrote one lady of the time to another, "I hope to be a dab at it by the time I see you." And so enormous was the popularity of chintz, or painted India calicoes, that in 1700 Parliament forbade their importation to save the English textile industry from ruination. In good time all this excitement reached America and stirred the colonists to emulation.

During the last decades of the seventeenth century the colonists had their separate preoccupations, which did not always encourage the importation of English notions. In 1675 and 1676 New England suffered the most devastating war in its history—King Philip's War as it was called after Metacom, or Philip, sachem of the Wampanoags, who started the conflict. With that gory business out of the way and, particularly, with the recall of the Massachusetts Bay charter in 1684 (among other considerations, Charles was annoyed by the minting of the pine-tree shillings) and the appointment of a royal governor, forces that had been latent in the colonies for some years past came to active life. With the reign of William of Orange the colonies were brought not only into the orbit of world

Above: portrait of Charles II on an English delft cup. At left: English ladies, in calico gowns, drinking tea

politics but into the main current of world thought. In any case, in those years around the turn of the century, very roughly from about 1685 to about 1720, remarkable changes were taking place throughout the colonial scene; changes that not only revealed the far-reaching authority of English taste but also proclaimed the vitality of New World attitudes. New cities, notably Charleston and Philadelphia, sprouted in the wilderness and almost overnight flowered into vital centers of trade and culture. The colonists now occupied most of the Atlantic coastal plain from the "Arctic braced" forests of northern New England to the wide deltas of southern Carolina. Within a generation after its founding in 1670 Charleston (then known as Charles Town) won the reputation of a "wealthy place"; pirates swarmed about the port, and in that benign, subtropical climate a great mixture of peoples—Barbadians, French Calvinists, English dissenters, Scottish Covenanters, Negroes, Dutchmen from New York and from Holland, Quakers, New England Baptists, Irish Catholics, and Jews among others—soon were fused into a unique cosmopolitan society.

From left to right: portraits of William and Mary on a delft jug; Indian warfare, detail from an engraved map; the great fire of London, 1666; portrait of Sir Christopher Wren; engraving of the steeple of St. Mary-Le-Bow, one of Wren's London parish churches

Philadelphia was founded in 1682 and very soon became a prodigy among cities. William Penn had widely advertised his land of freedom on the European continent as well as in England, and Philadelphia became a port of entry for great hordes of expectant immigrants. It was a carefully planned city, neatly laid out as a gridiron, and it soon boasted an impressive number of brick dwellings, "generally three stories high after the mode in London." No urban center in history had ever grown so rapidly and so gracefully as it did. By 1720 the city was so "full of all Country business and Sea affairs" that it had outdistanced all its colonial rivals except Boston.

In older communities as well, modern buildings were rising beside their old-fashioned neighbors and adding a new look to the cityscapes. "When any new houses are built," an English observer wrote of Boston in 1686, "they are made conformable to our new buildings in London since the fire." He was referring to the holocaust of 1666 that had virtually wiped out medieval London and to the more formally designed structures that replaced the charred ruins—structures whose basic character and whose ornamental detail were derived from Renaissance formulas as these were translated by English architects.

The most influential practitioner of the new order was Sir Christopher Wren, whose plan—never consummated—for re-creating the stricken city was the prototype of the one developed more than a century later for Washington, D.C. Among his many buildings, the fifty-two London churches he designed, with their tall, graceful spires (Gothic forms in classical guise) rising high above low-pitched roofs, set a general pattern for the Georgian churches and meetinghouses that would become such a prominent and engaging feature of the American landscape in the following century and a half. It was reported from Virginia that Wren drew the plans for the first William and Mary college building at Williamsburg, begun in 1695—probably the largest structure to have been built in the colonies. In 1699 the capital of Virginia was transferred from Jamestown to land adjoining the college, and here another new, planned city of imposing civic buildings and trim dwellings quickly sprang up from a flat and empty countryside. It is one of the most deliberate accomplishments in colonial town planning, as today's restoration so dramatically reveals. The capitol building may have been designed by one of King William's Dutch architects. At least it shows

strong Dutch influence and is remarkably similar to the New York City Hall that was erected around 1700 when Dutch influence was still strong in that city.

Practically none of the fine houses that were built in the years around the turn of the century have survived in their original form. They introduced elements of both style and comfort that became standard for American domestic architecture for the remainder of the colonial period. On the exterior of such houses, the windows—sliding-sash now, instead of casement windows—were rhythmically arranged on a façade whose central feature was a more or less elaborate doorway framed with classical moldings and detail. Inside, the kitchen was separated from the other rooms. To keep the increased number of these rooms as warm as might be, two chimneys were built at the ends of the building, allowing for a wide hall to run from the front to the back door, which often opened on a formal garden. Fireplaces relieved of their kitchen duties were smaller and somewhat more efficient.

In the older buildings the structural elements of the house had been left exposed and for the most part undecorated. The functions of posts and beams, fireplaces and doorways were frankly expressed. In the newer houses the posts and beams were encased or concealed in the plaster, fireplaces and doorways were

Top: the main building of the College of William and Mary, built between 1695 and 1702. Above: New York's second City Hall. Below: a panel from the parlor of the house built in 1712 for William Clarke, on Garden Court Street in Boston, depicts the house's façade.

framed with architectural moldings, walls were often handsomely paneled. As the years passed, these features became more refined. Architectural guidebooks illustrating the "proper" details and proportions were published in growing numbers. But the change was one of degree rather than kind, and architecture of this general and basic character is now referred to as being in the Georgian style. With these structures the influence of the Italian Renaissance, with its emphasis on symmetry, formal order, and classical motifs, found its first significant expression in British America.

The great London fire, opening the way as it did to a massive modernization of that capital's architecture (more than thirteen thousand buildings had been destroyed), no doubt popularized the new style in America sooner and more effectively than might otherwise have been the case. Still, in each passing season the winds of change swept across the Atlantic following the trade routes. By the turn of the century the impact of new modes and manners was marked in all the burgeoning centers of colonial civilization. The major transformation in the trappings and accessories of daily life that England had experienced with the return of Charles II, and again with the advent of William and Mary, was now giving new shape to the patterns of American culture. And the presence of royal governors heightened interest in the latest fashions from abroad—fashions in hair styles and costume as well as in masonry, woodwork, and silverware.

Not all the colonists suffered the changes gladly. In 1679 Increase Mather warned his compatriots that the younger generation of New Englanders was looking abroad to the English Gomorrah in search of "*Courtly Pomp and Delicacy*." No sooner was a "proud Fashion" introduced into the country, he lamented, than "the *haughty Daughters* of Zion in this place are taking it up, and thereby the whole land is at last infected." That substantial merchant Samuel Sewall regarded the frivolous lives and wicked extravagance of those who led the fashionable world in and about Boston with indignation; and he took the local notary public severely to task for shaving his head and "wearing a Perriwig of contrary Colour"—an abominable affectation favored by those who took the royal governor and his intimates for their models.

But the old order inevitably gave way. Sewall himself, although he decried the morals of those men of fashion, had ample respect for their high social station. He even looked with some awe on Governor Edmund Andros in his "Scarlet Coat Laced" and behaved with full deference on the memorable occasion when he was introduced to His Excellency. Like many of his fellow merchants, Sewall had traveled abroad. As a result of such exposures to society overseas, one visitor reported, the conversation of Boston was remarkably "polite." And "those that stay at home," he added, had "the Advantage of a free Education with Travellers. . . ." Before many years had passed, Sewall was drinking tea quite as casually as any Englishman and ordering from London furniture "of the newest Fashion (if the Fashion be good)"—as well as a gown of Chinese silk, such as was not available in Boston, for his third wife. He was also repairing occasionally to one of the local coffeehouses. The first of these was opened in Boston as early as 1676. Around the turn of the century all the larger cities had such public houses, modeled after those of London, where merchants assembled to do their business and exchange news of interest while they sipped the fragrant brew. And presumably, as in London, the air in those establishments grew ever blacker with the smoke of Virginia tobacco.

Because of its mixed population and its intimate associations with continental

Left: Elisha Cooke, Sr., a public figure in Boston, in a periwig. Above: the ship, Nassau, *in which Captain Giles Shelley sailed to Madagascar for pirates' treasure*

Europe, New York continued to be the most cosmopolitan and worldly of colonial cities. Shortly after he assumed office in 1668, Governor Francis Lovelace reported to Charles II with astonishment, "I find these people have the breeding of courts, and I cannot conceive how such is acquired." At the club where he associated with other royal officials and members of the leading New York families, one might have heard polite conversation in an easy medley of English, Dutch, and French. And in the houses, most of them still crowded together below "the Wall Street" at the tip of Manhattan Island, one would have found a variety of furnishings brought from distant lands to satisfy the demands of sophisticated New Yorkers.

Almost every New York household of any pretension seems to have displayed porcelains, lacquers, silks, and other items of eastern origin. When she died in 1696, Margharita Van Varick, for example, left behind her a large quantity of Chinese porcelains, a number of "East India" cabinets, cane baskets, ten India looking glasses, and "eleven Indian babyes [dolls]," along with an impressive array of ebony chairs, lacquer trays, and other exotic wares—all sorts of those strangely beautiful things that had been adopted with such excitement in England starting with the Restoration. Captain Giles Shelley, a local merchant and sea captain whose silver tankard is illustrated on page 105, also had a sizable collection of Oriental treasures, some of which he undoubtedly acquired through his close association with the pirates who trafficked heavily in luxuries from the East and who found New York an especially congenial port of call.

In 1697 the Earl of Bellomont, then royal governor of New York, Massachusetts, and New Hampshire, reported to London that in New York, as in other colonial cities, the merchants "not onlie wink at, but Imbrace Pirats, men and shippes." (Buccaneers even walked the streets of Quaker Philadelphia.) The celebrated Captain William Kidd was a respected and valued New Yorker when he advised Bellomont that "he knew the pyrats hants so well, that he could sail directly to 'em." That he did when he headed straight for their major rendezvous at Madagascar, charged by the government with suppressing piracy for once and all. However, Kidd suffered such difficulties and temptations that he turned pirate himself and in 1701 was hanged by the neck for his crime.

Pirated gold and silver oiled the colonial economy, and any government action to control such activity was unpopular with the merchants. Pirated gold and silver also provided the colonial silversmiths with the essential materials of their craft, which were otherwise not easy enough to come by. As it turned out, the first quarter of the eighteenth century was the pirates' heyday, in spite of England's efforts to put an end to their activity.

The introduction of novel beverages—of tea, coffee, chocolate, and punch—put a demand upon the silversmith for a variety of entirely new forms for the service of those drinks; and the influence of the "international" school of design introduced by the Restoration produced new styles of ornament and decoration not dreamed of in the preceding generations, as the following pages will illustrate. One further encouragement to silversmithing in the early decades of the eighteenth century was the increasing value of silver itself; in 1710 an ounce of the metal in New England was valued at eight shillings, in 1719 at twelve shillings, and by 1724 at seventeen shillings. Thus, wealth converted into usable plate proved to be a safe and profitable investment.

In any event, every colonial city and town of any size supported an ever increasing number of silversmiths, most of whom seem to have prospered in their work and many of whom were distinguished members of their communities. Boston supported a dozen silversmiths before it found employment for a single lawyer, and almost as many smiths were working in New York before the seventeenth century ended, men of Dutch, French, and German descent who were soon joined by craftsmen of English stock. Philadelphia's earliest silversmiths, César Ghiselin and Johannis Nys, were apparently both Huguenot *émigrés* who found haven in the Quaker city. There, it was reported in 1698, "silversmiths . . . have between Half a Crown and Three Shillings an Ounce for working their Silver and for Gold equivalent," a very fair return for their skills.

Penn had promised that his would be a "free colony for all mankind," and some years later a traveling European observed, "it has not been necessary to force people to come and settle here [in Pennsylvania]; on the contrary, foreigners of different languages have left their country, houses, property and relations and ventured over wide and stormy seas in order to come hither. . . ." From the beginning those "schismatical [and] factious" Quakers, a sect whose members had earlier been whipped and dragged through the streets of Boston and hanged on the Common, formed a very substantial element in Philadelphia society. Their sober purposefulness and industry brought those people a solid prosperity, and their generous patronage of local artisans made Philadelphia a center of fine craftsmanship almost simultaneously with its founding. Between 1682 and 1722 more than one hundred furniture makers alone—including clockmakers, upholsterers, and japanners—worked in the city and its environs.

In some ways Virginia seemed less like a threshold to the New World than a back garden of the Old. It remained largely a rural world and, as in the Carolina low country, affluent families continued to look to England for their furniture, furnishings, clothes, and many other necessities and luxuries of life. "The habits, life, customs, computations, etc. of the Virginians," wrote the Reverend Hugh Jones in 1724, "are much the same as about London, which they esteem their home." (Another earlier and more critical commentator pointed out that even the small planters imported much of their furniture. "Though their country be over-run with wood, yet they have all their wooden-ware from England," he caustically observed.) Jones went on to say that the planters spoke good English, by which he meant they did not have outlandish accents like the Scots and the provincial English, and that their clothes were of the best.

Among the most urbane of those planters, and among the wealthiest, was

William Byrd II of Westover. A seasoned traveler, a graduate of the Middle Temple and a member of the English bar, and also a member of the Royal Society, Byrd was a distinguished and powerful figure in Virginia's ruling group. Like his fellow tobacco aristocrats, he furnished his house with everything necessary for his comfort and taste after the latest fashion from England. Between his many and more serious activities he played billiards, cricket, and whist, watched the horse races, threw dice, and drank tea, punch, and French and Rhenish wines (the latter with sugar). And when he visited Williamsburg on official and personal business, he frequented the coffeehouse and the theatre. In London, Byrd had spent the rakehell years of his youth in the lingering atmosphere of Restoration gaiety and gallantry. As a mature adult with many responsibilities he was the very model of a Virginia aristocrat. The home he built in his later years, which housed his enormous library and his fine furnishings, remains a superb example of colonial architecture in the style of that later day.

In spite of the remarks quoted at the beginning of this chapter, and in spite of the close watch such colonists as Byrd kept on the London scene, it usually took longer than three or four months for the latest London fashions to strike roots in America; and once they were firmly rooted, they tended to persist long after the mode had changed abroad. Very little furniture in the William and Mary style, probably, was in the colonies during the reign of those monarchs; and most of the American-made adaptations of the style surely date from the period of Queen Anne and even later. Whatever the delays in transit may have been, however, sooner or later what was accepted in London as good taste and progress in the domestic arts found favor in the colonies, and native or immigrant artisans responded to demands for the latest thing. By 1720 most of the innovations that delighted Restoration England and the further refinements of the William and Mary style had become part of the colonial domestic scene.

In the course of settling down on American soil, after a long ocean crossing, the style underwent some marked changes in the hands of native craftsmen. It is not always easy to account for these since at times, when so disposed or so instructed, the colonial craftsman could apparently duplicate an English model to the slightest detail. There are examples of intricately carved caned furniture, in any case, whose place of origin—England or America—cannot easily be determined. However, at other times, various elements of the style were combined in ways that were rarely or never attempted in England. These colonial idioms would probably have been considered unstylish and rustic overseas, although such combinations seem as agreeable to us today as they undoubtedly did to the original owners of those pieces. In some cases the freedom from imported conventions reached the point where entirely fresh inventions emerged, such as the so-called butterfly table and the elaborately decorated silver tankards made in New York, which bear a clearly discernible stamp of the New World.

As in the case of other foreign fashions adopted in this country, the William and Mary style lingered on in its various phases well into the century. And, far more generally than in our day of rapid change, furniture and furnishings were considered property of enduring usefulness and value and were passed on from generation to generation. One revealing sidelight on this conservatism appeared in the advertisement of a Philadelphia chairmaker in 1734, whose major business, it seems, was not so much in chairs newly made as in the "old Chairs caned or Holes mended (if not gone too far)," which he offered to do "at reasonable rates" at his shop next to the "Sign of the Pewter Platter in Front Street."

Above: a portrait of William Byrd II, done in London, 1715–20, by Sir Godfrey Kneller. Opposite: as famous as Captain Kidd, Edward Teach, commonly known as Blackbeard for an obvious reason, was one of the most enterprising and most bloodthirsty pirates of the Spanish Main.

68. *A quillwork, or paper filigree, sconce with a crest on the frame*

69. *Tall-back, caned chairs were at first used around the tea table.*

The New Elegance

The William and Mary period marked the end of the medieval heritage in colonial design. The massive, rectilinear Jacobean forms were supplanted by furniture with a new lightness, finer carving, and surfaces decorated with veneer and inlay. Special attention was given to the choice of woods used in order to present beautiful grains immediately attractive to the eye. Walnut, in particular, replaced oak. These fresh concepts not only reflected seventeenth-century European baroque, that "unrestrained decorative orgy" introduced to Restoration England by way of France and the Low Countries, but also expressed the influences of the Orient. In the colonies the prosperity of the rising middle class created a demand for luxuries enjoyed in the Old World. Fashions from abroad were eagerly imitated. To fill these demands, cabinetmakers—a new order of artisans skilled in making fine case furniture—were appearing in the colonies. Unlike the urban English cabinetmakers, those in America turned their hands to everyday jobs and to a wide variety of carpentry work. The departure from the Jacobean is strikingly seen in chairs of the William and Mary period. This one (69) was made in New York around 1690. The pierced crests on the front stretcher and on the back are a Flemish design that characterized Restoration chairs; the caning is Far Eastern; the S-scrolls on the front legs are baroque, as is the rich carving on the back, "cutt with scrowles all over." The crested sconce (68) further illustrates the new taste for elegance. The decoration is "quillwork," an exacting filigree made of myriad strips of paper rolled into tiny scrolls, colored, gilded, or dusted with mica. Quillwork, a fifteenth-century craft, was revived in the seventeenth century and became a fashionable hobby for ladies of leisure in England and the colonies. The New England walnut dressing table (70) shows the new trends in cabinetwork and design: trumpet-shaped turnings on the legs; a serpentine, X-shaped cross-stretcher; narrow, double-arch moldings to trim the drawers; a curved profile to the skirt; and veneer to create an attractive surface.

70. A William and Mary walnut dressing table, an example of a new, specialized furniture form

A William and Mary armchair with its elaborate turnings, pierced crestings, and curved, carved arms bears little resemblance to the Gothic solidity of wainscot and Brewster armchairs of earlier colonial days. The chair shown here (71), indicative of the growing taste for sophisticated design and gracious living, is believed to have belonged to Captain Peter Schuyler, who was appointed the first mayor of Albany in 1686. (As head commissioner of Indian affairs for New York, Schuyler took several Iroquois chiefs with him on his visit to the court of Queen Anne in 1710.)

Leather upholstery was popularized in England during Cromwell's regime and continued to be used on armchairs, such as this one, as well as on side chairs in the same general style. But for both these types of chairs, woven cane on seats and on backs was characteristic of the William and Mary period and was extensively seen in Europe and the colonies. Cane, or rattan which grows in tropical Asia, was introduced to the western world by the Dutch and the Portuguese, and it came to England with the Restoration. The vogue for caned furniture reached such heights that English textile makers around 1690, suffering a loss of trade in upholstery fabrics, petitioned Parliament requesting the suppression of the cane-chair makers' thriving business.

71. An armchair probably made in colonial New York

71a. A detail (opposite) of the carved cresting with its repeated C-scrolls connected by formalized carved leaves

One of the first-known colonial clockmakers settled in New Haven in 1638, and Boston had a tower clock by 1657, as shown by a record of thirty shillings paid for its repair in that year. But clocks continued to be a rarity in the average household, despite the increasing number of skilled craftsmen in America at the turn of the century. Earlier timepieces were imported largely from England and Holland. The use of pendulum-driven works, invented toward the end of the seventeenth century, soon spread to America, and many old-model clocks were converted, as was the English lantern clock shown below (73), into "wag on the wall" mechanisms. Also, with the advent of longer pendulums, tall cases were devised to enclose and protect the works. This example (72) was made by John Wood, Sr. The case with its columned hood, by an unknown cabinetmaker, is similar to several others made around 1700 in and about Philadelphia.

Also among the new luxuries prized in the colonies during the William and Mary period were looking glasses, not yet widely produced in America. The example shown here (75), made in England between 1700 and 1710 during the reign of Queen Anne, is typical of the framed glasses that were exported to the New World at that time. The walnut table (76) was made in New England, but the slate and marquetry top (74) of a similar table is presumed to be a Swiss import because work of this sort can be seen in Swiss museums.

72. A walnut case encloses this pendulum clock made in Philadelphia.

73. A brass English lantern clock

74. *An imported slate and marquetry table top*

75. *An English looking glass with walnut frame*

76. *A William and Mary walnut dressing table with finials on apron and stretcher*

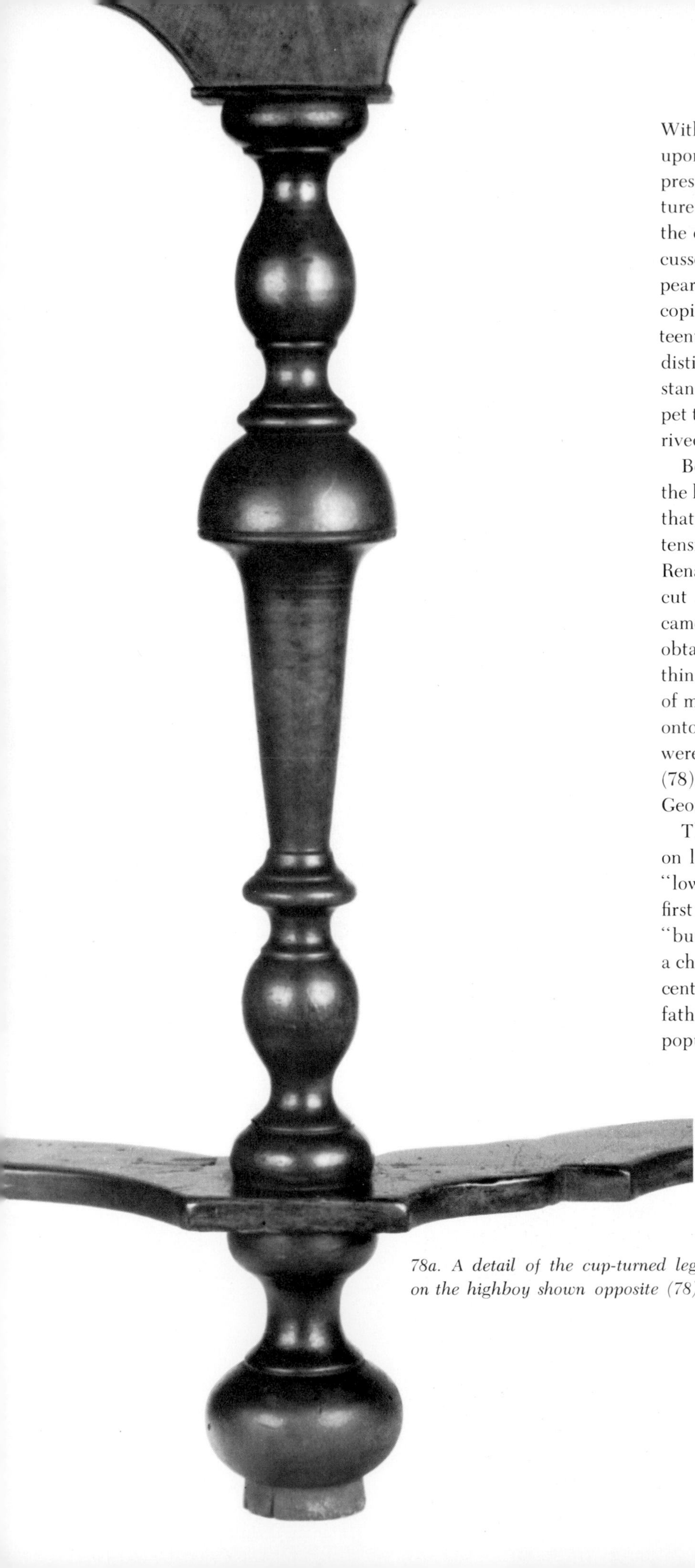

With the William and Mary period, a chest of drawers set upon a stand took the place of the Jacobean court and press cupboards as the most imposing single piece of furniture in a colonial household. A logical development from the comparatively primitive Jacobean chest-on-frame, discussed earlier on page 27, high chests of drawers first appeared in England after the Restoration and were soon copied in America. The "curious passion of the late seventeenth century for supports with many legs" became a distinguishing earmark of William and Mary chests on stands (77 and 78), as did the curved stretchers, the trumpet turnings (77), and the cup turnings (78), all designs derived from the baroque styles of Europe.

Both examples shown here are veneered with walnut, the leading wood for both William and Mary furniture and that of the forthcoming Queen Anne style. First used extensively for fine furniture during the Italian and Spanish Renaissance, walnut was durable, light in weight, easily cut and carved, and readily polished to a rich finish. It came in a variety of colors, and beautiful patterns could be obtained by cutting root and burl sections of a tree into thin strips suitable for veneer, the highly skilled technique of matching, fitting, and gluing decorative sheets of wood onto a solid surface. Inlaid strips of a contrasting grain were often used for borders, as on the New England chest (78), said to have been owned by Mary Ball Washington, George Washington's mother.

The term "highboy" to describe a high chest of drawers on legs was first used in the nineteenth century, as was "lowboy" to describe the dressing table—a new form that first came into fashion in Restoration England. The word "bureau" referred to a secretary or desk and came to mean a chest of drawers (but only in America) in the nineteenth century. Similarly, tall case clocks were not called grandfather clocks during this period; the phrase came from the popular song "Grandfather's Clock," published in 1875.

78a. A detail of the cup-turned leg on the highboy shown opposite (78)

77. The band of molding at the top of this walnut highboy conceals a drawer.

78. A highboy with decorative walnut veneer. Both chests have brass pulls, probably an English import, and both are from New England, 1700–1720.

79. *Col. Jonathan Warner, of His Majesty's Council*

80. *Macpheadris-Warner house, Portsmouth, N.H.*

81. *Murals in the Macpheadris-Warner house showing two of the five Iroquois sachems who were presented at the court of Queen Anne by Captain Peter Schuyler in 1710*

82. *Captain Peter Schuyler by an unknown painter*

One of the earliest Georgian houses still standing in New England, and reputedly the first brick house in Portsmouth, New Hampshire, was built about 1716 by Captain Archibald Macpheadris, a prosperous Scottish fur trader. The fluted Corinthian pilasters that frame the central doorway and the broken-arch pediment that caps it, the relatively large sash windows regularly disposed on the façade, and the horizontal band between the first two stories all reflect the influence of Renaissance patterns that would predominate in colonial architecture during the rest of the century. Later occupied by Captain Macpheadris' daughter and her husband, Colonel Jonathan Warner (79), the house cost six thousand pounds to construct. Murals adorn the staircase walls; two are life-size representations of Iroquois sachems (81).

From the Farthest East

Early in the sixteenth century Portuguese mariners, feeling their way around the southern tip of Africa and probing deeper into uncharted seas, opened new trade routes to the Far East. When the lumbering, square-rigged carracks of those pioneering seafarers brought back the exotic freight they gathered in such distant lands, Europe's imagination stirred with new excitement. There followed a wild scramble among western nations seeking treasures from the Orient —porcelains, lacquers, and other prized commodities that beguiled Europeans but that were beyond the skill of Europeans to produce. The trade was immensely profitable.

England was slow to join this competition in a serious way; but when Catherine of Braganza delivered Bombay to Charles II as part of her dowry, the English had a foothold that quickly led to a great advance in their trade with China and the East Indies. When they were installed in her royal apartments at Hampton Court, the objects included with the rest of her dowry created a sensation among her new countrymen. Along with other things, John Evelyn noted in 1662, "the Queen brought over with her from Portugal such Indian cabinets as had never before been seen here." He was referring to examples of lacquer ware that in the Occident was variously known as Indian, Chinese, or Japanese depending upon the locality of the Oriental seaport from which it was shipped to the western markets.

This initial astonishment gave way to a spreading desire to collect and own such precious rarities. In 1697 the English East India Company recorded one order alone for almost two thousand lacquer tables. Even so, supplies were too limited—and prices remained too high—to satisfy the English public that craved goods of the sort. So less expensive, more readily obtainable imitations were fabricated at home to meet the demand. Late in the seventeenth century the term "japanned" was coined to designate this substitute for the true lacquer—figures in low relief, modeled in gesso, covered with metal leaf, and disposed on black and red painted grounds. Many manuals were published to guide the amateur and professional alike through the mysteries of design and production; the first, by Stalker and Parker, appeared in 1688.

Oriental wares of all sorts found their way to the colonies as well. Some were channeled through the English East India Company, which monopolized England's trade with the East; others were smuggled in and came by way of pirating. One unfortunate ship's captain, when he reached Virginia from Madagascar in 1721, was seized "to be carried Home for his Tryal, not for any Dealings with the Pyrates [which he had had], but for having on Board East India goods," in violation of the company's monopoly. In the colonies also relatively inexpensive approximations of true Oriental work were produced to satisfy the demand for "exotica." In 1712 Nehemiah Partridge advertised that he could provide "all sorts of Japan work" for Bostonians, and he was followed by others who claimed that "no damp air, no mouldring worm or corroding time" could ever deface their handiwork. Some excellent samples (83) have indeed survived in good condition over the centuries since.

83. A japanned highboy, made in Massachusetts about 1700, with "Steps for China Ware"

84. *Chased detail with exotic figures from the base of a candlestick made about 1705 by Cornelius Kierstede (1674–1757) of New York*

85. *An India painted cotton (right), called a palampore, with the tree of life design*

86. *A Japanese porcelain bowl (below) with mounts marked by an unidentified silversmith*

87. *Tapestry (opposite) by John Vanderbank*

Once established, the vogue for *chinoiseries*, as these imaginative western adaptations of Oriental designs and motifs are called, affected virtually every phase of craftsmanship. In England during the 1670's and 80's fantasies in the Chinese manner were a fashionable form of engraved or chased decoration on silverware. Actually, these were purely fanciful scenes in which bizarre birds, beasts, and insects, fantastic shrubs and flowers, and caricatures of Oriental people were disposed in frivolous arrangements. In a few rare instances the colonial silversmith created similar versions of such pleasant whimsies (84), which may originally have been inspired by the romantic *chinoiserie* dramas that were staged in Restoration England.

Some of this vague but colorful imagery was woven into tapestries, such as those produced by John Vanderbank (87), the "most successful English tapestry manufacturer" of the early eighteenth century. Later in that century a touring American colonist noted a piece of tapestry "done by Vanderbank" in a sumptuous home in Massachusetts.

The painted calicoes, or chintz, from India (85), which were so immensely popular in England, apparently found their way to the colonies in some quantity. Before she was executed for witchcraft in 1656, Mistress Anne Hibbins managed to beautify the bed in her Boston home with "five painted calico curtains and valence," no doubt similar to those mentioned by Pepys in his diary for 1663: "Bought my wife a chint, that is a painted Indian calico, for to line her new study."

During the second half of the seventeenth century the Dutch East India Company brought to Europe from Japan porcelains—the so-called Imari porcelains—whose designs strongly influenced Europe's own porcelain industry in the years to come. No one knows how much of this ware reached the colonies, although the silver-mounted bowl shown here (86) may have been one example. Interestingly, a porcelain bowl with a notched rim was one of the objects forfeited or lost by Eliakim Hutchinson, a member of a distinguished Boston family, during the Revolution.

88. An octagonal Delft vase made in Holland about 1697. *89. Dutch Delft wig-stand made in the late 17th century*

Of all the products from the Far East porcelain was the most widely and variously imitated in Europe. Late in the seventeenth century a new wave of importations from China freshened public interest in this precious ware and supplied new models for European potters to copy or, indeed, provided them with ideas for novel developments of their own. As the illustrations on these pages suggest, forms in a wide variety—some derived from the Orient, others western in origin—were produced by English, Dutch, and other European potteries. Whatever their shape or function, a large proportion of these

90. Dutch Delft cube bottle, about 1685

91. Early 18th-century Delft wall plaque

92. English delft posset pot, 1690–1710

pieces owe their decoration, at least, to Oriental influences. Meanwhile, Europeans continued their own efforts to produce a true porcelain.

Judging from colonial inventories and other contemporary evidence, a sizable quantity of English and Dutch glazed earthenware—delftware—found its way to America in the seventeenth and eighteenth centuries, quite possibly including examples similar to those shown here. In any event, the unsymmetrical quality of Oriental design and decoration, its "antic" character as it appeared to western eyes, represented a new concept of beauty that challenged the orderly, measured classic styles of the time and that seemed to some critics to threaten the stability and progress of western art.

Comforts & Conveniences

The most important single contribution of the William and Mary period to solid comfort was the wing chair—or easy chair, as it was then called, introduced to Restoration England from the Continent. Such constructions, with their padded frames and with "wings" designed to ward off drafts, provided a soft and welcoming seat. No more completely easy chair has ever been devised. The boldly turned stretchers of the example shown here are a survival from earlier designs. The carved Spanish feet, sometimes known as Braganza feet, recall the tastes and trends introduced by Charles II's queen, Catherine of Braganza, that were still popular in the William and Mary period. The curved outline of the front legs, an adaptation of the earlier baroque scrolls, later developed into the cabriole leg, one of the most characteristic and graceful features of the Queen Anne style. The printed pattern of the covering fabric reflected the influence of the India chintzes that were such popular imports to the colonies in the late seventeenth century.

During the Restoration, with its emphasis on luxury, the art of upholstering became a thriving trade. In one brief twenty-one month period the crown ran up a bill of ten thousand pounds with the King's Upholsterer. The craft was soon established in the colonies with at least four upholstery shops in Boston, for instance, by 1688 and quickly gained in importance as the new styles in furniture spread. In the portrait above of Captain Johannes Schuyler and his wife—attributed to the Scottish immigrant John Watson—a prosperous colonial couple are presented in a setting of elegant comfort. The painting dates from about 1730, but the styles are of the William and Mary period. Madame Schuyler, in a loose overgarment with a hood—a mourning costume—sits in an upholstered chair, her arm casually resting on a tasseled cushion. The captain, who fought the French in early intercolonial wars and was a peacemaker between the Iroquois and the English, wears a bushy, powdered periwig and a long, deep-cuffed velvet coat.

93. Prosperous colonist Captain Johannes Schuyler and his wife

94. A wing chair made in New England early in the 18th century

Upholstered stools were uncommon in America during the William and Mary period despite their popularity in England; possibly court etiquette at the time decreed that those privileged to sit in the king's presence must sit upon stools. The unusual colonial example shown here (95), found in New Hampshire and made of maple, is covered in flamestitch embroidery, a pattern of Italian origin, or *bargèllo* work, also known as Hungarian work. Often seen in upholstery fabrics of this period, flamestitch continued in favor through the years up to today's needlework guides.

Corner chairs, or roundabout chairs (97), were a development of the William and Mary period. They were used at the card table but more often at a desk, hence the alternate term, writing chair. Their open fronts served to accommodate the voluminous skirts of women and the flaring coats of the men as well. In the example shown here, from the early 1700's, there are no splats between the seat and back rail. That comfortable addition was introduced in years to come. The center leg of this chair and the legs of the upholstered stool (95) terminate in Spanish feet.

A day bed (96) of "Cain," or "India" style, usually covered with cushions and with a canted back for added comfort, was designed for repose during the day. This rather formal concession to ease was first seen in England during Henry VIII's reign and reintroduced during the Restoration. The reverse-scroll carvings on this one are handsome illustrations of this highly fashionable motif.

95. Upholstered stools were rare in the William and Mary period. 96. A caned Massachusetts day bed with Flemish scrolls, 1690–1710

97. *A William and Mary corner chair, early 1700's*

Until the Restoration, writing furniture in England and America consisted largely of the portable desk with a slanted front, a heritage from the Middle Ages, sometimes known as a scholar's box. Convenient and comfortably designed desks in their varied forms had evolved by the close of the seventeenth century. This William and Mary fall-front desk with drawers (100), made in Massachusetts in the early eighteenth century, was veneered with walnut burl. Its teardrop drawer pulls are characteristic of the period, as is the "seaweed" cresting on the walnut-veneered frame of the looking glass above the desk.

The standish, or inkstand, wrought in silver for the first time at the end of the seventeenth century, created a rich and elaborate accessory for the newly fashionable desks. This one (99) was made by the Boston silversmith John Coney for Jonathan Belcher, governor of Massachusetts, New Hampshire, and, later, New Jersey. In the front is a shaker for pounce, a fine powder used to prevent the ink from spreading. Behind it to the left, engraved with Belcher's crest, is the container for wafers, disks of dried paste used for sealing letters. To the right is the inkwell. A fine hand became an admired skill, and calligraphy books gave extravagant samples of this art (98).

98. *Detail of calligraphy, from* Penman's Paradise, *printed in London about 1695*

99. *A silver inkstand made by John Coney*

100. *A slant-top desk and crested looking glass (opposite), both veneered in walnut*

Among the new forms of the period was the desk-on-frame (102), which developed, in effect, by setting the medieval scholar's box upon legs. This one from New York has a Dutch inscription (unfortunately, illegible) inside the lid, which opens upward; the interior is faced with pigeonholes. Another more elaborate form was the secretary, the upper part designed as a cabinet with a fall-front writing surface and drawers below. The skill of colonial cabinetmakers is handsomely shown in this example (105), made in New York about 1690–1710 and originally owned by the Brinckerhoff family. The body of the piece is cedar with beech and walnut inlays. This brass candleholder (104) offered concentrated lighting suitable for a desk.

Judging from the prodigious amount of writing by such diarists as Samuel Sewall and William Byrd II, and the vast output of such authors as Cotton Mather (101), the Boston divine, these men spent many hours at their desks. Byrd evidently owned one of the new desk forms of the period. In 1709 he noted in his diary: "We played at billiards in the afternoon. Then I mended the locks of my. . .secretary." Mather and Byrd possessed the largest personal libraries in the colonies at this time, each with three or four thousand titles. Many books were imported, but many were being printed locally. The first colonial press began in Cambridge in 1639; the second was set up at the Library Company in Philadelphia in 1692.

101. The Reverend Cotton Mather

102. A red gumwood desk-on-frame made around 1700

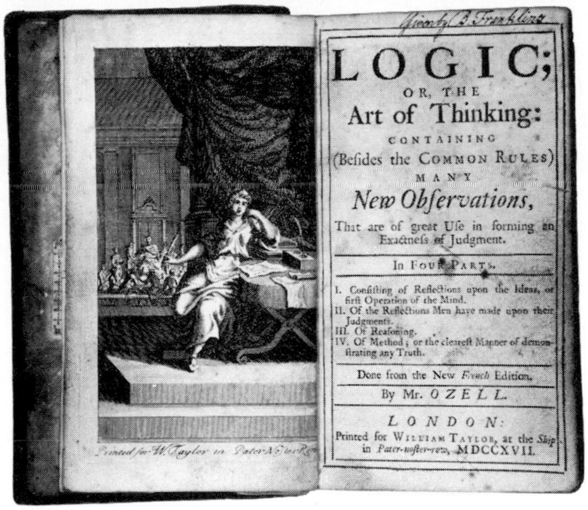

103. An English book on logic owned by young Franklin

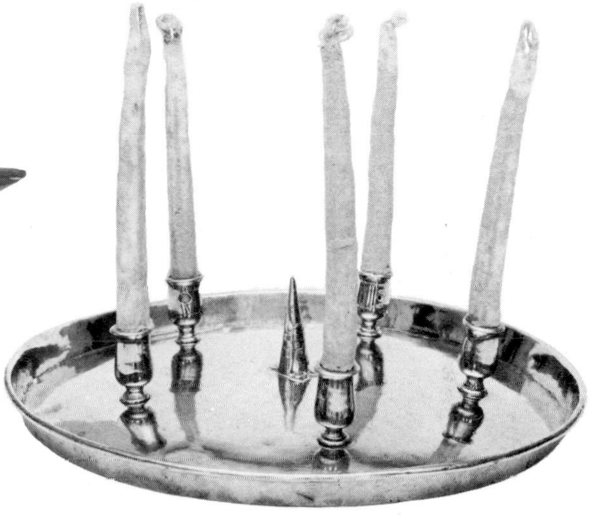

104. The brass candleholder is perhaps Dutch in origin.

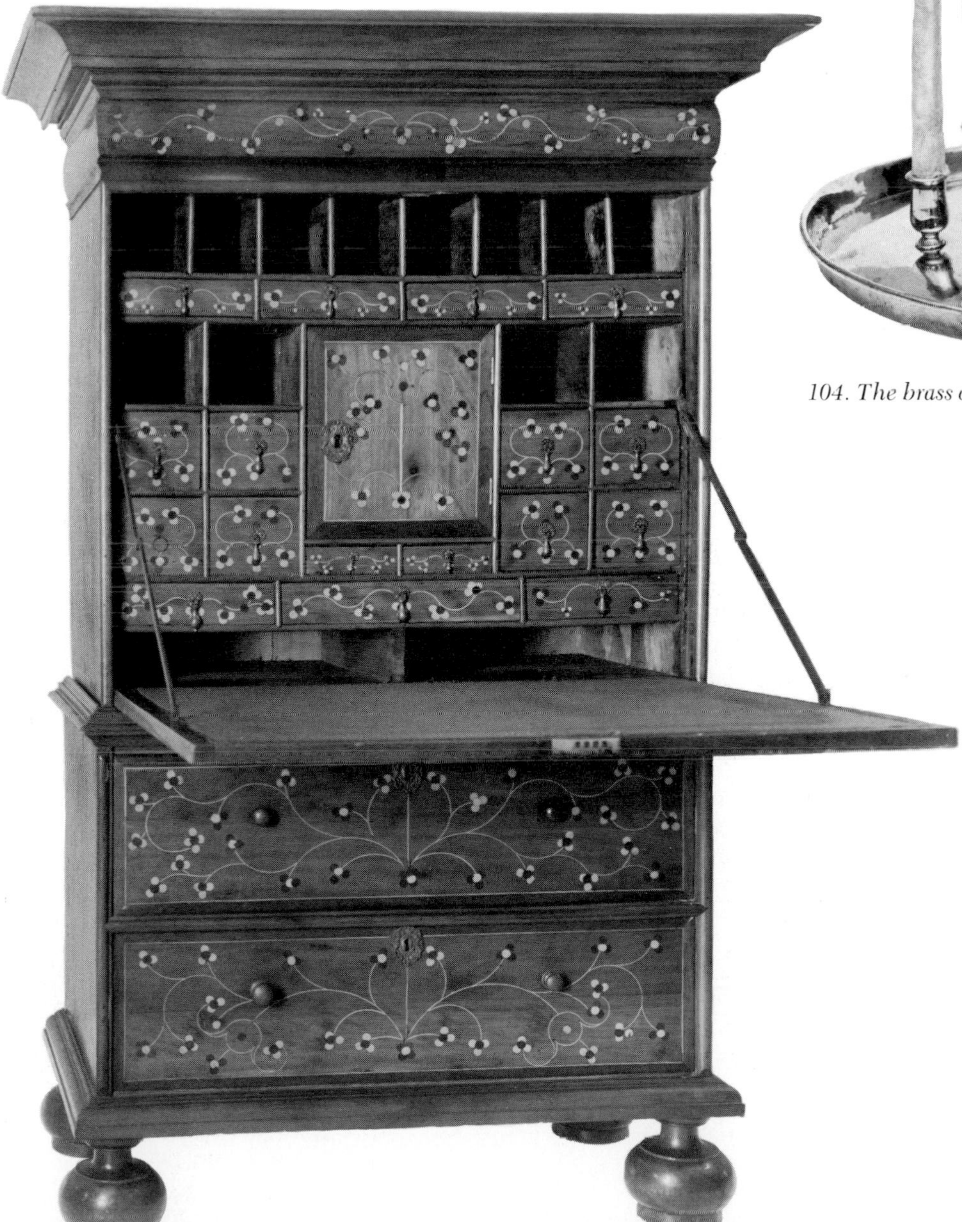

105. This New York secretary is ornamented with inlay.

Craftsmen & Apprentices

In colonial America no sharp line divided the crafts from the fine arts. Before he quit Boston for good on the eve of the Revolution to perfect his talents overseas, John Singleton Copley, the most accomplished of our early painters, found it mortifying that "people generally regard it [painting] no more than any other usefull trade... like that of a Carpenter, tailor or shew maker." For the eighteenth century the arts in general, emphatically including what we now call the crafts, were the means by which civilization was to gain in accomplishment and comfort—to progress, in short.

As the word was commonly used and understood in the eighteenth century, art was a useful, social accomplishment; it had a shared purpose. Colonial records mention, for example, that the town of Lancaster, Massachusetts, chose "an *artist* [a surveyor]...to lay our towne bounds"; that a pinnace sailed from Boston "under the conduct of Mr. Wm. Aspenwall, *a good artist* [a shipmaster and a navigator]"; and so forth. Today we feel the need to bring the artist into a more useful relation to society at large. The colonial world accomplished that by elevating every responsible and competent workman to the dignity of an artist.

The skills of the colonial artisan were solidly based on an ages-old tradition of training. By the late thirteenth and the early fourteenth centuries a carefully regulated system of apprenticeship in the various crafts and trades had been established in England. Municipal and guild authorities were charged with enforcement of the regulations. During Elizabeth's rule, in 1563, by the passage of a Statute of Artificers, this system was made uniform and general.

There were no guilds in America corresponding to those of England, but the colonists brought with them the essential features of the English apprenticeship system. In the New World, where so much work needed doing and where manpower was limited in relation to the resources of the land, the temptations to skimp the traditional regulations always remained great. However, town and colony authorities undertook to supervise such operations in the interest of the community. In 1660 the Boston town meeting decreed, "Whereas itt is found by sad experience that many youthes in this Town, being put forth Apprentices to severall manufactures and sciences, for but 3 or 4 years time, contrary to the Customes of all well governed places, whence they are uncapable of being Artists in their trade, besides their unmeetenes att the expiration of their Apprenticeship to take charge of others for government and manuall instruction in their occupations, which, if nott timely amended, threatens the welfare of this Towne, Itt is therefore ordered that no person shal henceforth open a shop in this Towne, nor occupy any manufacture or science, till hee hath compleated 21 years of age, nor except hee hath served seven years Apprentice-ship, by testamony under the hands of sufficient witnesses. And that all Indentures made betweene any master and servant shall bee brought in and enrolled in the Towne's Records within one month after the contract made, on penalty of ten shillings to bee paid by the master att the time of the Apprentices being made free." A similar order was issued by the Common Council of New York City in 1694, although the stipulation there was that an apprentice must serve his master "not for a Less Terme than four Yeares." However, in 1711 such a short term was held inadequate—after only four years apprentices were "seldom masters of their trades"—and a seven-year period was established by law. Most of the colonies at least tried to maintain this standard, in spite of a serious shortage of craftsmen in some places.

The indentures governing the relationship of master and apprentice generally followed English precedent. Be-

sides faithfully teaching a lad the "art and mystery" of his craft, the master was obliged to provide him with bed, board, and clothing. He was also responsible for the moral welfare of his apprentice, and usually for his instruction in reading, writing, and ciphering. At times the master was required, in addition, to send his charge to night school either at his own or the parents' expense. In 1719 the New York silversmith Charles Le Roux agreed "to suffer" his fifteen-year-old apprentice, Jacob Ten Eyck, to go to the "Evening School at the Charge of his Father." Like other apprentices, young Jacob agreed to live with Le Roux for seven years, faithfully "serve his Secretts [and] keep his lawfull Commands" and "gladly Everywhere Obey." He was not to waste his master's goods, nor gamble, nor fornicate, nor marry; nor was he to "haunt Alehouses Taverns or Playhouses."

Youngsters were not always susceptible to such discipline. In 1754 a South Carolina printer had to discharge a very capable but "villanous" apprentice who for three years "pulled the contrary way; owing to an unhappy affection for Drink, Play and Scandalous Company." One New York apprentice broke his arm at "one of those disorderly riotous Frolicks, that are most unreasonably practised annually" at the New Year. And certain others, *The New-England Courant* reported in 1722, were known to have resorted to a notorious house near the Old South meetinghouse where they indulged in improper and frivolous antics and even danced "Naked . . . with young Girls." In Boston!

On the other hand, when young Kiliaen Van Rensselaer came to Boston from Albany to serve as apprentice to Jeremiah Dummer, he found life in his new home

disappointingly plain. Some apprentices ran away, as Benjamin Franklin did in his youth, because they felt they were treated poorly. Occasionally disagreements broke out between master and apprentice that resulted in violence. But on the whole the system worked out successfully and amicably.

Customarily, upon the satisfactory completion of an apprenticeship, the master gave the departing young man "Two Sutes of apparrell to all parts of his body, the one for working Dayes, the other for Lord's Dayes fitt & convenient" plus "Foure new Shirts and Two new paier of Shooes." These were his "Freedome clothes." With the expiration of one trainee's term, the Philadelphia silversmith Joseph Richardson wrote his brother, "Our Kelly's Indentures expired this day and he left us Since dinner full trim in his freedom suit, and if he is not a foot higher in reality... he is in his own imagination."

At its best this system produced many highly qualified, even superb craftsmen. A good proportion of the artisans who worked in colonial America were immigrants who had been trained abroad, but there is no real evidence that their products were in any way superior to those of our native-born and -trained craftsmen. As earlier observed, the circumstances of colonial life did not encourage narrow specialization in any of the crafts. Furniture makers who turned out the most magnificent chairs and highboys, on occasion also made ironing boards, rolling pins, and chicken coops for their customers. Silversmiths who fashioned communion cups and tankards also engraved currency, billheads, and political cartoons. Painters of portraits turned their hands to making shop and tavern signs and coach decorations. Indeed, Copley was one of the first colonial artists (in *our* sense of the word) to make a living solely by his brush. Many of the lesser and earlier professed artists limned the features of their neighbors as a sideline to other workaday jobs.

Versatility was an almost necessary virtue in colonial society, and opportunities for rising in the world tempted craftsmen, along with merchants and other tradesmen, to branch out into different activities or to leave an enterprise for another more promising one. Aside from "Benjamin Franklin, printer," as he called himself even after the world at large had heaped honors on him for his innumerable other accomplishments, Paul Revere is probably the most celebrated of colonial craftsmen. The variety of his achievements as a patriot and citizen as well as a many-sided artisan will be mentioned later in this book. Longfellow's familiar poem retrieved Revere from relative obscurity. It is generally forgotten that William Dawes, who also alerted the Massachusetts countryside that fateful night of April 18, 1775, was a craftsman in his own right.

There were numerous other crafts-

men—like John Hull, to be sure—who played important roles in the social, political, and economic life of colonial America. Generally speaking, such artisans were respected and often prominent members of the community. In the seventeenth and eighteenth centuries patron and craftsman, consumer and producer, usually rubbed shoulders intimately in the same society and both understood the amenities and necessities of life from much the same viewpoint. Production was aimed at essential use and the methods of production were generally understood by everyone. When the craftsman warranted that his output was "as good as any other sold," he meant that it would pass examination by a knowing public. When almost everyone was a good judge of the serviceability and fitness of an object, fooling people for profit simply was not profitable.

Opulence in Silver

Colonial silversmiths never attempted the very elaborate pieces on which their European counterparts lavished their greatest skills. Such extravagances as Nell Gwyn's bed of silver or Catherine of Braganza's toilet set "all of massie gold" would have been unthinkable in the New World. Nevertheless, shortly before the year 1700 a generation of native smiths had grown to maturity in the colonies who practiced their art with a virtuosity that brilliantly expressed the spirit of the years around the turn of the century. Their output included a number of the finest pieces and the most interesting and elaborate forms of silverware that have come down to us from the entire colonial period.

New dining habits and the popularity of new beverages called for new types of silverware. Beyond that, wealthier customers demanded more elaborate plate, and the sophisticated outlook of these patrons was reflected in the sort of work that was hammered up for them. Although of an unmistakably American character, and although they display marked regional characteristics, the best and most typical examples from this period reveal no trace of provincialism.

Two of the outstanding Boston silversmiths, Jeremiah Dummer and John Coney, were well into middle age at the turn of the century. (The men were brothers-in-law and both had been apprenticed to Hull and Sanderson.) However, many of their finest accomplishments date from these and the later years of their lives. The monteith (107) that Coney made for the rich Boston merchant John Colman about 1705 is one of the most ambitious surviving pieces by any colonial smith. A monteith was a form of bowl, newly fashionable in England during the last years of the seventeenth century, that was used for chilling drinking glasses; these were hung inward, their bases held by the scalloped rim of the bowl. It was so named after "a fantastical Scot called *Monsieur Monteigh*" who, wrote one reporter in 1683, "wore the bottome of his cloake...so notched."

Brewing punch was a custom that had been introduced to England from India. By 1685, according to one report, punch had become "the beverage most esteemed by everyone" in New England. In 1692 Dummer fashioned the earliest-known colonial punch bowl (108), a piece that with its boldly scalloped rim recalls Portuguese designs.

Dummer probably trained Edward Winslow, a younger man who was born in 1669 and who developed into one of the most brilliant and the most successful silversmiths of the first half of the eighteenth century. It was he who made the punch ladle, a detail of which is shown here (106).

106. Detail of a punch ladle by Edward Winslow (1669–1753

107. A bowl for chilling glasses made by John Coney (1655–1722)

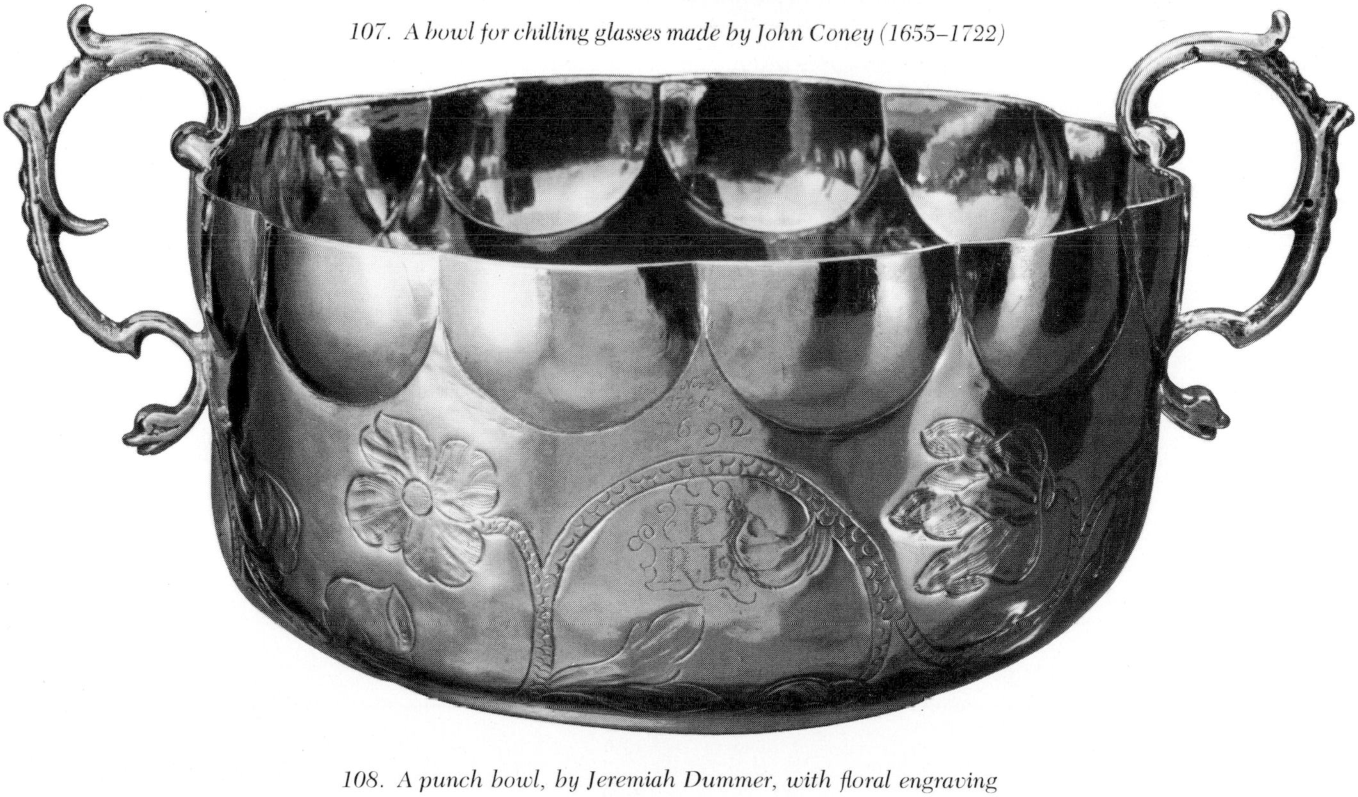

108. A punch bowl, by Jeremiah Dummer, with floral engraving

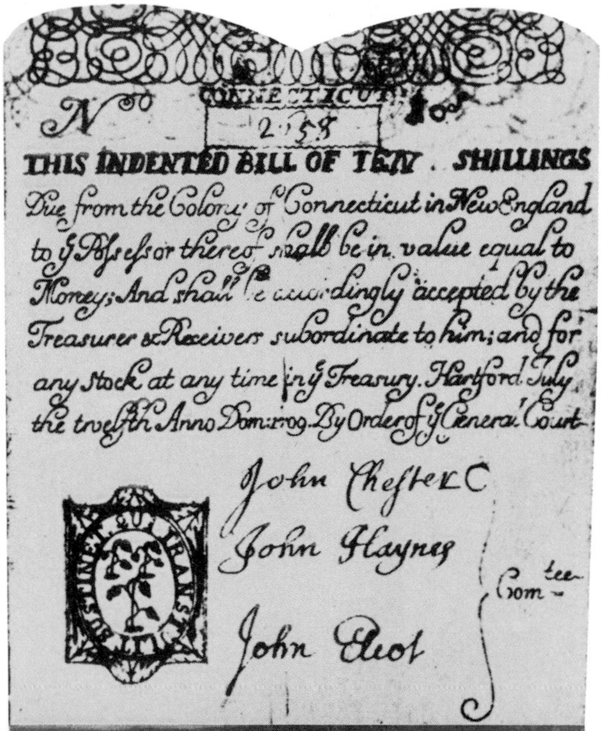
CONNECTICUT
No 2·58 10s
THIS INDENTED BILL OF TEN SHILLINGS
Due from the Colony of Connecticut in New England to ye Possessor thereof shall be in value equal to Money; And shall be accordingly accepted by the Treasurer & Receivers subordinate to him; and for any Stock at any time in ye Treasury. Hartford July the twelfth Anno Dom: 1709. By Order of ye General Court
John Chester LC
John Haynes
John Eliot
Com-tee

109. *Example of the currency commissioned by the colony of Connecticut in 1709, engraved by Jeremiah Dummer*

110. *Portrait of Edward Winslow painted by John Smibert*

111. *Chocolate pot made by Winslow*

112. *Silver peg tankard by John Coney*

113. Dummer's mark and a cup made in 1700, a gift to the church of Eastham

114. Silver standing salt by Winslow

Like so many of his fellow silversmiths, Winslow (110) was a prominent member of his community; before he died at the age of eighty-four he held a wide variety of public offices. And he made superb silver, including the standing salt (114) with its four scrolled brackets to support a dish or napkin, a survival of Elizabethan and earlier times when such forms—often monumental in size and architectural in character—served a ceremonial function at the "high table." Winslow also made one of the earliest and most elaborate colonial chocolate pots (111).

Chocolate was introduced to Europe from the New World by the conquistadors. Montezuma, Aztec emperor at the time of the Spanish conquest, is said to have had fifty pitchers of "chocolatl" prepared daily for his own consumption. He ate this frothy potation, mixed with vanilla and spices to about the consistency of honey, with a spoon from a golden goblet and in lonely splendor. (In Aztec Mexico cocoa beans served as a form of currency.) In somewhat modified form the beverage became popular in England during the last decades of the seventeenth century and the opening years of the eighteenth. Pepys found that with plenty of sugar and served hot "jocalette" made a rich but good drink. Some years later Samuel Sewall savored a pot of "chockalette" along with the venison that he shared at breakfast with Lieutenant Governor William Stoughton at Dorchester.

The chronic shortage of dependable metallic currency in the colonies led the Massachusetts legislature in 1690 to issue paper notes, which may have been engraved by John Coney as a similar issue in 1702 definitely was. That earlier printing represented one of the first official issues of paper money in the western world. In 1709 Dummer, who was well known in Connecticut for the silver vessels he made for the churches there (some similar to his communion cup (113) shown here), was chosen by the government of that colony to engrave and print 6550 sheets of bills of credit (109) to the value of £10,000.

Occasionally colonial tankards were made, after the fashion of those most popular in northern Europe, with a vertical row of pegs arranged on the inside (112)—a device which served to measure each draught of the beverage so that no one should have more than his fair share when the vessel was passed around. From this measured performance we have derived the expression "to take down a peg."

115. An ornate sweetmeat box made by Winslow

115a. St. George and the dragon, detail from above

116. Left: porringer, Wm. Cowell, Sr. (1682–1736)

117. Below: a christening basin made by Coney

118. Mark, with initials and a cony, used by Coney

119. Engraved matching spoon and fork by Coney

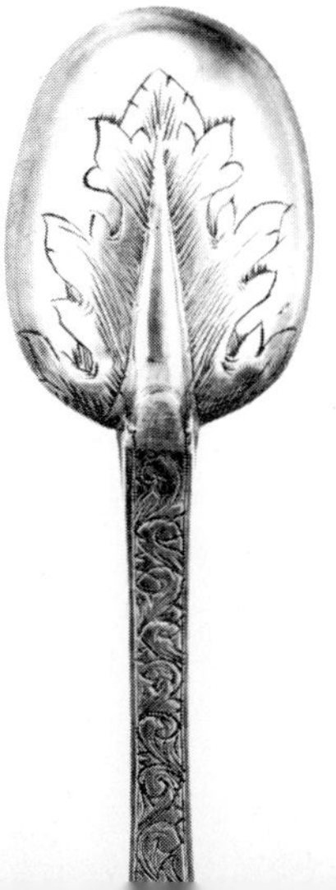

120. Tankard detail, Samuel Vernon (1683–1737)

One of the most opulent silver forms of the period was the sweetmeat, or sugar box (115). Sugar remained a luxury until, with the widespread use of tea and coffee in the eighteenth century, it was developed as a food staple. In the early colonies it was served with wines and other alcoholic beverages.

The shallow bowl with a single flat and pierced handle, commonly known as a porringer (116), grew in popularity as the eighteenth century advanced, to judge from the number that have survived.

It took a long time for Englishmen, and longer for most colonists, to appreciate the usefulness of forks. At first they seem to have been primarily reserved for serving food. Early, two-tined examples were occasionally made to match a spoon at the table (119). The fig-shaped bowl of the earlier spoons became more oval in shape with a reinforcing "rat-tail" extending down the back; and the handle, flattened out, ended in a three-lobed shape.

111a. Detail of the chocolate pot shown on page 98

121. William Stoughton with Harvard's first Stoughton Hall in the background

William Stoughton was one of the most munificent early benefactors of Harvard College, "which Nursery of good learning," he wrote, "hath been an inestimable blessing to the Churches and People of God in this Wilderness." He provided the funds for the erection of the original Stoughton Hall (121) in 1698–99, and in 1701 he presented to the college a magnificent silver cup (122) bearing his own arms. He was too ill to make the presentation and Samuel Sewall acted in his stead. "After Dinner and singing," the diarist recorded, "I. . .had it fill'd up, and drunk to the president, [in] the absence of him who was the Firmament and Ornament of the Province, and that Society. . . ."

In New York, with its conglomeration of peoples, a variety of international traditions were fused into a distinctive regional style of silverware. Jacob Boelen made the earliest-known colonial teapot (126) for Frederick Philipse, a prominent merchant engaged in the Madagascar trade. "When Frederick Phillipp's ship and the other two come from Madagascar (which are expected every day)," Lord Bellomont reported to the London Board of Trade and Plantations in 1698, "New York will abound with gold." The teapot was probably made not long thereafter.

Tea was still a costly drink in the early eighteenth century. However, the Occident was gradually developing its own form of tea ceremony, distinct from the traditional ritual of the Orient. In the West tea was brewed in a teapot rather than in the individual cup, and kettles were required for replenishing the hot water in the pot. The first reference to a teakettle appeared in 1687; about twenty years later Cornelius Kierstede of New York made the earliest surviving example of the form in colonial silver (125).

Coffee drinking also grew in popularity in the colonies during the early decades of the eighteenth century. The earliest coffeepots were tall, tapered cylinders (124), a basic form that persisted with some modifications for most of the rest of the century. New York had its first coffeehouse in 1697, and others soon followed. Here the merchants of the city often transacted their affairs.

122. The silver loving cup given by Stoughton, a Harvard graduate of 1650, to his alma mater

123. An 18th-century London coffeehouse

124. A silver coffeepot made by Charles Le Roux (1689–1745) of New York

125. Above: earliest-known colonial teakettle, by Cornelius Kierstede

126. Right: an early teapot, by Jacob Boelen, with the Philipse arms

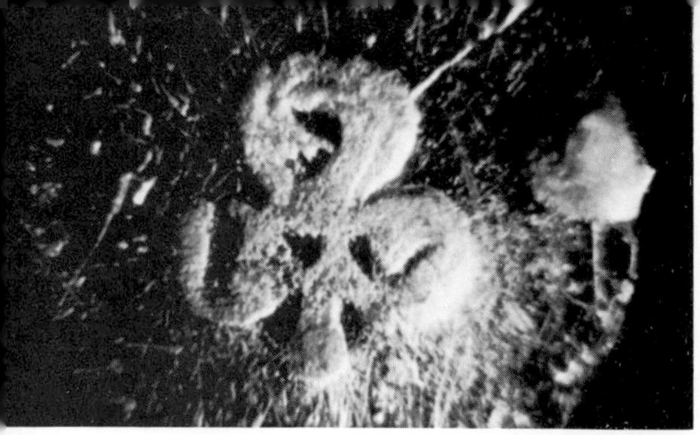

127. Silver tankard, by Jacobus Vanderspiegel (1668–1708), with elaborate decorations on the lid, handle, and base. Above: an enlargement of the maker's mark, ISV, *in a clover-leaf shape*

All the colonies tried to regulate tippling in public houses by carefully licensing the proprietors and imposing fines for disorderly behavior. As the cities grew in size and population it proved impossible to locate and suppress all the illicit groggeries and dramshops that often catered to a disreputable clientele, transient sailors among others. From its earliest days New York was a sailors' town, and in 1691 an ordinance was passed in an effort to control the "great Inconveniency [that] doth arise by trusting of Saylors whereby they Neglect their Attendance on board. . . ."

New York was a convivial place at every social level; "they all drink here," wrote one observer, "from the moment they are able to lick a spoon." The capacious silver tankards (127) made in that city early in the eighteenth century, with their flat lids often decorated with a commemorative medal or an engraved device (129), the little cast sculptures applied to their handles (127), and their ornamental base moldings were quite unlike anything produced in England, Holland, or France—or anyplace else for that matter. According to tradition a tankard (130), made by Gerrit Onckelbag (1670–1732), was presented by grateful New York merchants to Giles Shelley when he returned from Madagascar in 1698 in his ship, the *Nassau*, with a rich cargo of pirates' loot.

Another regional form developed by New York silversmiths was a two-handled bowl (132) divided into six panels and often decorated with bold floral motifs reminiscent of the exuberant styles of Holland. Such a vessel was probably used for punch or some other stimulating concoction, or—following a Dutch custom—it may have served to hold brandied raisins that were eaten with silver spoons.

At the dining table salt was losing its earlier, special importance, and sugar and spices were gradually gaining in popularity. Smaller, individual salts, like the one (131) by Jacob Ten Eyck (1704–93), replaced the ceremonial standing salts of former times; they were known as "trencher" salts because they stood beside the plate or platter which, when made of wood, had been called trenchers. Casters (128), sometimes in sets of three, evolved for dispensing sugar, pepper, and dry mustard.

129. An engraved monogram on the lid of a tankard made by Cornelius Kierstede

130. Above: a tankard by Onckelbag. 131. Below: a trencher salt by Ten Eyck

128. Caster by Bartholomew Le Roux (1665–1713), a Huguenot

132. A two-handled paneled bowl by Cornelius Kierstede

133. A footed salver, or tazza, *by Vanderspiegel*

Another silver form new to colonial households around the turn of the century was the salver (133), "a new fashioned peece of wrought plate," as it was somewhat earlier described in England, "used in giving Beer, or other liquid thing to save the Carpit or Cloathes from drops." (Carpets were used as table coverings at the time, rather than on the floor.) Large, two-handled cups, such as the one made in the 1690's by Jurian Blanck (135), were especially favored in New York. Here, the knops on the lid served as feet when the cover was inverted and used as a tray or saucedish. Both these pieces, like others shown on the preceding pages, displayed the style trends of the time; elaborately ornamented areas contrasted with plain surfaces, and curves and moldings often emphasized by spiral, ropelike bands or by fluted decoration.

The skills of these silversmith-engravers occasionally got them into trouble. The temptation to counterfeit both hard currency and paper notes was always present and sometimes irresistible. Although he belonged to an old and socially prominent family, in 1703 Onckelbag was found guilty of coining false money. He got off with a fine, but later counterfeiters had their ears clipped, were publicly whipped, or even hanged.

In these same years the brazier, or chafing dish, also made its first appearance in the colonies. The Philadelphia Huguenot smith Johannis Nys made one (136), appropriately pierced in a pattern of fleurs-de-lis, for Anthony Morris, early in the century. Nys' contemporary César Ghiselin, also a Philadelphia Huguenot, made the double-ended folding spoon shown opposite (134).

134. *Folding spoon, Ghiselin (1670–1734)*

135. *Cup with cover by Blanck (1666–99)*

136. *Brazier by Johannis Nys (1671–1734)*

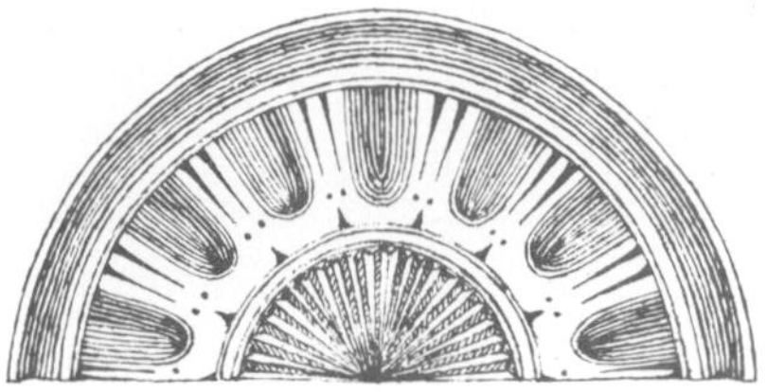

Workers in Wood

Those skilled woodworkers, so sorely needed at the beginnings of settlement in America to "make strong ware for the use of the countrie," had arrived in good numbers before the end of the seventeenth century—and they were doing a thriving business. Along with the "ingenious Carpenter" and the "cunning Joyner" called for in William Wood's summons of 1634, there were also "Cabenett Makers" listed as working in various colonies by the 1680's and others who specialized in making chairs. In some respects the problems and practices of these various types of artisans overlapped. The wood they used for surfaces that would show had to be smoothed down from rough, pit-sawn boards before it could be properly handled. For this purpose and for shap-

ing moldings of different contours a variety of planes were required—tools which, aside from their iron blades, were usually made of maple by the woodworker himself. Some molding

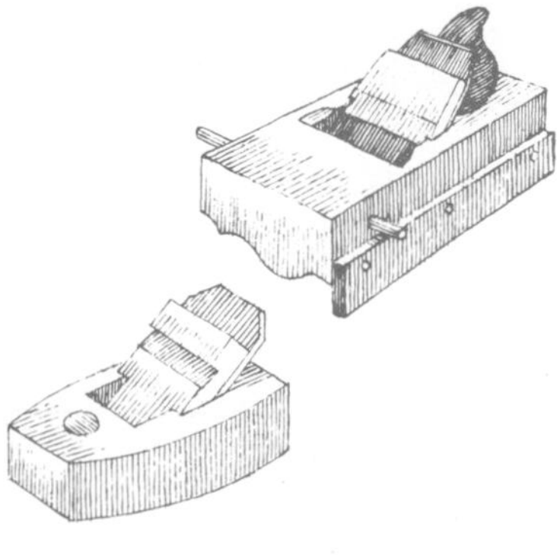

planes were so large they had to be towed with a rope by an apprentice while the master craftsman pushed and steadied the instrument on its way. In 1759 George Washington ordered a long list of tools for the furnishing of Mount Vernon, including about fifty molding planes of various descriptions, as well as a large number of bench and fitting planes.

The increasing use of wood-turning lathes late in the seventeenth century resulted, then and later, in a profusion of turnery for chairs, decorative spindles, table legs, stretchers, and other forms and devices. These elementary machine tools were either individually pedal-driven, spring-pole lathes or big-wheel lathes powered by a helper. In either

case the rotating wood was cut away to the required shape by long-handled chisels of various forms. For shaping the curves and corners of flat surfaces—

chair seats, table tops, and the like—the craftsman used a frame saw whose cutting blade was always conveniently visible as he worked the saw.

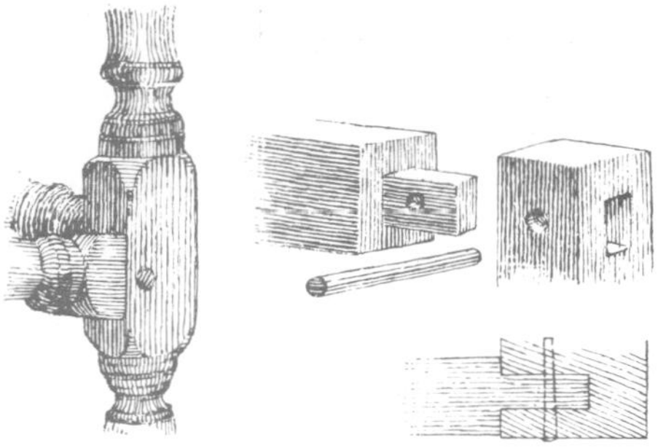

Chair and table stretchers, like the framework of timber buildings and other wooden elements that needed to be firmly fastened together, were joined by mortise and tenon. The tenon, or tongue, of one piece was slipped into the mortise, or hole, of the other and the two were then firmly locked by a hardwood pin that was inserted through both. For appearances' sake the mortise often did not go entirely through to the outside surface of a member—hence the term "blind mortise." Shoulders on two or more sides of the tenon kept this element at a fixed angle with the mortised piece. (The craftsman may have used heated animal glue as well, but if a piece was not properly and securely fitted together in the first place no amount of glue would have made a sound joint of the separate elements.)

The most common eighteenth-century device for securing the fronts to the sides of drawers was the dovetail joint, a detail of construction as old in its origins as ancient Egypt. This form of rigid joint, requiring neither nails nor pegs, was also used at other points in the construction of cabinets, boxes, and tables, although the labor involved in tightly fitting the triangular projections into the slots that were cut to receive them was considerable.

These traditional methods of furniture making, a basic but far from inclusive list of procedures, were all involved in the design and construction of such forms as the butterfly table shown here, one of the most pleasing and typical examples of native craftsmanship.

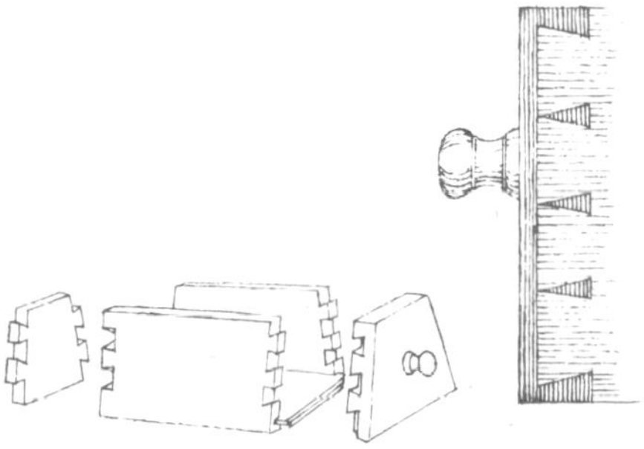

Until the introduction of furniture pattern books about the middle of the eighteenth century the designs of most pieces were based on traditional forms, with such variations as the individual craftsman or his customer may have thought agreeable or necessary. Even in the case of more sophisticated and elegant examples of the late colonial period, derived from engraved patterns, most pieces were endowed with an individual character which distinguished them from others made in the same style.

137. *A gentleman seated in a caned chair*

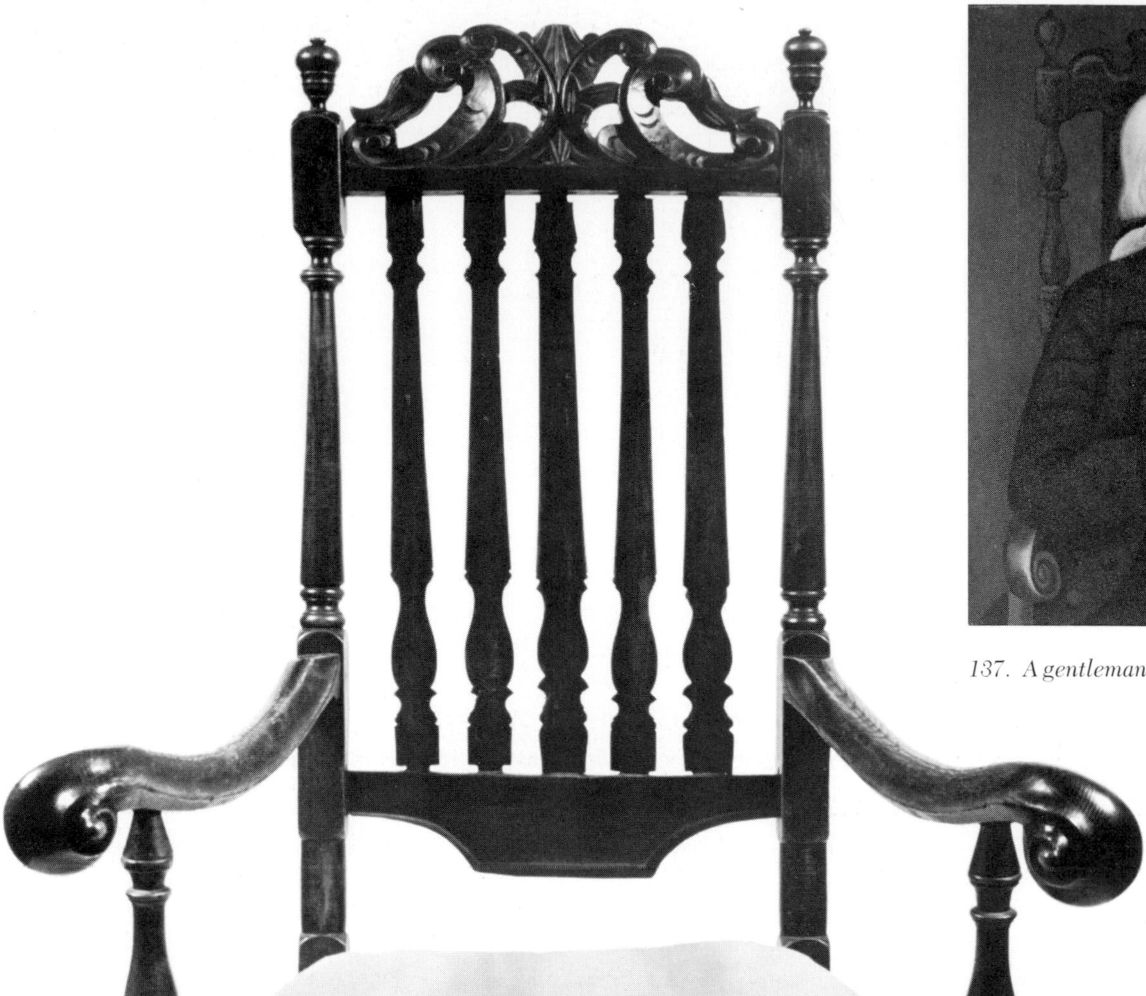

138. *A William and Mary banister-back chair, a colonial form, with ram's-horn detail on the arm shown opposite (far right)*

138a

139. A New England banister-back armchair

140. Below: a detail of a carved chair crest

The Native Strain

At the start of the eighteenth century furniture making rapidly expanded into one of America's leading industries, not only in the cities but in the country as well. Local craftsmen continued to re-create European fads and fashions, as can be seen in the caned chair in this anonymous portrait (137), of an unknown man, found in rural New England. Provincial forms, however, both in England and the colonies, continued their traditional simplification of urban embellishments. The armchairs shown on these pages, for example, were influenced by Restoration motifs—carved and scrolled crestings, Spanish feet, and the ram's-horn curl (above) on the arm. But with the use of split spindles in place of a caned center splat, urban elegance was modified into a new design—the banister-back chair. Narrow spindles, or banisters, were made by gluing two pieces of wood together, turning them on a lathe as one unit, and then separating them, thereby producing matching spindles, each with a flat side.

Whereas city cabinetmakers used such refinements as veneer, marquetry, or japanning, country craftsmen used simpler means to decorate furniture, such as the primitive but appealing designs painted on this William and Mary highboy (141). Roses, thistles, crowns, grapevines, and a fleur-de-lis are entwined on the drawer fronts. A caudle cup (much the same shape as the silver one shown on page 37) is depicted on the center drawer, a stylized tulip on the side of the piece, and trees across the apron. Such painted imitations of inlay were characteristic of the Guilford-Saybrook area in Connecticut where this highboy was made. In the Delaware Valley local artisans were refining a traditional design, the ladder-back chair, by arching the slats and setting them in graduated sizes (143). The ball-and-ring turnings on the front stretcher are a carryover from earlier styles. This Pennsylvania day bed (142) further exemplifies the simplification of elegance. There is no carving or Flemish scrollwork. The back is made with flat splats and raised or lowered by the functional expedient of a chain attached to the back rail.

Both the ladder-back chair and the day bed have rush seats, a thrifty substitute for imported cane. Rush has been used throughout history for chair seats, baskets, and rope; and candles, or rushlight, were made from the pith. Over two thousand years ago Indians in the Great Basin fashioned duck decoys from woven rushes.

141. A highboy (top) of tulipwood, white pine, and ash, painted to simulate marquetry, 1710–27

142. A walnut day bed originally painted blue

143. A Delaware River valley ladder-back chair, made of maple, with six graduated, arched slats

144. Splay-leg table with Spanish feet, Massachusetts, about 1710

The specialization of table forms—tavern tables, folding tables, dining tables, dressing tables, side tables, candlestands, tea tables—was by no means confined to wealthy households. All sizes and shapes were being produced by country craftsmen as well as by skilled artisans in the cities with their more sophisticated clientele. A single-gate table (147), frequently described as a tuck-away, was designed with a top that swung down when the gate was closed; tuck-aways were made from Maine to Virginia, and possibly farther south. Candlestands, too, were being made throughout the colonies. The one shown here (146) has a particularly rustic flavor with its coat of brown paint and the cross-base construction. Splay-leg tables (144) appear to have been a uniquely American form made not only in walnut, as was this example, but also in less prized woods, which were often painted. Possibly the most significant development of the period was the table designed specifically for dining, a direct result of the new concepts of spacious, gracious living with a room set aside for meals. Large gate-leg dining tables became extremely popular, whether in mahogany (145) or in native woods.

145. A large gate-leg dining table (left), here made in imported mahogany, a wood rarely used in this period

146. One of the many forms (above) of candlestands

147. Small tuck-away tables (below) with a single gate folded for easy storage and were useful space savers.

148. *A butterfly table made of maple, about 1700*

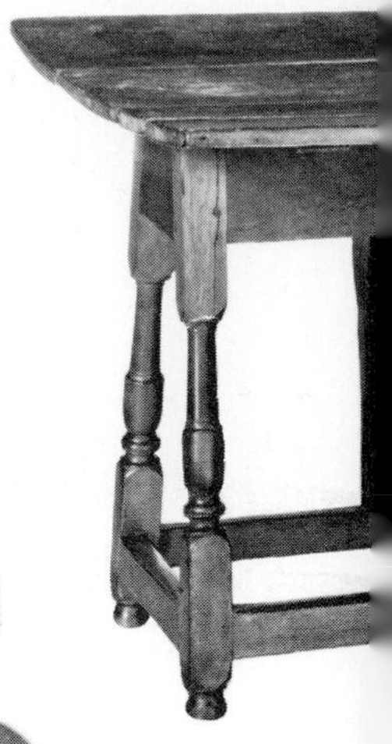

An American variation of the gate-leg table, that perennial favorite first noted in early Tudor inventories, is the butterfly table, so called because of the wing shape of the brackets. Since there is no firm precedent for this design, it is considered a purely colonial innovation. Butterfly tables were made in a variety of lengths and widths: round (148), square (151), or oblong (150), the latter with its four brackets being an unusual example of this form.

The continuing specialization of writing furniture led to desks-on-frames with fall-fronts. In the one shown here (152), the interior finely fitted with curved drawers and arched pigeonholes, the fall-front rests on square pull-out slides, a characteristic of early desks. The shielded candlestand (149) and the side table with a drawer (153) are further illustrations of the diversity of forms produced by native craftsmen.

For some settlers, of course, furniture was roughhewn at best. In 1704 Madam Sarah Knight, the intrepid traveler from Boston, described a dirt-floored Rhode Island "Hutt" that contained only a "Bedd...an earthan cupp, a small pewter Bason, A Bord wth sticks to stand on, instead of a table, and a block or two in y[e] corner instead of chairs." In an account of a backwoods free-for-all William Byrd II wrote that a North Carolinian tried to brain a Virginian with "a Limb of our Table, big enough to knock down an Ox."

149. *A candlestand with a shield*

150. *A cherry butterfly table.* 151. *Turned stretchers (right) are rare on butterfly tables.*

152. *A maple desk-on-frame, 1680–1710, with a fall-front.* 153. *A New England maple stretcher table (above), early 1700's*

Chairs from Boston

New England ships carrying New England products were putting in at ports of call from the Mediterranean to South America; the Caribbean and coastwise trade continued to expand. By 1733 colonial commerce had cut so sharply into the English export market that the commissioners for the Board of Trade and Plantations complained to Parliament: "such Improvements have been lately made there [New England] in all Sorts of Mechanic Arts, that not only Scrutores, Chairs, and other Wooden Manufactures, but Hoes, Axes, and other Iron Utensils are now exported from thence to the other Plantations, which, if not prevented may be of ill Consequence to the Trade and Manufactures of this Kingdom. . . ." New England's industries and commercial shipping had, in fact, become so extensive that the first lighthouse in the colonies had been built in 1716 at the entrance to Boston's busy harbor "to direct and guide the vessels att sea."

Among New England's exports one type of chair made in and near Boston since the early years of the century became extremely popular in the Middle Colonies, especially in Philadelphia. Boston chairs, as they were called, were usually made of maple, often painted red or black, and generally covered in leather. In two examples shown here, the turned front legs terminate in Spanish feet (154) and in button feet (155). Both these chairs are distinguished by a shaped curve to the back, an innovation of the period sometimes called a "spoon-back," which created an exceptionally comfortable chair. This painted maple armchair (156) with cabriole legs, its center splat and seat caned in lieu of leather upholstery, is a variation of the basic form. Boston chairs, a style that persisted well beyond the William and Mary period, were frequently listed in Philadelphia inventories up to the Revolution, and large numbers have been found in that area. Many, of course, were copies of the New England exports, widely copied by Philadelphia chairmakers as a 1742 advertisement in *The Pennsylvania Gazette* shows, "Made and to be sold by Plunket Fleeson...black and red leather Chairs, finished cheaper than any...imported from Boston." The Van Rensselaers in Albany owned a set of eight Boston chairs branded with family initials. The S.V.V.R. brand shown above is for Solomon Van Vechten Van Rensselaer.

154. Left: a New England side chair with Spanish feet. 155. Center: a side chair with button feet, also from New England

156. Right: a maple William and Mary armchair with caning. 157. Philadelphia's port and "brave, brick houses," about 1720

The Triumph of the Curve

The Queen Anne Style (1720-1750)

In 1702 Anne, second daughter of James II, succeeded to the English throne. She was the last of the Stuart monarchs. Anne was not a brilliant queen, but the twelve years of her rule were distinguished by some memorable achievements. On the Continent the Duke of Marlborough won the great victories at Blenheim and Ramillies that led to the signing of the Treaty of Utrecht in 1713, ending the bloody War of the Spanish Succession and at the same time halting the expansion of France, which for almost a century had been the dominant power in Christendom. By that treaty the prestige of England was sharply accelerated throughout the western world, and that rise of prestige was to be one of the strong historical currents of the eighteenth century. The influence of English customs and forms exerted a pervasive authority everywhere—even in France, and above all in the colonies. Also during Anne's reign Scotland was joined to England to form that lasting political entity, Great Britain.

The war had greatly stimulated economic activity in Europe. New capital was needed for fresh ventures in industry and trade and various steps were taken to provide it. In 1711 the South Sea Company, a monopolistic trading organization, was formed in England to exploit the resources of South America and the Pacific islands. A similar company was organized in France under the direction of the Scottish financier and promoter John Law to drain the riches of the Mississippi Valley. The initial success of such ventures encouraged numerous imitations, and vast amounts of money were invested by eager subscribers. George I, who succeeded Anne in 1714, was himself governor of the South Sea Company; and it was rumored that his mistresses and favorites were let into the speculation "on the ground floor." Unlimited riches seemed to be in prospect for all concerned. But in 1720 those gigantic "bubbles" burst with shattering consequences for innumerable shareholders. (Out of the operations of Law's company, however, the Crescent City of New Orleans had been founded in 1718. In years to come that settlement became the major entrepôt for the trade of the entire Mississippi River basin—and one of the most colorful and enchanting urban communities of the United States.)

As one result of the widespread financial disasters, Robert Walpole assumed a leading role in the British government. Largely because of his financial genius and his mastery of politics, Great Britain enjoyed increasing material prosperity in the decades to come. Only four years after the great crash George I reminded

Opposite: furniture and objects of the Queen Anne period; for descriptions see p. 373

his subjects that they possessed "peace with all powers abroad, at home perfect tranquillity, plenty, and an uninterrupted enjoyment of all civil and religious rights." Walpole was the first of the "great commoners" to rule Great Britain, the first of the British prime ministers. Under his leadership middle-class Englishmen benefited widely from a continued growth of commerce and industry. In his poem *Summer*, written in 1727, James Thomson took note of the growing affluence of Englishmen. Apostrophizing Britannia he wrote:

> . . . Thy Country teems with wealth,
> And Property assures it to the swain,
> Pleas'd and unwearied in his guarded toil.

In that increasing circle of the well to do, the cabinetmaker, the glassmaker, the silversmith, and other artisans, as well as the artist and the poet, found an unprecedented and growing market for their wares.

Even before the accession of Anne so much of the coin of the realm had been melted down to be wrought into silver plate for the homes of the wealthy that steps had to be taken to alleviate the shortage of hard currency. In 1697 an Act of Parliament raised the cost of the raw material by decreeing a new and higher than sterling standard for silverwork. This so-called Britannia standard (wrought pieces made under this stricture were stamped with the figure of Britannia) remained in effect until 1720, by which time the desired result was achieved. Another result of that temporarily imposed standard was to increase the softness of the metal by reducing the proportion of the copper alloy. This made some difference in the handling of the metal and encouraged the production of relatively simple forms. The silver styles thus advanced by legislation continued to be popular through the reign of George I. Although the Britannia standard did not apply to America, colonial styles in time followed the English fashion, and the Queen Anne style in silver persisted here until the middle of the century. It was gradually superseded by more elaborate designs in the following decades.

It was during Anne's rule that the alien strains of design that had been brought into England so freely in the preceding generation or two were thoroughly domesticated. For, although they periodically succumb to "foreign excesses," the English are inherently averse to extravagant design. In any event, the baroque details of foreign origin—the intricate patterns of broken and reverse scrolls and curves, and the other elaborations—popular in the reigns of Charles II, James II, and William and Mary were gradually replaced by the more sober and typically

Six so-called Mississippi Bubble plates, Chinese export porcelain copies of Delft designs, which lampoon the land speculation schemes of John Law in Louisiana

English Queen Anne style. The change of taste was described by Lord Shaftesbury in 1712: "In short we are to carry this remembrance still along with us," he wrote, "that the fewer the objects are besides those which are absolutely necessary in a piece, the easier it is for the eye by one simple act, and in one view to comprehend the sum or whole." The Queen Anne style achieved this simplification of form, this greater unity in the design of chairs, tables, and case pieces. In all craft products of the period the curve triumphed—an undulating, graceful curve that pleased the eye as well as it served the needs of solid construction. The single most conspicuous element of this construction was the cabriole leg, a form of support originally derived from the profile of an animal's hind leg—and a form used in ancient Egypt almost five millenniums earlier. The term cabriole stemmed from the Italian *capriola*, goat's leap.

It has been said that chairs reveal more about the habits, the fashionable tastes, the manners, and the customs of people than any other household article. Strong, simple, and handsome, the typical early Queen Anne chair achieved a classic harmony of form and function; a harmony analogous to that achieved by the writers of the time and that led Doctor Samuel Johnson to call this the Augustan Age of English literature. Every trace of Tudor and Puritan stiffness disappeared into a flow of gentle curves; the twisted turnings gave way to plain arms, legs, and stretchers; carving was reduced to a minimum; and the back with its solid splat was curved to accommodate the contour of the human spine. For a while, until mahogany superseded it, walnut was the most popular wood, and its warm color and pleasant texture contributed to the handsome appearance of furniture in general.

Many modern ideas of utility and comfort in the home had their origins in the years of Anne's rule. Englishmen of that time were learning to live more easily and conveniently with their household equipment. Old forms were taking on new grace and new forms were being created to satisfy an increasing number of needs and wants. The design and construction of chairs, tables, coffeepots, and other accessories were worked out so well that we can still live happily with reproductions or adaptations of the household equipment of that period—or, indeed, with the originals if we are fortunate enough to own them. A growing variety of dressing tables, card tables, looking glasses, and tea tables, as well as other accessories for the serving of tea, all reflected the changes in manners and customs that affected an ever-widening public as the century advanced and as the general standard of living improved.

English walnut armchair showing the curvilinear character of the Queen Anne style

Top of a Queen Anne highboy, or high chest of drawers, from Massachusetts, around 1725–40

The title page from William Kent's The Designs of Inigo Jones, *which was published in 1727*

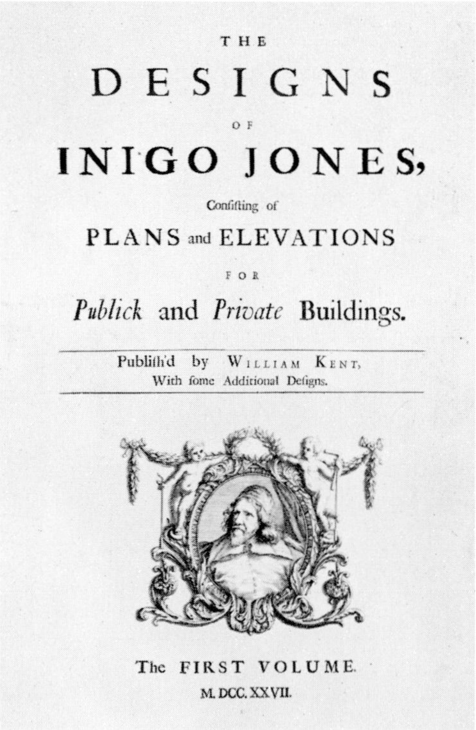

THE
DESIGNS
OF
INIGO JONES,
Confifting of
PLANS and ELEVATIONS
FOR
Publick and *Private* Buildings.
Publifh'd by WILLIAM KENT,
With fome Additional Defigns.

The FIRST VOLUME.
M.DCC.XXVII.

Large pieces of furniture had scrolled bonnets or pediments that repeated the characteristic curve of the period. Larger and taller pieces were both practical and appropriate now that the ceilings of rooms were higher, and with their solid proportions and molded detail they assumed the quiet dignity of architecture. With general prosperity new buildings sprouted all over the British Isles. The rich, *nouveaux riches*, and many who could not afford it raised stylish dwellings that were often more splendid than they were comfortable or convenient. Every educated man professed an interest in architecture, and those who built had a growing number of architectural books to advise them on everything from the framing of timbers to the just proportions of the classical orders. The most elaborate of these works were English versions or adaptations of the works of Andrea Palladio, the great architectural designer of the Italian Renaissance, and of his English disciple, Inigo Jones. In England the champion of Palladianism was the third Earl of Burlington, whose enthusiasm for the revived Renaissance and classical forms gave rise to a cult among his admirers and followers. Although Burlington was not a professional architect, he was the most lavish of the aristocratic amateurs and had under his patronage several of the most gifted professionals of the time. For his generous contribution to the art he was widely praised. In an adulatory epistle to the earl, Alexander Pope exclaimed:

> You show us Rome was glorious, not profuse,
> And pompous buildings once were things of use.

And he added with keen perception:

> Yet shall, my lord, your just, your noble rules
> Fill half the land with imitating fools. . .

So great was the interest in architecture in the new and "proper" taste that according to Horace Walpole one important lady had Burlington's follower William Kent design a birthday gown featuring "a petticoat decorated with columns of the five orders." A flood of other design books and practical handbooks followed the publications sponsored by Burlington, a flood that spread to America and left in its wake a deposit of handsome structures, domestic and public, in the cities and across the countryside.

By the dawn of the eighteenth century America had been drawn into the strong currents of international affairs. Queen Anne's War, fought principally on the Carolina and New England frontiers and in the West Indies, was the New World counterpart of the War of the Spanish Succession. On its conclusion in

1713 the colonies also entered a period of peaceful growth and expanding trade. In this increasingly prosperous society there began to emerge many of the patterns of life that are familiar to us today.

Building operations were constantly changing the appearance of urban communities, but there were housing shortages at times. Some Philadelphians had to walk "up one Pair of Stairs" to their quarters in multi-family tenements, and female shoppers in Boston had to climb stairs occasionally to buy shoes, laces, and ribbons "Just Imported from London." Stores and shops in general carried an increasing variety of consumer goods, both homemade and imported. One New York emporium, a precursor of the modern department store, offered a line of commodities ranging from chairs, beds, and tables, to pictures, drugs, and medicines. Not many years later a Philadelphia craftsman opened a mail-order business. In numerous communities traffic laws were passed to control such public nuisances and dangers as "Excessive Galloping, Trotting & paceing of Horses" and "the great Disturbances Occasioned by Horses and Chaise in great Numbers Crouding into Town and also out...till Nine, Ten, and sometimes Eleven a clock at Night." In all the colonial cities the gentry traveled about in their coaches and other vehicles, or hired such conveyances on occasion. Coachmakers enjoyed a flourishing trade; when requested to do so they would emblazon their patrons' coats of arms on the body of a vehicle.

To avoid the congestion and clatter of city life some Philadelphians moved to newly developed suburbs. Outside the central area of the city several large privately owned tracts of land were divided into small building lots. On the farther outskirts of Philadelphia and other cities, gentlemen of means built their countryseats, impressive testimonies both to their taste in architecture and their substantial resources. One such rural retreat, called Stenton, was raised during the 1720's by James Logan, former secretary to William Penn. In 1725 Logan wrote to Mrs. Penn that his wife earnestly beseeched "I may be allowed to live with her on our Plantation near Germantown under no other obligation to public affairs than to ride once a week to town to advise and assist in your affairs for which she hath a great Zeal, yet more for her husband's peace." Stenton still stands, an enduring ornament of the Germantown countryside.

Many of the most admirable surviving colonial dwellings, mainly country houses, were erected during the building boom of this period, roughly between 1720 and 1750. It was in the 1720's that Thomas Lee, an explorer and later the governor of Virginia, raised his great house, Stratford, on the banks of the Potomac (it was later to be the birthplace of General Robert E. Lee); about the same time Frederick Philipse, whose grandfather had accumulated a fortune by trade in New Amsterdam, built the major wing of his stately Manor Hall in Yonkers, New York. In the next decade John Drayton, a member of the king's council, erected Drayton Hall on the banks of the Ashley River just outside Charleston, South Carolina; and in Westover, on the James River in Virginia, William Byrd II constructed the most famous Georgian house in America.

Like his English counterpart, every colonist of cultural pretension considered a knowledge of architecture an essential aspect of his education. In his great library Byrd had ten of the architectural books of the sort earlier mentioned; Logan had four; and other copies were increasingly available at bookstores and libraries throughout the colonies. At least eighty-seven different titles were known in America before the Revolution, and it is safe to say that from the 1720's to the end of the century hardly a house of any consequence was built in the

The five classical orders taken from William Salmon's Palladio Londinensis, *published 1727*

colonies and the new nation that did not reveal a debt to those manuals.

The interiors of such large and luxurious houses were fitted with marble fireplaces, paneled walls, and other adornments of a fashionable nature. In 1744 colonial America's wittiest and most urbane tourist, Dr. Alexander Hamilton of Maryland, en route to Boston, visited "a house about half a mile out of town [Newport], built lately by one Captain Mallbone." (Godfrey Malbone was a Virginia-born merchant who had made a fortune in the West India trade and in privateering.) "It is the largest and most magnificent dwelling house I have seen in America," Hamilton reported. "It is built intirely with hewn stone of a reddish colour; the sides of the windows and corner stones of the house being painted like white marble. It is three storys high, and the rooms are spacious and magnificent. There is a large lanthern or cupola on the roof, which is covered with sheet lead. The whole stair case, which is very spacious and large, is done with mahogany wood. . . . Round it are pritty gardens and terrasses with canals and basons for water, from whence you have a delightfull view of the town and harbour of Newport with the shipping lying there."

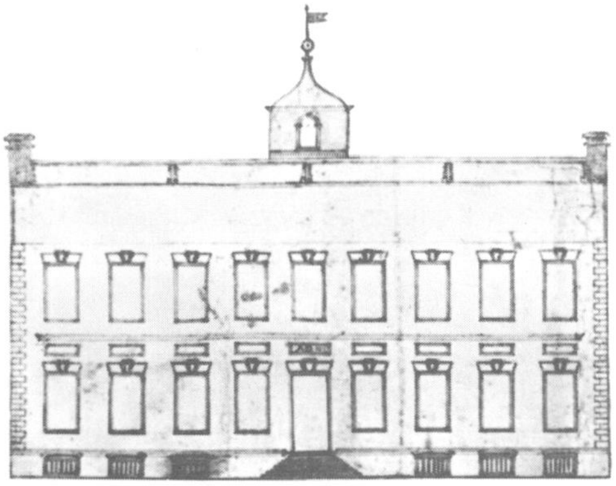

Malbone's great house, like most of the superb town houses of that time, has long since been destroyed. In the late 1730's Thomas Hancock built a handsome mansion on the south slope of Boston's Beacon Hill, overlooking the Common, that set a standard of elegance and sophistication throughout New England. It was probably the most architecturally advanced house of its time in the colonies, but in 1863 it was torn down to make room for more modern structures. Until recent generations Americans have had little respect for such monuments of the past. Fortunately, public buildings have had on the whole better fortune, and we can still admire Faneuil Hall in Boston, Trinity Church in Newport, and Independence Hall in Philadelphia, among other handsome survivors from those years. But it is sad to remark that there is less left standing of eighteenth-century New York than there is of Periclean Athens.

In 1724 a number of the leading housewrights of Philadelphia, some prominent citizens among them, founded a company modeled upon the Worshipful Company of Carpenters of London, chartered in 1477, which they called the Carpenters' Company of the City and County of Philadelphia. It was America's first

builders' guild. It was formed "for the purpose of obtaining instruction in the science of architecture and assisting such of their members as should by accident be in need of support, or the widows and minor children of members." One of their first acts was to draw up and publish a *Book of Prices* to assure fair charges to owners and adequate recompense to workers. They also issued a *Manual* of architectural designs, constructional details, and other matters for the guidance of their members.

The Carpenters' Company no doubt contributed importantly to the architectural distinction of Philadelphia and its environs as well as elsewhere. When the trustees of the little College of New Jersey, later renamed Princeton University, planned the erection of a major building, Nassau Hall, Robert Smith of the company was entrusted with its design. The building itself served its purpose so admirably that it became a model for University Hall in Providence—the nucleus of what was to become Brown University—Dartmouth Hall, and other college structures of later years.

It was during the years in which the handsome dwellings mentioned earlier were rising, from about 1720 to 1750, that the Queen Anne style in furniture took root and flourished in the American colonies. Older styles lingered on, of course. In 1720 Samuel Sewall ordered "a Duzen of good black Walnut Chairs, fine Cane, with a Couch," a suite that must have been in the William and Mary fashion. Twelve years later furniture of this sort was still offered at an auction where, as a newspaper advertisement stated, "Buyers may depend upon having fair play, good liquor, and if they please good bargains." Before this period ended there were signs that heralded developments of the Chippendale period, but the prevailing fashion was for the Queen Anne.

Anne herself, of course, was long since dead; and, in fact, the style that evolved in England during her reign was not associated with her name until a much later date, and then by students and antiquarians. (To the men of earlier times the terms we use for the various periods and styles would be completely confusing.) But, loose as it is, the term Queen Anne has won general acceptance and it serves as a useful label. In the colonies, as earlier in England, the sensuous curved line that characterized the style became the line of fashion. (Except, per-

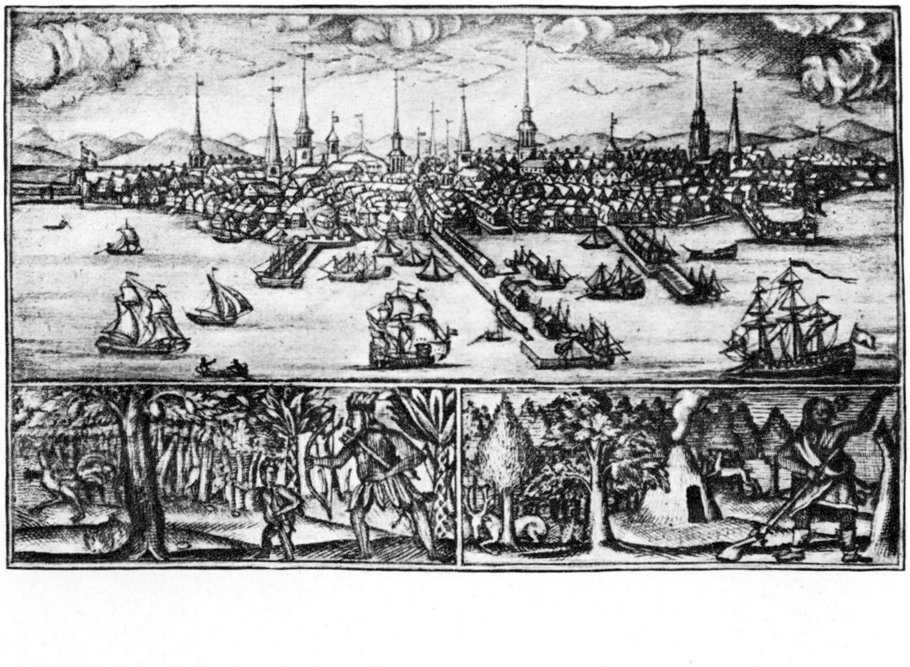

Opposite: drawing (top) of the Pennsylvania State House, now Independence Hall; (bottom) the Thomas Hancock house, to the right is the beacon on the top of Beacon Hill

Left: a rare line engraving of Boston in 1744

An engraving of the city of Philadelphia, before 1754, viewed from the Jersey shore

Girl made to look "strait" by wearing stays

haps, in ladies' figures; in 1730 one Philadelphia tradesman guaranteed that he could provide stays "to make Women look Strait that are not So.") Practically all the forms that tended to make the daily life of a prosperous Englishman so comfortable, gracious, and convenient were produced in America for those who could afford the best—and they were a growing number. Governor James Glen reported that Charleston annually imported "a considerable quantity of fine laces of Flanders, the finest Dutch linnens, and French cambrick, chintz, Hyson Tea, and other East India goods, silk, gold and silver laces, etc." Such was the extravagance of the Carolinians, he averred, that they were going the way of the ancient Romans. When George Berkeley, dean of Londonderry, arrived at Newport in 1729 he noted "a rage for finery" among the merchant aristocrats of that flourishing city. One Quaker boasted to the dean that he owned a solid gold teapot such as even the queen of England did not possess. Even the Indians seem to have been given at times to fashionable performances. At one point on his travels Dr. Hamilton met two "Mohooks on horseback, dressed *a la mode Francois* with laced hats, full trimmed coats, and ruffled shirts. One of them was an old fellow, the other a young man with a squaw mounted behind him. The squaw seemed to be a pritty woman all bedaubed with wampum."

As the price of tea was progressively lowered over the years, more and more people found it within their means to indulge in that pleasant beverage. At midcentury one traveler noted that tea was drunk morning and afternoon in the colonies, "especially by women." It was so common, he added, that "there is hardly a farmer's wife or a poor woman who does not drink tea in the morning. I was confirmed in this opinion when I took a journey through some parts of the country which were still inhabited by Indians....Indians who lived close to the European settlements had learned to drink tea....When the English women drank tea, they never poured it out of the cup into the saucer to cool it, but drank it as hot as it came from the teapot. The Indian women in imitation of them, swallowed the tea in the same manner." He concluded that the Indian women who drank too much of the beverage lost their teeth prematurely, "in the

same manner as the European women." As the ritual of tea drinking developed, more and more equipment was produced to serve it in the proper fashion. Sugar bowls, milk and cream pitchers, among other novelties, as well as special tables to hold the service became the indispensable equipage of the well-to-do home. Indeed, the tea table offered increasing competition to the tavern table—a circumstance, it has been claimed, that contributed to the growing control of social life by women and to the encouragement of polite conversation. Dr. Hamilton noted in Boston particularly the ladies appeared conspicuously in public and they dressed elegantly. They were, he commented, "free and affable as well as pritty," and, he concluded, "I saw not one prude while I was here."

Not all colonists enjoyed these refinements of life. There were then, as now, the poor as well as the rich. Devereux Jarratt, who was born in Virginia in 1733, recalled that during his youth his family "made no use of tea or coffee; meat, bread, and milk," he added, "was the ordinary food of all my acquaintance. I suppose the richer sort might make use of those and other luxuries, but to such people we had no access." He went on to remark that his class looked upon "*gentle folks* as beings of a superior order" who wore periwigs. (In later years Jarratt became a prominent evangelistic preacher who warned rich and poor alike about the perils of worldliness.)

In 1728 the rise of the cost of living, caused by the depreciation of paper currency, set off a lively argument in the pages of *The New-England Weekly Journal*. Bostonians of ordinary means were charged with "Inadvertence to their own Expences," which led them into troubles with their budgets. In the course of the ensuing controversy (which might have been an editorial device to stimulate circulation), on what might be called the family page of the paper, it was revealed that a "Family of but middling Figure" could not expect to indulge in tea, coffee, or chocolate—or wine and spirituous liquors. But they might afford a maid, whose yearly salary was only slightly greater than the annual cost of candles for the household.

However, the colonial economy was on the whole sound, and it was rapidly expanding. Families that were of "but middling Figure" in one generation were frequently families of substance in the next, with tea, wine, and other comforts and delights well within their reach. It was during the years considered here that Benjamin Franklin, a runaway Boston printer's apprentice, rose to become a highly distinguished and prosperous craftsman and citizen of Philadelphia. As early as 1737, when he was only thirty-one years old, he advertised in *The Pennsylvania Gazette*, his own newspaper, requesting the return of his copy of Colin Campbell's *Vitruvius Britannicus*, which he had lent long since to some negligent person. This book was one of the large architectural tomes that Byrd, Logan, and other prominent gentlemen were collecting for their libraries, a very expensive volume for a young printer to own and pass about.

While Franklin was rising to prominence and prosperity, Philadelphia continued to be a booming city, soon to become the most populous urban center in the colonies. When he visited there on his tour up and down the coast in 1744, Hamilton found the place rather shabby, its streets obstructed with rubbish and lumber. This, however, he excused as a consequence of the extensive building operations. A few years later the Swedish traveler Peter Kalm remarked on the "grandeur and perfection" of the city, which, he stated, was "by no means inferior to those of any, even of the most ancient, towns of Europe."

No two people reporting on the colonial scene saw it quite the same. Looking back on his tour, during which he traveled 1624 miles, Hamilton concluded that "as to politeness and humanity, they [the colonists] are much alike except in the great towns where the inhabitants are more civilized, especially at Boston." On the other hand, Franklin, who knew the colonies as well as anyone, pointed out that each of them had "peculiar expressions, familiar to its own people, but strange and unintelligible to others."

Above: a 1748 woodcut of a sea captain delivering a letter. Opposite: provincial armchair by John Gaines of Portsmouth, N.H.

Traffic between the different colonies, by land as well as by sea, was steadily increasing as the century advanced. Daniel Henchman of Boston published in 1732 the first American road guide, *The Vade Mecum for America: Or a Companion for Traders and Travellers*, which described the highways and listed taverns from Maine to Virginia; it also gave the location and dates of the principal fairs held in the northern colonies. For all this there apparently was a serious need. Before mid-century Peter Kalm reported that the people of New Brunswick, New Jersey, reaped "a considerable profit from the travellers, who every hour pass through on the highroad." By 1728 a regular packet service had been established between New York and Charleston to handle the provision trade between those two cities; and in these and following years numerous small vessels plied the coastal waters between the larger settlements. The fact that in 1759 more than five hundred letters went unclaimed at the Philadelphia post office alone indicates how busily the mails were operating by mid-century.

But in spite of improved communications and the growing convenience and speed of travel, distinctively regional patterns of life persisted; and as the colonial population spread out, this diversity was reflected even more clearly in the design and construction of furniture and other furnishings that were produced in different sections of the country. Sometimes the elements of style and workmanship that distinguish the forms of one area from those of another are very subtle. As in the case of the "Boston" chairs mentioned in the last chapter, furniture was shipped out of New England ports for sale and for use in other sections of the country, where it was at times imitated. Nevertheless, it is often easily possible to say whether a chair or a lowboy, for example, was made in or about Boston, Newport, New York, or Philadelphia by its proportions, the character of its carving, or some other element of its design or structure.

The basic English tradition that nurtured American craftsmanship was constantly refreshed in the colonies by the importation of English products and by the immigration of English artisans conversant with the latest fashions from London. During the reigns of the first two Georges the early simplicity of the Queen Anne style in England gave way to more ornate and pretentious design. The influence of the fashionable architect William Kent, among others, reached to "all who were emulous for distinction by an ostentatious display of their consequence and wealth," and for such patrons he "changed the fashion of their chairs and tables."

The colonies, as usual, did not pretend to emulate the extremes of English style, for economic and practical reasons. America was remote from those institutions, the crown and the privileged aristocracy, that so strongly influenced the decorative arts abroad. Yet it is probable that our colonial ancestors took the same delight in restrained forms and clean, finished surfaces that we do today.

In any case, the Queen Anne style in some of its aspects lingered on in America until the end of the eighteenth century. At its best it represents the most satisfactory expression colonial craftsmanship ever found, as the following illustrations should demonstrate. The height of sophistication in this style was achieved in Philadelphia; but in the other large northern cities—in New York, Newport, and Boston particularly—local versions of distinctive merit also evolved, all having a strong American accent. Far up the river valleys and in villages distant from the large centers the Queen Anne style was translated into a vernacular often of highly individual charm.

The Grace of Chairs

In no other area of furniture design can the Queen Anne style be so clearly demonstrated as in the shape and construction of chairs. Here the transition from the right angle to the curve, completed in this period, is variously expressed in cabriole legs, serpentine stretchers, horseshoe-shaped seats, rounded splats and rounded supporting stiles, undulating crests, and aprons arched in cyma curves—cyma itself being taken directly from the Greek word for wave.

Most importantly, these curved elements were not superimposed upon a basically rectangular form, as they had been up to this time, with the use of carved and scrolled ornaments on flat surfaces. The structure of the Queen Anne chair—from the ground up, so to speak—was one of subtly shaped component parts. Carving became a secondary statement of the curved line, a graceful addition to an inherently graceful construction.

Certain features of the Queen Anne style may well have been drawn from Oriental sources. For centuries the Chinese had been making chairs with rounded crests and backs shaped to fit the spinal column. The outline of the splat of the Queen Anne chair has been attributed to the contour of a Chinese vase; and the claw-and-ball foot (158), first used in this period and later to become a popular Chippendale motif, was an ancient Chinese device—the talon of a dragon grasping a pearl. Ornaments used by the Greeks and Romans, such as the acanthus leaf, were revived during the Renaissance and were incorporated into Queen Anne designs. The acanthus, a prickly herb from the Mediterranean region, is shown opposite on a chair cresting. The scallop shell, a predominant Queen Anne motif (upper left), was also used in many forms of ancient art—Phoenician coins, Greek ceramics, Roman altars, tombs, and perfume flasks, and also, incidentally, on Aztec and Mayan artifacts.

There was the influence of the European rococo as well, which was reaching dizzying heights of fantasy, particularly in French decoration. But colonial craftsmen modified the European extremes—the excessive use of gilt and carved masks, for example—to create an independent interpretation. Regional styles developed rapidly in America with Boston, New York, Newport, and Philadelphia as the principal centers of design. Generally speaking, chairs from Boston were spare and delicate, and stretchers persisted long after they had passed out of fashion in other areas. New York chairs were generously proportioned, the splat and stiles often in matching curves (158). In Newport the serpentine stretcher was favored, and the shell on the crest silhouetted, a pattern also used in New York. But it was in Philadelphia that the Queen Anne chair achieved its richest form with a rhythmic balance of interlocking curves and profusion of ornament which reflected the best of European design.

158. A side chair with carved shells on crest and knees. Tapering, footed rear legs are a New York feature.

159. Upper right: a Philadelphia chair with concave arms, scrolled splat, and three-toed feet in paneled "socks" (an Irish furniture motif)

160. Above: a New York chair with unusual carved crest. Its walnut-veneered back splat and stiles are cut in matching curves. This is one of a set of eight made for the Apthorp family.

161. Right: New England chairs had spare, slender proportions. This one has pad feet on the front legs and a cyma curve on the front apron.

162. Above: a Rhode Island corner chair upholstered in 18th-century French cut-wool velvet

163. Upper left: walnut side chair from Massachusetts, one of a set of six belonging to Edward Holyoke, president of Harvard College, 1737–69

164. Left: the pronounced curves of the legs and the pad feet with sharp-cut "shoes" characterize this Newport stool covered in flamestitch.

165. *A simple walnut side chair from Philadelphia*

166. *A Philadelphia chair*

167. *A Rhode Island chair*

168. *A Connecticut chair*

169. The front and rear view of a New England easy chair with original needlework on the back

170. Opposite: a maple chair, with crewelwork seat, from Connecticut. 171. Left: a painted chair of a type made in the Hudson River valley until the 19th century. 172. Right: cherry wood, a square seat, scalloped apron, and slim splat mark the Connecticut chair.

Services for Tea

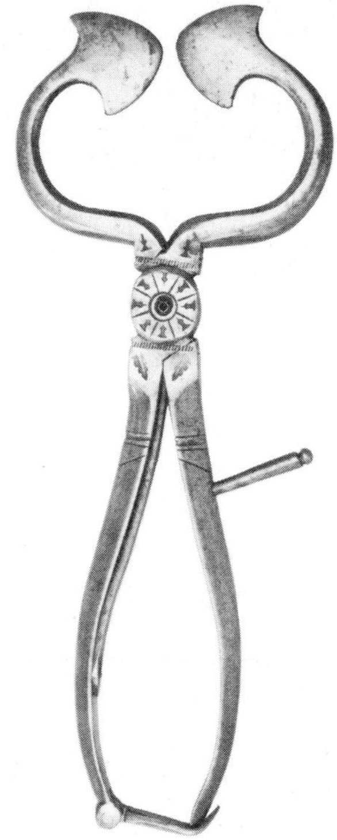

173

The ever-growing popularity of tea drinking carried a flood of new words into the English language. Starting in the seventeenth century and continuing until the end of the eighteenth, the appearance of these terms reflects the development of new social habits that the thirst for tea brought about in the British Isles and in England's colonies. Although the tea plant itself was mentioned as early as the sixteenth century, the beverage made from it was still something of a novelty several generations later. An early reference to tea as a drink appeared in an English newspaper advertisement of 1658: "That Excellent, and by all Physitians approved, *China* Drink, called by the *Chineans, Tcha,* by other nations *Tay alias Tee,* is sold at the *Sultaness-head,* a *Cophee-house* in *Sweetings* Rents by The Royal Exchange, London." Thereafter, over the decades to come, the vocabulary expanded to include, in rough order, *tea-spoon, tea-table, tea-stand, tea-equipage, tea-chest, tea-things, tea-saucer, tea-tray, tea-party, tea-house, tea-room,* and so on until the possible combinations were exhausted.

At the start, however, there were objections to the new custom on various grounds. In 1678 one Englishman deplored that some of his friends, instead of resorting to the pipe and bottle after dinner, had "fallen into the base, unworthy, Indian [sic!] practice of calling for tea." And before the end of the seventeenth century the Worshipful Company of Joiners in London protested that, to the disadvantage of their trade, 6582 tea tables had been imported from the Orient within four years. But the tide of taste and fashion was rising. As the eighteenth century progressed tea became the staple of the China trade.

Well before the middle of the century the popularity of the beverage was unchallenged in England—and in America, until colonial patriots gave their own native kind of tea parties in the years preceding the Revolution. In 1740 a tourist in Boston observed that "the ladies here visit, drink tea and indulge every little piece of gentility to the height of the mode and neglect the affairs of their families with as good grace as the finest ladies in London." Peter Kalm, the Swedish traveler, noted that in Albany, a large part of whose population was of Dutch origin or descent, and even among the Swedish population of Pennsylvania, tea had become a common drink by the middle of the century.

The troubles of the Revolution caused but a brief interruption in all this. Even before the peace was signed tea drinking had regained its old popularity. A visiting Frenchman noted in 1781 that "the greatest mark of civility and welcome" the Americans could show a guest was "to invite you to drink it [tea] with them."

The most popular form of colonial silver teapot during the second quarter of the eighteenth century, at least in New England, as in England itself, was a globular shape inspired by Oriental porcelain pots and European pottery imitations of them. The pot here illustrated (175) is handsomely engraved with the owner's coat of arms surrounded by decorative mantling, as are a number of other similar examples by the prominent Boston silversmith Jacob Hurd (1702/3–58).

174. An English family at their tea table, painted by Gawen Hamilton, about 1730

175. A silver teapot, by Jacob Hurd of Boston, engraved with the arms of its owner

176. Below: a metal trivet used by the fireside to support a kettle of hot water

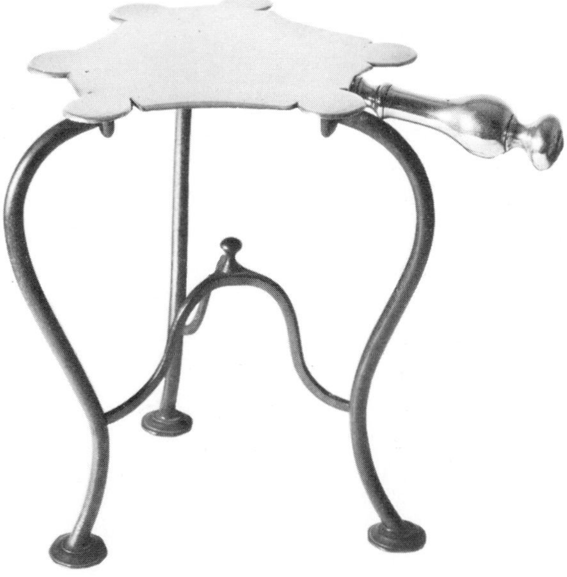

177. *Covered milk pitcher made by William Homes (1717–83)*

178. *A similar pitcher by Hurd*

179. *A teakettle made by Hurd, once owned by James Russell Lowell*

Adding milk or cream to tea was an English innovation that was quickly adopted in America. The custom was apparently common enough in England about 1720 when Matthew Prior wrote in his poem, *To a Young Gentleman in Love:*

> He kissed her on his bended knee;
> Then drank a quart of milk and tea.

Since there was no suitable Oriental form to copy or adapt, early milk or cream pitchers (177, 178) were designed in the shape of contemporary mugs with a spout added.

Even before America was directly engaged in the China trade, a few colonists were commissioning Oriental porcelain made to their order. A tea service made in the first half of the eighteenth century (180), and owned by Catharina de Peyster Rutgers, presents a combination of Chinese and western design. The cups, without handles, and the teapot are essentially Oriental forms; the other elements of the service, such as the milk pitcher and the sugar bowl, were made to accommodate Occidental usage. A slop bowl and a spoon tray not shown, forms not used in the Orient, are also included in the rest of the set. The similarity in outline of a Chinese porcelain covered bowl (181), made about 1717 for the tea service of the Right Honorable James Craggs, and a silver bowl (182), made by Simeon Soumain (1685–1750) of New York for Elizabeth Blair Cruger, provides a striking example of this interplay between East and West. In both cases the form is that of a Chinese rice bowl.

Although, as we have seen, a colonial silver teakettle was first fashioned early in the eighteenth century, few others seem to have been made here in the years up to the Revolution. This rare example (179)—the only one known to have been made in colonial New England—with its own spirit lamp, was stamped by Jacob Hurd. Many others were, of course, imported from England.

180. Top: part of a Chinese export porcelain tea set. 181. Above, left: export porcelain bowl. 182. Right: a colonial silver bowl

The kettle with its heating lamp was at times provided with its own stand (184), which had a sliding rest to hold the teapot as hot water was poured into it. Such stands were similar to, though smaller than, the tripod form that was so commonly used as a tea table (183). The top of the latter could often be tilted when the piece was not in use. Whatever their shape, tea tables were sometimes left standing, ready for use, with their equipage displayed on them. In 1728 while William Byrd II was visiting Mrs. Alexander Spotswood, the ex-governor's lady, her tame deer "spying his own figure in the [looking] glass...made a spring over the tea table that stood under it...shattered the glass to pieces, and falling back upon the tea table made a terrible fracas among the china."

Although they were outlawed in most of the colonies later, private lotteries were for a while in popular favor. In 1727 the highest prize in one of them included "an Eight square Tea-Pot," wrought by the silversmith Simeon Soumain—no doubt similar to one by Peter Van Dyck (185) who was an appraiser at that same lottery. This octagonal, pear-shaped form, similar to Dutch models, was especially popular in New York.

So long as it remained expensive tea was often kept in "small chests and trunks, with lock and key" for security's sake. Canisters intended to fit into such cases were usually made in sets of two or three to hold different sorts of tea. The example shown here (186) was engraved "Bohea Tea"; its companion piece, "Green Tea." In time the word "caddy"—derived from the Malay *kati*, a weight more than a pound—was introduced to refer to such containers.

183. Above: a painted table, in the Queen Anne style, with an octagonal tilt-top

184. Right: a teakettle stand with slide

185. Right: an octagonal teapot made by Peter Van Dyck (1684–1750) of New York

186. Below: one of a pair of tea caddies by Thauvet Besley (made a freeman, 1727)

190

187a,b. *Front and back of teaspoon by Wm. Simpkins (1704–80)*

188. *Middle: mote spoon made by an unidentified silversmith*

189. *Below: a painted table with inlaid top of Delft tiles*

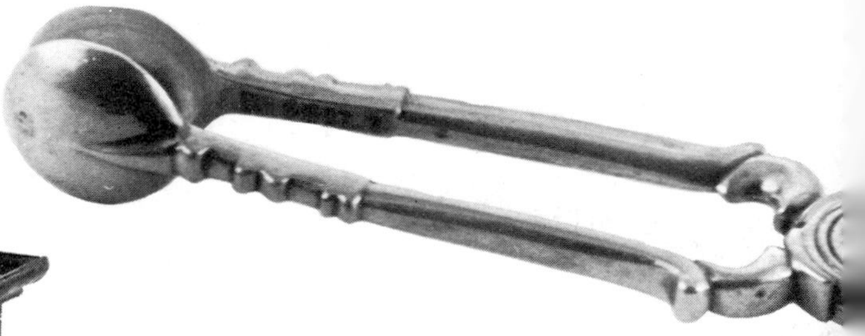

191. *Above: a tea strainer by James Butler (1713–76)*

192. *Below: tongs by George Fielding (working, 1731)*

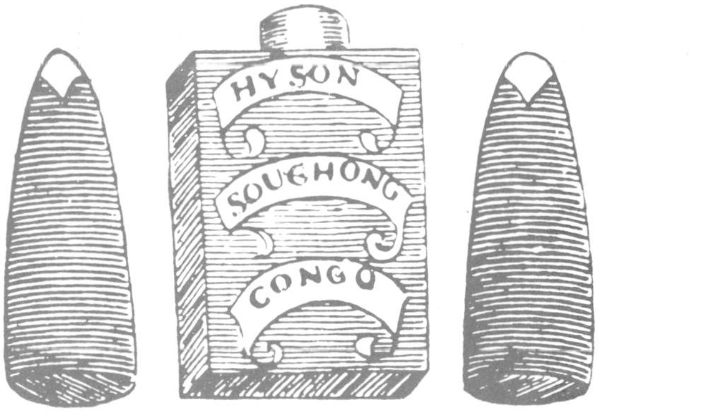

The practice of taking sugar with tea was another European innovation that was quickly copied in the colonies. Steel nippers (173) were used to cut sugar that came as a loaf, as shown in the advertisement above, into convenient lumps. In 1749 Peter Kalm recorded that the Dutch in Albany "never put sugar into the cup, but take a small bit of it into their mouths while they drink," a custom perhaps about to be followed by the young Susanna Truax (190), as shown by an anonymous painter. A highly critical Frenchman remarked later in the century that Americans used "great quantities" of sugar in their tea.

Before the middle of the century most of the useful paraphernalia for serving tea western style had developed into forms that are more or less familiar to us today: teaspoons (187), sugar tongs (192), and tea strainers (191), along with other equipment. One device, known today as a mote spoon (188), may have been used to skim off the foreign particles that were inevitable in tea in the eighteenth century (such matter is now removed before the tea is packaged); the sharp-ended handle, also, may have been used to unclog the strainer of a teapot's spout.

While sipping tea from a saucer was probably deemed gauche behavior, that quaint aberration of formal etiquette recalled in the phrase "a dish of tea" was not unknown in the colonies. Although, as Peter Kalm observed, colonists of English descent were not guilty of such impropriety, by his implication those of other backgrounds were. In any event, the custom remained a fairly common one well into the nineteenth century.

Delft tiles were laid into the top of one of a small number of unusual tables (189) that may have seen duty in the service of tea, although they are commonly termed mixing tables. In any event, such a surface was not marred by hot or strong liquids that left so many wooden table tops scarred and stained after years of use, and the blue and white patterns of the tiles added a colorful contrast to their polished or painted wooden frames.

The Japanner's Art

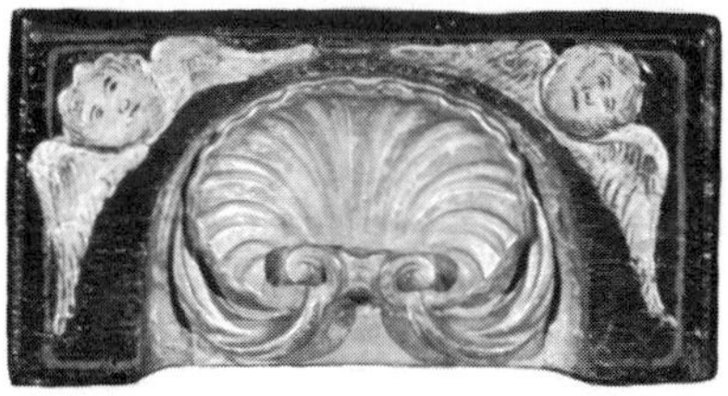

Classicism and Orientalism met head on in Europe, and the controversy over these seemingly disparate styles raged in England for many years. In 1688 anti-classicists John Stalker and George Parker in *A Treatise of Japaning* wrote, "Ancient and modern Rome must now give place: The glory of one Country, Japan alone, has exceeded in beauty and magnificence all the pride of the Vatican at this time, and the Pantheon heretofore." In the 1730's *The Universal Spectator* satirized classicism with an imaginary gentleman who "talks all day long of frieze, cornice, and architrave, [and] there is not a gate-post near his house nor a broom-stick in it which he has not had...carved according to some one of the five orders." The classicists countered with comments on the "horrible shapes" of eastern art, and one wryly stated that fox hunters would be aggrieved to break a leg jumping a fence that was not made in the Oriental style. Another wrote, "every hovel for the cows has bells hanging at the corners," and further cited the artistic heresy of a mythical Lady Fiddlefaddle who replaced her Italian paintings with "great-bellied Chinese Pagods...and red dragons." While the intelligentsia wrangled, English and colonial furniture makers, with no academic qualms whatsoever, freely used elements from both styles "according to fancy." This Queen Anne highboy (194) from New England is ornamented with adaptations of classical motifs—a broken pediment, urn finials, shells, and Corinthian columns; the surface is decorated with japanned depictions of the Orient as a colorful dreamworld. The cupids on the matching lowboy (193) and highboy suggest the japanning was done by Thomas Johnston, who practiced the craft in Boston between 1732 and 1767 at the sign of the "Golden Lyon in Ann Street" and adorned his trade card with similar cupids. Colonial japanning was simpler than European techniques. Rather than oak or deal, which required a gesso fill, Americans used fine-grained maple or yellow pine, which could be painted upon directly. (When a tortoise-shell effect was desired, vermilion was streaked with lampblack.) The raised design was built up with whiting (a chalk compound) and polished, all surfaces sized, and metal dust or leaf affixed. "Lay on your gold," the *Treatise* rhapsodized, "if your work be sufficiently moist, you'l perceive how lovingly the gold will embrace it, hugging and clinging to it...." For the final step a coat of varnish was applied over the entire piece.

193. A japanned lowboy from New England

194. A japanned highboy with classical decorations

195. Above: a Queen Anne chair made in Massachusetts, about 1750. The decoration was applied at a later date.

196. Left: a japanned clock with the raised and gilded figures on a red and black "tortoise-shell" background

197. This looking glass is set in a japanned pine frame with Queen Anne scrolling on the crest and on the apron.

The majority of japanned colonial furniture was made in Boston, the first records of the craft in that city dating from 1712. In 1735 Gerardus Duyckinck advertised in *The New-York Weekly Journal*, "Looking-glasses new Silvered and the Frames plaine, Japan'd or Flowered." Since Duyckinck was the only japanner advertising in the city at that time, he possibly did the gold-on-black Chinese designs on the frame of this Queen Anne looking glass (197), made between 1735 and 1745, and originally owned by Isaac Van Keuren of New York. In Greek and Roman times and on into the Middle Ages, looking glasses were usually polished metal and were designed to carry in the hand; a wall glass was a rarity. The process of silvering glass with tin and mercury to create a mirror was perfected by the Venetians in the fourteenth century. Not until the late nineteenth century did the term mirror come into use for all forms of looking glasses. Until that time a "mirror" was a hand glass.

After Duyckinck's death his son, Gerardus Duyckinck, Jr., announced in a 1746 New York paper that he was continuing the family business, "Limning, Painting, Varnishing, Japanning, Gilding etc." The decorations on the classically designed oak case of this clock (196) have been attributed to young Duyckinck. The works were made by Bartholomew Barwell, who advertised himself as "lately from the City of Bath" and worked in New York between 1749 and 1760.

Japanning was the western adaptation of the highly complex and time-absorbing Oriental method of applying lacquer, which required many months, often years, of alternate drying and polishing. This Queen Anne walnut chair (195) is one of a set of six originally owned by the Winthrops and shipped, according to family legend, to China in 1795 to be lacquered. They are brilliantly decorated with birds, landscapes, and flowers in gold, green, and red on a black ground with the Winthrop coat of arms, flanked by acanthus leaves, on the apron.

Table Types

198

Variations on table styles continued. This one in walnut (200), of the type known as a "handkerchief" table because of the triangular drop leaf, was designed as a breakfast table. The marble-topped Massachusetts table (201), also of walnut, was finished on all four sides to stand in the center of a room. The tilt-top stand (203) was made in the Queen Anne manner in 1784 by Jonathan Gavet, a Salem cabinetmaker. Three-legged tables were popular throughout the eighteenth century; they balanced well on wide, uneven, colonial floor boards and could be used for a number of purposes, as well as being extremely decorative. The drop-leaf dining table (202) was made in Newport, between 1730 and 1750, of Santo Domingan mahogany, which would become the favored wood of Rhode Island furniture makers.

The use of Turkey "carpitts" as table covers persisted into the Queen Anne period, as can be seen in Robert Feke's 1741 portrait (199) of the Isaac Royall family. The "Transylvania" rug (198), so called because of the number found in Transylvanian churches, is strikingly similar to that in the painting. But fashions were changing; imported Turkish carpets were being placed underfoot instead of being used on table tops. Floorcloths—canvas or linen heavily painted, sometimes in imitation of marble tiling—were also being used for carpeting and by such prominent figures as Governor William Burnet of New York, Peter Faneuil of Boston, and, as late as 1796, by General George Washington.

199

200. Above: a folding "handkerchief" table

201. Left: the table top is Brescia marble.

202. Right: drop-leaf dining tables were a Queen Anne variation of the gate-leg table.

203. A mahogany three-legged tilt-top stand

Lost Landmarks

Many of the finest homes built in the American colonies have been destroyed. These lost landmarks included, unfortunately, some buildings that were more imposing than all but a very few of those that have survived from the same time. One, destroyed a century ago, was the splendid mansion the merchant Thomas Hancock began building on Beacon Hill in 1737. When completed three years later it was the most distinguished house in Boston and was widely admired. It stood just outside the settled part of the city on a site overlooking the Common that had been used for pasturage since the founding of Boston more than a century earlier. To landscape the property Hancock ordered a great number of seeds and fruit trees, walnut trees, yew trees, "Jessamin Vines," among other bushes and assorted plants from London. "My Gardens all Lye on the South Side of a hill," he wrote, "with the most Beautifull Assent to the Top & it's allowed on all hands the Kingdom of England don't afford So Fine a Prospect as I have both of Land and water. Neither do I intend to Spare any Cost or Pains in making my Gardens Beautifull or Profitable."

Who designed the house is not known, but many of the details, if not indeed the general plan, were undoubtedly derived from one or another of the English architectural books of the time. (At one point Hancock inquired about the cost of having Corinthian capitals carved in London, but whether he actually ordered such work done is uncertain.) In any case, the finished building was a superb example of the Georgian style.

The doorway with its engaged columns set against a rusticated frame was unprecedented in the colonies, and the use of projecting brackets to support the balcony was another unusual feature. Some elements of the design were widely imitated throughout New England in years to come. A broken-scroll pediment crowned the balcony window, which was flanked by Corinthian pilasters also set against a rusticated frame. The stone for this window was cut to specifications in Middletown, Connecticut, which may account for the appearance, up and down the Connecticut River valley, of numerous doorways that follow this general pattern trans-

lated into provincial woodwork (see page 157). Two large wings of the house housed an "elegant ball-room" and a "kitchen and other domestic offices."

For the fifty-odd windows of the house Hancock ordered forty dozen panes of glass from London, along with three marble hearths, twenty dozen blue and white Delft tiles, looking glasses with walnut frames, a chiming clock, and various other items of furniture in the latest style. He also sent a pattern for wallpaper, instructing his agent to have it made "as Cheap as Possible, & if they can make it more Beautifull by adding more Birds flying here & there, with Some Landskip at the Bottom [I] should Like it well." In 1739, as befitted a gentleman who could commission such a luxurious establishment, Hancock wrote a friend in London to go to the herald's office and order a coat of arms. "Lett it be well cutt," he added, the "Crest & Arms in Silver."

Hancock was a self-made man. When he was twenty-one years old he opened a stationery store, or bookshop, on Ann Street in Boston. Clever, industrious, and diplomatic, he soon had friends among the leading local men of affairs. One was Daniel Henchman, Boston's most prominent bookdealer. With Henchman and other merchants Hancock participated in a successful paper manufacturing business and other ventures. And in 1730 he married Henchman's daughter, Lydia, who brought with her a very comfortable dowry.

At about this time he also began to import the various English goods such as he advertised in *The Boston Weekly News-Letter* in 1736: "Just imported, and sold by Thomas Hancock...Callicoes of two and three Colours, blew and white ditto, purple and white Chints... fine India Damasks...Green Tea, large Bibles, Paper, and most sorts of Stationary and Cutlary Ware," and several other items. He exported fish, whale oil, and potash; and he provided the Newfoundland fishermen with rum, molasses, tobacco, and other provisions.

Because the Acts of Trade and Navigation prohibited the colonies from importing a variety of goods from any country but England, Hancock occasionally smuggled goods into Boston—as did many other merchants of the time. Taking care that the news of one of these trips would not leak out, he wrote to the captain: "I hope ere this, you Safe arrived at Surranam, & your Cargo to a Good Market. I Press you make the best dispatch possible...& Closely observe when you come on our Coasts not to Speak with any Vessells, nor let any of your men write up to their wives, when you arrive."

The bulk of Hancock's fortune was made during the French and Indian wars by supplying the British troops. The provisions were not always of the best quality, apparently, for at one point a supply was refused by one of the posts. They wrote that "having carefully surveyed a Barrell of Pork in the Stores sent here by Thomas Hancock Esqr & Co...we found same Stinking decay'd and intirely unfit for use." A solution to the problem of bad meat was found in another instance when the commissary of one of the posts wrote "I have got rid of the Old Pork...without any difficulty to the French."

In 1761, when Daniel Henchman died and left his large estate to his daughter and son-in-law, the Hancocks were very rich indeed. That same year Thomas began to consider following the example of some of his wealthy neighbors to "sell all & Go to England & spend my days in quiet." His wife, he added, was "quite willing." However, before he could execute such a plan he died (in 1764), leaving his house and estate to his widow and to their nephew John Hancock.

As a matter of course John took over his uncle's business, but having none of his uncle's merchandising ability (despite the advantage of a Harvard education) he eventually put it in the hands of an associate to run for him. He then devoted more and more of his attention to the political affairs of the colony, and in the years directly preceding the Revolution he was celebrated as a public hero and a patriot in every town from Boston to Philadelphia. When the break with England came it was his signature, written large and bold "so that George the Third may read without his spectacles," that headed the list of signers of the Declaration of Independence.

The year before that great statement was made Hancock's stables and house had been used as a British hospital and as a residence by Generals Sir Henry Clinton and Thomas Gage while the redcoats occupied Boston. It was from an upstairs window of the house that Sir William Howe's officers spied (using Thomas Hancock's old telescope) the entrenchments of the colonial forces on Dorchester Heights and concluded that "neither Hell, Hull, nor Halifax could afford them worse shelter than Boston."

When John Hancock returned to the house he found that the unwelcome occupants had "totally defac'd & Ruined" all his carpets, and he ordered new Wilton carpets from England to replace them. In 1793, racked with gout and "swathed in flannel from head to foot," he gave up this life. Before his death he had expressed a wish to give his mansion, of which he was then sole owner, to the state of Massachusetts (he had been elected its first governor in 1780), but that intention was never carried out. Part of the contents were sold within three weeks of his death, the rest at various sales and auctions over subsequent years up to 1863. That year, in an effort to save the house from destruction, a suggestion was made that it become the residence of the governors of the state, or a museum for a collection of Revolutionary relics. But neither purpose was achieved. On June 26, 1863, an auctioneer's poster announced:

The Old Hancock House
At 4 P M on the Premises

All the materials of the old Hancock House of Revolutionary Fame, on Beacon Street consisting of red cedar, oak joists, hard wood finish doors, carvings, window blinds, flooring etc comprising many antique curiosities & materials to be fashioned into many useful & ornamental parlor mementoes. Also the stone, brick work, masonry etc.

The house was then quickly demolished.

Architectural Woodwork

The early settlers in America (and the later generations who moved westward into the continent) encountered forests on a scale Europe had not known for centuries. Wood was everywhere; it was the colonies' most immediately available and most plentiful resource: wood for houses, furniture, and tools, and for ships. In the forty years between 1674 and 1714 New England alone built no fewer than 1332 oceangoing vessels. Many were sold abroad. Because of the demands of naval warfare with Holland, France, and Spain, England's royal forests were seriously depleted. The colonists, on the other hand, could turn to what seemed like an inexhaustible source of oak, pine, and spruce timber large enough for building both men-of-war and merchantmen. According to one contemporary report, New England turned out seven hundred ships in the single year of 1723, and similar construction went on up and down the coast. If this trend continued, complained the master builders of London, things might end with England's ordering all its merchantmen from the colonies—and losing all its best shipwrights to colonial shipyards. The pay was better there, for one thing, and opportunities in general were greater in America. But England needed ships. By the eve of the Revolution almost one third of all the vessels in the English merchant marine were made in the colonies.

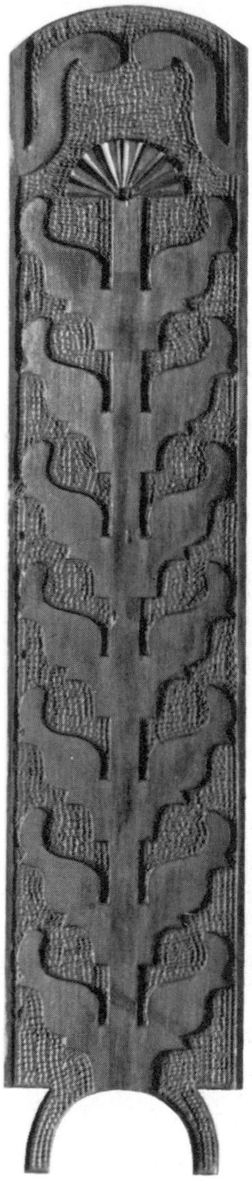

Wood for shipbuilding and other purposes was also brought to England from the New World. In 1721 England abolished the heavy import duty on virtually all timber from the North American and the West Indian colonies. Until mahogany replaced it in popularity, black walnut, called "Virginia" walnut in England, was extensively used in English cabinetwork and chairmaking. But in spite of all the cutting of timber required for this purpose and for building in the colonies, in spite of the clearing of wooded lands for farms and towns, one widely traveled French visitor who had journeyed the length and breadth of the new nation late in the eighteenth century observed that compared with France, at least, the landscape of America was still "one vast wood."

As a consequence of all this plenty, many things have been made of wood in America that in other lands were more often fashioned of brick or stone. Although numerous important colonial mansions were constructed of the latter materials, frame houses remained the typical American architectural form, particularly in New England. There, until well after the Revolution, buildings of large size and imposing appearance continued to be made of wood. Most of the designs for exterior architecture represented in the English building manuals were intended as guides to the stonemason. In the colonies these models were freely adapted in woodwork, often with very engaging effects.

Just how free such adaptations of formal patterns could be is apparent in the carved wood doorway (204) from Westfield, Massachusetts, shown on the opposite page. It is a particularly elaborate example of a distinctive regional style that was confined to the Connecticut River valley and that, as mentioned on the previous page, was probably inspired by the balcony window of the Hancock house whose stone elements had been cut in the valley. Such ornate work had not been seen in that area before and undoubtedly attracted the attention of housewrights for miles up and down the riverway.

But here is only the most general approximation of that elegant window. Where detailed memory failed, a vigorous imagination was applied. In the hands of a country carpenter or housewright the stately language of Renaissance architecture as it was expressed in the Hancock house was translated into a lively vernacular. The wooden frame of the doorway was regularly gouged to simulate cut stone, but the fluted Corinthian pilasters of the original model have been converted into an exercise in flat carving. The leafy tendrils that run up their length and that form the capitals are a local invention; the cushion frieze above the doorway opening and the broken-scroll pediment above that follow the contours of available molding planes; and the outlines of the entire doorway are duplicated in miniature on the base of each pilaster, an ingenuous provincial pattern.

204. A painted pine doorway, a country housewright's version of Renaissance design, from the Connecticut Valley

205. Left: a walnut corner cupboard. 206. Right: the walnut speaker's chair from the House of Burgesses in Williamsburg, Va.

The numerous architectural manuals that were published in England from about 1715 to about 1760 influenced furniture as well as building design. Almost all of them indicated or insisted that a real understanding of the classical orders and a proper regard for good proportions were essential to the housebuilder. In 1740 Batty Langley issued the first edition of *The City and Country Builder's and Workman's Treasury of Designs*, a manual intended for and largely subscribed to by craftsmen, cabinetmakers included. "Cabinet Makers," the author observed, "originally, were no more, than *Spurious Indocible Chips*; expelled by Joiners, *for the Superfluity of their* SAP...'tis a very great Difficulty to find, one in Fifty of them, that can make a Book-Case, &c. indispensably true, after any one of the Five Orders; without being obliged to a Joiner, for to set out the Work.... If these Gentlemen persist much longer thus to despise the Study of this Noble Art; the very Basis and Soul of their Trade, which now to many Joiners is well understood; they will soon find the bad Consequences of so doing: and have Time enough on their Hands, to repent of their Folly. And more especially, since that our Nobility and Gentry delight themselves now more than ever, in the Study of Architecture."

The petulant tone of that outburst hardly seems justified, since much of the surviving cabinetwork of this period both from England and America was handsomely proportioned, stoutly constructed, and showed proper regard for the principles of architectural design. In any event, the three illustrations on these pages reveal the close relationship between cabinetwork and architecture that was observed in the colonies. The free-standing triangular corner cupboard (205), with its fluted pilasters and classical moldings, and the shell-topped cupboard (207), actually incorporated into the fabric of the wall, serve the same purpose in much the same way. The throne-like speaker's chair (206) from the House of Burgesses at Williamsburg, with its paneled sides and back and its crowning pediment, is more an element of interior architecture than a piece of furniture. It may have been from this same chair that in 1759 Speaker John Robinson, to spare the embarrassment of a newly elected burgess, about to be cited for his bravery in the French and Indian War, said, "Sit down, Mr. Washington; your modesty is equal to your valour, and that surpasses the power of any language I possess."

207. A shell-top cupboard built into the paneled wall of a room

The room of Cotton Mather's house where Benjamin Franklin, neglecting to stoop, bumped his head on a beam (referred to on page 13) would not have accommodated the furniture illustrated on these pages. Before 1700 the beams in a lower-story room were often less than six feet from the floor. However, from about 1720 until the Revolution, ceilings—in finer homes, at least—were usually between ten and thirteen feet in the clear, and the scale of various furniture forms increased proportionately.

Seventeenth-century clocks, largely, were designed to strike the hour on a bell rather than to "tell the time" by the hands on a dial. Before the second quarter of the eighteenth century accuracy was much improved and a minute hand became an important feature of larger and more elab-

208. Left: walnut-veneered tall clock by William Claggett of Newport. 209. Right: a cherry secretary from Connecticut

orate clockfaces. In this example (208) the face is revealed between two Doric columns supporting an arch. The hoods of the imposingly tall cases that housed the mechanism were raised in steps, as here, or sometimes rose in a scrolled pediment, surmounted by finials.

Each of the secretaries here illustrated (209, 210) is over seven feet tall; with its broken-scroll pediment and arched panels each reflects the prevailing architectural fashions. The leafy-tendril pilasters of the example (209) from Connecticut (see also page 156) very obviously recall the treatment of the doorway from Westfield. Even looking glasses at times exhibited an architectural character (211), with moldings and scrolls duplicating those of doors, windows, and cornices of the rooms in which they were hung.

210. Left: a walnut secretary, with ornamental inlay, from New England. 211. Right: a carved and gilded looking glass

In the 1720's America entered a period of peaceful prosperity and tremendous commercial expansion. New fortunes were made in grain, salted fish, lumber, molasses, rum, and slaves, particularly in Newport, which would soon rival Boston in the Caribbean trade. One such Rhode Island merchant prince was Metcalf Bowler, whose Newport mansion, Vernon house, is noted for its *chinoiserie* frescoes. Bowler also enjoyed the luxury of a summer home in Portsmouth, Rhode Island; a fireplace wall from his country house is shown here (213). The chimney opening is faced with blue and white Delft tiles, and Delft plates are displayed in the overmantel cupboard with sliding doors. The stile-and-rail paneling is set between pilasters with stopped fluting, a provincial demonstration of the classical architectural motifs revived in Europe during the Renaissance. The walnut chairs with out-curving arms are from New York.

The Portsmouth house was set in eleven and a half acres of formal gardens landscaped with fish ponds, fountains, rare plants and trees, and "hothouses with exotics from all parts of the world." Among Bowler's numerous horticultural treasures was a legendary apple tree from the Garden of Eden. One of Bowler's ships had "Chanced to rescue from shipwreck a prince of the royal blood of Persia, whose father, in the fervor of his gratitude...presented to the captain from his own garden...a young apple tree growing in a porcelain tub, which was declared to be one of the few direct lineal descendants of the tree of knowledge." Cider made from the fruit of this tree, transplanted in Rhode Island soil, was said to surpass the finest French wines. At dinner parties in the handsome room where this paneled and tiled fireplace once stood, Metcalf Bowler supposedly served—and amazed—General Washington, Marquis de Lafayette, and Comte de Rochambeau with his home-brewed "Eden champagne."

In such households many furniture items, such as looking glasses, continued to be imported. This English one (212) has a walnut veneer frame decorated with a gilded gesso scallop shell, the upper part of the glass cut in a floral pattern. Sheets of looking glass were still being made from blown cylinders that were split and flattened, a process that necessarily limited their size, hence the piecing of two and sometimes three sections in early looking glasses.

212. Above: a Queen Anne looking glass, an English import

213. Opposite: an interior with a paneled wall typical of early Georgian woodwork designs in colonial America

Comfortable Accommodations

Four-post beds from the Queen Anne period are extremely rare. This fine example (214) was made in Rhode Island of maple, a wood not often employed by cabinetmakers of that area. All four tall posts have cabriole legs and pad feet, an unusual feature in colonial four-post beds; as a rule, only the two foot posts were shaped and carved, and the two head posts were left plain. The mid-eighteenth century hangings and bedspread are of homespun linen embroidered in crewelwork. The trellis-patterned New England spread was originally owned by Thomas Hancock, and later by his nephew and heir, John Hancock.

Another rare piece from the Queen Anne period is this Philadelphia walnut sofa (215) with its arrow-shaped stretchers. The feet in paneled "socks," like those on the chair (159) earlier described, is a Philadelphia design introduced by immigrant furniture makers from Ireland. The upholstery is a brilliant blue eighteenth-century Italian brocatelle, a popular contemporary fabric best described as a heavy damask in which the silk figure of the warp is woven against the linen or woolen background of the weft. The word sofa is of Arabian origin and in the Near East referred to an alcove raised from the floor and "furnished with rich carpets and cushions, where honourable personages are entertained."

The dressing table (216), made of Connecticut cherry wood, has a delicately scalloped top, possibly to parallel the cyma curve in the apron. An inscription on the side of one drawer reads, "Mary A. Woodruff from Mother."

214. Above: a Queen Anne four-post bed. 215. Right: a Queen Anne sofa, distinguished from a settee by its greater size and comfort

216. A cherry dressing table from Connecticut

The day bed continued to be an important piece in a well-furnished house. In this example (218), made of walnut in Philadelphia, the design is clearly derived from chairs of the Queen Anne period with splat backs and upholstered seats. Here the scrolled splat is doubled. The carved shell on the crest is repeated on the knees of the front legs.

Carved shells also appear on the cabriole legs of the walnut settee (219), again from Philadelphia. The tall back and curved outline of this settee are reminiscent of chair backs of the late seventeenth century. It was made about 1735 for Stenton, the Germantown home of James Logan, statesman, scholar, and botanist, who amassed a fortune in land investments and in trade with the Indians. The walnut side chair (217), with flat stretchers and upholstered in black leather, is still another Pennsylvania piece from Logan's house. The pointed front feet are overlaid with a single carved panel, or "tongue." These upholstered low-seated chairs, usually armless, are called slipper chairs.

The walnut shaving stand (220), or toilet mirror—later called a dressing glass, or shaving table—is from Rhode Island. The four tiers of concave drawers are exceptional in furniture of the Queen Anne period.

217. Above: a walnut Queen Anne slipper chair

218. Below: an upholstered walnut day bed

219. An upholstered settee from Philadelphia

220. A shaving stand with an adjustable looking glass

On the Lighter Side

It has been said that in the early colonial years a gentleman of leisure was unknown in America, unless "he were a jailbird or a redskin." But the colonists found time to play. There were quilting bees and husking bees, the latter described as "Riots" by a Salem clergyman; house-raising, wedding, funeral, and christening parties; dances, sleigh rides and waffle frolics, with "kissing... a great part of its entertainment," wrote one young man in 1744. There were fairs, lotteries, parades, and illuminations; traveling acrobats and trained animal shows. Country men enjoyed "hunting, fishing and fowling, with which they entertain themselves in an hundred ways," as well as shooting matches and wolf hunts: "All persons to... meet upon the hill at the meetinghouse by the beat of the drum."

In eighteenth-century New York turtle barbecues were a diversion for the "chief gentry in town"; and in 1744 Dr. Hamilton described a man-of-war crew, on a "festival day," roasting a whole ox and "getting drunk as fast as they could." For Governor William Burnet of New York there was golf; his 1729 inventory listed "Nine Gouff Clubs, one iron ditto and seven dozen balls." The game, in those days, appears to have been a form of miniature golf (221). Children, of course, had their pastimes and toys, such as the wooden tops shown here (223), found in Williamsburg excavations. In the engraving at the right (222), *Youthful Amusement*, an eighteenth-century child plays with a top and a string.

222

221. An 18th-century Dutch cartoon (opposite) shows a companionable game of golf between French, American, and Indian players.

In the 1750's young John Adams wrote in his diary: "Let others waste the bloom of Life, at the Card or biliard Table, among rakes and fools." But the Puritan conscience was not universal; George Washington, at the same age, enjoyed both diversions. Card playing, despite fines and prohibitions, was popular everywhere, and billiard tables were standing furniture in many taverns and private homes. The one above (224) was engraved on the trade card of E. Turpin, candlemaker, 1752. Backgammon, draughts, shuffleboard, skittles, bowls, and "dicing" were also played, particularly at taverns, the social centers of the day where, John Adams also wrote, "Yet if you set the evening, you will find the House full of People, drinking Drams, Phlip, Toddy, Carrousing, swearing."

Cockfighting and animal baiting, the "butcherly sports...a rude and dirty pastime," as diarist John Evelyn termed them in England in 1670, were crude colonial diversions. A bullbaiting, for example, was held by the keeper of the DeLancey Arms in Bowery Lane in 1763, a cockfight in the Salem townhouse in 1744. Philip Vickers Fithian, tutor to the Carter children in Virginia, wrote in 1774, "I was before Dinner very strongly urged by Mr. Taylor, Mr. Randolph, & some others to attend a Cock-Fight, where 25 Cocks are to fight, & large Sums are betted, so large at one as twenty five Pounds but I choose rather to stay at Home." On the frontier men let each other's blood in maiming, eye-gouging, "sporting" matches—or rough-and-tumbles, as they were called.

In direct contrast were the gentle diversions of singing and music. Early in the 1700's public concerts began in the South, New York, and Philadelphia; choral societies sprang up in New England towns; spinets, harpsichords, guitars, violins, and organs were enjoyed throughout the colonies, as well as jew's-harps and a primitive form of the banjo. Jefferson played the cello, Washington the flute, and Franklin rang out tunes on an instrument made of musical glasses.

225. Right: a cribbage board dated 1735 and decorated with inlays of the four suits

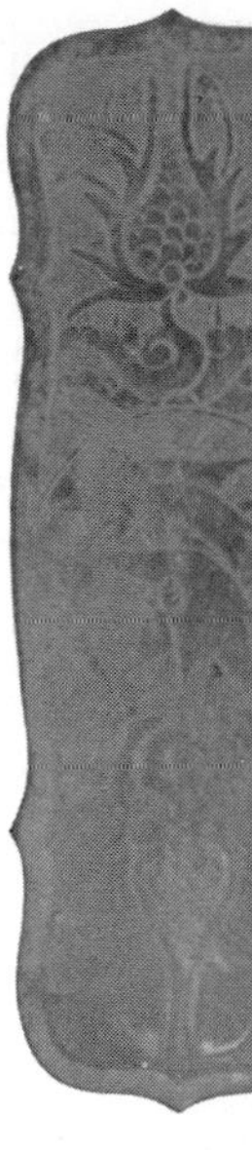

226. *A 1756 sampler (above) shows a wedding party arriving before a New England church.*

227. *Edging the page are an assortment of counters, or "fish," used in lanterloo, or loo.*

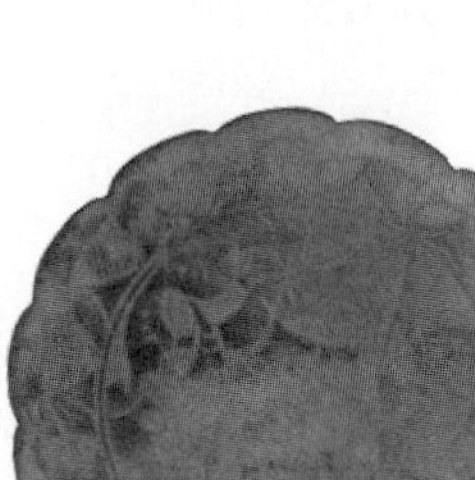

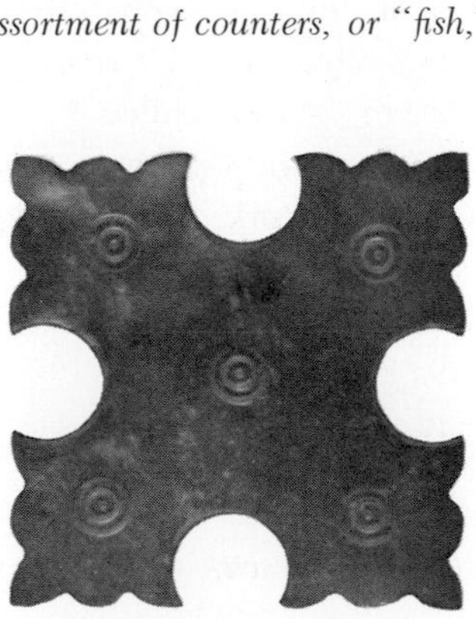

228. Above: 18th-century playing cards for the popular games of whist, all fours, put, piquet, and loo

229. Below: the top of a gaming table embroidered with flowers, coins, cards, and Chinese fish counters

230. Opposite: a 1670 board for goose, an Italian pastime similar to parchesi. Goose was enthusiastically played in England and the colonies by gamesters of all ages, and often as a gambling game by adults.

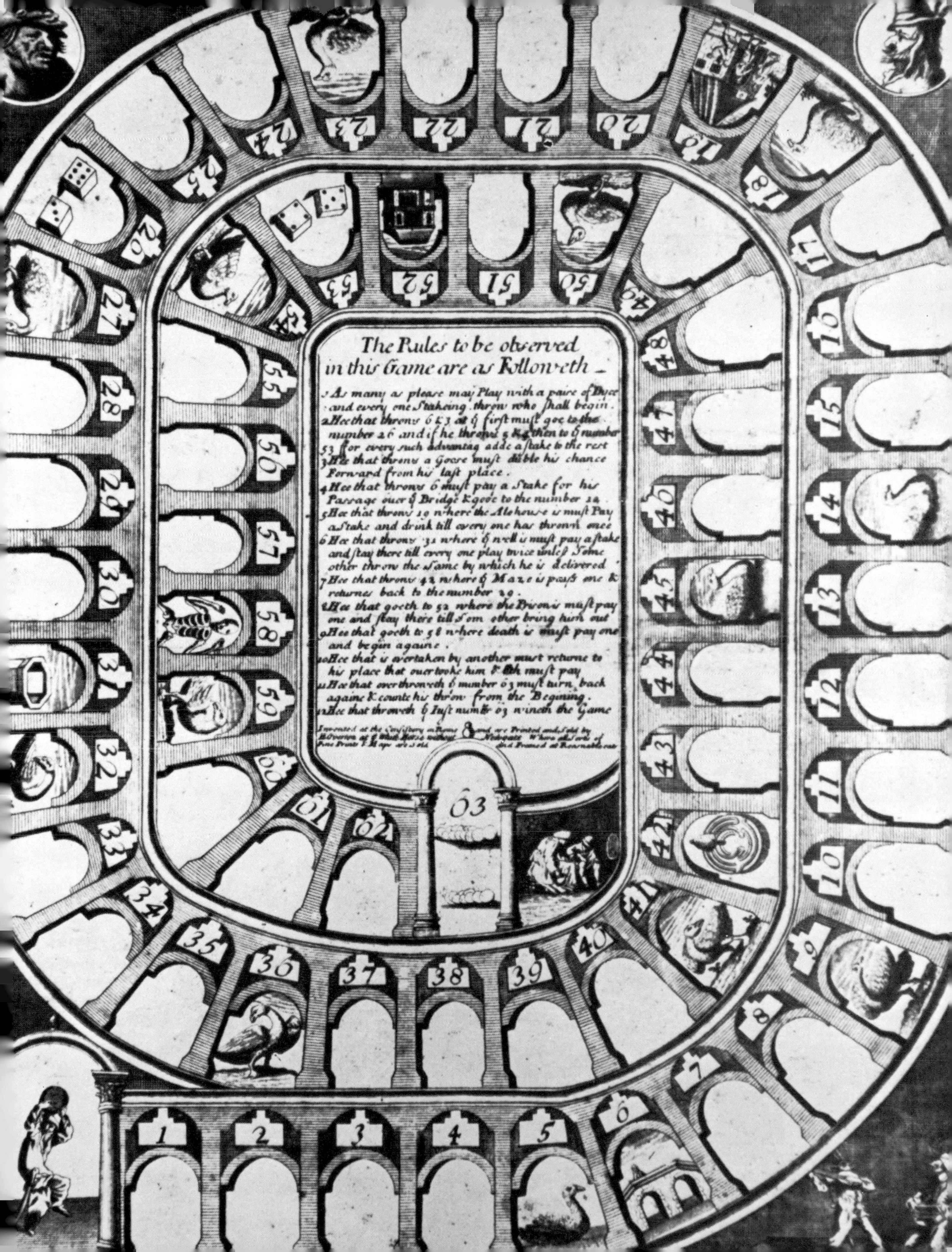
The Rules to be observed
in this Game are as Followeth
1 As many as please may Play with a paire of Dyce
and every one Stakeing throw who shall begin.
2 Hee that throws 6 & 3 at ÿ first must goe to the
number 26 and if he throws 5 & 4 then to ÿ number
53 for every such advantag adde a stake to the rest
3 Hee that throws a Goose must dubble his chance
Forward from his last place.
4 Hee that throws 6 must pay a Stake for his
Passage over ÿ Bridge & goe to the number 12
5 Hee that throws 19 where the Alehouse is must Pay
a Stake and drink till every one has thrown once
6 Hee that throws 31 where ÿ well is must pay a stake
and stay there till every one play twice unless some
other throw the same by which he is delivered
7 Hee that throws 42 where ÿ Maze is pays one &
returnes back to the number 29.
8 Hee that goeth to 52 where the Prison is must pay
one and stay there till som other bring him out
9 Hee that goeth to 58 where death is must pay one
and begin againe.
10 Hee that is overtaken by another must returne to
his place that overtooke him & both must pay
11 Hee that overthroweth ÿ number 63 must turn back
againe & counte his throw from the Begining.
12 Hee that throweth ÿ Just number 63 wineth the Game
1
2
3
4
5
6
7
8
9
10
11
12
13
14
15
16
17
18
19
20
21
22
23
24
25
26
27
28
29
30
31
32
33
34
35
36
37
38
39
40
41
42
43
44
45
46
47
48
49
50
51
52
53
54
55
56
57
58
59
60
61
62
63

231. The English sport of fox hunting was inevitably transplanted to America. In New York, for example, soon after the English took that colony from the Dutch in 1664, meets were held during the autumn months in Flatbush. In 1780 a New York paper advertised: "Gentlemen fond of fox-hunting will meet at Loosely's Kings Head Tavern at day break...." George Washington, like other Virginians, was an enthusiast, riding to hounds on six successive days in the winter of 1769. The hunting party shown below is a colonial overmantel painting of the late 17th century.

Horses were a vital part of colonial life. In this detail (232) from an overmantel painting from the Martin van Bergen farmhouse, built in 1729 in Leeds, New York, two horsemen gallop through the Van Bergen farmyard. Racing became widely popular throughout the colonies. A 1670 description of Long Island stated: "Towards the middle of Long Island lyeth a plain sixteen miles long and four broad...where you shall find neither stick nor stone to hinder the horse heels, or endanger them in their Races, and once a year the best Horses in the Island are brought hither to try their swiftness, and the swift is rewarded with a silver cup." This silver trophy (233) celebrates a flat race won in 1751 by Old Tenor, belonging to Lewis Morris, Jr., who owned one of the finest stables in New York. At other meets prizes ranged from "A Holland smock and Chintz Gown full-trimmed," for the winner of a ladies' race, to William Byrd III's wager of five hundred pistoles "against any that could be brought." But somber days were ahead. On the eve of the Revolution the Continental Congress urged the colonies to discourage "horse racing and all kinds of gaming, cockfighting, exhibitions of plays, shews and other expensive diversions...."

232

233

234. Top, right: Mr. Neilson's battle, with the Royalist Club

235. Above: The Royalist Club. *Both are satiric sketches of colonists gathered at their favorite taverns to "Philosophize, harangue, pun, sing, dance...nay we are really in fact a club."*

236. *Upper right: silver mug, made by Francis Richardson, Jr., with a view of its base (above)*

237. *Silver caster by Adrian Bancker*

Modes in Silver

On April 5, 1734, *The Boston Gazette* printed the complaint of an anonymous critic who felt, as proper Bostonians have before and since, that the ancient virtues of his community were being undermined by immoderate and unnecessary innovations. "It is too well known," he protested, "how our Extravagance in Apparel and Luxury at our Tables, are hastening the ruin of our Country, and are evils which call loudly for a remedy." His indignation had been triggered by a proposal to introduce a dancing assembly, but obviously he was concerned with broader issues.

Among the luxuries at the table he may well have had in mind the abundance of fine plate that, judging from contemporary inventories and surviving examples, adorned not only tea tables but dining tables—and that was also distributed elsewhere throughout the colonial home. During the second quarter of the eighteenth century an increasing variety of forms added to domestic convenience and served new habits of dining, drinking, and living in general. When he died in 1729 Governor Burnet of New York left silverware which included, aside from his tea equipment, twelve candlesticks, a set of three casters, eight salts, two "canns" (mugs), a chafing dish, two porringers, two coffeepots, shoe and garter buckles, spurs, a toothpick case, and three dozen each of knives and forks. The list continues but that is enough to suggest the wide range of household and personal needs the silversmith was called upon to satisfy.

By this time the elaborate designs of the William and Mary style had largely been discarded or modified, and the relative simplicity of the colonial version of the Queen Anne style prevailed. The style was marked by a reliance for effect on carefully considered proportions, and an increased use of casting for candlesticks and for the spouts and handles of other forms.

The "canns" listed in Governor Burnet's inventory of plate may have resembled the vessel shown opposite (236), made by Francis Richardson, Jr., of Philadelphia (working 1729–38), a traditional English form that was popular as an ale or beer mug in all the colonies. As was often the case in colonial silver, the exact weight of the finished piece was engraved on its base. For many years it was assumed that the little hole at the end of the handles of such mugs and tankards (236) was used as a whistle to summon a servant. Actually this was a vent to allow for the escape of hot air when the two hammered strips that composed the hollow handle were soldered together, and for the ingress of cool air after the soldering was completed.

Also, the casters listed in the same inventory could have resembled the one shown opposite (237), one of a set of three designed to contain sugar, pepper, and dry mustard. They were made by Adrian Bancker (1703–72), son of the mayor of Albany. With its graceful baluster-shaped body, readily grasped and not easily overturned, its tall, decoratively pierced slip-on cover fastened with a bayonet clasp, and its attractive, cast, acorn-shaped finial, this illustrated piece epitomizes the functional beauty of the Queen Anne style.

During the early years of the eighteenth century, London silversmiths felt the competition of the Huguenot craftsmen who had fled to England to escape religious persecution in France. As was observed earlier, some of these skilled French craftsmen, as well as seasoned merchants and traders, found their way to the American colonies. Peter Faneuil, American-born son of the first of the French family of that name to engage in New England commerce, rose to prominence during the period covered by this chapter. About the time Faneuil gave the historic hall that bears his name to his adopted city, Boston, Jacob Hurd fashioned a pair of candlesticks, one of which is shown here (238). This unusual pair is so distinctly French in style that it has been assumed they were cast in a mold imported from France by Hurd or an agent.

238. Silver candlestick made by Jacob Hurd

239. A silver saltcellar made by Charles Le Roux, silversmith and the official seal maker of New York

240

The name Le Roux frequently appeared in records of Paris silversmiths over the centuries. Bartholomew Le Roux was the first of the name to practice in the colonies, starting around 1687. His New York-born son and apprentice, Charles, made a pair of individual salts (239), which—with their cast garlands, masks, and feet in the form of dolphins—rank among the most sophisticated examples in colonial silverwork.

241

Sauceboats made their first appearance on colonial tables around the middle of the eighteenth century and grew in popularity over the years to come. The example shown opposite (246) is one of a pair made by Joseph Richardson (1711–84) of Philadelphia for Sarah, daughter of James Logan of Stenton.

The classic simplicity of the Queen Anne style is handsomely demonstrated by the coffeepot (247) fashioned by Jacob Hurd in the form of a tapered cylinder with a gracefully curved handle and spout and a slightly domed lid. It bears the engraved arms of the Clarke family within a cartouche in the rococo style that became a prevailing fashion in the decades preceding the Revolution.

242

Throughout the colonial period the porringer remained one of the most familiar forms in American silver, used, like its medieval predecessors, for porridge, broths, berries and milk, and the like. For a time the piercings of the handles varied from region to region. Some like those by Adrian Bancker (240) and Thauvet Besley (241) are typical of New York workmanship. Examples by Johannis Nys of Philadelphia (244) and Samuel Vernon of Newport (242, 243) show other regional styles. Jonathan Clarke (1705–70) also of Rhode Island adopted the so-called "keyhole" pattern (245) that became popular everywhere by mid-century.

243

246. Above: a sauceboat, by Joseph Richardson, with the Logan arms engraved on its side

247. Below: a silver coffeepot by Jacob Hurd

244

245

248. *A New York tankard detail*

249. *A silver brazier by John Burt*

250. *Saucepan made by Jacob Hurd*

The piercings of chafing (warming) dishes, or braziers, were more elaborate and more varied than those of porringer handles. Similar devices, using charcoal to supply a mild heat to whatever plate or receptacle that was placed upon them, had a long history in Europe. Examples in silver, often in pairs, were frequently mentioned in colonial inventories of the Queen Anne period. The handsome piece shown here (249), with its hoof feet and turned wooden handle, is one of such a pair made by John Burt (1691–1745) of Boston who, to judge from the large estate he left upon his death, enjoyed a great commercial success. He also left three sons who practiced his craft after him.

Saucepan-like vessels, often called brandy warmers, such as the one by Jacob Hurd (250), were probably used for holding hot foods and liquids. They were no doubt kept on a stove in the kitchen or on a spirit lamp or a chafing dish in the dining room until their contents were served.

To judge from the number that have survived, tankards were a consistently popular form of silver throughout the eighteenth century. Each of the principal colonial silver-making centers had its own distinctive style for these capacious vessels. Except in New York, the lids of tankards tended to assume a domical shape as the century progressed, as indicated by the example (251) made in Newport, Rhode Island, by John Coddington (1690–1743).

Colonists who could boast coats of arms, and some who had no right to them, had such heraldic devices engraved on their best plate. The example shown (248) is from a tankard by Peter Quintard (1699–1762). One of the most accomplished colonial engravers was Nathaniel Hurd, silversmith son of Jacob. His portrait by Copley shows him, with books of heraldic and cipher designs before him.

251. Tankard by John Coddington

Patterns of Elegance

The Chippendale Period (1750-1785)

Twice in the generation that preceded the American Revolution England took to the battlefield against its enemies on the Continent, and each time the colonies were swept into the conflict on their side of the ocean. This was partly because of their dependent status; as colonies they could not avoid being implicated in Britain's imperial problems, especially when both their own security and possession of a large part of the North American continent were at stake. But it was also the matter of self-determination that in good time brought about their political independence. The European War of the Austrian Succession, which France and England joined in 1744, is known in America as King George's War. The threat of French competition for land and furs and fish—for empire, in short—hung over the entire length of colonial America. Benjamin Franklin, ordinarily a calm man, raised his voice in alarm, alerting his compatriots to the real and ever-present menace of French and Indian raids on their homes and settlements.

In 1745 after the unsuccessful attack by the French on Port Royal, Nova Scotia (renamed Annapolis Royal after it was taken by the English during Queen Anne's War), Governor William Shirley of Massachusetts took the offensive. To protect New England's trade and fisheries he organized an expeditionary force to reduce the strong French fortress at Louisbourg on Cape Breton Island. It was a "mad scheme," but seven colonies responded to his call to join a co-operative enterprise that was unique in colonial experience. Connecticut, Massachusetts, and New Hampshire provided troops; New York supplied cannon; and Pennsylvania and New Jersey sent provisions. Rhode Island agreed to send troops, but they were organized too late to join the expedition. The "troops" were recruited from farmers, fishermen, shopkeepers, artisans, and others with virtually no experience in military matters. They are remembered in history as "Pepperrell's Yokels," after Maine's Kittery Point merchant, William Pepperrell, who was chosen as commander although he himself had never led troops in battle. However, Pepperrell was a popular figure and his appointment attracted volunteers.

The spirit of the expedition was expressed by one youth who wrote: "The News of our Government's Raising an army (Together with the Help of the other Neighbouring Governments) In order to the Reduction of Cape Breton. (Viz) Louisbourg, which was Like to prove Detremental if not Destroying to our Country. So affected the minds of many. (together with The Expectation of Seeing Great things, etc.)—As to Incline many, yea, Very Many to Venture themselves and Enlist into the Service Among whom, I was one, which was the, 14th of March 1745. I And having had the Consent of my friends, (and asking

---

Opposite: a group of furnishings of the Chippendale period; descriptions on p. 373

their Prayers), (Which was A great Comfort to me. Even all the Time of my being Asent.) I set out for Boston, Tuesday March 19th."

Although, like most of the other landlubbers, he was probably miserably seasick en route, he did see those "Great things"; the "Yokels" performed heroically and successfully. A motley fleet of about ninety transports carried the small all-American army to its destination, and after a forty-nine-day siege the "Canadian Gibraltar" surrendered. However, in the European peace settlement of 1748 Louisbourg was returned to the French, and the colonists were back on the defensive. Another war was brewing, again on both sides of the Atlantic. At the Albany Congress in 1754, Franklin called for a necessary union among the colonies. "Join, or Die," he advised his compatriots. On July 4 of that same year Lieutenant Colonel George Washington of the Virginia militia, who had been dispatched to halt the French advance into the Ohio Valley, was forced to surrender the meager defenses of Fort Necessity (in what is now western Pennsylvania) and return to his home base in bitter defeat. (A year still later Washington was the only unwounded officer of General Edward Braddock's staff in another retreat from that same area.) "Such was the complication of political interests," wrote Voltaire of that earlier brief but vital skirmish, "that a cannon shot in America could give the signal that set Europe in a blaze."

More than Europe was set ablaze. The war—known as the French and Indian War in America and as the Seven Years' War abroad—spread to India and the distant Philippines; it was, in short, a world war, and one with enormous consequences. The climactic episode in the conflict's American phase was General James Wolfe's great victory over the Marquis de Montcalm on the Plains of Abraham in 1759, with which Quebec, the keystone of French America, fell to the British. With this event England challenged Spain as the world's supreme

A detail from a manuscript map showing the plan of Louisbourg on Cape Breton Island in 1758, shortly before the French surrendered this "Canadian Gibraltar." The attacking British troops, just landed, are being fired upon by French soldiers from behind their protective earthworks.

colonial power, and the pattern of international relationships around the world was decisively changed. In his *History of the English People* John Richard Green wrote that it was no exaggeration "to say that three of its many victories [of the Seven Years' War] determined for ages to come the destinies of the world. With that of Rossbach began the re-creation of Germany.... With that of Plassey the influence of Europe told for the first time since the days of Alexander on the nations of the East.... With the triumph of Wolfe on the Heights of Abraham began the history of the United States of America." It was true that with the French conclusively defeated in America the colonies felt free of an awful menace for the first time in generations and found new confidence in their own future. Some, English statesmen among them, wondered whether with this new freedom the colonies might even feel free and confident enough to shake off their dependence on the mother country. One English clergyman, who was touring America at this time, remarked that most of the colonies had already fallen into such "errors of independency."

Yet, paradoxically, during the quarter of a century before the Revolution, America depended on England more heavily than ever before or since for cultural models and standards. The separate colonies in many ways remained closer to the mother country than to one another. In matters of dress, literature, art, architecture, and home furnishings London set a common standard that was accepted in all the colonies. Even the alien strains that had been added to the American melting pot were affected by the influence and authority of the parent culture. That staunch patriot John Adams was himself susceptible to what one of his contemporaries resentfully called the "evil Itch of overvaluing Foreign parts." While he was attending the First Continental Congress in Philadelphia, he paused in his efforts to plan his country's freedom from English constraints to write his wife, Abigail, that the Bostonian's manners were superior to the Philadelphian's because they were "purer English." During his prolonged stay in England Benjamin Franklin felt so strongly the allure of life on that "petty island," with its "sensible, virtuous and elegant Minds," that he seriously considered moving there for good—if he could "persuade the good Woman to cross the seas." However, he subsequently concluded that "*old Trees cannot safely be transplanted*," and his permanent home remained in Philadelphia. In time, as he became ever more deeply involved in the question of American rights, his admiration for England diminished, although to his dying day he continued a spirited correspondence with a number of those "elegant Minds" as well as others in France and elsewhere abroad.

A sizable number of wealthy colonists were returning "home" to Britain to improve their education, to read law at the Inns of Court, to study medicine at the universities, or to take orders in the Anglican Church. Some went there to conduct business, others to sample the gracious ways of life in England, still others to learn the art of painting from their eminent expatriate countryman, and the king's intimate friend, Benjamin West. The Revolution interrupted but did not halt that flow of touring Americans. When the war was over they again swarmed overseas. In the 1780's Abigail Adams wrote from London that she saw so many Americans about her, she could hardly believe she had left home.

One of the most persuasive forms of English influence, so far as furniture and furnishings were concerned, came to the colonies in the various pattern books designed to guide and instruct craftsmen and their patrons. In the same year, 1754, that Washington suffered his sharp defeat in the western wilderness Thomas Chippendale of London issued his first edition of *The Gentleman and Cabinet-Maker's Director*. This was the most complete and comprehensive furniture manual that had appeared to date, and it provided a stimulus to crafts-

Newly created baronet Sir William Pepperrell, "The Victor of Louisbourg," by John Smibert

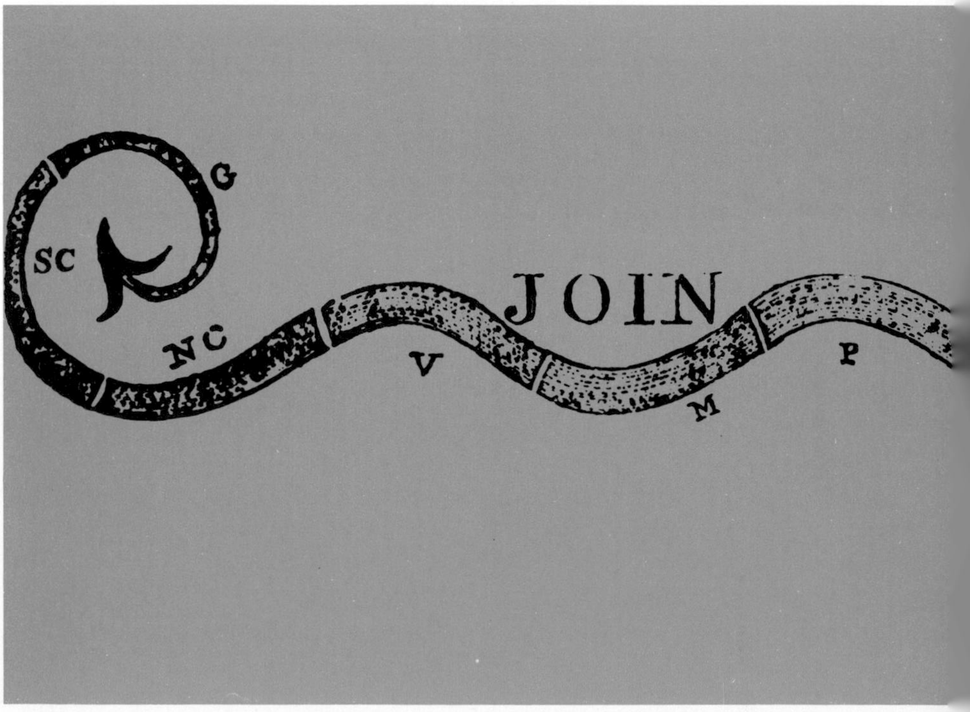

manship—in the American colonies and in other countries, as well as in England—that endured for a generation after its publication. It was, to be sure, only one of a number of such books that were published during that period, but the fame it acquired in later times has associated Chippendale's name with the trends of design and fashion that dominated the several decades before the Revolution.

"Chippendale style" is a very loose term, but a handy one. Actually, the style originated in England before Chippendale was heard from. It amounted to a gradual translation into English terms of the earlier French rococo style. "Rococo" is derived from *rocaille*, a word that refers to the rock and shell forms that were so popular in French ornament during the reign of Louis XV. The word "rococo" was applied to the style after its vogue had passed. At the time the English version was characterized rather as being in "the Gothic, Chinese and Modern [meaning French] Taste."

French influences are direct and obvious enough in the designs of Chippendale, his precursors, and his contemporaries. The other elements, however, are only remote and whimsical suggestions of anything authentically Chinese or Gothic. In any case, the total effect of the style was one of endlessly curving patterns, asymmetrical ornament, and—as decorative motifs—natural and organic forms. It was as though the simple, undulating forms of the Queen Anne style had suddenly been infused with an almost uncontrollable vigor and variety.

The year before Chippendale issued the first edition of the *Director*, William Hogarth issued *The Analysis of Beauty* in which he referred to the undulating line, the S-curve, as the "line of beauty." Such flowing lines he discerned at every hand among those things that pleased the eye, from the curved stays that gave proper shape to a woman's figure to the "winding walks and serpentine rivers" that graced the cultivated English countryside. Also, he remarked, "the lines that form a pleasing smile about the corners of the mouth have gentle

Left: the version of Franklin's historic slogan from Boston's The Massachusetts Spy, *July 7, 1774. The dragon represents Great Britain.*

Below: Colonel George Washington of the Virginia militia by Charles Willson Peale, 1772

windings" (but not excessive laughter which distorted such graceful patterns).

Variety and intricacy, elements that characterized the Chippendale style, Hogarth deemed essential aspects of beauty. "There is scarce a room," he wrote, "where one does not see the waving-line employ'd in some way or other. How inelegant would the shapes of all our moveables be without it? how very plain and unornamental the mouldings of cornices and chimney-pieces without the variety introduced by the *ogee* member, which is entirely composed of waving-lines." Rococo decoration had made such lines familiar aspects of design before he wrote, but his words no doubt helped strengthen their prestige and encouraged the acceptance of Chippendale's patterns.

Over these same years the colonies developed and improved their resources at a phenomenal rate. At mid-century Franklin observed that the population of

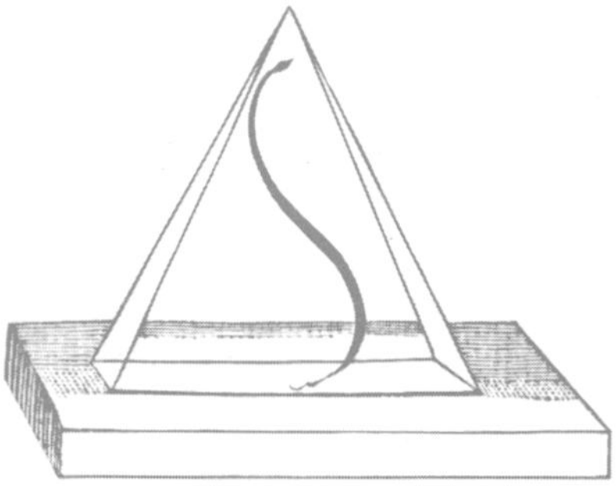

British America was doubling in size about every twenty years; and, he added, the demands of the colonists for material goods were growing even faster. At the time he made that observation almost a million and a half people occupied the eastern seaboard. Some of them were moving on to cheaper lands in the West, a trend that disturbed the government in London. Until some practical system of imperial organization could be devised for that unimaginably vast inland area, and some effective way of dealing with the Indians be found, it seemed wiser to keep the colonists east of the Appalachians. In the Proclamation of 1763, King George III did "strictly forbid, on pain of our displeasure, all our loving subjects from making any purchases or settlements [in that western region] . . ." and that proclamation was reaffirmed by the Quebec Act in 1774. But, as one proverb put it, "if hell lay to the West, Americans would cross heaven to reach it." Neither the Crown nor Parliament could stop them.

In the burgeoning seaports and the spreading plantations of the East sizable fortunes were being made. About the time Franklin remarked on the population growth the Swedish visitor to America, Peter Kalm, reported that "the English colonies in this part of the world have increased so much in their riches that they almost vie with Old England." This was an exaggeration, to be sure, but it pointed to the truth. When he died in 1764, Thomas Hancock, as already described, was one of the wealthiest citizens of New England. He could have vied with the affluent gentry of London had he retired to England, as he once intended to do, to enjoy his means. Upon his death in 1744, William Byrd II of Westover, Virginia, left his heirs 179,000 acres of the best land in that commonwealth. "In most articles of life," one observer concluded, "a great Virginia planter makes a greater show and lives more luxuriously than a country gentleman in England, on an estate of three or four thousand pounds a year." Hancock and Byrd, like other wealthy, prominent people throughout the colonies,

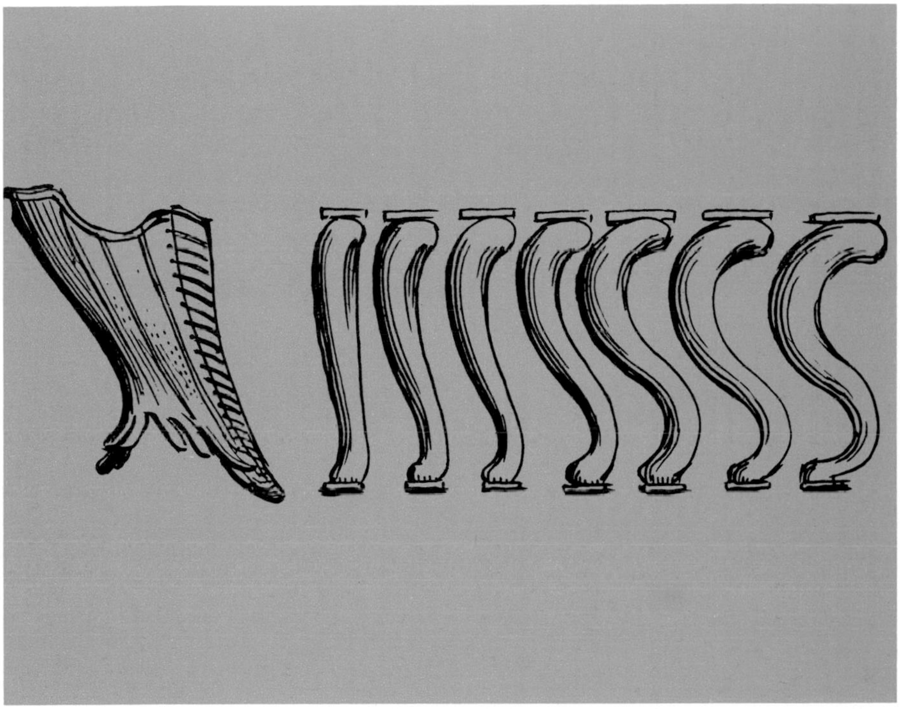

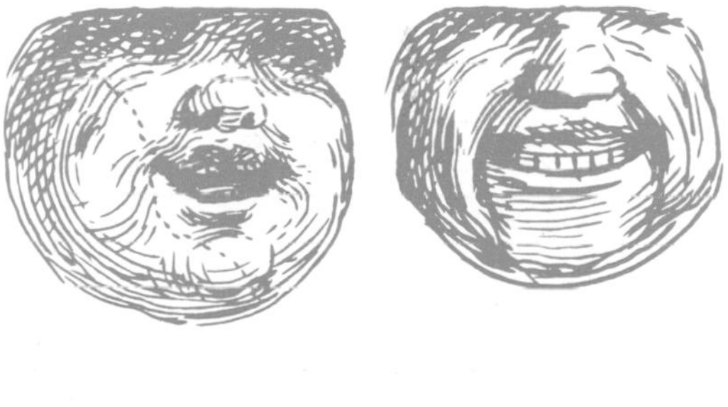

From left to right: the illustration from the title page of Hogarth's The Analysis of Beauty; *a 1742 Hogarth engraving that satirizes popular fashions; the "line of beauty" illustrated by a woman's stays, variations on the ideal line using chair legs, a pleasing smile and a distorting laugh, all from Hogarth's essay*

represented an elite, to be sure, but it was an elite whose ranks remained open to newcomers. The names of the "great" families were open to change and the list of those who had risen to riches and importance was always growing. In New England by the middle of the eighteenth century a few distinguished names familiar in the seventeenth century still appeared on the roster of those in high places, but most of the names of repute were new.

Nicholas Boylston was one of them. In his diary under the date of January 16, 1766, John Adams reported: "Dined at Mr. Nick Boylstone's, with the two Mr. Boylstones, two Mr. Smiths, Mr. Hallowel and the ladies. An elegant Dinner indeed! Went over the house to view the Furniture, which alone cost a thousand Pounds sterling. A Seat it is for a noble Man, a Prince. The Turkey Carpets, the painted Hangings, the Marble Tables, the rich Beds with crimson Damask Curtains and Counterpins, the beautiful Chimny Clock, the Spacious Garden, are the most magnificent of any Thing I have ever seen."

Another Bostonian, Josiah Quincy, Jr., visiting Charleston just before the

Detail of the woodwork from the Powel house

A rococo design from Chippendale's Director

Revolution, found a disturbing warmth and excitement in the social life of that southern city. In the "grandeur, splendour of buildings, decorations, equipages, numbers, commerce, shipping, and indeed in almost everything," he added, Charleston surpassed all he had seen or hoped to see in America. And for many others that gay and hospitable community seemed to be, according to the canons of the eighteenth century, the most cultivated and civilized center in the New World. The fact remains that each of the growing cities had its distinctive aspects, its own local and regional variant of the prevailing culture.

To accommodate the swelling population, new houses were rising everywhere, in country and city alike. Or, from time to time, changes and additions were made to old structures until, as in the case of Mount Vernon, large and impressive mansions were developed from very modest beginnings. As in the past, housewrights equipped with building manuals were at hand to guide and help the home builder. But now, discerning and well-to-do patrons could also call upon the services of professional architects. In 1755 George Mason, who subsequently composed the Virginia Bill of Rights, had brought to America under contract one William Buckland, "citizen and joiner of London," to assist in the construction of his handsome new home, Gunston Hall. After his service with Mason was concluded, Buckland, equipped with a substantial library of English architectural books for guidance, set himself up as an independent architect. As such he created the Hammond-Harwood house in Annapolis, among other distinguished structures in the same area. Other competent architects, for the most part immigrants who, like Buckland, had been trained in England, contributed their professional talents to the building boom that persisted throughout the colonies during the pre-Revolutionary years.

The demand for artisans to furnish the new and the enlarged homes, as well as to build them, tempted an increasing number of craftsmen in every medium to come from the Old World to the New to practice their specialties—men and women who promptly advertised in a growing assortment of newspapers that they were prepared to supply the most discriminating customers with all manner of goods in the latest London fashion. Not to be outdone, native artisans advertised that their wares were also comparable in quality and style with London-made products, and there was truth in their claims. In 1765 Samuel Powel, a wealthy Philadelphian then in London who was later a friend of and host to George Washington, was advised by his uncle, Samuel Morris, not to import furnishings from England for the elegant mansion he planned to have built. "Household goods may be had here as cheap & as well made [in Philadelphia] from English patterns," wrote Morris. "In the humour people are in here, a man is in danger of becoming Invidiously distinguished who buys anything in England which our Tradesmen can furnish. I have heard the joiners here object this against [those]...who brought their furniture with them."

People were in the humor Morris described because three months earlier Parliament had passed the Stamp Act, quite casually and with no suspicion that this hated legislation would quickly bring the American colonists almost to the point of open revolt. Before the act was repealed a year later, nonimportation associations had sprung up in virtually every section of the land. At least one New York silversmith was forced out of business for his "daring Infractions of the Non-importation Agreement."

Yet, in spite of this and in spite of the "long train of abuses" cited in the Declaration of Independence, and which led to the Revolution, America continued to find in England its cultural models and standards. Even while Washington was leading the cause for political independence on the battlefield, his workmen at home were using English architectural manuals for reference in the renovation of Mount Vernon. And, as Samuel Morris indicated in his advice to Powel, the furniture makers relied as heavily on various pattern books compiled by English designers, Chippendale's *Director* among a number of others, to produce their most stylish pieces. The sofa, tables, chairs, and other forms illustrated as samples on the trade card of Benjamin Randolph (see pages 200–201) are all derived from models pictured in three different English books that had been brought to Philadelphia shortly after publication.

At this point Philadelphia had become the most progressive city in America —and the largest; its population had tripled during the twenty-five years preceding the Declaration of Independence—and Morris' high opinion of its craftsmen was completely justified. Philadelphia "Chippendale" furniture represented the most ambitious achievement of colonial craftsmanship. There, at least, the prevailing style was executed with the greatest exuberance and vigor. The carved woodwork and the stucco ceiling decorations of the Powel house, largely copied or adapted from Abraham Swan's *Designs in Architecture* (first published in London in 1757), show the verve with which local craftsmen worked in the "modern taste."

It was in this "splendid seat" that John Adams dined with distinguished company one evening on his first visit to Philadelphia. "A most sinfull Feast again!" he reported in his diary, "Every Thing which could delight the Eye, or allure the Taste, Curds and Creams, Jellies, and Sweet meats of various sorts, 20 sorts of Tarts, fools, Trifles, floating Islands, whippd Sillabubs &c.&c.—Parmesan Cheese, Punch, Wine, Porter, Beer, &c." Upon his arrival Adams had looked with a cold Boston eye on the prodigality of Philadelphia life. (It was his first trip away from his native New England.) For all its "Trade, and Wealth, and Regularity," he concluded, Philadelphia was *not* Boston. "The Morals of our People are much better," he confided to his diary; "Our Language is better, our Spirit is greater, our Laws are wiser, our Religion is superiour, our Education is better." Adams brought with him from staid Boston a

Left: Copley's portrait of Nicholas Boylston in a morning robe and cap, painted in 1767

Right: William Buckland, as painted by Peale, drafts the plan of the Hammond-Harwood house.

Front door of the Hammond-Harwood house, designed by William Buckland, built in 1774

measure of local pride that "tinctured his judgment and clinched his prepossession." However, by the time he left for home "in a very great Rain" at the conclusion of the First Continental Congress, his attitudes had softened and he bade a regretful adieu to "the happy, the peacefull, the elegant, the hospitable, and polite City of Phyladelphia."

The Philadelphia-made furniture Adams saw on that visit may have been strongly influenced by English design books, but it was unmistakably a local product. Cabinetmakers, chairmakers, and other woodworking artisans, here as elsewhere in the colonies, rarely copied any single design. Rather, by a selective rearrangement of different elements and often with an independent, personal contribution, they created distinctive native and regional styles. It was in this period, for example, that the highboy, frequently with its matching lowboy, was elaborated into a form of great distinction. The block-front, shell-carved furniture that was developed to such a degree of perfection in Rhode Island seems to owe little or nothing to any of the published design books. Just how this very sophisticated style originated remains something of a mystery. But in passing it might be recalled that in 1770 Newport's foreign trade was greater than New York's, and that thriving little city supported more than fifty cabinetmakers and wood carvers. And it was also during these years that the Windsor chair evolved as one of the most flexible, graceful, and characteristic of all American furniture forms, decidedly different from and more handsome than any English prototypes and analogues.

The growing custom of labeling furniture with the makers' names, and with more abundant documentary evidence of other sorts, has made it possible to identify the work of individual craftsmen of this period more often than in the case of earlier years. A list of the accomplished furniture makers who are known to have practiced this craft during the decades before the Revolution would indeed be too long to include in a book such as this, although specific examples of the work of a number of them are illustrated and described in the pages that follow. Pewterers and glassmakers assumed important roles in the colonies during these years, and their work can also often be identified.

Since silversmiths traditionally punched their wares with a mark bearing their initials or, in later years, their full surnames, a large proportion of the colonial silverwork that has survived can be ascribed to individual makers. In pre-Revolutionary years almost every community of any consequence supported at least one silversmith, and most of the large cities found work for dozens of them. And, as ever, these craftsmen ranked among the important citizens. It was on December 17, 1773, that Boston's Committee of Correspondence chose Paul Revere to ride posthaste to New York and Philadelphia with the committee's report of the Tea Party, which had taken place the day before in the local harbor. On December 27 one John Boyle wrote in his diary: "Mr. Paul Revere returned from New York and Philadelphia, performing his journey in a much shorter time then could be expected at this Season of the year. The inhabitants of these Cities were highly pleased with the Conduct of the People here in destroying the Tea and they were determined that when the Tea Ships expected there arrive, they should be immediately returned to the Place from whence they came." And so it happened when tea arrived at those posts.

In the following years Revere along with many other craftsmen were called from their work to perform various duties in the Revolutionary cause. Revere's activity in this direction has been widely told, but there were others who were no less involved in public service. Marinus Willett, cabinetmaker of New York and great-grandson of that city's first English mayor, was a leading spirit in the local branch of the Sons of Liberty. On June 6, 1775, he was one of a group that seized arms from the British forces which were evacuating New York. Two years later, when he was serving as lieutenant colonel in the army, Congress awarded him an "elegant sword" for his bravery at the siege of Fort Stanwix in New York. Another craftsman, Charles Willson Peale, probably the most versatile of all colonial craftsmen, saw action as a lieutenant at the battles of Trenton and Princeton and, among other public services, acted as chairman of the Constitutional Society. While in the field he exercised one of his numerous talents by painting miniature portraits of his fellow officers. Benjamin Frothingham, whose label (engraved by Nathaniel Hurd) is illustrated below and who is known to have been a superb cabinetmaker, was a major of artillery in the colonial army and a personal friend of George Washington. His house and shop were destroyed when the British burned Charlestown in 1775, but he rebuilt them after the war and resumed his trade. In 1789 Washington honored Major Frothingham, as he was called following the Revolution, by calling upon him at his rebuilt home. It was apparently the only private visit the Father of his Country made in that town, which must have added to the major's local distinction.

Some of these craftsmen-warriors did not return to their trades after hostilities had ceased, like Willett who went on to become mayor of his native city. In any event, the war interrupted the earlier constant flow of communications with England. In England new styles were being introduced with the publications and other activities of the brothers Adam, neoclassic styles that eclipsed the popularity of Chippendale's designs. Chippendale himself was associated with the Adams and in his later years worked in the manner they had made popular. But largely because of the war, such fresh currents were slow in reaching America and the familiar colonial styles prevailed for years after the peace was signed in 1783 and America became a nation.

Above: a portrait of Colonel Marinus Willett with an "elegant sword," done by Ralph Earl

Left: B. Frothingham's label. It is initialed in the lower right corner by Nathaniel Hurd, well-known Boston silversmith and engraver.

252. *Above: design for the "Ribband Back Chair" from the third edition of the* Director

253, 254. *Below: designs for two "Couches" from the same edition of Chippendale. All three illustrate the "modern [French] taste."*

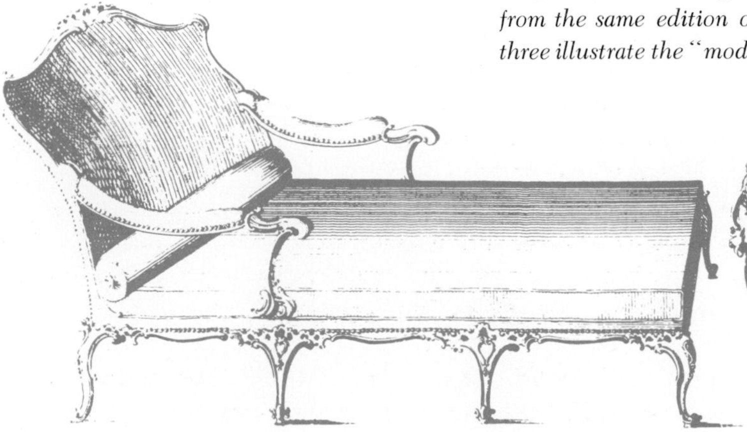

Designs for Living

Two factors of major importance influenced the development of colonial furniture styles from about the middle of the eighteenth century until the end of the Revolution. The first was the general use of mahogany for the finest pieces; the second was the publication of a variety of pattern books addressed specifically to the cabinetmaker and chairmaker and designed with the working properties of mahogany clearly in mind.

Mahogany was a New World product but its widespread popularity in London, where styles were set, by and large determined the development of new forms and ornamental details made with that wood. The wood was known in England since the sixteenth century, but it was the abolishment of import duties on timber, in 1721, that encouraged its use in cabinetwork. The value of mahogany shipped to England in 1720 had been a mere £43. In 1735 the figure had risen to £6430, and in 1750 it was almost £30,000. By then mahogany had supplanted walnut as the fashionable wood for many types of furniture.

There were good reasons for its popularity. Far more than walnut, it was worm resistant. It was almost as strong as metal and it could be carved in the most intricate patterns, features which significantly affected the design and construction of chairs particularly. The great width of the boards obtainable from mahogany made it an ideal wood for the tops of tables and the doors of cabinets, secretaries, and similar case pieces. Also, it came in a range of beautiful colors and developed attractive patinas that improved with use and rubbing. Writing of his experiences in the New World, the English naturalist Mark Catesby reported in 1743 that the "Excellency of this wood for all Domestick Uses is now sufficiently known in England." And, he might have added, it was as well known in the colonies.

Up until the middle of the eighteenth century the English pattern books, issued mainly in the interest of architects, builders, and their patrons, included few designs for furniture. Although it was not the earliest, Chippendale's *The Gentleman and Cabinet-Maker's Director* was the first important manual devoted entirely to furniture and ornament and illustrating almost every type then in use. The change of emphasis is obvious and dramatic (252, 253, 254). Instead of an insistent reference to the five orders of classic architecture (although he conceded their basic importance), his engraved designs offered an extravagance of curved and interlaced elements, cockleshells, and bits of pierced and scrolling foliage in the rococo manner of the Louis XV style and other motifs that he claimed were inspired by Chinese or Gothic art. This sort of free and curious invention aroused the scorn of the king's surveyor, Isaac Ware, who considered it a misfortune of the times "to see an unmeaning scrawl of C's inverted and looped together, taking the place of Greek and Roman elegance even in our most expensive decorations. It is called French," he complained, "and let them have the praise of it! The Gothic shaft and Chinese bell are not beyond nor below it in poorness of imitation."

Chippendale himself was aware that at least some of his suggested designs seemed extravagant to the point of impracticality. In the concluding paragraph of the preface to his first edition he advised his readers: "Upon the whole, I have here given no design but what may be executed with advantage by the hands of a skillful workman, tho' some of the profession have been diligent enough to represent them (especially those after the Gothic and Chinese manner) as so many specious drawings, impossible to be work'd off by any mechanic whatsoever. I will not scruple to attribute this to malice, ignorance and inability: And I am confident I can convince all Noblemen, Gentlemen, or others, who will honour me with their commands, that every design in the book can be improved, both as to beauty and enrichment, in the execution of it, by Their Most Obedient Servant. Thomas Chippendale."

He convinced enough noblemen, gentlemen, and others to enjoy a thriving trade. It seems that he did little woodworking himself, once he was established, but ran a well-organized shop of craftsmen who turned out the furniture and accessories necessary to fill the commissions from his wealthy customers. The furniture Chippendale supplied for Nostell Priory, Harewood House, and other houses in England is still in its original position. It is likely that Chippendale's firm supplied furniture "in the Chinese taste" for the house of Theresa Cornelys, a well-known singer whose entertainments were notorious until she went bankrupt in 1772. Fanny Burney visited the house on one occasion and reported that "the magnificence of the rooms, splendour of the illuminations and embellishments" exceeded anything she had ever seen before. In later years his shop produced work for clients of Robert Adam, work in the neoclassic style that bore little or no relation to the illustrations in the three editions of his publication, the *Director*.

255. *Top: a chair design from Manwaring's* The Cabinet and Chair-Maker's Real Friend...

256. *Above: mahogany chair, made in Massachusetts about 1770, adapted from Manwaring's design*

257. *Right: a carved cabriole leg, with claw-and-ball foot, from a Philadelphia mahogany highboy*

258. Left: Philadelphia dressing chest. 259. Right: design from the 1762 edition of Chippendale's Director

260

261

Chippendale never won royal patronage, as did some of his competitors in the furniture trade, and before the end of the century the designs of the *Director* were "wholly antiquated and laid aside," although it was conceded that they had great merit "according to the times in which they were executed." Nevertheless, his publication was an immediate success and it was quickly put to service by colonial craftsmen. Occasionally, an engraved design was almost literally translated into wood, as in the case of the dressing chest, or commode (258, 259). The carved pine wall bracket (261), illustrated on this page, closely follows a design (260) of Thomas Johnson, a contemporary of Chippendale.

Ironically, the cabriole leg with claw-and-ball foot (257), considered almost a hallmark of colonial furniture in the Chippendale style, is virtually ignored in the *Director*. By the time furniture pattern books appeared this feature had passed out of style in England. In 1765 Robert Manwaring, a London designer and craftsman who did not underevaluate his own accomplishments, published *The Cabinet and Chair-Maker's Real Friend & Companion*, a book that was advertised for sale in *The Massachusetts Gazette, and Boston News-Letter* of January 1, 1767. Manwaring paid Chippendale tribute by borrowing from the latter's engravings. In any event, his intention was to convey to the workman "full and plain Instructions, how he is to begin and finish with Strength and Beauty, all the Designs that are advanced in this Work." From plate nine of this publication a Massachusetts craftsman borrowed the design of a chair back (256), but subtly altered its proportions, and substituted the cabriole leg with claw-and-ball foot, so popular in America, for the straight, square-section examples shown in Manwaring's pattern (255).

Chippendale did not introduce the rococo style into England, but the three editions of his *Director* did much to widen the acceptance of that "modern taste" both for furniture and for decoration in general. Guided by one or another of various published pattern books, colonial engravers made free use of rococo motifs on silverware and in the design of trade cards, broadsides, and similar announcements, as in the heading (264) of a summons to a meeting of the "Hand-in-Hand Fire Company" held in New York in 1762.

Several books issued in London by Abraham Swan and incorporating elements of rococo ornament had a marked influence on colonial interior architecture. The chimney piece of the "mahogany room" in the Jeremiah Lee house (262) in Marblehead, Massachusetts, follows a plate in Swan's *The British Architect* (263) almost line for line. This book, first published in London in 1745, was reprinted in Boston and Philadelphia in 1775. Other plates engraved for Swan's handbooks were followed in the decoration of the Samuel Powel house in Philadelphia, Kenmore near Fredericksburg, Virginia, the Brice house in Annapolis, Maryland, and numerous other colonial mansions, including Mount Vernon on the Potomac.

An overmantel at Mount Vernon displays a carved relief illustrating Aesop's fable of the fox, the crow, and the cheese—allegedly at Washington's suggestion, to serve as a moral to his nieces and nephews. Various English and French editions of *Aesop's Fables*, some illustrated with wood (266) or copper engravings, were available in the colonies; at least nine American editions were printed in Philadelphia alone during the second half of the eighteenth century. Some engravings of the fables appeared in the second (1755) and third (1762) editions of the *Director*. And these classical stories, enframed in rococo scrolls, were occasionally carved on the finest furniture made in Philadelphia in the Chippendale period. The lower center drawer of the highboy illustrated opposite (265, 265a) depicts the familiar fable of the fox and the grapes, undoubtedly following a contemporary engraving.

262. Upper left: chimney piece in Jeremiah Lee house, Marblehead, Mass.

263. Left: chimney piece design from Swan's The British Architect *(1745)*

264. Above, right: decoration from an announcement engraved in New York

265. *Above: a mahogany highboy made in Philadelphia*

265a. *Below, left: detail depicting one of Aesop's fables*

266. *Below, right: 18th-century woodcut of the same fable*

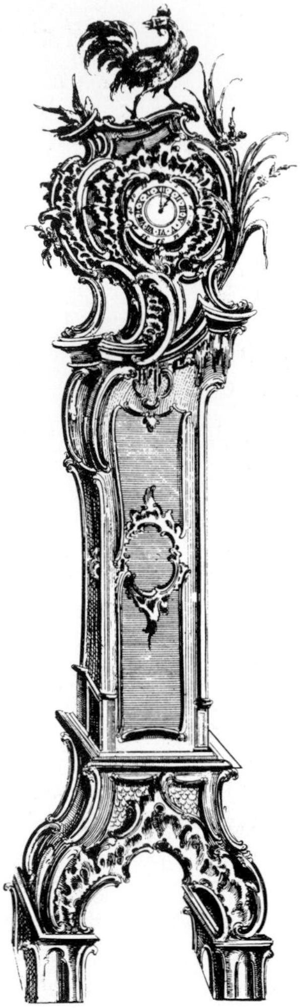

Nothing better illustrates how conversant the colonial craftsman was with English designs of the Chippendale period than the trade card of Benjamin Randolph, who purchased a shop on Chestnut Street in Philadelphia in 1767 and who was favored by commissions from the leading families of that city. The card itself, with its elaborate rococo frame, was undoubtedly copied from some English model. Specifically, virtually every piece illustrated on the card was copied more or less directly from one of several different English pattern books. The design of the bust in the upper left corner and of the secretary in the lower center were both apparently based on a plate in Chippendale's *Director.* In the upper right corner, the tall clock was taken from *Designs for Furniture* by Thomas Johnson, first published in 1758. Next to it, the sofa was an adaptation of two similar forms shown in *Household Furniture in the Present Taste...by a Society of Upholsterers*, a publication that was advertised for sale in New York in 1760, the same year it was issued in London. Both the toilet table in the lower right and the square table above it at the right, the fire screens, the stools, and the tilt-top table are also adaptations from plates that first appeared in this same publication. By his skills Randolph won the patronage of Thomas Jefferson, among others.

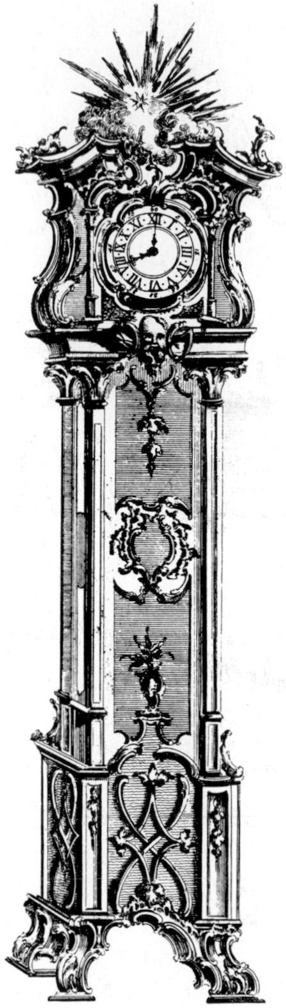

Illustrations from the various contemporary English pattern books used by Benjamin Randolph for his trade card

Opposite: Randolph's trade card. Among other pieces, he made the desk on which Thomas Jefferson drafted the Declaration of Independence.

B·R's Ware Room
Benj.n Randolph
Cabinet Maker
at the Golden Eagle in Chesnut Street
Between third and fourth Streets.
PHILADELPHIA,
Makes all Sorts of
Cabinet & Chair work
Likewise Carving, Gilding, &c
and Modern
Perform'd in the Chinese
Tastes

Philadelphia Rococo

In 1771 two young Philadelphia poets attending Princeton hailed their home city as the "mistress of our world, the seat of the arts, of science, and of fame." That same year John Singleton Copley, in search of commissions, wrote that Philadelphia was "a place of too much importance not to visit." The artists and craftsmen of that city were in fact blessed with lavish patronage. Furniture makers there developed the most elaborate colonial variations of the Chippendale style. Philadelphia highboys were especially ornate with their handsomely carved pediments (267) and drawer fronts. Except in their decorative details such forms bore no relation to the designs illustrated by Chippendale. Tilt-top tables standing on tripod bases with claw-and-ball feet (269) were also richly carved. The edges of the round tops of the most highly developed examples were molded and carved in a so-called piecrust pattern. Drop-leaf tables (268) were used for dining. At times several identical tables were extended and placed end to end to accommodate large numbers of diners. Chairs were more commonly based on designs in the *Director*. Upholstered chairs with open arms like the example here (270) were called "French chairs" by Chippendale in his publication.

270. *Below: an upholstered armchair that follows Chippendale's design for a "French chair"*

267. *Opposite: carved detail of a mahogany highboy made for the Hollingsworth family, possibly by Thomas Affleck*

268. *Top: drop-leaf dining table; swinging legs support the leaves when raised*

269. *Above: tea table with tripod base and tilting, scallop-edged top. There was "a tea table upturned in the corner of the parlor" in Franklin's Philadelphia home.*

The transition from the Queen Anne to the Chippendale style was gradual, as such developments usually are. Rococo elements associated with the Chippendale style were apparent in colonial craftsmanship (and in English work, to be sure) before the publication of the first edition of the *Director*. Familiar features of the Queen Anne style continued to appear in colonial design until well into the second half of the eighteenth century. The chair illustrated (272) is an attractive medley of motifs; its horseshoe-shaped seat and arched back rails are in the earlier manner, its pierced splat and claw-and-ball feet in the later style.

But in time the lively play of scrolls so characteristic of Chippendale ornament—intricate designs which, William Hogarth remarked, led the eye "a wanton kind of chase"—replaced the quiet curves of the Queen Anne style. Nowhere in the colonies was this exuberance of design more successfully mastered than in Philadelphia, as in the carved and gilded frame of this looking glass (271). In 1763 John Elliott, "Cabinet-maker in Chestnut-street, the corner of Fourth-street" in Philadelphia, advertised that among the other services he offered, "He also quicksilvers and frames old glasses, and supplies people with new glasses to their own frames; and will undertake to cure any English looking glass that shews the face either too long or too broad or any other way distorted." With an eye to a potential market for his wares in the local German population, Elliott often printed his labels both in German and English.

In October, 1768, Plunket Fleeson, a Philadelphia upholsterer and merchant who had immigrated from London some thirty years before, advertised for sale "American Paper Hangings, Manufactured in Philadelphia, of all kinds and colors, not inferior to those generally imported; and as low in price." The imports he referred to were usually either English papers or, on occasion, rolls that were shipped via England from China. Imported papers were advertised in colonial papers at least as early as the 1730's. Although he never actually hung it, Robert Morris, a financier of the American Revolution, ordered a set of Chinese wallpaper for his home in Philadelphia. By about this time, however, one colonial manufacturer boasted of a "most beautiful assortment of 1500 Pieces Paper, in 600 different patterns, from one to twenty six colours."

271. Opposite: a carved and gilded Philadelphia rococo looking glass; the 18th-century wallpaper was a Chinese import

272. Right: a walnut armchair, made in the 1750's, combining elements of both the Queen Anne and Chippendale styles

273. Above: Peale's portrait of the Cadwalader family; the father offers his nine-month-old daughter a peach from his orchard

274. Right: carved card table, with hairy-paw feet, shown in the painting by Peale

275. A lowboy, or dressing table, a companion to the highboy shown opposite

Plunket Fleeson supplied much of the upholstery material for the Philadelphia house of John Cadwalader, "a Gentleman of large Fortune," in the words of John Adams, "[with] a grand and elegant House And Furniture." (Washington described Cadwalader as "a military genius, of a decisive and independent spirit, properly impressed with the necessity of order and discipline and of sufficient vigor to enforce it.") The very "elegant" card table (274) from that house, with its hairy-paw feet and elaborately carved apron and legs, is pictured in Charles Willson Peale's portrait of Mr. and Mrs. Cadwalader and their infant daughter, Anne. The artist reported to a friend that this painting was "greatly admired," presumably by the Cadwaladers and their friends. It has been assumed that the table was made by Benjamin Randolph, whose trade card is illustrated on page 201 and who did work for the Cadwaladers.

"After all," Nathaniel Hawthorne wrote more than a century ago, "the moderns have invented nothing better in chamber furniture than those chests which stand on four slender legs, and send an absolute tower of mahogany to the ceiling, the whole terminating in a fantastically carved ornament." He was referring to those carved colonial highboys (then known as high chests of drawers) that sometimes soared to more than eight feet. The form was long outmoded in England when, during the decade or so preceding the Revolution, it was carried to its extreme development in America, most spectacularly in Philadelphia. The lower center drawers of the so-called "Pompadour" highboy (276) and its matching lowboy (275) are carved with scenes illustrating Aesop's fables. One of the engravings for a mantel block in the 1762 edition of Chippendale's *Director* has as its subject the fable of the two pigeons from Aesop, and this may have been the inspiration for these carved decorations. On the drawer front of another lowboy (277) appears the figure of a swan, probably representing another of the fables of Aesop.

276. Above: a highboy with a carved bust, resembling Mme Pompadour, on the pediment. 277. Below: detail of a Philadelphia lowboy

278. A mahogany sofa with reverse-curved back, rolled arms, and bold cabriole legs

279. An extravagantly carved easy chair made by Benjamin Randolph of Philadelphia, about 1770

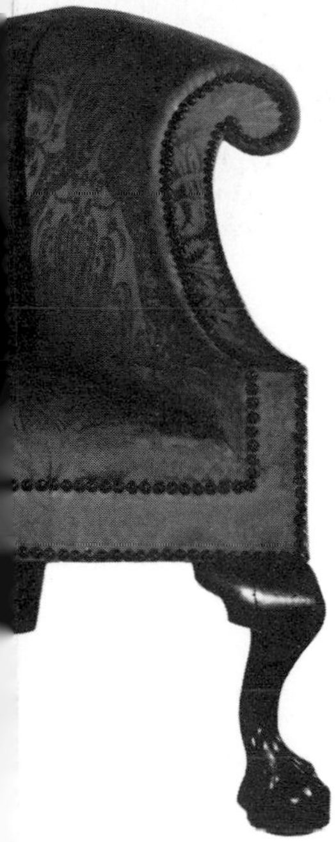

The exceptional length of the sofa at left (278) provided an ample opportunity for the designer to develop a series of sweeping curves across the back. Another Chippendale "Sopha of Green flowered Damask with two Cushions," made about the same time as this one, but not so long, "sloped across the Green drawing Room" of President Washington's temporary home on High (now Market) Street when Philadelphia was the national capital.

Without documentary evidence it is usually not possible to attribute a piece of furniture to a specific maker. However, students of the subject have associated the three other forms on these pages with three outstanding Philadelphia craftsmen: the very highly developed easy chair (279) with Benjamin Randolph; the card table (281) with Thomas Affleck; and the chest of drawers (280) with Jonathan Gostelowe. Randolph and Gostelowe saw active service in the Revolutionary cause. Affleck, a native of Aberdeen, Scotland, who owned a copy of "Shippendale's Designs," was a loyalist. However, he received many important commissions, including some furnishings for the Pennsylvania State House (now Independence Hall).

280. Chest of drawers attributed to Jonathan Gostelowe; on it, a gilded "swinging glass"

281. A serpentine-front card table of a kind known to have been made by Thomas Affleck

The strength of mahogany led furniture carvers to attempt daring pierced designs on chair backs. In Philadelphia scores of intricate variations on the prevailing theme were worked in the richly colored wood until it seems that every invention and combination of motifs were exhausted (282, 286). There were craftsmen who specialized in carving and with their special skills ornamented the chairs, case pieces, and other forms made by their colleagues.

Except for the elaborate carving that featured the finest examples (284), clockcases changed very little in character during the Chippendale period. The workman who constructed the cases for clocks, incidentally, was never the same as the mechanic who made the works and inscribed the face with his name.

The first edition of the *Director* included numerous designs illustrating furniture with straight, square-sectioned legs, apparently known as Marlborough legs, instead of the cabriole support that had been so widely popular since the days of Queen Anne. Some of the finest examples of Philadelphia furniture, such as the unusual writing table shown here (283), followed this more advanced style. Philadelphia inventories of the time repeatedly mention mahogany "Scrutores with Glass doors," referring to tall secretaries. Shortly after the Revolution Governor John Penn had "a very elegant" one in his home on Third Street; the description nicely fits the example here illustrated (285).

282. Above: side chair with carved shells, ornamental pierced splat, and claw-and-ball feet

283. Below: a mahogany writing table with a gadrooned skirt and paneled Marlborough legs

284. Right: a detail of a mahogany tall clock

285. Above: secretary with glass doors, bracket feet, and richly carved pediment

286. Below: detail of the back of a chair

With the close of the Anglo-French conflicts in North America New York emerged from the war "almost vulgarly rich" with fortunes made on government contracts, shipping, and privateering. After 1760 hundreds of thousands of pounds of New York money were spent in the construction and furnishing of mansions and country estates, and on "French and Spanish wines, portrait-painting, carriages from London." In the years between 1765 and 1768 Stephen Van Rensselaer II, the seventh patroon of the manor of Rensselaerswyck, built one of the most impressive Georgian houses in the colonies. The great central hall (289) was decorated with wallpaper specifically made to measure in London and ordered through Van Rensselaer's father-in-law, Philip Livingston, who wrote: "I think it very Handsome indeed... I am told You Intend to gett Stucco work on the Ceiling of Your Hall which I would not advise You to do, a Plain Ceiling is now Esteemed the most Genteel." The wallpaper, hand painted in tempera, remains one of the rare surviving examples of this type of eighteenth-century paper "hangings," and handsomely represents the rococo elements of the Chippendale style. Four large panels of romantic seascapes and landscapes, all derived from contemporary European paintings, alternate with smaller cartouches of the four seasons (autumn is shown here on the left, winter on the right).

289

287. Left: a New York armchair. 288. Right: a New York side chair. Both pieces were originally owned by the Van Rensselaer family.

Hudson Valley Chippendale

290. A Chippendale chair is shown in John Mare's Portrait of a Man.

291. Left: a New York side chair with acanthus leaves carved on the cabriole legs

292. Above: a drop-leaf dining table retaining the oval form of the early 1700's

"Samuel Prince...has on hand, for sale, A parcel of the most elegant furniture, made of mahogany, of the very best quality, such as chest of drawers, chest upon chest, cloath presses, desks, desks and book cases of different sorts, chairs of many different and new patterns." Prince's advertisement in 1775 was typical of those placed in New York newspapers by local cabinetmakers, such as his former apprentice, Thomas Burling, and by Gilbert Ash earlier in the century. At the sign of the "Royal Bed and Star in Wall-street," Joseph Cox advertised his wares in the "cabinet and upholstery branches: All finished in the newest Taste." Cox's label appears on the settee in the hall from the Van Rensselaer Manor House (289). From the workshops of these craftsmen and their contemporaries came the "rich" furniture that so impressed John Adams during his visit in 1774 to the "Opulence and Splendor" of New York, although he testily countered his comments by declaring that he had not seen "one real Gentleman" since his arrival.

The New York interpretation of Chippendale designs created distinctive regional characteristics. Gadrooning was often used on the skirts of chairs. Claw-and-ball feet were carved in square, box-like shapes. Carved tassels and ruffles were popular on the back splats of chairs (287, 288). As in the Queen Anne period New York furniture had heavier, more solid proportions than that made elsewhere in the colonies. These generous, comfortable forms were from New York's Dutch heritage, which was still vital in the city's life. (Dutch was still spoken from the pulpit of the Reformed Protestant Dutch Church, for instance, until 1824.) The walnut side chair (291) and the mahogany armchair (293) are fine illustrations of the New York style: gadrooning on the skirts, square-cut claw-and-ball feet, and an over-all appearance of solidity. The pattern of the splat of the side chair, a particular favorite in New York, was based on plate twelve of the third edition of Chippendale's *Director*. In the same edition plate nine appears to have suggested the pattern of the chair in *Portrait of a Man* (290) by John Mare, who painted in New York, Albany, and Boston between 1760 and 1774. The eight-legged, oval-topped mahogany table (292) again demonstrates the square-cut claw-and ball foot, as does the mahogany easy chair (294), upholstered in yellow damask.

293. Above: this New York armchair has leafage carved across the top of the crest.

294. Right: a New York easy chair with deep "wings" and rolled cone-shaped arms

295. *Above: a fall-front mahogany desk in the New York Chippendale style*

296. *Below: a five-legged gaming table made of mahogany veneer on beech*

In case pieces—desks, secretaries, highboys, lowboys, and chests of drawers—New York cabinetmakers rarely used the *bombé*, block-front, or serpentine lines favored by New England craftsmen. The straight lines of this desk (295) typify the New York Chippendale style. Two gaming tables (296, 298) of New York workmanship are again identifiable by the boldness of the curves and over-all sturdiness of their proportions. The table (298) with the square depressions for candlesticks and the oval "fishponds" for counters is one of two matching tables presented by General Washington to Judge John Berrien, whose New Jersey home was one of Washington's headquarters in 1783.

Bracket, or table, clocks became extremely popular in England following the invention of the short pendulum in 1658, but they were rarely made in America. The brass dial of this unusual colonial example (297) is signed by Charles Geddes, New York, who advertised himself as a "clock and watchmaker and finisher from London." Bracket clocks, fitted with handles at the top and mounted on small feet, supposedly received their name because matching brackets to hold them were often designed. Wall brackets were an important eighteenth-century ornamental device for the display of porcelains, candelabra, and the like; the 1754 *Director* gave patterns for "Brackets for Bustoes."

297. Above: a walnut-veneered clock on a contemporary bracket

298. Below: a gaming table of mahogany veneer on an oak frame

The straight lines and square shapes of New York's case pieces often had fluted, chamfered corners as illustrated by the chest-on-chest (303), similar to one on New York cabinetmaker Samuel Prince's label, and by the highboy (300) made of bilsted, or sweet gum, a wood used extensively in colonial New York. During the Chippendale period very few highboys were made in this region; New Yorkers seem to have preferred the chest-on-chest.

A popular English design, found particularly in New York, was the spider-leg table (301), a delicate modification of the gate-leg table adapted for use in the drawing room. A spider-leg table appears in Copley's portrait of Mr. and Mrs. Isaac Winslow (302), painted around 1774.

The straight leg, which returned to fashion in England about 1750, is shown here in the New York mahogany side chair (299), with upholstery of eighteenth-century Italian silk damask. William Ince and John Mayhew's *Universal System of Household Furniture* and Chippendale's *Director* gave various names to this type of upholstered chair, such as "French" or "back stool," the latter a term dating from Tudor inventories. A colonial advertisement in 1772 listed "six elegant French Back-Stools covered with very rich brocade."

299. Left: New York Chippendale side chair upholstered in Italian damask

300. Above: simplicity of design denotes a New York Chippendale highboy.

301. *Mahogany spider-leg table, a favored New York design*

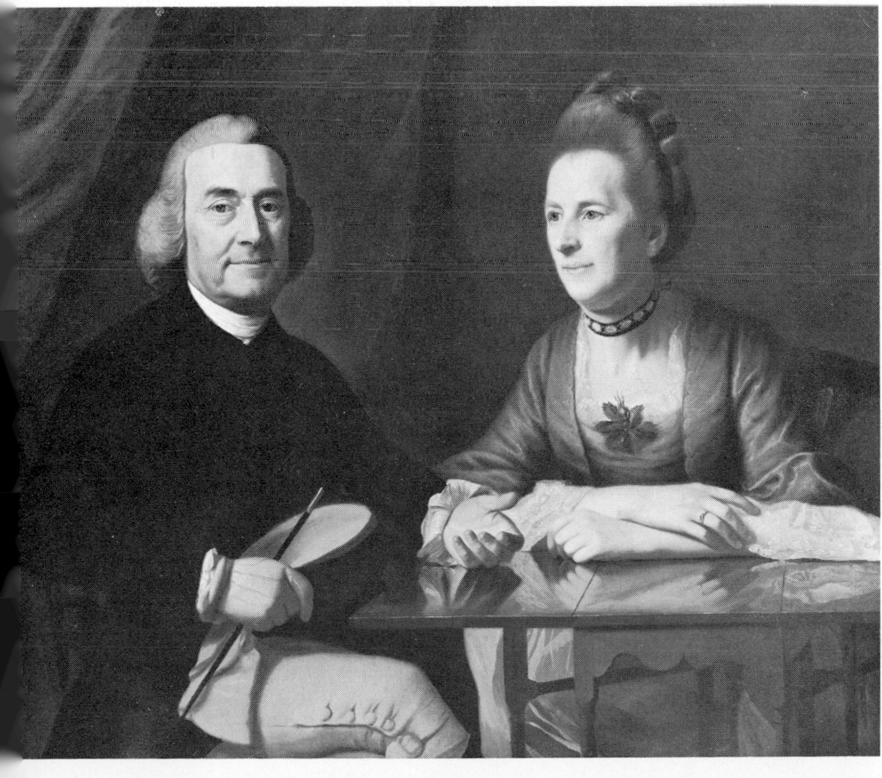

302. *Above: the Isaac Winslows sit beside a highly polished spider-leg table.*

303. *Right: the chest-on-chest was another form favored in colonial New York.*

304. A bombé *secretary, richly ornamented with rococo and classical elements*

New England Variations

With the new wealth of the merchant class and the rising prosperity of the middle classes Bostonians evinced a highly unpuritanical interest in worldly goods. The Bay colony's creed of restraint and thrift was cast aside, and, like New York and Philadelphia, Boston was caught up in the expression of elegant living. By 1760 the city was encircled with gentlemen's estates; the view from Beacon Hill was described by an English visitor: "gently rising hills & vallies, thick planted with Churches and country seats." In 1782 the Marquis de Chastellux wrote of one such estate: "The house is very handsome and perfectly furnished, and everything breathes that air of magnificence accompanied with simplicity, which is only to be found among merchants." During the Revolution the ladies of Boston's fashionable world were described by Abbé Robin, a chaplain with the French troops in America: "the church is the grand theatre where they attend, to display their extravagance and finery. There they come dressed off in the finest silks, and over-shadowed with a profusion of the most superb plumes. The hair of the head is raised and supported upon cushions to an extravagant height."

Among the cabinetmakers who made furniture in the Chippendale style for moneyed Bostonians were such names as Benjamin Frothingham, John Cogswell, and George Bright, to whom this *bombé* secretary (304) is attributed. The *bombé*, or kettle-base, form so handsomely interpreted in the Boston area was adapted from Louis XV furniture forms. Slender cabriole legs, as shown on the tea table (305), continued to be a Massachusetts characteristic. Claw-and-ball feet were carved with the side talons angled away from the front center talon, a regional pattern illustrated by the secretary, the tea table, and the upholstered chair (306). The arms of this chair, which is one of a pair, end in bird-head carvings (306a).

306a

305. A deeply scalloped mahogany tea table

306. A mahogany armchair made in Salem, Massachusetts

The persistent appeal of japanned furniture, particularly in the Boston region, is shown in the tall case clock (311) with its *chinoiserie* decorations raised against a red and black "tortoise-shell" background. The band of fretwork set into the curved hood is a Chippendale motif. The clock is dated 1766 and signed by Gawen Brown, who was born in England, had settled in Boston by 1749, and made and installed the tower clock in the Old South meetinghouse about 1770. The tower clock, according to an issue of *The Boston-Gazette* of that year, ran "with great regularity and exactness."

Fretwork, as seen on the japanned clock, also appears as a border on the top and drawers of this chest (307) made by William King of Salem, where many outstanding pieces of Massachusetts furniture originated. Despite his skill as a cabinetmaker, King was once apprehended as a horse thief and frequently abandoned his family "to ramble unincumbered."

The delicate mahogany tea table (309) has the fluted straight leg with lattice brackets, newly fashionable in the Chippendale period. The table originally belonged to Francis Borland, a Boston Tory who died in a fall from his roof, according to family legend, while watching the Battle of Bunker Hill.

The pierced splat side chair (312) shows another innovation of the period, the French scroll foot, or whorl foot, a pattern also used in the curving cross stretchers of the tea table (309). Hairy-paw feet, found in the finest examples of Massachusetts furniture, were used on the desk (310), whose block-front drawers end squarely, rather than being topped with shells as in most Connecticut and Rhode Island block-front case pieces.

307. Top: a Chippendale chest of drawers by Wm. King. 308. Above: a New England settee with characteristically slender proportions

309. Left: a tea table. 310. Right: a desk with a fall front

311. Left: a japanned tall case clock. 312. Right: a walnut side chair

Throughout most of the eighteenth century Newport, Rhode Island, was one of the five major cities in the colonies serving not only as an active seaport for European and West Indian commerce but also for the coastwise trade. Fortunes were also made by "the fine art of evading revenue officers"; chests of tea were smuggled in between hogsheads of molasses, East Indian goods were camouflaged as cargoes of herring, and Madeira wines and Barcelona silks were disguised as shipments of salt. In 1763 on nearly a mile and a half of Newport's water front, docking facilities were offered at sixty-six wharves.

A Virginia visitor in 1771 described the town: "It far surpassed the idea I had formed of it...a very agreeable prospect from the water, being situated on an easy rising hill." Robert Melville, governor of Grenada in the West Indies, praised the Newport gentry as "celebrated for their hospitality to strangers, and extremely genteel and courtly in their manners." Many of these genteel and courtly folk were refugees from religious persecutions—Baptists, Congregationalists, Quakers, and Sephardic Jews from Spain and Portugal, who enjoyed the freedom of Rhode Island's "miscellaneous theology."

Rhode Island's temperate climate was a further attraction to settlers, and the shore line was dotted with country estates built by the successful and prosperous. Fine gardens were laid out "belonging to gentlemen of fortune and taste, having fish ponds of perch, trout, etc." Newport's lure as a summer resort had already begun with growing numbers of "wealthy inhabitants of the Southern Colonies, and the West Indies, seeking health and pleasure." The names of important visitors were printed in capitals in eighteenth-century issues of *The Newport Mercury*, the names of ordinary visitors in small type.

Within Newport's thriving community of merchant princes and wealthy summer visitors were the Townsends and the Goddards, an extraordinary dynasty of gifted cabinetmakers allied by marriage and apprenticeship. Over the course of a century nineteen craftsmen from three generations of Townsends and Goddards worked together, or singly, to produce much of Rhode Island's best furniture from a Queen Anne lowboy attributed to Job Townsend, Sr. (1699–1765) to a mahogany cabinet in the Empire style attributed to John Goddard II (1789–1843).

Both families were Quaker and lived and worked on Easton's Point, where Newport's Quaker colony was centered. Among their best patrons were Newport's prosperous Jewish colonists, as well as such prominent Providence figures as Governor Stephen Hopkins, Moses Brown, and his brother, John Brown, the original owner of this roundabout chair (314). It is likely that John Goddard I (1723–85) made this particular Newport piece since it is known that he made furniture for the Browns.

Like all cabinetmakers of the era, the Townsends and Goddards did not confine themselves to fine furniture. The ledger of Job Townsend, Jr. (1726–1818), for example, lists such odd jobs as a "wigg box," a checkerboard, a bird cage, a "Wooden Horse," billiard sticks, and "a Coffin for Mr. Coit." As was customary in those days Townsend sometimes dealt by barter; in one instance, he gave three tables and a corner cupboard to a local barber in exchange for "A Year's Shaven, a Cutt Wigg, a foretop to the Wigg, and 24 feet of mahogany." John Goddard I, known for his block-front secretaries and kneehole desks, "Costly as well as ornimental," also invested in the coastwise venture trade, sending out a line of inexpensive chairs and tables to be sold on consignment from Connecticut to the West Indies. Early New England furniture, it is worth noting, has been found in various parts of the world—a tea table in Bermuda, a bedstead in Haiti, a desk-bookcase in Cape Town, South Africa.

313. Detail of shell carving on the mahogany kneehole chest of drawers (313a, on page 227) made by Edmund Townsend (1736–1811)

314. *A mahogany roundabout chair of Newport origin*

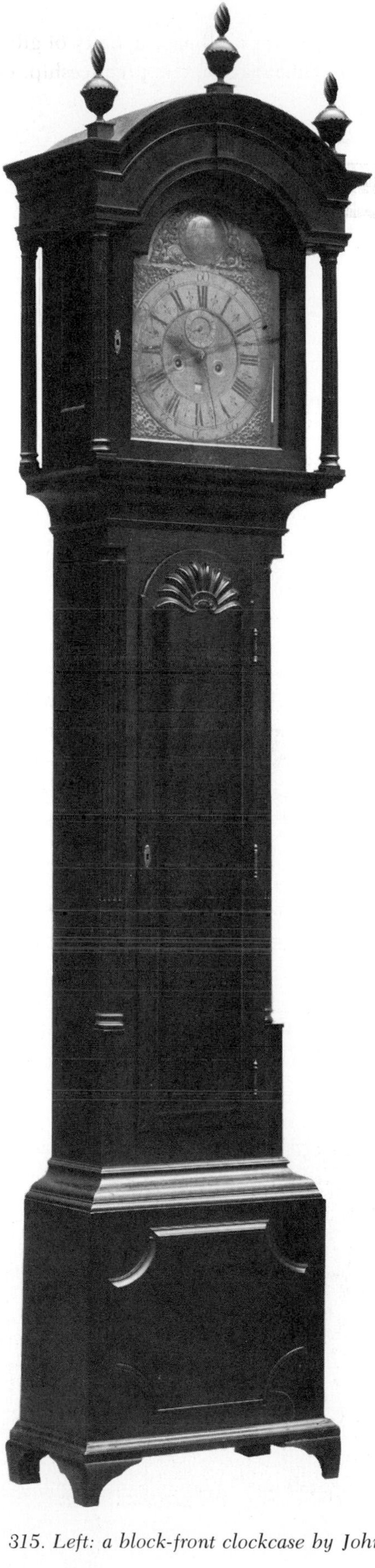

315. *Left: a block-front clockcase by John Townsend.* 316. *Right: a Newport gaming table with French scroll feet*

317. *Top: a chair by John Townsend, the straight front legs carved in stopped fluting*

318. *Left: tea table with a rococo fretwork rim and geometrically pierced stretchers*

319. *Right: a mahogany block-front secretary with side handles to facilitate moving*

The most significant innovation of Rhode Island's Chippendale period was the block front with shell carving, a development that appears to have no distinct precedent in European furniture and is attributed to the creative abilities of the Townsend and Goddard cabinetmakers. The tall case clock (315) on the preceding page, the secretary (319) attributed to John Goddard I, and the kneehole chest of drawers (313a) by Edmund Townsend are examples of this design, in each case the blocking topped with the shell. As a general rule, block-front panels were cut from a single piece of wood, usually solid mahogany.

Another design, which was not often copied by other New England craftsmen but remained the particular signature of the Townsends and the Goddards, is the bracket foot with a scroll. This device is fully expressed on the kneehole chest of drawers (313a); the curved brackets, set between the front legs, end in carved whorls that curl onto the feet. On the secretary (319) the brackets end in a moderate curve rather than a spiraled scroll. The urn finials with corkscrew flames are a Townsend-Goddard design.

Both the secretary and the highboy (320) have the bonnet, or roofed, top favored in Rhode Island design rather than the open pediment used in other regions and best described as a façade type of construction. The highboy also illustrates the undercut claw-and-ball foot, an opening being carved through between the talons and the ball. This refinement was used on the best pieces of English furniture during George II's reign but was rarely attempted by colonial cabinetmakers other than in Newport.

The tea table (318) is one of several such tables known to have been made by John Townsend (1732–1809), all with the stretchers in this pattern and straight legs carved in stopped fluting. This example has a fretwork "fence."

320. Top: a mahogany highboy with carved shell and flame finial

313a. Above, right: a kneehole chest of drawers with block front

321. Right: a lowboy with knees carved in John Goddard's style

Cabinetmakers in New England's inland towns created highly individual patterns in their furniture. Eliphalet Chapin of East Windsor, Connecticut, made graceful, simplified adaptations of ornate Chippendale motifs upon his return from Pennsylvania, where he had lived for five years—apparently to avoid a "marriage of necessity" in his home town. The cherry highboy (323) with entwined scrolls on the top and lower drawers, a lattice pediment, and a central "sea horse" cartouche illustrates Chapin's distinctive modification of Philadelphia's rococo styles. Benjamin Burnham of Colchester, Connecticut, also "sarvfed his time in Felledlfey," as is inscribed in his cherry desk (324); the unusual three-tiered bank of interior drawers follows an especially robust curved design. Aaron Roberts of New Britain, Connecticut, is generally credited with the development of pin-wheel and rope-twist carvings (326) found in that area. Among rich provincial case pieces were those made by the Dunlap family of New Hampshire. This highboy (322) typifies the Dunlap manner with its many carved fans, the fretted gallery, the double-scroll skirt, and slim-ankled legs—the latter also on (325).

322. A "tiger-stripe" maple highboy from New Hampshire

323. *A pedimented Connecticut cherry highboy*

324. *A Connecticut desk with shells and block front*

325. *Left: a chest of drawers made by a Dunlap.* 326. *Right: a cherry chest-on-chest with carvings in the Connecticut style*

Country Chairs

In small towns, villages, and rural farming areas of colonial America furniture was made by local carpenters and joiners, many of whom were skilled artisans, or often by householders themselves, who were both "cultivators and artisans." Pieces made by trained country craftsmen would have been found, for example, in a wayside tavern such as the one visited by the Marquis de Chastellux in 1782, "a very pretty room, adorned with good prints and handsome mahogany furniture."

This provincial furniture, simply wrought for unpretentious homes, frequently followed the patterns of the moment, as do these chairs with the pierced Chippendale splats (327, 328, 331). In two other illustrations (334, 336) the chairs are forthright versions of elaborately carved ladder-back designs made in urban areas. An appealing potpourri of styles is found among the other examples. The rush-seat chair (329) has the turned front legs with Spanish feet from the William and Mary period combined with a splat and curved crest of the Chippendale period. The New England armchair (330), made around 1750, has turned front legs ending in pad feet and a vase-shaped splat all in the Queen Anne manner, and once again a Chippendale crest tops the back. The straight, narrow lines of the two New Hampshire chairs (332, 333) with fluted legs create a particularly provincial air. The more ornate chair (332) with fan carvings and Chippendale "ears" has been attributed to the Dunlap family.

327. Top, left: cherry wood, Conn. 328. Top, right: Charleston chair

329. Above, left: painted pine. 330. Above, right: New England chair

331. Top, left: walnut chair, N.J. 332. Top, center: maple chair, N.H. 333. Top, right: maple chair, N.H. 334. Above, left: cherry, Conn. 335. Above, center: a turned maple chair. 336. Above, right: mahogany, N.H.

Benjamin Franklin, Printer

Throughout his long life Benjamin Franklin was never far from a printing press. Although he retired from active business as a printer when he was forty-two years old, wherever he was he continued to practice the craft, as time permitted and as it pleased him, almost to his last days. Some of his most engaging works were the satires and bagatelles he printed, to amuse himself and delight his friends, on his press at Passy when he was in France as minister plenipotentiary of the United States. He was then in his seventies. In 1788, when he was eighty-two and covered with most of the honors an admiring world could bestow upon a mortal, still proud of the craft to which he had been trained as a youngster, he began his last will and testament with the words, "I, Benjamin

Franklin, of Philadelphia, printer...."

He was, of course, a great deal more. Franklin was the most cosmopolitan spirit of his age. He was as much at home in England, where he lived for eighteen years, and in France, where he lived for nine, as he was in Philadelphia, where he passed the greater part of his life. To the people of Europe Franklin was not only a symbol of America, a sage and genial philosopher from a dimly envisioned overseas Arcady; he also personified the most cherished ideas of the Age of Enlightenment, ideas that would liberate mankind from its long past of prejudice and error and establish its "natural right" to freedom from oppression. This self-made republican with long gray locks, a tallow chandler's son, a printer and a many-sided tradesman, who moved with ease and honor among the powdered heads of Europe, who quipped with royalty, and who exchanged thoughts with the most advanced and able minds of the day—this man more than any other American of the time caught the attention of the world at large. When John Adams joined Franklin in France he reported that his elder colleague enjoyed a reputation "more universal than that of Leibnitz or Newton, Frederick [the Great] or Voltaire, and his character [was] more beloved and esteemed than any or all of them." Franklin's name, Adams continued, "was familiar to government and people...to such a degree that there was scarcely a peasant or a citizen, a *valet de chambre*, coachman or footman, a lady's chambermaid or a scullion in a kitchen who was not familiar with it, and who did not consider him as a friend to human kind. When they spoke of him, they seemed to think he was to restore the golden age."

Long before his sojourn in France Franklin had attracted the attention of the world to Philadelphia, particularly with his scientific experiments. But even before that, with his printing press, his remarkably lucid literary style, and his uncommon good sense, he was an unsurpassed propagandist for worthy causes. The maxims of Poor Richard, his most popular brainchild, were immediately and repeatedly republished in the colonial press from Boston to Charleston. They were translated at least three times into French, and in 1784 a Russian edition was published at St. Petersburg. Such maxims as "Keep thy shop, & thy shop will keep thee," "Fish & visitors stink in 3 days," "God heals, and the Doctor takes the Fees" were quoted everywhere. For more than a generation before 1776 they constituted something like a common primer for the man in the street. And in the trying times of the Revolution such disparate personalities as Abigail Adams and John Paul Jones found inspiration in recalling one or another of the sayings of Poor Richard.

There were no limits to Franklin's searching interest in the world about him, in the skies above him, and in the depths of the ocean he crossed so many times. On a single day in 1772 he wrote thirteen letters to as many different persons on subjects ranging from the employment problems of a glass factory and the problem of silk culture to the selection of books for the Philadelphia Library Company (an outgrowth of a club he had earlier organized) and the principle of oath taking. At times he almost covered as much ground in a single letter; in one brief note, for example, he discussed variations in climate, smuggling, taxation, swamp draining, storms, and sea-shell rocks among other things. To facilitate keeping a record of his correspondence he made a duplicating machine—"a rolling press, for taking the copies of letters or any other writing," a visitor to his house reported in 1787. "A sheet of paper is completely copied in less than two minutes, the copy as fair as the original, and without effacing it in the smallest degree." He also designed a chair for his library, with a ladder concealed beneath a hinged seat for getting at volumes in the upper tiers of his bookcases, and for fetching others that were out of reach he devised a mechanical hand at the end of a pole, similar to the instruments used today in grocery stores for bringing down packages from the topmost shelves.

And, as his eyes grew weary with age, he thought of bifocal eyeglasses to ease the strain. "I imagine it will be found pretty generally true," he wrote a friend from Passy in 1785, "that the same convexity of glass, through which a man sees clearest and best at the distance proper for reading, is not the best for greater distances. I therefore had formerly two pair of spectacles, which I shifted occasionally, as in travelling I sometimes read, and often wanted to regard the prospects. Finding this change troublesome, and not always sufficiently ready, I had the glasses cut, and half of each kind associated in the same circle, thus. By this means, as I wear my spec-

tacles constantly, I have only to move my eyes up or down, as I want to see distinctly far or near, the proper glasses being always ready. This I find more particularly convenient since my being in France, the glasses that serve me best at table to see what I eat not being the best to see the faces of those on the other side of the table who speak to me; and when one's ears are not well accustomed to the sounds of a language, a sight of the movements in the features of him that speaks helps to explain; so that I understand French better by the help of my spectacles."

These were, to be sure, among the minor accomplishments of a man who had, in the words of one contemporary, "snatched the lightning from the sky, and the scepter from tyrants"—referring to his studies of lightning and his successful efforts in the revolutionary cause. But Franklin's interest in homely details was as keen as his concern for the large issues of life. While he was abroad he sent frequent messages to his wife advising her in matters concerning the furnishing and decoration of their Philadelphia home. In 1758 he sent her, "To show the Difference in Workmanship...something from all the China Works in England," along with an apple corer, and "Breakfast Cloths...to spread on the tea table." For, he wrote, "no body breakfasts here on the naked Table, but on the Cloth [they] set a large Tea Board with the Cups." He also sent carpeting for the floor of the best room, with careful instructions as to how to lay it. And, among still other household objects, he sent "a Pair of Silk Blankets, very fine. They are of a new kind...they are called Blankets: but I think [they] will be very neat to cover a Summer Bed instead of a Quilt or counterpain."

On a later occasion, in 1770, he advised the mayor of Philadelphia of new fashions in interior decoration. "Of late, indeed," he wrote, "they begin here to leave off wainscoting their rooms, and instead of it cover the walls with stucco, often formed into pannels like wainscot, which being painted, is very strong and warm." In another letter he had already instructed his wife in this matter. Regarding one of the rooms in their home, he explained, "I would have you finish it as soon as you can, thus. Paint the Wainscot a dead white; Paper the Walls blue, & tack the Gilt Border round just above the Surbase and under the Cornish. If the Paper is not equal Coloured when pasted on, let it be brush'd over again with the same colour; and let the Papier machée musical Figures be tack'd to the middle of the Cieling; when this is done, I think it will look very well." He further advised her that the London fashion was "to make one Curtain only for each Window," and sent her some "blue Mohair Stuff" for hangings.

Franklin had planned the construction of his house in 1763, but he left Philadelphia later that same year and commissioned Samuel Rhoades of the Carpenters' Company to supervise building operations in his absence. Actually, because of his long sojourns abroad, he barely lived in it at all until the last five years of his life. There he died, rich in years and fame, in 1790.

337. Above: hammered and engraved pewter dish by Francis Bassett (1690–1758) of New York

338. Below: detail of a pewter porringer made by David Melville (1775–93) of Newport, R.I.

Everyman's Alloy

Before the first American colonies were settled pewterware had largely replaced wooden trenchers and horn and leather drinking vessels on the tables and cupboards of middle-class English homes. Pewterers in England enjoyed a prosperous trade and, for a while, The Worshipful Company of Pewterers ranked high among the London livery companies. To protect their advantage London pewterers even as early as 1532 were insisting that no Englishman should "at any time hereafter resort to any strange Regions or Countries, there to use, teach or exercise the said Craft of Pewterers," as some had done "for their singular Lucre." Significantly, the Virginia Company of London omitted any mention of the pewterer's trade in appealing to virtually every other type of artisan to emigrate to America. Pewterers are not mentioned in the early records of the Massachusetts Bay colony, either. The London pewterers were out to supply the New World and to a considerable degree they were successful. At one point, in 1760, the value of the pewter shipped to America far exceeded that of all English furniture, silverware, and tinware sent to the colonies. As a further discouragement to colonial manufacture a five per cent ad valorem tax was placed on tin, the principal ingredient of pewter—until the bitter complaints of the tin suppliers of Cornwall persuaded Parliament to rescind the tax.

Nonetheless, by that time pewtering had long since become an established craft in the colonial world. The nature of the metal itself in part subverted London's monopolistic policy. Pewter is a relatively soft and destructible alloy, but also it may be melted and remolded easily and at little expense. Within a generation after the first settlements colonial artisans were at work recasting "damnified" wares, and by 1725 there were ten pewter-making shops in Boston and six both in New York and Philadelphia. Relatively little colonial pewter made before 1750 survives.

339. Right: tankard by Joseph Leddell (died, 1753) of New York

340. Below: a bowl by Leddell or his son and namesake (1718–54)

Although pewterware was inexpensive to make, the brass molds into which the molten metal was cast were costly. As a consequence, these often passed from one generation of craftsmen to the next (secondhand molds were frequently advertised for sale in colonial newspapers). This continued re-use of the molds, in turn, tended to retard the evolution of new styles, unlike designs in silver which changed continually. Some pewter forms continued to be made as much as a century or more after they were first introduced.

To make a piece of hollow ware, such as a tankard, as many as four molds were required: one each for the body, the cover, the thumbpiece for opening the cover, and the handle. For a plate one mold of two hinged parts was all that was required. In any case, the nature of the metal and the molding process both encouraged a simplification of form. To smooth and finish the surfaces the casting was "skimmed," that is, turned on a lathe. It was then polished to a fair luster with rottenstone or some other abrasive.

341. Tankard by John Will; worked in New York about 1753–66. (Top, left to right: the marks of Henry Will of New York, Wm. Will of Philadelphia, John Will)

342. A pear-shaped teapot by William Kirby (worked from about 1760 to 1794) of New York. (At the top: two 18th-century pewter communion tokens and the mark of Frederick Bassett (1740–1800) of New York)

343. Marrow scoop, unknown maker. 344. Porringer by Peter Kirby (working 1736–88) of New York; a similar handle design in silver was popular at least fifty years earlier. 345. Spoon by Wm. Will (working 1764–98)

By the middle of the eighteenth century American-made pewter was serving a wide variety of needs from the nursery and bedroom to the kitchen and dining room, and from the tavern table to the communion table. Joseph Leddell, Jr., advertising in 1752 that he made "any uncommon Thing in Pewter, in any Shape or Form as shall be order'd," added that he also engraved pewter as well as other metals, ivory, and turtle shell "in a neat manner and reasonably." Neat the engraving may have been, but the nature of the metal did not lend such decoration on pewter the sparkle it gave to silver. However, one of Leddell's "uncommon" accomplishments was to engrave a silver tankard, which still survives, with scenes from classical mythology. (In another vein, the engraved device illustrated under the title on page 235, taken from a dish made by Francis Bassett, represents the legend of a great fish caught in Lake Geneva in 1740.)

Aside from its numerous uses in the household and tavern, pewter served one of the earliest and most important of New England industries by providing the metal for still worms in the production of rum. (In 1731 well above one million gallons of this strong popular drink were distilled in Boston from French West Indian molasses.) The use of lead, an occasional minor ingredient of pewter (as were antimony, bismuth, and copper), was forbidden in these worms because it could result in lead poisoning. The complaint of one colonist, suffering from that "miserable distemper, a twisting of the guts" after drinking rum, might indicate that, because it made the metal more easily workable, lead was occasionally used in spite of the prohibition.

Roughly speaking, the century from 1750 to 1850 was the heyday of the American pewterer. As vessels and utensils of crockery, glassware, and other metals were brought within the same price range, these materials gradually superseded pewter for most of the purposes it had served.

346. *Upper right: a standing cup, or communion chalice, by Johann Christopher Heyne (1715–81), Lancaster, Pa.*

347. *Upper left: tankard, Simon Edgell (active 1713–42)*

348. *Right: bed-warming pan with cover by Wm. Will*

349. *Roger Sherman in a Windsor chair*

Windsors

Windsor chairs were first produced in sizable quantities in the beech forests of seventeenth-century England where country artisans, moving their thatched workshops from one fall of timber to the next, made spindles, legs, bows, stretchers, and seats on the spot. The chairs were presumably named for the large market town of Windsor. The term "stick chair" describes their basic construction, stick legs and stick spindles driven into a plank seat. In the eighteenth century the low-priced, durable Windsor joined the English gentry in their gardens and on their verandas; Josiah Wedgwood, for one, bought Windsors at five or six shillings apiece. London cabinetmakers made a drawing room version in mahogany, usually embellished with cabriole legs and an ornately pierced center splat; several "richly carved" examples were made for St. James's Palace.

In the early 1700's Windsor chairs appeared in Philadelphia inventories, but whether they were imported or domestic is unknown. By mid-century, however, craftsmen of that city had developed the art of "Philadelphia" chairs, as Windsors were sometimes called, into an exacting and flourishing trade. The relatively heavy English design was transformed into light, graceful proportions, thanks to the urban taste of Philadelphia furniture makers and the varied attributes of native woods. Hickory and ash, in particular, were tough and springy and could be shaped into slender bows and spindles. Chairmaker Josiah Sherald advertised in *The Pennsylvania Gazette* in the 1760's that he would pay "Five Pounds a Cord for Hickory Wood, split strait and clean...in four and an Half or five Feet" lengths. Knot-free pine and whitewood, for example, were easily carved into contour seats, and close-grained maple, a comparatively hard wood, was generally used for turned legs and stretchers. Neither screws nor nails were necessary in a well-wrought Windsor. Spindles and legs were set into seats of unseasoned lumber, which shrank as it dried and gripped the component parts in a sturdy all-wood construction. The first Windsors made in Philadelphia were low-backs (353), soon followed by comb-backs (352), bow-backs, or hoop-backs (351), and in New England, by the continuous hoop-and-arm design (350 and 359).

350. Opposite, left: a brace-back Windsor chair from Connecticut. 351. Opposite, right: a bow-back chair owned by James Monroe

352. Above, left: a comb-back chair with leg turnings typical of Philadelphia. 353. Above, right: a Pennsylvania low-back chair

354. Left: a braced Philadelphia fan-back Windsor chair with spiral ears

355. Above: a rare, triple bow-back settee with tapering legs, a characteristic of New England Windsors. The arms terminate in "knuckle" carvings.

After the 1750's the craft of the stick chair spread to every major city on the eastern seaboard, and the Windsor became one of the most popular articles of furniture in the colonies. Thomas Jefferson is said to have composed the first draft of the Declaration of Independence sitting in a Windsor chair. The Second Continental Congress (357) apparently sat upon them. George Washington bought twenty-seven in 1796 for the portico at Mount Vernon, at $1.78 per chair. Roger Sherman, the Connecticut cobbler who became the most influential figure in Congress toward the end of the Revolution and the only man of his time to sign The Articles of Association of 1774, the Declaration of Independence, the Articles of Confederation, and the Constitution, sat in a Windsor for his portrait (349) by Ralph Earl. John Adams had his favorite Windsor; James Monroe used one (351) in his Fredericksburg, Virginia, law office, and Windsor chairs were listed among household goods up for public auction in 1780—"Late the property of Benedict Arnold."

356. Right: this New England bow-back Windsor is the type pictured below.

357. Below: detail of Edward Savage's engraving, Congress Voting Independence, *with Benjamin Franklin and Charles Carroll in Windsor chairs*

The marks of quality in a Windsor are a contoured shape to the seat, a boldness to the turnings, an outward rake, or splay, of the legs, and an over-all balance of design, which must be sturdy but light in feeling. As a general rule, the greater the number of back spindles, the more prized the chair—nine spindles are excellent, eleven are exceptional.

To mask the assorted woods used in their construction and because American Windsors, like their English counterparts, were originally intended as garden furniture, chairs were painted in a variety of colors: Indian red, black, yellow, rose, gray, brown, blue, or "jappann'd and neatly flowered." Benjamin Franklin owned two dozen that were painted white, and Thomas Jefferson ordered four dozen for Monticello that were described in the bill rendered in 1801 as "Black & Gold." But most typically, Windsor chairs were "painted green like garden furniture in France," a comment recorded by Médéric Moreau de Saint-Méry in his book, *Voyage aux Etats-Unis de l'Amérique, 1793–1798.*

358. Top: a fan-back Windsor side chair made in Wilmington, Delaware

359. Above: a New England high chair, the back curving into the arms

360. Right: a comb-back writing chair presumably from Rhode Island

361. *A round Windsor table with three legs*

Variations on the Windsor were seemingly unlimited, even to the creation of a Windsor riding chair—an open, two-wheeled, one-passenger sulky with a Windsor affixed as the driver's seat. Many forms have persisted. The low-back Windsor, for example, known in the nineteenth century as a "firehouse" chair, is made today under the current name of "captain's" chair. In the colonial years shipments of Windsors were sold along the Atlantic seaboard and in the West Indies. This farflung trade was eulogized by Windsor chairmakers marching in New York's Federal Procession of 1788, in celebration of the Constitution. They carried a banner depicting a dockside shop from which their wares were being loaded onto ships. The motto read:

> 'Free Trade'
> The federal states in union bound,
> O'er all the world our chairs are found.

362. *A hooded maple and hickory cradle, made in Boston in the late 18th century, has spindles turned in a bamboo design.*

Revere & Others

In the score or more years that led up to and concluded with the Revolution colonial silversmiths found in the "modern style" a fresh opportunity to exercise their skills and their creative imagination. As with furniture, old forms were given fresh dress and new forms evolved to satisfy an expanding list of needs and modes. The repertory of scrolls, shells, and capriciously curved and contorted foliage of the current vogue enlivened the metal to a point where essential shapes were sometimes all but lost in a play of ornament. The teakettle (364) by Joseph Richardson, with its reverse-curved handle, inverted pear-shaped body almost completely covered with raised and chased designs, and cabriole legs ending with shell feet, illustrates the trend at its extreme best. A sugar bowl, teapot, and creamer (363) by Pieter de Riemer (1738–1814), each inverted pear-shaped and with corresponding spirited ornament, comprise an early example of a tea set designed *en suite*; in earlier periods the separate elements bore little relation one to another in their designs. Shortly after he came to New York from England in 1754 Daniel Christian Fueter (1720–85) fashioned a stand in the prevailing style (365) to accommodate a London-made set of casters and a pair of silver-topped glass bottles for oil and vinegar.

363. Tea set, with the Van Rensselaer crest, by Pieter de Riemer

364. Above: the richly ornamented teakettle, on a stand with a spirit lamp, made by Joseph Richardson

365. Below: cruet stand by Daniel Christian Fueter

366. Left: miniature portrait of Rachel Revere by Joseph Dunkerly

367. Right: Paul Revere (1735–1818), painted by Copley around 1768

The colonists who sat to John Singleton Copley for their portraits constituted an early American aristocracy of sorts, so many of them were distinguished in various ways during pre-Revolutionary years. Most of the artist's subjects were pictured candidly and realistically, but carefully garbed in their best clothes. Long before Longfellow hallowed his name, and before he rode to fame as a patriot "On the eighteenth of April, in Seventy-five," Paul Revere had the special distinction of being portrayed by Copley, sitting at a table in his working-shirt sleeves and thoughtfully regarding a silver teapot he was in the course of completing (367, detail 367a). A pot of almost identical form, chased and engraved with rococo embellishment (372), suggests the finished character of the piece he has in hand.

Working in the style of the day Revere hammered out almost every form of silver and gold that was then in use, from thimbles (370), spoons (368, 369), and spurs (371), to trays (375), tankards (377), and coffeepots (376). In 1768, the same year that he undertook dentistry, he made one of the most historic pieces of colonial silver and cut in copper one of his most memorable engravings. The silver piece was a bowl (373) commissioned by fifteen Sons of Liberty to honor the "glorious NINETY-TWO Members of the Hon^{bl} House of Representatives of the Massachusetts-Bay, who, undaunted by the insolent Menaces of Villains in Power... Voted NOT TO RESCIND" a circular letter they had sent to the other colonies protesting the Townshend Acts—and it is so inscribed. A detail of the engraving (374) depicts the arrival at Boston's Long Wharf later that same year of the British expeditionary forces, formed, as the print explains, "for supporting ye dignity of BRITAIN & chastising ye insolence of AMERICA." That was an odd statement to be inscribed by a colonial patriot. However, the inscription further remarks on the "insolent Parade" of the troops up King Street. It would seem that Revere aimed at a buying public in both camps.

368. Left: teaspoon. 369. Right: saltspoon. Both are by Revere.

370. Below, left: gold thimble made by Revere for his daughter

371. Below, right: one of a pair of silver spurs made by Revere

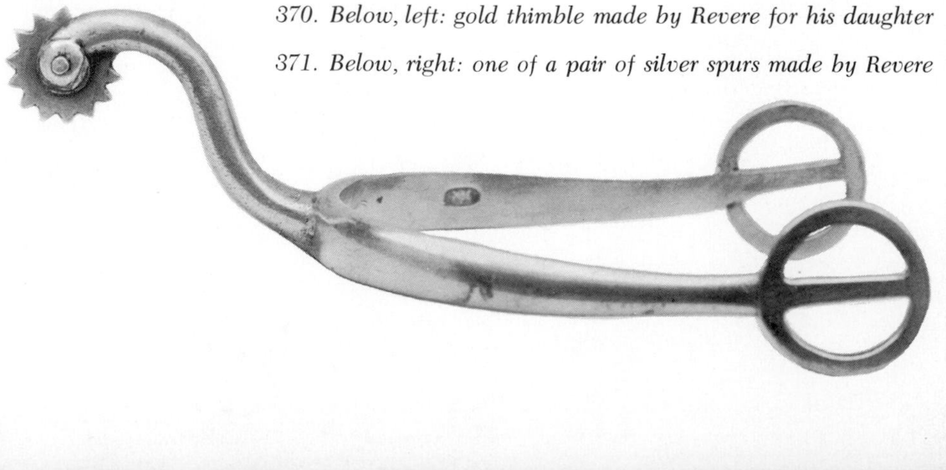

372. *Above: finished teapot similar to that in the Copley portrait*

367a. *Below: detail from the Copley portrait of Revere shown opposite*

373. Silver bowl engraved with the names of Sons of Liberty

374. Opposite: in 1770, The Boston-Gazette *advertised for sale Revere's engraving,* A View of Part of the Town of Boston in New England and Brittish Ships of War Landing their Troops! 1768, *a detail of which is shown here. Revere added to the print a description of the troops that paraded, "Drums beating, Fifes playing... Each Soldier having received 16 rounds of Powder and Ball."*

375. Above: silver tray made by Revere about 1761

376. Below: coffeepot made by Paul Revere in 1781

377. Above: silver tankard made by Revere

377a. Top: a detail from the tankard above

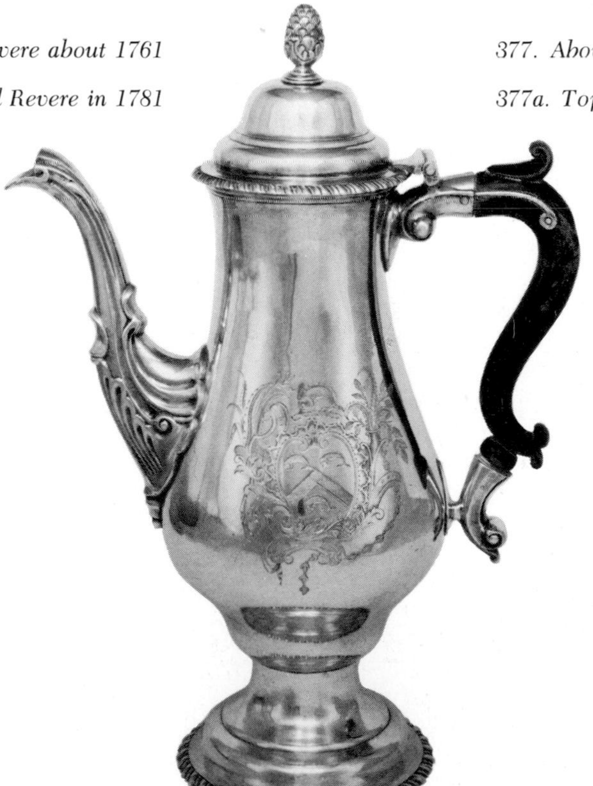

Another piece of great historic interest is the inkstand (383) made in 1752 by Philip Syng, Jr. (1703–89) by order of the Assembly of Pennsylvania at a cost of £25.16.0. In 1775 it was relinquished to the Continental Congress, and it was used by the signers of the Declaration of Independence and the Constitution. The dish cross (380), also made in Philadelphia, by Richard Humphreys (working 1771–96), was an ingenious, newly developed device for heating and supporting dishes at a safe distance above the top of a table. The arms were made adjustable to fit dishes of various shapes and sizes.

Following the unsuccessful invasion of England by "Bonnie Prince Charlie" and his Jacobite supporters, 1745–46, the Stuart pretenders to the British throne, exiled in France, continued to enjoy some sympathy but to incur more rancor. The scene engraved on a beaker (382) by Daniel Christian Fueter offers a graphic commentary on anti-Jacobite sentiment. (Fueter himself was a political exile from Switzerland, but he was pardoned and returned there to die.) Another highly engraved piece (379), made by Fueter's son Lewis, was presented to one Captain Thomas Sowers in 1773 for having successfully repaired the battery at the tip of Manhattan Island. Myer Myers (1723–95), who made the pierced cake basket illustrated here (381), was a prominent Jewish silversmith; he also made many pieces for services in colonial synagogues.

378. Scales used by Syng to weigh gold and silver coins

379. Engraved salver by Lewis Fueter of N.Y. (1746–85)

380. A dish cross with a spirit lamp by Richard Humphreys

381. *Pierced cake basket made by Myer Myers*

382. *The engravings on this beaker, by the senior Fueter, show the devil leading the Stuart pretender and the pope to the fiery mouth of hell.*

383. *The inkstand made by Syng for the Pennsylvania Assembly*

385. *Right: porcelain bowl made in China for export*

386. *Opposite, left: a delft dish celebrating Wilkes*

387. *Opposite, right: teapot protesting the Stamp Act*

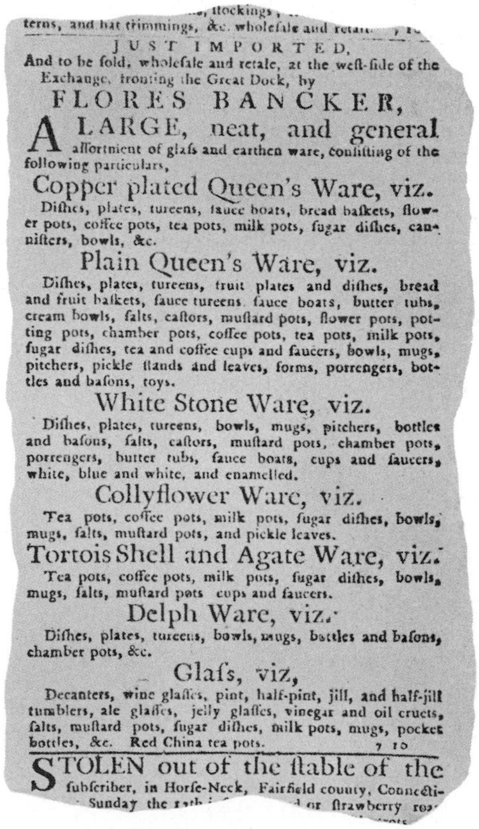

terns, and hat trimmings, &c. wholefale and retail

JUST IMPORTED,

And to be fold, wholefale and retale, at the weft-fide of the Exchange, fronting the Great Dock, by

FLORES BANCKER,

A LARGE, neat, and general affortment of glafs and earthen ware, confifting of the following particulars,

Copper plated Queen's Ware, viz.

Difhes, plates, tureens, fauce boats, bread bafkets, flower pots, coffee pots, tea pots, milk pots, fugar difhes, canifters, bowls, &c.

Plain Queen's Ware, viz.

Difhes, plates, tureens, fruit plates and difhes, bread and fruit bafkets, fauce tureens fauce boats, butter tubs, cream bowls, falts, caftors, muftard pots, flower pots, potting pots, chamber pots, coffee pots, tea pots, milk pots, fugar difhes, tea and coffee cups and faucers, bowls, mugs, pitchers, pickle ftands and leaves, forms, porrengers, bottles and bafons, toys.

White Stone Ware, viz.

Difhes, plates, tureens, bowls, mugs, pitchers, bottles and bafons, falts, caftors, muftard pots, chamber pots, porrengers, butter tubs, fauce boats, cups and faucers, white, blue and white, and enamelled.

Collyflower Ware, viz.

Tea pots, coffee pots, milk pots, fugar difhes, bowls, mugs, falts, muftard pots, and pickle leaves.

Tortois Shell and Agate Ware, viz.

Tea pots, coffee pots, milk pots, fugar difhes, bowls, mugs, falts, muftard pots cups and faucers.

Delph Ware, viz.

Difhes, plates, tureens, bowls, mugs, bottles and bafons, chamber pots, &c.

Glafs, viz,

Decanters, wine glaffes, pint, half-pint, jill, and half-jill tumblers, ale glaffes, jelly glaffes, vinegar and oil cruets, falts, muftard pots, fugar difhes, milk pots, mugs, pocket bottles, &c. Red China tea pots. 7 10

STOLEN out of the ftable of the fubfcriber, in Horfe-Neck, Fairfield county, Connecti- Sunday the ... or ftrawberry ro...

384. *Left: shell-top cupboard displaying the types of English pottery listed in the advertisement from* The New-York Gazette, *1771*

Culture & Conflict

Throughout the colonial period America continued to rely upon Europe, upon England particularly, for fine tablewares of pottery, porcelain, and glass. By the middle of the eighteenth century technical improvements had made possible a great expansion of the English pottery industry, mainly in Staffordshire; from then until the Revolutionary War discouraged such commerce, the colonies were deluged with the varied wares of those factories. The newspaper advertisement opposite gives some indication of the different types that were imported here; in the cupboard shown next to it (384) examples of these types are displayed.

"Queen's Ware" refers to the plain cream-colored pottery developed by Josiah Wedgwood, and so named after he had won the patronage of Queen Charlotte in 1765 with this innovation. The "Copper plated" variety was decorated by transferring an impression from a copperplate engraving to a pottery surface before it was glazed. Most of the names of the other wares mentioned are self descriptive; "Collyflower," "Agate," and "Tortois Shell" earthenware simulate those natural materials.

Josiah Wedgwood met Benjamin Franklin and was sympathetic to the American cause during the growing dispute over colonial liberties. He was concerned about the constitutional rights of Englishmen wherever they were. At one point he wrote his partner, Thomas Bentley, "Mr. Greenville [George Grenville, the prime minister from 1763 to 1765] & his party seem determin'd to Conquer England in America, I believe...I tell them the Americans will then make Laws for themselves." One day in February, 1765, the yawning members of Parliament passed the Stamp Act with hardly a show of serious interest or a word of debate. "There has been nothing of note in Parliament," Horace Walpole reported, "but one slight day on the American taxes." But with that gesture Parliament had in fact put a torch to the times. Even Franklin was surprised at the vehemence of American resistance. As leader of the opposition, William Pitt warned the ministry, "America is almost in open rebellion! Sir, I rejoice that America has resisted. Three millions of people so dead to all the feelings of liberty as voluntarily to submit to be slaves would have been fit instruments to make slaves of the rest."

English merchants, dismayed to see their overseas markets shrinking, added their voices to the colonists' complaints. John Wilkes, a formidable agitator and reformer, openly denounced Britain's policy. In 1763 he wrote an essay in his periodical, *The North Briton*, that challenged statements made by George III and so enraged the king that he had the author thrown into jail. As a consequence of this and other protestations Wilkes was celebrated as a defender of English liberties, at home and abroad. For a decade, as the dispute raged, English potters found a ready market on both sides of the ocean for wares decorated with symbols and slogans that expressed such popular public attitudes (386, 387). Even porcelain ordered from China (385) was emblazoned with similar spirited designs. The odious Stamp Act was repealed the following year. One London artist made a small fortune satirizing the defeat of Parliament in a cartoon that sold for sixpence.

The same year that Wilkes issued his controversial pamphlet young Samuel Powel of Philadelphia went to England and was presented to the king. Like many other affluent young colonists, he then made the grand tour of Europe. In the course of his further journeys he was received by the pope in Rome and presented to the king of Sardinia in Turin; before he turned homeward he paid a visit to Voltaire. A decade later Ralph Izard of Charleston, South Carolina, with his wife, Alice De Lancey, made a similar tour, but Izard declined to be presented at court because he would never "bow the knee...to mortal man." In Rome the Izards had their double portrait (388) painted by the expatriate American John Singleton Copley (389), against an assortment of classical elements that included the Colosseum, a cast of a Roman sculpture (*Orestes and Electra*), and a Greek vase. In London Izard made efforts to avert the coming conflict between England and her colonies, but soon felt obliged to leave the country for France. While there, in 1777, he was elected by Congress as commissioner to Tuscany, but was finally recalled after some bitter altercations with Benjamin Franklin. Meanwhile, America's indignant response to the tax on tea was only

one more of the rebellious acts and attitudes of the colonists that received publicity in London broadsides (390).

War had started when Copley returned to England from Italy. He never went back to his native country, but he predicted that it would win its independence and become a "Mighty Empire." "It is a pleasing reflection," he wrote, "that I shall stand amongst the first of the Artists that shall have led that Country to the Knowledge and cultivation of the fine Arts" and that the latter would "one Day shine with a luster not inferior to what they have done in Greece or Rome in my Native Country."

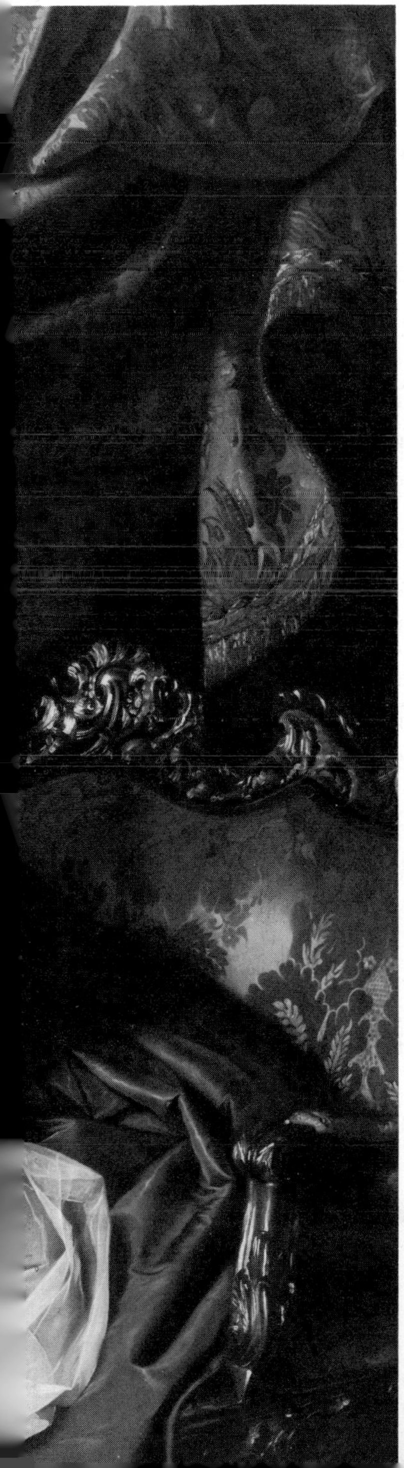

388. Left: Mr. and Mrs. Ralph Izard from Charleston, S.C., painted by Copley in Rome

389. Top: a pastel self-portrait of John Singleton Copley, executed in America in 1769

390. Above: the patriotic ladies of Edenton, N.C., pledging to drink no more tea, 1775

While the Revolution was being fought to its final decision new styles in furniture and decoration were gaining popularity abroad. The work of the Adam brothers "in the antique manner" represented the growing fashion. But, with the war, American shipping practically disappeared from the seas, and imports diminished to virtually nothing. Style changes in America had to wait for the peace.

When the fighting was over, the sea still offered the new nation its main road to recovery from the conflict and to economic independence. With familiar ports closed to American ships, new avenues of trade had to be found. On Washington's birthday, 1784, hardly three months after New York was evacuated by the British, and almost before the ink on the treaty of peace was dry, the *Empress of China* (391) sailed from New York for Canton to open direct trade with China. The 360-ton ship carried a cargo of furs, foodstuffs, and ginseng, a wild root treasured in China as the "dose of immortality." Fourteen months and twenty-four days later the vessel returned with, as one newspaper reported, "a full cargo, and of such articles as we generally import from Europe." In the next six years twenty-eight American ships made that lengthy voyage. (Some of the American vessels, manned by youthful crews, were so small they were mistaken in Far Eastern ports for tenders of larger ships.) The American flag became prominent among those flown above the foreign "factories," or warehouses, that lined the Canton water front (394), and the China trade thereafter enriched the bank accounts as well as the minds and homes of Americans.

Europe had some time since learned the secret of making porcelain, both the true, or "hard-paste," porcelain such as that produced in China and the so-called "soft-paste" porcelain and "bone china" that approximated the Oriental product in their physical properties. ("True," or hard-paste, porcelain is white, fine-grained, and exhibits a conchoidal—that is, shell-shape—fracture when chipped; pottery is opaque, relatively coarse in texture, and friable. If a piece of glazed porcelain is broken, the glaze will be seen to have fused with the body, as both are made of the same materials; in pottery the glaze and the body remain distinct.) Although the European porcelains—including the products of the Chelsea, Derby, Worcester, and other English factories—won almost immediate favor among those who could afford it in America, the wares made in China for export to the western world were in increasing demand. As soon as Americans gained direct access to the source, they had these Oriental wares made to their order and decorated with all manner of scenes, motifs, and devices that reflected both their national pride and their personal interests, as well as prevailing fashions.

391. A Chinese fan showing the Empress of China *at far left*

392. *Above: a Chinese export porcelain coffeepot*

393. *Right: table screen of porcelain slabs depicting the signing of the Declaration of Independence*

394. *Below: a China-trade punch bowl showing the warehouses of Canton with foreign flags unfurled*

The Colonial House at Work

Functioning Forms in the Home

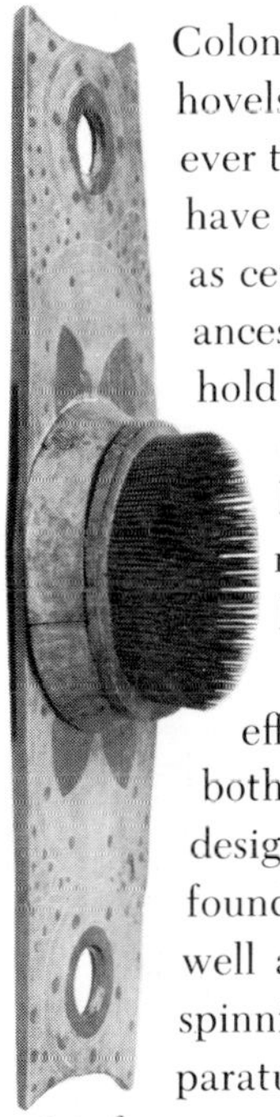

Colonial homes, like our dwelling places today, varied from the meanest hovels to mansions of most impressive grandeur. At every level, whatever the character of their furnishings, they lacked conveniences that have long since developed into necessities of our domestic routine, such as central heating, running water and plumbing, and electrical appliances. To warm his home, to light it, and to provide for other household needs the colonist resorted to means that were not always either efficient or effective by modern standards, but that met the problems with pleasing designs and involved the skilled efforts of craftsmen in every medium. The candle, for example, may have shed little light, but the device that held it in place was usually fashioned with conspicuous grace. Also, an open fire is neither the most efficient nor the cleanest way to heat a room, no less a house, but both the colonial fireplace and its necessary equipment were commonly designed with a care for appropriateness and handsomeness not to be found, let us say, in a modern radiator. The provision of comforts as well as necessities also involved the skills of the housewife with her spinning wheels, looms, reels, needles, dyes, and other household apparatus. A wide variety of imported fabrics were available to the colonists from an early date, but homespun and fancywork wrought by the ladies of the household added substantially to the warmth and color of the home.

While speaking of color it is well to remember that, in the eighteenth century at least, the woodwork of colonial rooms was more often than not painted in rich and varied hues. In 1753 a Boston house that was offered for sale boasted rooms "handsomely painted throughout"; one was green, another blue, still another simulated cedar and, among yet others, one apparently was marbleized. A room from a colonial house in New Hampshire was painted a strong mustard color, its door a rich chocolate brown. In 1748 Peter Kalm observed that the popular color in New York and vicinity was a gray-blue. Occasionally the woodwork of a room was painted with scenic designs. When fully paneled walls went out of fashion the areas above the dado were often covered with decorative papers or sometimes hung with fabrics. The upholstery fabrics used in these rooms were also strong in color. Frequently, the furniture covers and hangings of a single room matched, as contemporary references to green, blue, and yellow rooms indicate.

Opposite: a grouping of varied household forms; for detailed descriptions see p. 373

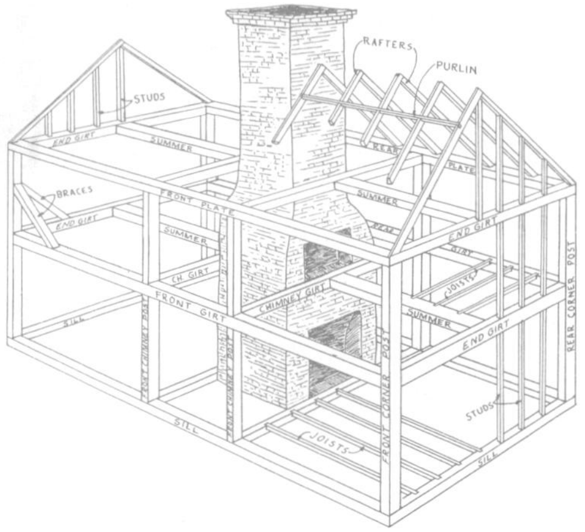

Above: the structure of a colonial frame house

Below: raising a framed wall with pike poles

In a surprising number of instances the walls of colonial rooms seem to have been hung with a profusion of pictures, more than we might feel comfortable with today and disposed in ways contrary to modern notions of decoration. There were at least thirty-nine pictures hanging in four of the rooms of Cornelis Steenwyck's house in seventeenth-century New York. About a century later in Boston Dr. Thomas Bulfinch, "on ye stair Case" of his entrance alone, displayed thirty-eight pictures; the staircase of Henry Vassall's house in Cambridge boasted eighty-four "Great & small" pictures. When lightning struck the Boston house of Jacob Wendell in 1745, it "scorch'd the Cieling and some Pictures that hung up near it," an unlikely place for them in our day.

The functioning of the house as "a machine for living," apart from its purely architectural style, changed character over the years. Like the furniture and furnishings they contained, rooms gradually developed more specialized purposes and assumed more convenient attributes. As already remarked, in the first permanent colonial dwellings life tended to center in the hall, a room of all purposes, particularly in cold weather. (What we refer to as a hall was then termed an entry.) In the course of time, however, those various purposes were served by separate areas—by the kitchen, the buttery, the bedroom, the parlor, the hall (in our sense of the word), the dining room, the library, and so on according to the size and pretension of the structure.

With this evolution, and with furnishings adapted to more special uses, the house became progressively more comfortable and convenient. Beyond that, privacy, an almost unknown concept in earlier years, came within the range of possibility. Before it did become a practical possibility within the home, privacy simply had not been a serious consideration of life. In 1704, on her adventurous journey to New York on horseback, Madam Sarah Knight, an altogether proper lady from Boston, seemed not to think it scandalous to sleep in the same room with several men in a Connecticut inn. "Down I laid my poor Carkes (never more tired) and found my Covering as scanty as my Bed was hard," she wrote. "Annon I heard another Russelling noise in Y^e^ Room—called to know the matter—Little miss said shee was making a bed for the men; who, when they were in Bed, complained their leggs lay out of it by reason of its shortness—my poor bones complained bitterly not being used to such Lodgings, and so did the man who was with us...." Thus she passed the cold December night.

The increased specialization of rooms was gradual and the degree of specialization undoubtedly varied with family circumstances. A visitor to Boston in the seventeenth century reported of one house that the poultry was given its "breakfast" in the kitchen in cold weather. As also earlier observed, the Samuel Sewalls entertained nine persons for dinner in Mrs. Sewall's chamber in 1708; and in 1737 an upstairs bedroom in another Boston house contained, aside from its bed and other bedroom facilities, fifty-five pieces of "small coarse China," apparently for use at the dining table in this same room. Late in the eighteenth century, in simpler houses at least, upstairs rooms were still used for various sorts of storage as well as for sleeping and dining. In 1791 the Reverend William Bentley of Salem observed that since the "effluvia from the human body by fair experiment did render cheese, butter, &c. rancid," the custom of lodging in rooms where such things were stored was "detrimental to the cheese, &c." (Closets for storage were not unknown in colonial homes, but the word often referred to a small room with its own window, occasionally used as an "office," or study, or as a dressing room, that opened from a larger room.)

Bathrooms were practically nonexistent. (The effective sanitary regulation of "privy houses," "houses of ease," "houses of office," or "necessary houses," as toilet conveniences were variously termed, was a matter of continued public concern of cities throughout the colonial period.) Within the house, closestools with their concealed pots were indispensable adjuncts of the bedroom or adjoining chamber, and as often as not followed the fashions of the day in their general design and construction. In 1723 one resident of Newport brought running water into his house "underground from the Spring," and sixty years later the little Moravian town of Bethlehem, Pennsylvania, had an "excellently contrived waterworks" that piped water into its homes. But for the most part, colonists, in city and country alike, had to go to the nearest well or hand pump for their necessary water supplies, not always without danger—as in the case of Mary Coffey of Philadelphia who in 1736 "pitch'd" into her well and was drowned when the rope on her bucket gave way unexpectedly.

Although floor plans and architectural styles of houses changed over the years, the basic construction methods remained essentially the same. The various elements of the colonial frame house were hand hewn from massive oak timbers, meticulously and securely joined by mortise and tenon, like the furniture of the period, with wooden pins run through the joints to tighten them further. Thus fitted together the several wall frames were arranged flat on the ground in preparation for the raising. The principal members were often more than a foot square and only a communal effort would raise such heavy forms and assemble them in position. The frames first were lifted as high as possible by hand, then were raised to the required elevation by the use of "pike poles," at which point some agile young man mounted the corners to guide the tenons of one frame into the mortises of another and pin them together. It could be dangerous work, and there were frequent accidents, as contemporary records make clear.

The day of a raising became a social occasion, with the prospect of the frolic that invariably followed completion of the job, and of the strong drink that as invariably flowed, speeding the work at hand. In 1774, after more than a year of preparation—cutting and squaring timber, cutting shingles, gathering stone for foundations and chimney pile, digging the cellar (which took sixty-six days), and so on—a house was thus raised on Gardiners Island, New York. "Raised the House," the owner laconically reported; "Elias Mulford brought over in his boat 13 Men & wife, Daniel King in his 9 Men, come over in Mine 14 Men. the Carpenders & my servants 15 more, 49 in the whole, some of which was by standers raised it in rather less than 6 Houres, none much hurt, no notice given of raising untill the Night before for fear of a heard of grog brusers, not a man but invited."

Such early houses were built more solidly than was required for any of the stresses and strains they were likely to endure even over a long period of years. Spared the hazards of fire and purposeful demolition most of them would, with ordinary care, still be standing. Where they have survived and been cared for, or understandingly restored, they provide insights into aspects of colonial experience that can be realized in no other way. "The true character of the Americans," wrote one eighteenth-century *émigré* to this country, "is mirrored in their homes." A few years later, from much the same point of view, Gouverneur Morris wrote to George Washington, "I think it of very great importance to fix the taste of our country properly, and I think your example will go very far in that respect. It is therefore my wish that everything about you should be substantially *good and majestically plain*, made to endure...."

View of the Ashley house, Old Deerfield, Mass.

395. *Right: three fireplace flues joined to the main chimney of a Cape Cod house*

396. *Far right: stovewood stacked outside the Pennsylvania State House, 1799*

397. *Below: 17th-century stone fireplace*

398

House Warming

"The snow lay, from November 4th to March 23rd, half a yard deep about the Massachusetts, and a yard deep beyond Merrimack, and so the more north the deeper, and the spring was very backward." Governor Winthrop's *Journal* made reference upon reference to New England's bitter weather. He wrote of snowflakes "great as shillings," of a "tempest of wind and snow," of colonists who "starved to death with the cold."

The hearth was the center of the house. From their first temporary shelters, underground burrows with a "smoaky fire against the earth at the highest side," the colonists built their homes around massive chimneys with wide fireplaces (397). Here the cooking was done, meat turned on a spit, bread baked in the built-in ovens, and pots hung over the flames—from green-wood lug poles in early years, when metal was scarce, and later from wrought-iron swinging cranes. In front of these huge fireplaces the colonists "made shift to rub out the Winters cold...having fuell enough growing at their very doores." Reverend Francis Higginson, arriving from England's scant wood supplies, said of the thickly forested New World that here was "good living for those that love good fires."

Cast-iron firebacks came into general use before the 1800's, not only to protect chimney masonry, but also to reflect precious heat; this one (398) depicts a fort with cannon and a British flag. Franklin, however, would decry the open hearth as responsible for "damaged furniture, sore eyes, and skins almost smoked to bacon." The use of stoves, popularized in the 1700's as an alternative to open fireplaces, is shown in a detail from an engraving of the Pennsylvania State House (396); cordwood is stacked by the back door, stovepipes protrude from the windows.

Dutch settlers constructed fireplaces (399) of "patriarchal magnitude" with tile facings, no jambs, and with mantel ruffles to deflect the smoke up the chimney. "The fire is in the room itself," wrote the Marquis de Chastellux describing a house "built in the Dutch fashion" that served as Washington's headquarters in Newburgh, New York, in 1782.

399. A Dutch fireplace without jambs, from the Schenck house, built in Brooklyn about 1675

400. *Above: a brass kettle, with wooden handle and gooseneck spout, to be set on a hearthside trivet*

401. *Left: Dutch copper chocolate pot with mixer*

402. *Below: this silver-plated brass brazier held coals which warmed dishes supported on the prongs.*

403. High-back settles, like this 17th-century example in pine, kept out drafts and provided a warm seat before the fire.

404. Above: a warming pan. 405. Lower left: a stove plate. 406. Lower right: tin fire scoop

Fireplace equipment and accessories took varied forms, many artfully decorated, but all highly practical. The foot warmer (407), pierced in a heart-shaped pattern, holds a metal drawer which carried hot coals, thus creating a small, portable stove. Foot warmers were deservedly popular—in fact, quite necessary—during lengthy services in unheated colonial churches. One chill Sunday Samuel Sewall wrote in his diary: "This day so cold that the sacramental bread is frozen pretty hard, and rattles sadly." Long-handled warming pans (404), usually hung beside the fireplace, also held hot coals and would be slipped between cold sheets to warm them before the household retired. The brass lid of this example is engraved and pierced with scrolls, flowers, and a rooster. The decoration on the cast-iron stove plate (405), dated 1741, is typical of Biblical themes so often used by Pennsylvania Germans. Here the scene depicted is the death of Abel at the hand of Cain.

Fire scoops, such as this one (406) made of tin with a maple handle, were used to transfer live coals from one hearth to another in order to light a fire instead of taking the pains of kindling a flame with a tinderbox. When a fire blazed, a spit of meat could be set across the hooks on the andirons (408) at the desired height.

407. *Above: this curly maple foot warmer, in which hot coals were carried, has a punched decoration.*

408. *Right: 17th-century andirons with spit hooks*

With the progressive specialization of living space, each room planned to serve a particular purpose, the kitchen became an entity in itself. The massive fireplace, in which all cooking was done and around which the family gathered for warmth, was no longer the single focal point of the house. The other rooms were built with smaller, more efficient and economical, and less smoky fireplaces.

The ballroom from Gadsby's Tavern in Alexandria, Virginia, was constructed in the symmetrically balanced, classical fashion of the 1700's. Its chimney piece (412), with the broken-scroll pediment and other elaborations, represents the formal architectural style that was given to what had once simply been a large functional opening in the chimney pile. It was in the Alexandria ballroom that Washington attended his last birthday ball in February, 1798, a celebration in his honor which had become a yearly event throughout the country at the close of the Revolution. It was also at Gadsby's Tavern that Washington dined, shortly before his death in 1799, and ordered canvasback duck "with a chafing-dish, some hominy, and a bottle of good Madeira, and we shall not complain."

The stylistic attention given to fireplaces was extended to fireplace equipment as well. Bellows were often handsomely carved (409) or otherwise decorated. The brass andiron (410), one of a pair, has claw-and-ball feet and spiral turnings ending in a spiral finial; this pair was made, and stamped, at the foundry operated by Paul Revere and his son. The coal-burning grate (411) is made of iron with a bottom band of brass trim and front legs of brass, which were again designed with claw-and-ball feet and flamelike finials. Coal grates, introduced in the 1700's, offered a new source of heat; colonial cities were no longer bounded by "unending" wood supplies. Towns such as Boston and Newport had to transport much-needed and expensive cordwood from more and more distant places. As early as 1737 the continued recession of the forests led to the first proposal for conservation in this country.

409. Top, right: 18th-century wood and leather bellows

410. Above, right: andiron marked "Revere Son, Boston"

411. Right: an iron and brass grate used to burn coal

412. *An 18th-century fireplace, with pedimented chimney breast, from Gadsby's Tavern, Alexandria, Va.*

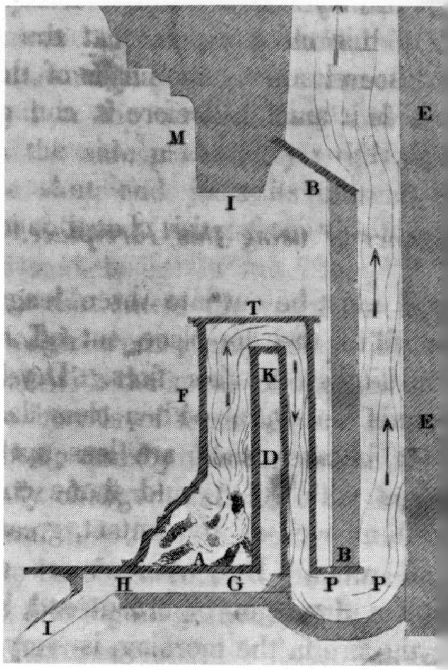

413. *Above, left: a Franklin stove.* 414. *Above, right: cross section, Pennsylvanian Fire-Place* (416)
415. *Below: cast-iron "box" stove.* 416. *Opposite, right: Franklin's Pennsylvanian Fire-Place, 1742*
417. *Opposite, far right: a marbleized tile stove made at a Moravian pottery in North Carolina*

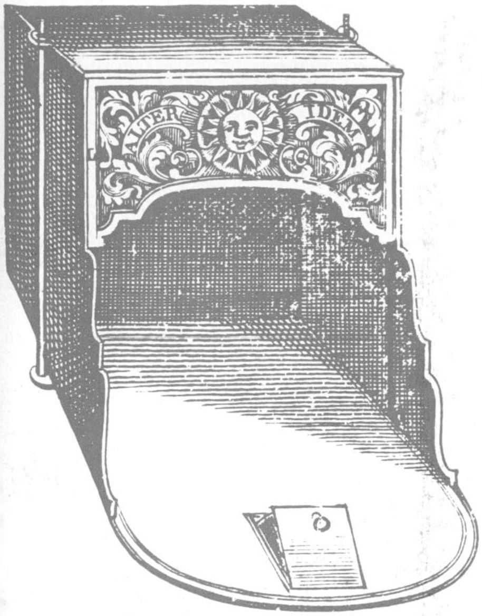

Cast-iron stoves, which heated by radiation, were introduced to America largely by German settlers, who also reproduced the ceramic stoves of their homeland. This example (417) is of marbleized yellow tiles, fired by Gottfried Aust, an immigrant Moravian potter. In 1742 Benjamin Franklin designed his Pennsylvanian Fire-Place (416) that brought in outside air through a duct and warmed it in a series of passages at the back of the frame before releasing it into the room. By conveying the combustion heat of the fire behind the fireback before releasing it up the chimney he utilized it three times instead of losing it up the flue at the moment of combustion. The so-called Franklin stove (413), extensively produced up to this day, does not have the repeating chimney pattern of his original model, but is in effect nothing more than a cast-iron fireplace. A smaller stove (415), cast in one piece, appeared around 1750. It was later adapted by the ascetic Shakers, to whom an open fire denoted "passion."

With a medium-sized colonial household consuming fifty or more cords of wood annually, it is small wonder that shortages were acute in urban areas. Although fifty wood boats might arrive in Manhattan in a single day and "upwards of one thousand" sleds carried wood to Boston on a January day in 1760, shortages continued. Since coal was not yet extensively mined in America, most that was used was shipped from England and was consequently expensive. Innumerable advertisements of "choice" Newcastle, Scottish, Welsh, and Swansea coal appeared in eighteenth-century newspapers; Peter Kalm, visiting New York from Sweden in 1748, wrote that "in many parts of the town coal is used both for kitchen fires and in other rooms."

The use of stoves, a traditional form of heating in northern European countries, became widespread in the colonies during the 1700's. Whether fueled by coal or wood, a stove warmed a room more efficiently and economically than a fireplace, which sent most of its heat up the chimney.

Light at Night

Toward the end of his long, inventive life Benjamin Franklin suggested that the most practical solution to the problem of artificial illumination was to do without it. He urged sensible people to go on daylight-saving time. Candles were "smoky, unwholesome, and enormously expensive," but no better means of lighting had yet been developed—except, perhaps, for the bright and flickering light from the fireplace. From the earliest days of settlement colonists had supplemented firelight with simple lamps of timeless design (420, 421), in which cotton or tow wicks stemmed from an illuminant that ranged from fish oil and kitchen grease to whale or vegetable oils. (Bring "cotton yarn for your lamps," Edward Winslow advised new colonists in 1621.) But those who burned such midnight oil over their books and papers must literally have smelled of the lamp, more or less unpleasantly according to the oil they used. Colonists also on occasion burned "the wood of the pine tree cloven into little slices something thin," stuck in the brickwork of the hearth or in wrought-iron holders (419, 422). These, wrote Francis Higginson, burned "clear as a torch." They also gave off much "fuliginous smoak" and dropped "a pitchy kind of substance" wherever they were placed. Rushes—stripped, bleached, and dipped in fat—were burned in similar holders.

418. Top: a 16th-century water lens used to intensify candlelight

419. A 17th-century wrought-iron rushlight, or candlewood, holder set in a wooden base

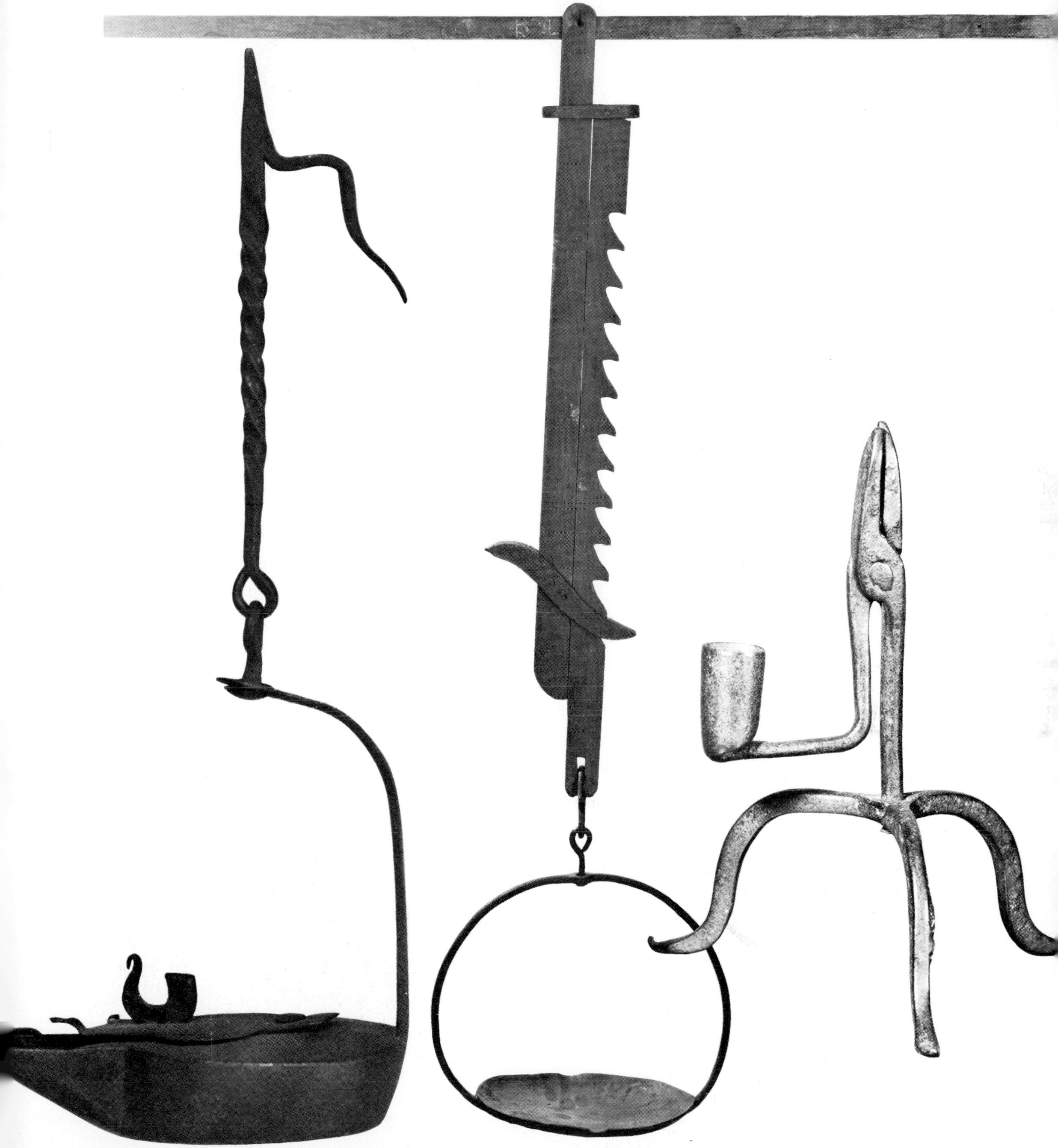

Left to right: 420. Hanging "Betty," or grease lamp, with prong for fixing to a wall. 421. Open two-wick grease lamp suspended from a trammel. 422. A combined candle and rushlight holder

423. *Left: 17- and 18th-century brass candlesticks.* 424. *Right: a European brass candleholder and tinderbox*

For ordinary Americans any attempt at bright lighting was not worth the candle; that is, the need of more light than would illuminate the page of a book or a section of needlework was secondary to the cost and inconvenience of providing it. Lighting an entire room was not a common performance. One evening in 1773 Robert Carter had as many as seven large candles lighted in his dining room, and Philip Fithian, Princetonian tutor to the Carter children, thought the room "looked luminous and splendid." Carter was a wealthy man and could afford such extravagance, but, as Fithian's exclamation reveals, the ordinary colonial household got along with much less light. Even George Washington, an affluent planter and generous host, counted the cost of his candles. He usually retired "soon after candlelight" and got up at dawn as wealthy Romans had done two millenniums earlier. Poor Richard's axiom, "Early to bed and early to rise," was ancient common sense that applied to all.

Homemade tallow candles, from by-products of the kitchen, were the cheapest sort, albeit they needed constant trimming and stank when extinguished. Those made from the berries of the wax myrtle, bayberry candles, yielded "a pleasant fragrancy," especially when put out, but gathering enough berries was laborious and the cost was proportionately high. Beeswax was rarely used for domestic purposes. Best of all were spermaceti candles made from a crystalline substance found in the head of the sperm whale: they lasted a long time, their odor was not disagreeable, and their relative brightness brought objects "close to the Sight, rather than causing the eye to race after them." Washington preferred them although they were expensive. For awhile the process of their manufacture was kept a secret of the "United Company of Spermaceti Candlers," who exercised a monopoly.

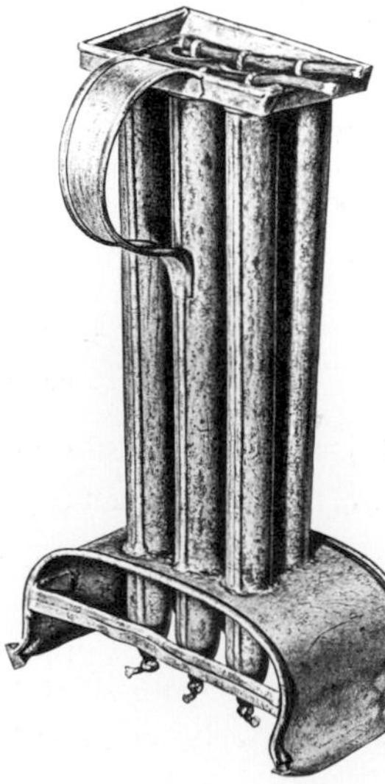

425. *Left margin: adjustable wood candlestand. Above, left to right:* 426. *Early 19th-century tin candle mold* 427. *English delft candlestick.* 428. *English brass candlestick. Both of the sticks date from the 17th century.*

429. Upper left: a wooden candlestand with a threaded shaft for raising and lowering the candles on the arm

430. Upper right: English brass taper jack; the taper, a wick soaked in wax, supported by the jaws of a clamp

431. Left: an 18th-century Philadelphia candlestand, with a drawer and protective screen, on a tripod base

432. Above: a revolving candle-dipping stand with ten disks for holding wicks while they were dipped in tallow

433. A European brass candleholder with snuffers

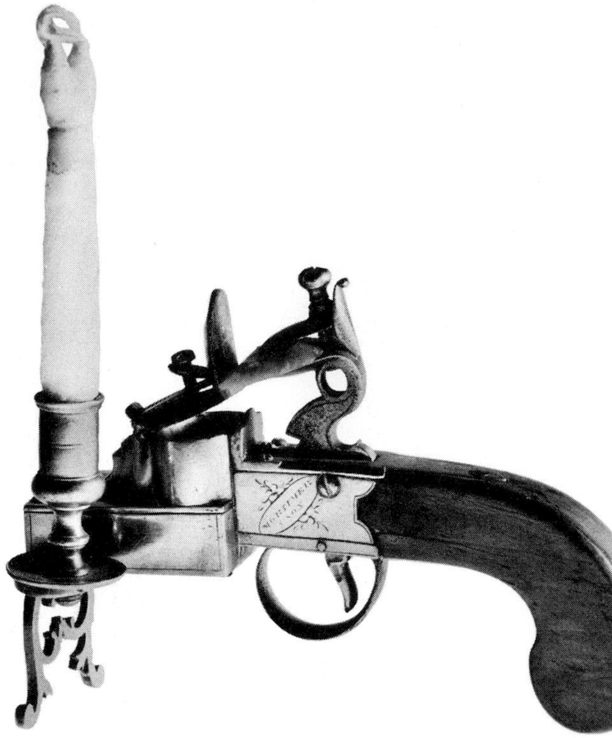

434. An 18th-century candlestick, with a flint and steel lighter, made by Mortimer & Son, Ludgate Hill in London

We enjoy candlelight today (from odorless, wick-consuming candles), so long as we do not have to depend upon it for general illumination. However, it seems an anachronism that our ancestors had to put up with its inadequacies long after their other household gear and living arrangements had directed domestic life toward modern notions of comfort and convenience. By way of compensation candleholders and their attendant equipment, such as snuffers and their stands, were often designed with elaborate style and with great ingenuity. Imported examples of silver, brass, and other metals, and of pottery and porcelain, supplemented the output of native craftsmen. Candles were indeed supported with every dignity, although none of this—except mirror reflectors—increased their practical efficiency.

Judging from his own figures, it would have cost George Washington about eight pounds a year to burn a single spermaceti candle five hours each night. Even the best candles had to be frequently snuffed, that is trimmed, to keep them burning at an optimum level and with a minimal odor. This point was remarked by Jonathan Swift in his *Directions to Servants*, where he sardonically suggested that they snuff the candles at the supper table since the burnt wick might by luck fall in the soup, sack posset, or rice-milk and thus be extinguished "with very little stink."

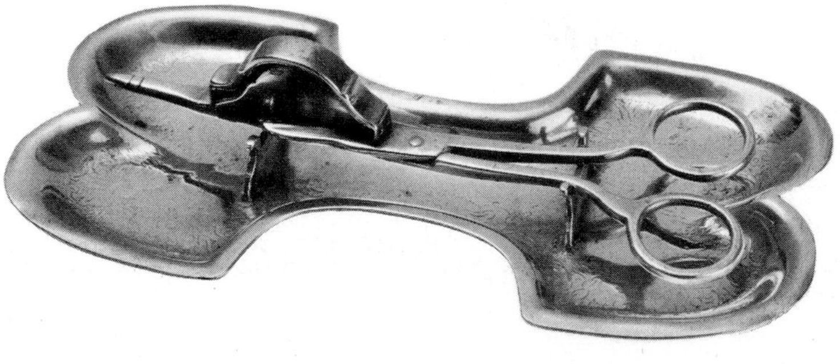

435. Above: an English engraved brass snuffer and tray

436. Below: a "Chimney looking-glass" with sconces

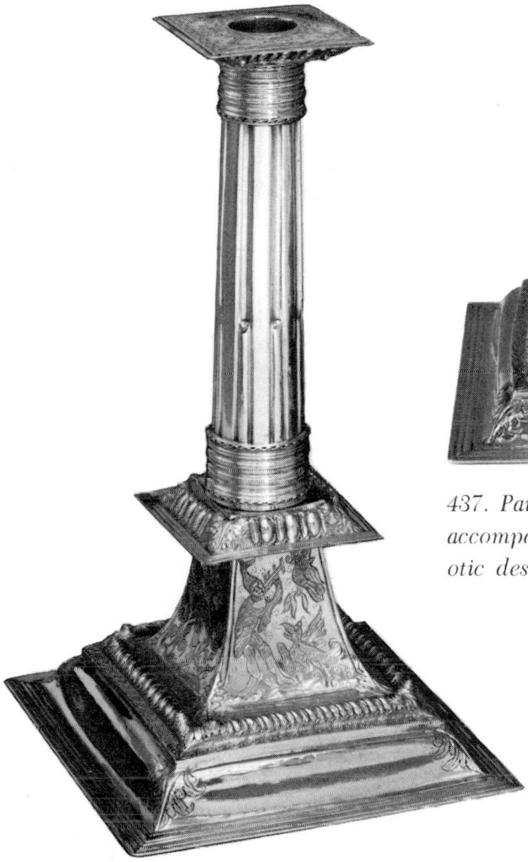

437. Pair of silver candlesticks with their accompanying snuffer stand, chased with exotic designs, made by Cornelius Kierstede

438

439

440. *Tin chandelier with fifteen branches, made in New England*

Outdoors, tin lanterns enclosing candles (439) or open lamps (438) did little to pierce the dark, and could not compete with moonlight. The street lamps of early New York, one of the inhabitants observed, "exhibited the somnified gloom of a sepulchral taper," and then only on moonless nights. Indoors, chandeliers were introduced as early as the seventeenth century for homes and institutions that could afford them and that had room to hang them. Those that were imported became increasingly numerous and elaborate in the course of the next century. In 1778, while Washington endured at Valley Forge, the British staged a fabulous pageant in Philadelphia. To light one room they were able to borrow from the houses of the city "one hundred branches with three lights in each,...eighteen lustres, each with twenty-four lights, suspended from the ceiling, ...and three hundred wax tapers," which they "disposed along the supper-tables." It was a prodigious concentration of light and one almost doubts the record when it neglects to describe the heat that must have been generated.

In 1784 the Argand lamp, an invention of Aimé Argand, a Swiss, and the first radically improved lighting device in history, was put on the market. It fed oil from an elevated container to a tubular wick in a way that gave air to both its outer and inner surfaces. When glass chimneys were added, serving as blowers, such lamps provided illumination equivalent to that of six freshly snuffed tallow candles. They also consumed their own smoke. Franklin and Jefferson, who were in Paris at the time, each bought several of the lamps and shortly afterward Washington was using them at Mount Vernon (441). Lighting had entered a new era, although to some the glare of the Argand lamp was "too vivid for weak or irritable eyes."

441. *A silver-plated Argand lamp owned by George Washington*

442. *English brass chandelier in St. Michael's Church, Marblehead, Mass.*

443. *An 18th-century English or Irish glass sconce*

444. *One of a pair of silver-plated Argand lamps*

445. *Top: gilded weather vane by Shem Drowne*

446. *Left: weathercock from a church in Albany*

Of Time & Weather

447. *Above: an iron weather vane from Pennsylvania*

448. *Below: hourglass made early in the 18th century*

449

The ingenuity and imagination of the colonial metalworker had their freest expression in the shaping of the weather vanes that played against the skies atop so many private and public buildings. Their infinite variety is merely suggested by the three examples shown on these pages. Most famous of all the men who hammered out these early mobiles was Shem Drowne, who made the dazzlingly gilded Indian warrior (445), poised to release the arrow from his bow, that long crowned the cupola of the Province House in Boston. In 1742 Drowne also made the celebrated copper weather vane in the form of a grasshopper for Boston's Faneuil Hall.

Little in the way of precision was expected of the earliest clocks used in colonial America. With a single hand that moved about a dial indicating nothing shorter than quarter hours, those mechanisms were probably not models of constancy either. However, by the aid of a sundial (449) clock time could always be checked against solar time with a table of equations to compute the difference between the two. For less exacting measurements of the passage of time the hourglass provided a handy expedient that was frequently resorted to in churches. Reliable clocks remained relatively expensive until the nineteenth century. As late as 1786 so few people in Salem, Massachusetts, owned clocks or watches that public notice of the time was given throughout the town at one in the afternoon. At that hour, it was proposed, school should start, which would prevent the children from going swimming when they were "too much crammed with animal food."

450. Above, left: flax spinning wheel

451. Above, right: baptismal certificate detail showing a spinning wheel

452. Below: niddy noddy, a wool reel

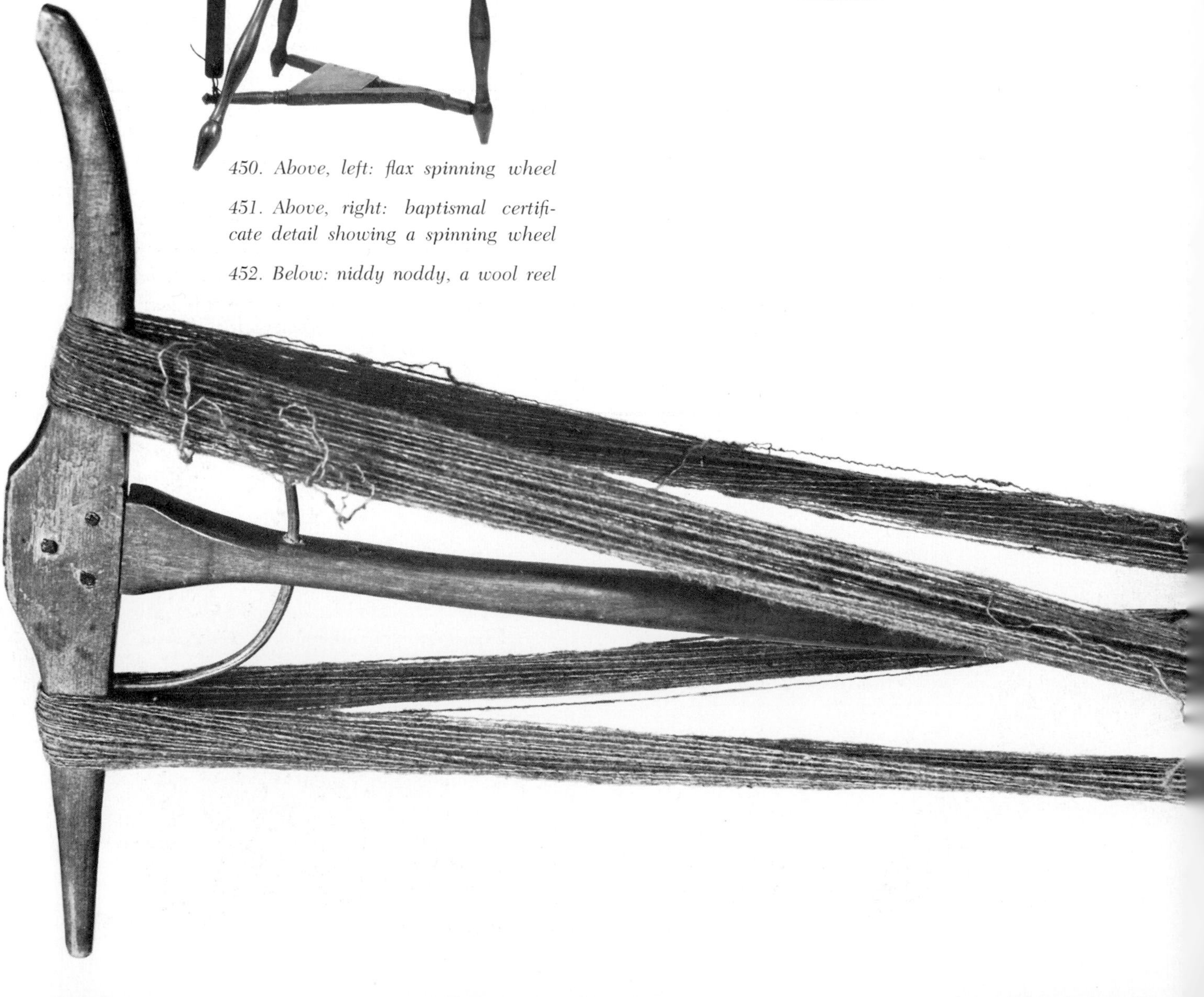

Woman's Work

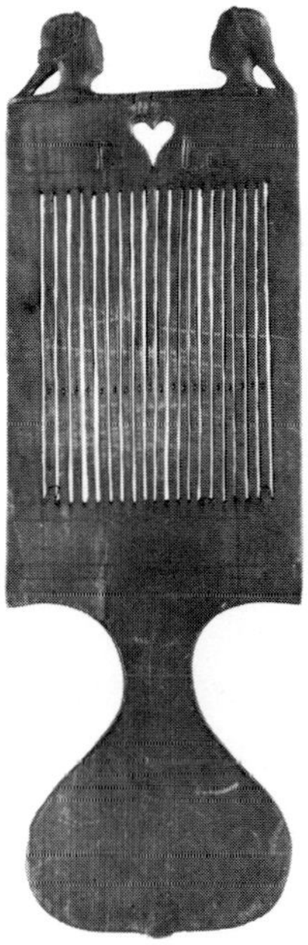

"The weaving loom is the pastime of the women, even among those who consider themselves of rank," a Hessian officer wrote from Connecticut during the Revolution, "And the man of the house considers it an honor to wear cloth that has been made on his farm." A French officer in Massachusetts during the war was told by a farmer: "My daughters and my wife spin, and for sixteen years I have not bought an ell of cloth." Spinning and weaving skills had been early established in America by self-sustaining colonists without ready cash for English textiles. In the 1640's all families in Massachusetts and Connecticut were required to grow flax or hemp, Massachusetts towns increased the number of sheep, and spinning quotas were assigned by village selectmen. By 1743 one Philadelphian could write that "a vast deal of linen and woolen" was made by Pennsylvania's country craftsmen, who "hawked" cloth as far east as Rhode Island. Similarly, Sir Henry Moore, governor of New York, wrote in the 1760's: "every house swarms with children, who are set to work as soon as they are able to Spin and Card, and as every family is furnished with a Loom, Itinerant Weavers then... put the finishing hand on the work." The art of spinning, so deftly practiced by colonial women, is the twisting of loose fibers into a continuous strand. To prepare wool for the large wheel on which it was spun into yarn, the heavy winter fleece of the sheep was carefully processed through successive stages of cleaning and carding, or combing. After being spun, the woolen yarn was wound off into hanks on a wooden frame called a niddy noddy (452). The preparation of flax for the small flax wheel (450), also known as a Saxon wheel, was an arduous, heavy task performed by the men of the family. The desired fibers, lying between the bark and the core of the plant, were separated through soaking, pounding, scraping, and combing, then spun into linen thread by the women. A full-size loom, upon which these yarns and threads were woven into cloth, was the size of a four-post bed and all but filled a country kitchen. Often they stood in an attic, a shed, a loom room, or—as in the southern colonies—a weaving house. The small tape loom (453), an ancient weaving device, was used to make decorative narrow bands of ribbon and trimming or shoe laces.

453. Above: wooden tape loom with two heads carved in profile and initials, RL, on either side of a heart

454. Right: a contemporary sketch of a dyer at work

455. Above: bed hangings and cover in 17th-century crewelwork

456. Below: mahogany closestool, made in the Chippendale style, with the chamber pot concealed behind the deep, scalloped skirt

Despite the daylong round of chores accomplished by colonial housewives, whose tasks could range from the routine jobs of cooking and baking to such special projects as soapmaking and candle-dipping, these women found time to create brightly patterned, richly colored needlework. The cloth on which they stitched their brilliant designs might have been imported from England or made by professional local weavers, but much of their material was spun and woven at home. Although there were professional dyers in the colonies (454) the glowing colors found in colonial fabrics were often the work of the housewife.

Dyes were concocted from indigenous plants. To list a few, there was red from pokeberry, dogwood, sumac, and bloodroot, the latter a wild plant used by certain Indian tribes to paint their faces. Orange came from bittersweet, yellow from onionskins, black from alder bark and poison ivy, purple from iris petals and blueberries, and green from the pressed blossoms of the goldenrod. Blue, a favorite and predominant color in colonial textiles and needlework, usually came from the indigo plant, either imported or domestically grown, particularly in the southern colonies. Indigo peddlers traveled through the countryside selling from village to village. This is the blue so frequently found in early crewelwork.

Crewelwork, one of the oldest forms of embroidery, is a pattern of varying stitches in woolen yarn, usually against a ground of bleached linen. The Bayeux tapestry is a notable medieval example. Colonial designs, by and large, were adaptations of Oriental textile motifs—vines, leaves, flowers, birds, and insects—popularized in England in the 1600's. These designs were worked in crewel yarns onto cushions, chair seats, dresses, petticoats. However, lavishly embroidered bed curtains and coverlets offer the most impressive expression of crewelwork (455). Beds were enclosed with curtains in most colonial homes, not only for privacy, but for warmth. And in bedrooms such as this, specifically planned as sleeping quarters with utmost care paid to details of decoration, closestools (456) were generally included among the furnishings.

Decorative bed rugs were also used, vividly designed in warm colors. This one (457), made by Mary Avery of North Andover, Massachusetts, in 1722, was hooked with heavy wool looped through a loosely woven linen. The next example (458), made in Connecticut by Hannah Johnson in 1796, was hooked with wool on a coarse woolen ground. The original shades of brown, green, and rose have faded to a pale brown over the years, but the strikingly Oriental floral pattern remains.

457. Above: bed rug of wool on linen patterned with flowers and hearts

458. Below: bed rug with the maker's initials, her age, 26, and the date, 1796

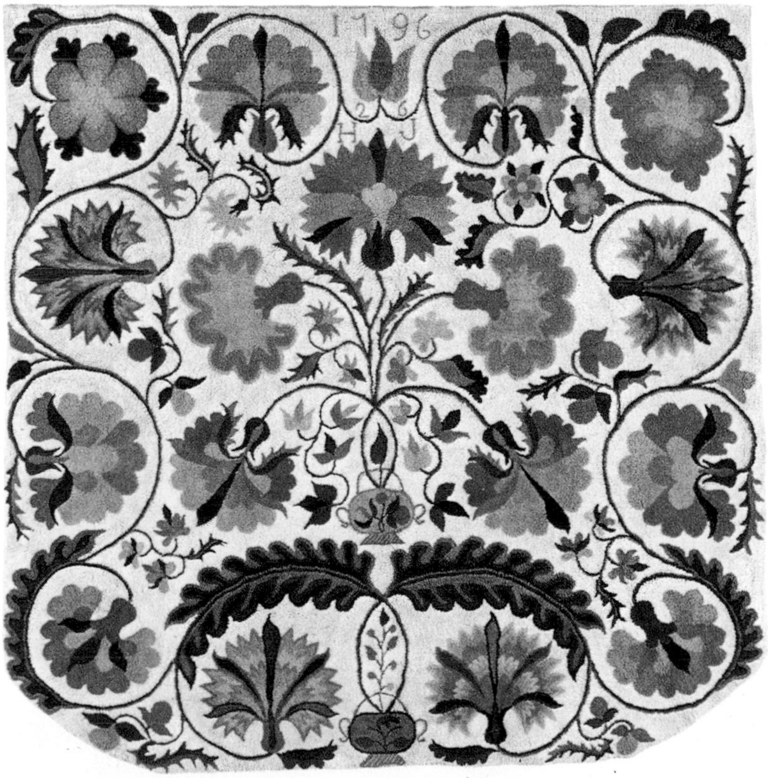

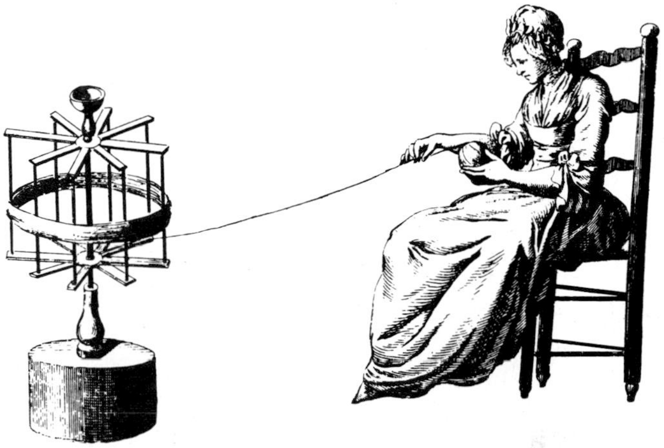

459. Opposite: crewel yarn on linen, Mary Sarah Titcomb, 1760

460. Above, left: needle-point sewing case, monogrammed silver clasp with thirteen linked rings circling "we are won," which may refer to the union of the colonies, or perhaps to marriage

461. Above, right: yarn was often wound from a rotating frame.

462. Below: hair-curling iron in its decorative tripod stand

463. Bottom: an iron engraved with leaves and flowers, which is dated 1756, and a pierced trivet upon which to rest a hot iron

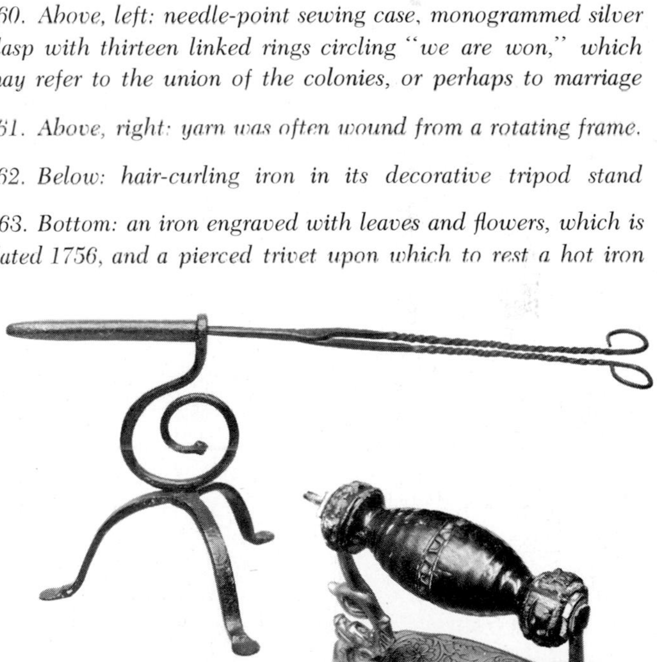

The tutor to the Carter children in Virginia, Philip Vickers Fithian, wrote in his diary in December, 1773: "Spent most of the Day at the great House hearing the various Instruments of Music. Evening, at Miss Prissy's Request I drew for her some Flowers on Linen which she is going to imbroider for a various Counterpane."

In the colonial period little girls were taught needlecrafts at an early age—both ornamental embroidery stitches and the practical skills of sewing hems, seams, and buttonholes. Knitting, for example, was one of the first lessons in domesticity, and many children who had not yet learned to read and write could knit socks, stockings, and mittens. The painstaking lessons in embroidery were demonstrated by samplers, a familiar form of needlecraft mostly done in cross-stitch but also displaying a "sampling" of other intricate stitches mastered by the young embroiderer. Samplers were usually patterned with the alphabet, a pastoral landscape that might include a house, trees, birds, and family pets, and were completed with a Biblical quotation or a motto. One popular verse ran:

> When I was young and in my Prime,
> You see how well I spent my Time.
> And by my sampler you may see
> What care my Parents took of me.

Adam and Eve was also a popular theme (459). In another surviving example, from eighteenth-century Philadelphia, Adam and Eve were decorously clothed in colonial dress.

464. Opposite, top: crewel peacock, detail on a coverlet

465. Opposite, center: needlework pictures were often copied from engravings. This scene, embroidered in silk by Sarah Derby of Salem, Mass., in the 1760's, was taken from a 17th-century French engraving by Jean Lepautre.

466. Opposite, bottom: a crewelwork picture, about 1750

467. Below: an embroidered country scene with a staghunt

468. Right: an adjustable mahogany fire screen from Newport, the embroidery cross-stitched on a piece of canvas

Lessons in needlecrafts were by no means limited to samplers and the knitting of socks and mittens. Colonial newspapers abounded in advertisements of sewing classes. In 1719 *The Boston News-Letter* announced a school where young gentlewomen and children could learn "all sorts of fine Work...embroidery in a new way." In 1773 a New York paper advertised a boarding school where Mistress Sarah Hay would not only teach reading, both prose and verse, and instruct students in the "strictest principles of religion," but would also teach needlework, "all in the neatest manner and newest taste."

The patterns used in different types of handiwork came from a variety of sources. Many were traditional, such as the majority of designs woven into hand-loomed coverlets or used in quilting. Others were freely designed, such as the flowers drawn by Philip Fithian for Miss Prissy. Still others, most in fact, came from pattern books or from needlework shops, which advertised "Drawings on Sattin or Canvis for Embroidering," or "All sorts of beautiful Figures on Canvas...the Patterns from London."

469. Below: crewel purse by Mary Eaton, Newbury, N.H.; dated "April 3, 1764" in the design

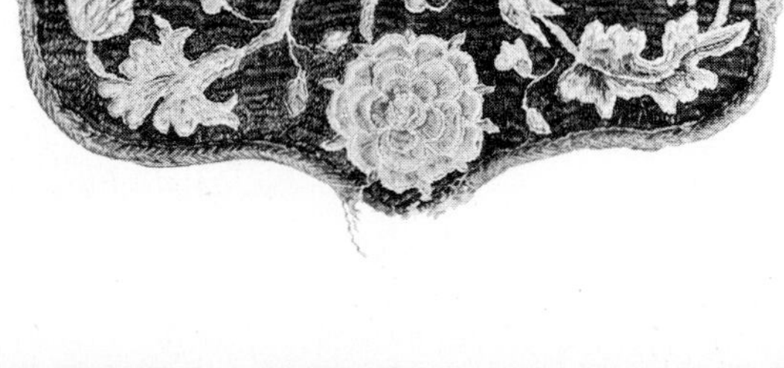

470. *Prudence Punderson's needlework picturing her window hangings*

471. *Left: the looking glass, table, and inkstand may be those depicted in the needlework panel, where the looking glass is shrouded as for her funeral.*

472. *Above: an 18th-century painting, by Benjamin Wilson, shows slip covers.*

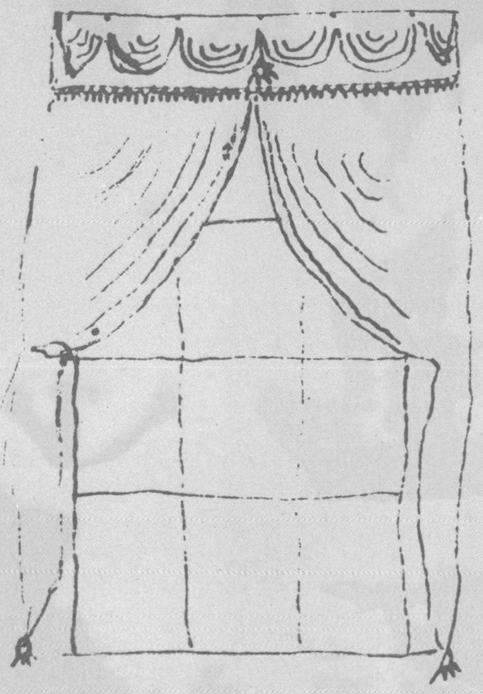

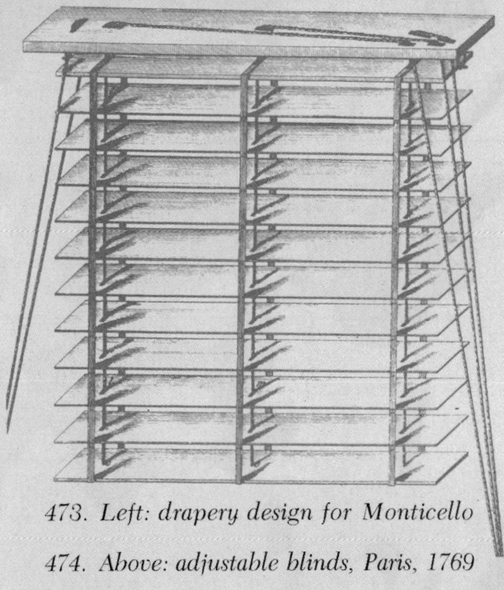

473. Left: drapery design for Monticello

474. Above: adjustable blinds, Paris, 1769

475. Right: detail of Edward Savage's engraving of Congress Voting Independence, *showing Venetian blinds at the windows*

Shades of Our Ancestors

Contemporary pictures showing the interiors of colonial homes are extremely rare. In a most unusual needlework panel shown opposite (470), Prudence Punderson (1758–84), later Mrs. Timothy Rossiter, of Preston, Connecticut, depicted herself successively as an infant, a lady preparing her needlework, and a corpse within a closed coffin. Aside from the grim expression of her own mortality, she revealed as accurately as she could with her needle the fittings of her room, some of which (471) have survived along with the picture she so faithfully stitched.

This panel also provides virtually the only representation of colonial window hangings. Apparently curtains and draperies of any sort were relatively uncommon before 1750, even in homes of the well to do. However, Thomas Jefferson was prompt to install window curtains in some of the rooms at Monticello before the Revolution. Later in the century he sketched a plan for sill-length hangings (473) in blue damask for one of his rooms, and other plans for dimity curtains at the still-unfinished President's House in Washington when he moved there in 1801. George Washington and Jefferson both ordered Venetian blinds for their windows. In 1767 a Philadelphia newspaper carried an advertisement for such "Venetian sun-blinds for windows... stain'd to any colour, moves to any position, so as to give different lights, screens from the scorching rays of the sun, draws a cool air in hot weather, draws up as a curtain, and prevents from being overlooked...."

Slip covers for furniture were used by colonists as early as the seventeenth century. In the next century they were offered in newspaper advertisements as "loose cases for washing." In 1757 Washington received from England an easy chair with "a Check Case."

476. Peter Manigault and guests toast one another. At the window, folding paneled shutters may have served instead of curtains.

Although there are no shades, curtains, or draperies on the window shown in the sketch above (476), the furniture, glassware, and other tableware used at this supper party represent the current fashions of the mid-eighteenth century as well as the artist could depict them. Peter Manigault, graduate of the Inner Temple, was one of the best-equipped and most accomplished hosts in Charleston's brilliant society. How close even that highly cultivated center was to the rawness of the New World is suggested by the fact that two of Manigault's rollicking guests were later killed by Indians on the near-by frontier.

In less serious moments of life, wherever men gathered to share one another's company and conversation, the pipe and the bowl went together. Long before recent reports on the dangers of smoking, King James I protested that it was "A custome lothsome to the eye, hatefull to the Nose, harmefull to the braine, daungerous to the Lungs, and in the blacke stinking fume thereof, neerest resembling the horrible Stigian smoke of the pit that is bottomelesse." But in spite of that prescient royal warning Europe's addiction to American tobacco increased with each generation. About 2500 pounds were exported from the Old Dominion in 1616; in 1775 over 100 million pounds were shipped overseas from this country.

480. An English trade card advertising the tobacco grown in Virginia

477. Above: cherry box for holding pipes

478. Below: an extended steel pipe tongs

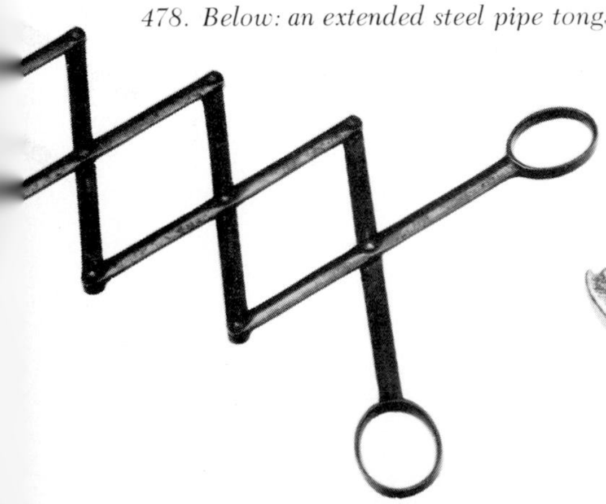

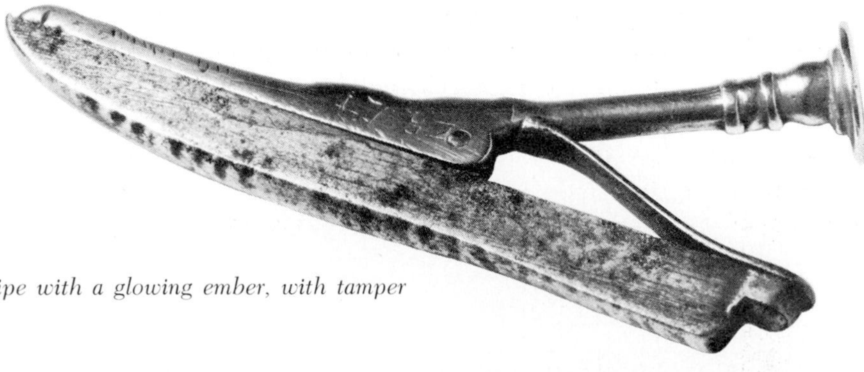

479. Right: tongs, used to light a pipe with a glowing ember, with tamper

Woodenware

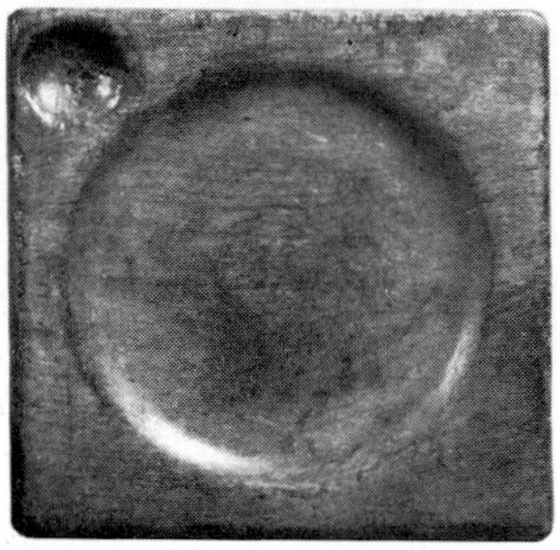

Before Elizabeth's reign, when pewter became widely used in England, ordinary folk ate from wooden tableware, or treen ("made of tree"), or served food upon thick cuts of bread called trenchers, from the French *tranche*—a slice or slab. With the passing of this medieval custom the word trencher came to mean a heavy wooden plate, whose basic form (481), whether English or colonial, varied little over the centuries. From contemporary accounts treen was not merely an inexpensive alternative to pewter, the poor man's silver, but was an acceptable item in table furnishings. Samuel Pepys, however, seems to have preferred more elegant settings. An entry in his diary in 1663 sourly described a dinner held at the London Guildhall on Lord Mayor's Day: "It was very unpleasing that we had no napkins, nor change of trenchers, and drank out of earthen pitchers and wooden dishes." Colonial inventories of comfortable households repeatedly list treenware, "two dozn & halfe of trenchers, four Wooden dishes." Miles Standish left twelve trenchers among his effects; Harvard purchased trenchers for use in the dining hall; and advertisements for "Wooden Trenchers" appeared as late as 1775 in *The Connecticut Courant*.

In the early days of colonization, in keeping with medieval tradition, trenchers were often shared by a husband and wife, by two children, or by a newly engaged couple as an announcement of betrothal. The story is often told of a Connecticut deacon who was accused of vanity because he had made a trencher for each of his children on his turning mill. The colonists also fashioned a wide assortment of other small utensils and implements from wood, which was readily available and easily shaped. Besides bowls, cups, plates, spoons, and standing salts they made egg whisks, ladles, cheese presses, butter stamps, funnels, soap dishes, and a host of other small useful objects. Wooden drinking tankards were copied from the traditional European form, hooped staves with a hinged cover. Noggins, small drinking vessels, were carved in one piece. Maple was most frequently used for treenware; the burls, or knots—irregular growths on the tree—produced curling and twisting grains that were particularly handsome in bowls and other rounded shapes. In the early years Indians also made and sold treen carved from maple knots. The use of wood for tableware continued in rural areas and on the frontier until late in the 1800's.

481. Opposite, top: a birchwood plate, or trencher, with a small depression for salt, possibly imported from England

482. Opposite, far left: sugar bowl turned from maple burl

483. Opposite, left: a bowl with fitted lid in maple burl

484. Above: an oval-shaped bowl of maple burl made with rectangular cutout handles, from New England, 1775–1800

485. Left: covered bowl, maple burl, 14 inches in diameter

From the Rhine to the Susquehanna

The Pennsylvania Germans

About two generations after the Pilgrims landed at Plymouth Rock the people of the Rhine Valley first heard of the promise of the New World. In 1671–72 and again in 1677 William Penn visited the Rhineland as a Quaker missionary and several years later started to advertise there his "free colony for all mankind." By his earnest exhortations, and by letters and brochures which were translated into German and widely distributed, he aroused an immediate interest in America—an interest that rapidly spread and, in time, sent a vast flow of German peasants, craftsmen, and sectarians streaming across the Atlantic. "Along the Rhine a number of families have banded together to accept the invitation of an Englishman named William Penn, who recently visited that community, to settle in that beautiful land [America]," wrote a resident of Heilbronn in 1681 to his son in New York. "We, as also the Platenbach family, are only awaiting a good opportunity when the dear Lord will take us to you...America is the only dream of Elisabeth. Catherine, only six years old, asks us daily, 'Will we soon be going to our brother in America?' " Two years later the ships *America* and *Concord* arrived at Philadelphia carrying several scores of persons from the Rhineland, who established a permanent settlement on the outskirts of Philadelphia, which they appropriately named Germantown.

The Rhine Valley is one of the garden spots of Europe. For this reason it was a land contested for over many centuries, first by warring migrant tribes and Roman legions, and later by warring emperors and princelings. In the course of the seventeenth century, especially during the Thirty Years' War, and again during the War of the Spanish Succession, the population of the area suffered unspeakable horrors and hardships at the hands of invading armies; in their wake followed famine and pestilence. When the burdens of excessive taxation and then religious persecution were added to this list of woes, these people of strong Protestant faith quit their homeland in hordes to seek salvation in Penn's promised land. So many of the Germans who shipped to America via England came from the Palatinate, an area including much of the Rhine Valley and neighboring lands stretching from Switzerland to Holland, that the name Palatine was used as a general term for all German emigrants.

Opposite: 18th- and 19th-century Pennsylvania German objects; descriptions on p. 373

Not all the Palatines headed for Pennsylvania. Queen Anne tried to attract them in large numbers to the Hudson River valley, where they were to help in the production of naval stores. Several thousand did in fact arrive at New York in 1710, but they considered themselves ill-treated in this colony and many of them, at the invitation of Governor Sir William Keith, moved on to more hospitable regions in Pennsylvania. Others who landed in Georgia, the Carolinas, New Jersey, and other colonies also seem to have found their way to Penn's lands. But Philadelphia remained the principal port of entry.

These immigrants were by no means all peasants. The arrivals in Philadelphia in April, June, and July of 1709, who numbered 1838 in all according to one early chronicler, included 56 bakers, 87 masons, 124 carpenters, 68 shoemakers, 99 tailors, 29 butchers, 45 millers, 14 tanners, 7 stocking weavers, 6 barbers, 4 locksmiths, 95 cloth and linen weavers, 82 coopers, 13 saddlers, 2 glass blowers, 3 hatters, 8 lime burners, 2 engravers, 3 brickmakers, 2 silversmiths, 48 blacksmiths, 3 potters, and 6 turners; enough skilled workmen to sustain a diversified society. Many of these craftsmen no doubt stayed on in Philadelphia to serve the needs of that expanding community. Largely, however, the newcomers were husbandmen, families whose ancestors had for countless generations tilled the soil and cared for livestock and who instinctively recognized the richness of the land that awaited them in Pennsylvania. Unlike their British antecedents and contemporaries, who followed the inland waterways to determine their place of settlement, they took to the trail of limestone soil where the tall trees flourished and good farming awaited only the clearing of the land. And there, by industry and perseverance, they prospered. "The farmers or husbandmen live better than lords," reported Georg Wertmüller, they "pay no tithes nor contributions.... Handicraftsmen earn here much money." Such statements and other reports of religious liberties circulated in printed form throughout Germany and impelled thousands more to seek such peace and plenty in the New World.

To pay their way many came as indentured servants, selling themselves into servitude, usually for two to seven years, before they would be free to strike out independently. Many did not make it at all. The ships on which they took passage were often hardly seaworthy and the passengers were packed in "like herring," exposed to filth, disease, and vermin. The voyage took anywhere from six weeks to six months and provisions at times gave out. On one such passage, while the ship "sailed about the sea twenty-four weeks," more than two thirds of the travelers died from hunger. On another, the passengers turned on the mice and rats in their extremity and ate all of them they could catch.

In spite of such hazards and hardships the stream of emigrants grew in volume, reaching a peak in the middle of the eighteenth century. In 1738 alone some nine thousand persons from the Palatinate landed at Philadelphia from whence large numbers fanned out into the Pennsylvania hinterland—to Berks, Lehigh, Lebanon, Dauphin, Lancaster, and York counties. For the most part they spoke only German and so great was the influx that even Benjamin Franklin, most liberal of Americans, was concerned for fear the basic English culture of the colony might be submerged. "Unless the stream of their importation could be turned from this to other Colonies...," he wrote, "they will soon so out number us, that all the advantages we have will not [in My Opinion] be able to preserve our language." Even in Philadelphia the street signs were printed and painted in both German and English, in some parts of the city only in German. (Franklin himself had earlier, in 1732, accommodated the newcomers by pub-

Playing cards bearing land advertisements, in verse, were distributed in England by The Pennsylvania Company.

lishing the short-lived *Philadelphische Zeitung*, the first German-language newspaper in America; in this project he was helped by Louis Timothée, a recent *émigré.*)

Like the Puritans before them these Germans came to America, for the most part, to preserve and enhance a cherished way of life and to maintain the precepts and practices of their religious faiths. More stubbornly—or faithfully—than the Puritans they persisted in their traditional ways, resisting the Anglicizing influences that tended to shape other non-British settlers into a common mold and preserving down to the twentieth century an enclave of rural folk culture in the heart of the urban and industrial East. In 1783 a visitor from Germany complained that the language of the "Pennsylvania Dutch" (the word Dutch is misbegotten from *Deutsch*, or German) had been corrupted into "a miserable, broken, fustian salmagundi of English and German." But the leaders of these people had already undertaken measures to check this degeneration of their native dialect. German-language newspapers were published at Germantown, Reading, and Lancaster, as well as at Philadelphia. Books were imported from Germany and others printed in German by local presses. (The first complete Bible printed in America—other than John Eliot's Algonquian translation—was printed in German on the press of Christopher Sower in 1743, thirty-nine years before the first English edition was produced in this country.) In their churches, schoolrooms, homes, and markets, the Pennsylvania German language prevailed over English. Only in 1911 did English become compulsory as a common language for pupils in their local schools. It has been estimated that almost a third of a million people in various states of the union and in Canada, as well as in Pennsylvania, still speak the dialect.

Over the years no other people of foreign nationality in America so steadfastly retained the customs and the manners, as well as the language, of the Old World. They were a conservative and deeply religious folk representing a wide variety of pietistic sects—Mennonites, Amish, Dunkards, Schwenkfelders, among others—and included in their members such "church people" as the German Lutherans, Moravians, and still others of Protestant persuasion. Although in the eyes of the world the sectarians, the "plain people," with their picturesque dress and quaint customs, and the Moravians, whose settlement at Bethlehem quickly became one of the show places of America, are the most typical Pennsyl-

Left: an illustration from a Pennsylvania German tract denouncing the slave trade

Below: Washington named as the "Father of his Country" for the first time in print in the Nord-Americanische Calendar, *1779*

vania German element, they represent in fact a minority of these people. Rather it was the Lutherans and members of the German Reformed Church that fed the mainstream of Pennsylvania German culture. Whatever the shade of their faith they all were firm in the belief that each individual was an equally endowed and responsible citizen of God's commonwealth. And like the Quakers who received them into their colony, they practiced a benevolent humanitarianism that helped earn that colony above all others a reputation for social progress. They also opposed slavery on moral and religious grounds. Francis Daniel Pastorius, the distinguished leader of the group that had settled Germantown, signed the first protest in 1688. "And those who steal or robb men, and those who buy or purchase them, are they not all alike?" read the message sent to a Quaker meeting that year. Penn was still advertising for settlers and Pastorius asked for assurance that he and his followers might "satisfie lickewise our good friends & acquaintances in our natif Country, to whose it is a terrour or fairfull thing that man should be handeld so in Pensilvania."

At the time the Palatines settled in Pennsylvania in large numbers, Philadelphia was a main center of the most sophisticated and stylish colonial craftsmanship. By extreme contrast the Pennsylvania Germans of nearby counties practiced the useful arts with a spirit that strongly and brightly reflected the deeply rooted, traditional culture of their homeland, a culture that still clung to the medieval past. Out of that remote past emerged the unicorns, from time immemorial the fabled symbols denoting purity, that appeared in confronting pairs as the principal motif on the painted dower chests of Berks County, and the peacock, ancient symbol of the resurrection of the dead, that was represented on pottery tableware, illuminated certificates, and stitched embroideries.

Detail from a water color, 1742, of Bethlehem, Pa., originally a Moravian settlement

Like the early settlers in other colonies, the Germans and Swiss who came to Pennsylvania could bring very little with them on the small, crowded ships that carried them from Europe. What they fashioned in the New World, they made and decorated in the memory of what had served them at home. Many of the other motifs, besides the unicorn and the peacock, had their origins in mythology and folklore. Still others reveal a constant awareness of the flowers, the birds, and the beasts which were so intimately part of their work in field and garden. The dove, symbol of conjugal bliss; the pomegranate, standing for fertility and regeneration; the fuchsia, rose, and forget-me-not, these and numerous other natural and geometric forms—such as stars, crosses, and interlaced circles—persisted as decoration in every medium well into the nineteenth century.

The most ubiquitous theme of all was the tulip, whose cup-shaped, richly colored blossoms had fired the European imagination when the plant was first introduced into the western world from Turkey in the mid-sixteenth century. In the next century the Dutch gave way to a frenzied speculation in these exotics—to the point where just a single bulb commanded an enormous sum. Vast amounts of money were gambled on the fragile plant—the craze was called tulipomania, and Alexandre Dumas (*père*) described the phenomenon in his story *The Black Tulip*—until the market crashed, one of the first market crashes in history. But in south Germany, and elsewhere, the tulip flower long remained a highly popular decorative motif, well remembered by immigrants to the New World. Whether they knew that the flower was an old Persian symbol of love or whether they thought of it as a variation of the holy lily or, grouped in threes, as a representation of the Holy Trinity can only be conjectured.

Memory blurs with time, and with few European prototypes immediately before them, the Pennsylvania Germans approximated and simplified the traditional designs that had been part of their birthright overseas. Indeed, many of the finest examples of this decorative art, the strongest statements of this colorful tradition, date from the decades after the Revolutionary War, more than a century after the first Rhinelanders settled at Germantown.

Purely secular sentiments reflecting the wry humor and collective wisdom of common folk also found their way into the arts, particularly in the inscriptions that often appear on the practical pottery that was produced in great abundance from local kilns. One potter expressed the cherished contention of the "man of the house" in almost any society with the legend, "Rather would I single live than my wife the breeches give." Another reflected on the wayward nature of youth with the worried phrase, "I am very much afraid my naughty daughter will get no man." Still another philosophically repeated a familiar German proverb, "Luck and misfortune is every morning our breakfast."

In reading such homely sayings as in looking at their colorful artifacts it is easy to categorize the Pennsylvania Germans as limited, conventional, and ingenuous in their outlook, which they were to a degree. However, there were aspects of their culture that contributed importantly to the broad currents of life in America. German craftsmen were among the first and the principal makers of musical instruments in this country. Music played a significant part in their religious life, and to a degree in their community life. The Moravian community at Bethlehem was organized into "choirs," and here too musical instruments were used in religious services virtually from the start. In his *Autobiography*, Benjamin Franklin wrote of his visit to Bethlehem in 1756: "I was at their Church, where I was enterteain'd with good Musick, the Organ being accompanied with Violins, Hautboys [Oboes], Flutes, Clarinets, &c." While they were still relatively new, in 1785, Franz Joseph Haydn's "Virgin" Quartets were performed in Bethlehem and *The Creation* some years thereafter.

A "shirt tail" soldier in his frontier garb

In spite of their devotion to old traditions, the Pennsylvania Germans were responsible for some innovations that played an important part in the destiny of Americans. It was their gunsmiths who developed the "Kentucky" rifle, that exquisitely fashioned instrument of precision which, in the hands of expert marksmen of the frontier, proved such a deadly weapon both in the Revolutionary War and in the War of 1812, at New Orleans. At the siege of Boston in 1775 George Washington called for reinforcements from the Pennsylvania back country, and companies of riflemen from Berks, York, Lancaster, and Northampton counties were the first to answer his summons. These were those "shirt-tail men [that is, with the fringed hunting shirts of the frontier] with their cursed twisted [rifled] guns" who were, according to one British soldier, "the most fatal widow-orphan-makers in the world."

It was also the Pennsylvania Germans who developed the Conestoga wagon—that boatlike, handsome, gaily colored "ship of inland commerce" drawn by at least four horses "of a peculiar breed" that proved such an invaluable transport during the Revolution. "In this waggon," observed one witness, "they convey to market over the roughest roads, between 2 or 3 thousand pounds weight of the produce of their farms.... It is no uncommon thing, on the Lancaster and Reading roads, to meet in one day from fifty to one hundred of these waggons...most of which belong to German farmers." It was an adaptation of these covered wagons that in the next century carried an untold number of Americans to a new life in the western reaches of the nation.

486. *Above, left: a Pennsylvania plank chair, dated 1770, decorated with a leaping stag and stylized heart*

487. *Above, right: a walnut wainscot chair made in the early 18th century, from Chester County, Pennsylvania*

488. *Above: walnut table with heart motif carved into the apron*

489. *Opposite: Pennsylvania German sawbuck table, about 1750*

Style & Tradition

The first homes built by the Pennsylvania Germans were generally log cabins, a type of building common to northern Europe and introduced to America in the seventeenth century by Swedes and Finns. The German colonists used such shelters on a large scale, both in villages and in the country, squaring the logs and notching the corners, as was their traditional practice in log construction, and whitewashing the mortar between the logs, according to an eighteenth-century account, "thus making the house in stripes of alternate white, and dusky wood color." The diligent Germans prospered, fulfilling the persuasive promises of William Penn's handbills circulated throughout Europe in the seventeenth century: "The Richness of the Air, the navigable Rivers, and thus the prodigious Increase of Corn, the flourishing conditions of the City of Philadelphia make it [the colony] the most glorious place." After the French and Indian wars German colonists began to build the fieldstone farmhouses and magnificent barns, as "large as pallaces," which still distinguish much of the countryside where these folk originally settled. The interiors of these later farmhouses were simple and effective—whitewashed plaster walls offset by paneled woodwork on doors, chimney fronts, and stairways. The Pennsylvania Germans cherished their warmth, and their houses were well heated in the German manner by cast-iron or tile stoves decorated with Biblical scenes and sayings. Their fondness for religious themes is illustrated here with the detail (490) from a carved walnut cooky board showing Adam and Eve.

In the solid walnut furniture made by these people traditional forms dating from the Middle Ages were combined with peasant designs remembered from the homeland; the addition of occasional motifs and design elements borrowed from Philadelphia's cabinetmakers created a unique regional expression. The medieval heritage is everywhere evident: in the wainscot chair (487); in the table with flat stretchers and a removable top (488), its odd-shaped drawers a Palatinate pattern; in the sawbuck table with its Gothic X-shaped supports (489); and in the plank chair (486), or Moravian chair, adapted from provincial German forms.

The most imposing piece in a prosperous Pennsylvania German household was the *schrank*, or cupboard, similar to the great *kas* introduced to New Amsterdam by settlers from Holland. This *schrank* (494), a masterpiece of Pennsylvania German craftsmanship, is made of black walnut with an exquisitely patterned inlay, which has the appearance of ivory, but was done with a paste of beeswax and powdered white lead. Wax inlay, a technique known in Germany as *wachseinlegen*, was never used extensively in either Europe or America, particularly in furniture of this size, and was generally restricted to small objects of carved wood or bone.

With this *schrank*, clearly made by a professional, the influence of contemporary fashions is shown in the use of the classic cornice and frieze to surmount a traditional German form. The looking glass (493) also shows an acquaintance with the styles of the moment in its Pennsylvania German interpretation of Chippendale designs. The overlapping of styles, typical of provincial furniture, is further illustrated by the walnut table (491). The fan carvings and the pad feet follow the style of the Queen Anne period; the varisized drawers were traditional in Palatinate tables—one size for cutlery, another for linens.

491. *Opposite, above: a table in the Queen Anne manner with its drawers patterned from earlier European provincial tables*

492. *Opposite, below: a pine settle is typical of the everyday type of furniture made by German settlers. Pieces such as this were made of soft native woods, rather than walnut, and usually gaily painted, although this example was left plain.*

493. *Above, left: the frame of this looking glass suggests the Chippendale style with its elaborate cresting with two hearts (reversed) and the stylized tulip. The band of dentil molding is a classical pattern; the swirling swastika on the apron originated in the ancient world as a symbol for the sun.*

494. *Above, right: a Pennsylvania German* schrank, *dated 1779, decorated in wax inlay simulating the inlay of rare woods*

495. Top: a spice cabinet inlaid with light-toned woods, around 1760

496. Above: richly decorated dower chests were traditionally given a young girl by her father. This example is of walnut with delicate inlay.

497. Top: a walnut watch box with architectural molding and pediment

498. Above: an 18th-century pine table in a traditional provincial form

499. Left: a Moravian side chair with a Queen Anne splat and the seat made of woven splint (thin strips of wood)

500. Below: walnut Bible box, satinwood inlay, from Chester County, Pa., where such inlay was commonly used

501. Center: a cupboard in the English style with hearts and border carved in a German folk pattern

502. Right: a clock with the walnut case in an English pattern, as is the shell inlay above the face; the star and tulip inlays are of folk origin

503. Far right: a Pennsylvania German easy chair covered in leather, with abbreviated wings and a shell with vines carved on the top crest, reputedly owned by "Baron" Stiegel

Like the pieces illustrated on the preceding two pages, this tall clock (502) and corner cupboard (501) reveal the crosscurrents of influences affecting the design of much Pennsylvania furniture. The basic form of these examples follow English styles, but in their inlaid or carved motifs and in minor elements of design they show a debt to continental traditions. The fusion of styles was inevitable. An eighteenth-century Scottish observer wrote, Pennsylvanians "are a people, thrown together from various quarters of the world." For Pennsylvania Germans migrating south, this statement continued to hold true. As one of a group of Moravians noted in his diary, written en route to a German settlement in North Carolina in 1753, an Irishman slept by their fire, an Englishman shared their tea, a Swede their food, a horse was shod by a "Free Negro," whose wife was Scottish, they bought hay from a Swiss, and chatted with a Silesian.

504. Above: the festive custom of decorating an evergreen tree at Christmas time was a German tradition brought to the colonies by German emigrants. As far as is known Lewis Miller's sketch is the first American picture of a Christmas tree. Beside it at the table sits a Negro nursemaid with her three active charges. Although it is not shown in this detail from Miller's crowded page of drawings, he wrote—in both German and English—that "Beef, broth, Salad, and Egs, and good wine, is good for the children." The remainder of the page portrayed three Pennsylvania German townsfolk. "Old Seifert" was shown dipping yarns into a vat of dye (454, page 285), a carpenter, Joseph Wampler, sat at ease with a walking stick in his hands, and the "chymist," Frederick Zercheer, stirred a smoking brew over an open forge. According to Miller's notation Zercheer was making gold in his shop, but the "composition blew up a full discharge."

505. Left: in this view of farm life a hog is strung up by its heels from an overhead branch and slaughtered by "Old Mrs. Hausman," who appears to be a husky, unsqueamish countrywoman, adept with her butcher knife and evidently well versed in the art of dressing an animal carcass.

The Living Past

A record of the day-to-day life of a community of Pennsylvania Germans has survived, remarkably, in a portfolio of nearly two thousand water-color sketches by a self-taught artist, Lewis Miller, who was a carpenter by trade and was born in York, Pennsylvania, in 1796. Although Miller's German neighbors are portrayed in the opening years of the nineteenth century, they represent a continuity of customs and events that would have been much the same during the colonial era. The brewer, the bootmaker, the snuff maker, the weaver enjoying a "Small Beer, and Eating pretzels, and Gingerbread," raccoon hunters returning from the field, all were portrayed by Miller's brush, even to the local fortuneteller at her cards. He drew himself (506) smiling and briskly busy at his carpenter's bench. In another self-portrait he drew a handsome, auburn-curled dandy with sideburns, a white stock and vest, and blue frock coat. No event in the town of York seems to have passed unnoticed, and Miller reported dates and facts in his notebooks, both in German and English. The unfortunate Anthony Ritz sawed through the limb on which he sat in a cherry tree and came down "Roaring most terribly." A steer escaped and ran into Jacob Rupp's kitchen, "Breaking and crushing the earthen ware to piece's." George Geistweit's pet fox came loose from his chain but was found entangled in thread spread to bleach on the grass in Philip Decker's lot. Christian Lehman grew a pumpkin so large "no man could lift it." Mrs. Schiley, who sold herring, hard soap, and candles, lived to be ninety-eight.

506

Miller included sprightly views of a Methodist camp meeting, of fairs, parades, a visit from the "Dover Riflemen," and Sheriff Kleinfelter riding up to the jailhouse with an armed posse. He also sketched "Immigrants on the Way through York" in their covered wagon, and a gentleman from France taking a spill into a York snowbank when the sleigh in which he was riding abruptly overturned. Miller painted an interior of the Lutheran church, its pews crowded with parishioners, "The Singing Choir" grouped around the pipe organ in the choir loft. And as Pastor Jacob Goering delivers his sermon, one member of the congregation stokes the stove that stands in the center of the church, and the sexton chases a stray dog from the service.

507. Top: Miller often did reminiscent scenes from his childhood. Here he showed himself, aged four, in the office of Dr. John Morris on Main Street, where he had been taken by his father to be treated for ringworm. The infection on his cheek was rubbed with spirit of vitriol, which "hurt and burnt me."

508. Above: against the setting of the Geiger farm with its log buildings and assorted livestock the strawberry pickers are led through the garden by the music of a shepherd's pipe.

509. Left: a small scholar sits on a bench to study, in this detail from Miller's memory of classes held at the Lutheran schoolhouse, as a music lesson was given the other students.

510. Above: a bucket brigade and a hand pump fight a York fire. "Mrs. Wilt was taken out of the window, out of the upper Story."

511. Below: "Stepfan a good violin player and his companien a German" at the dulcimer provide music for dancing at a York party.

512. Below: "Old Style cooking, the Bake oven, baking Bread," Miller noted in his praise of the good cooking at York's taverns.

513. Right: a trumpet quintet playing a hymn written by the village schoolmaster at the consecration of York's Moravian church

514

A Colorful Heritage

Although the art of illuminating manuscripts gradually died out in Europe with the widespread use of movable type, it continued to be practiced by Pennsylvania Germans in a vital and decorative expression of folk art known as *fraktur*. The word *fraktur* comes from a sixteenth-century German type face, which in turn was a copy of an ancient style of penmanship. Among Pennsylvania Germans the term *fraktur* was used for both illuminated calligraphy and for ornamental drawings, usually in the symmetrical form that typifies peasant art, as does the ink and watercolor *fraktur* above (514). Folk stories were also illustrated (528), this one being a humorous anecdote about the "Seven Swabians," the proverbial country bumpkins in German lore who set forth in fear and trembling to slay a monster, which turned out to be nothing more ferocious than a hare.

Birth and baptismal certificates, or *taufscheine*, often made by itinerant artists, were intricately and elaborately illuminated (515), and were favored by those sects that believed in infant baptism, such as the Lutheran and Reformed churches, whereas the Amish and Mennonites, for example, did not. The *taufschein* shown here is also embellished with two verses of a hymn often sung at baptismal ceremonies and frequently used on this type of *fraktur*: "I am baptised! I am in the Covenant Through baptism with my God." Biblical quotations, house blessings, copybooks, hymnals, and religious poetry were also patiently and brilliantly lettered and illuminated, particularly by clergymen, schoolmasters, and by members of religious communities such as the Ephrata Cloisters. The recurring motifs found in *fraktur*—traditional peasant designs—are the same motifs used by the Pennsylvania Germans in their lively and colorfully painted household furnishings.

515. Opposite: Catharina Seiffert's birth and baptismal certificate, 1789, topped with a merry band of dancing musicians

Verzeichnis dieses Tauffscheins daß
Catharina Seiffertin ist geboren den 10ten
tag Julius im Jahr unsers Herrn Jesu Christi
1789 in Lower Saccon Taunschip in Northampton Caunty
in dem Staat Pennsilvanien, ihr Vatter war Johannes
Seiffert und die Mutter Dorothea — Nach ihrer
burt haben ihre liebe Christliche Eltern sie nach d
Jesu Christi zur heiligen Tauffe bestätigen la
Herrn Pfarr Schwalbach getauft und in den heili
bund Jesu Christi einverleibet worden, da denn
Seiffert und Catharina Raubin ihr Tauff
gen waren und ihr den obigen Christlichen Namen gegeben.
Ich bin getauft, ich steh im bunde,
Durch meine Tauff mit meinen Gott,
So sprech ich stets mit frohen munde,
In Kreutz in trübsal angst und Noth,
Ich bin getauft, des freu ich mich,
Daß Jesus freud bleibt ewiglich.
Ich bin getauft, ob ich gleich sterbe,
Was schadet mir das küle grab,
Ich weiß mein vaterland und erbe,
Daß ich bey Gott im himmel hab,
Nach meinem tod ist mir bereit
Die himmels freud die seligkeit.
Gott geb ihr glück und segen Gesundheit allerwegen,
ihr schild soll Jesus seyn und Jesum zum Trost allein

516. Above: the paneling on this Pennsylvania chest of drawers, as well as the birds and the angels, is characteristic of Germanic styles.

517. Right: clockcase decorated with a bird, urns, flowers, leaves, and blossoming vines

518. Opposite: this flowered detail comes from one panel of a blanket chest made in 1794 for Elizabeth Hockessen, Dauphin County, Pa.

519. *Above:* fraktur *of gaily clad women, trimly uniformed soldiers, stout trumpeting angels, and mythical birds amid flowers and hearts*

520. *Opposite: the brightly painted lid of an oval wooden splint box, presumably a bride box, traditionally given the bride by the bridegroom*

OVERLEAF: *left, top to bottom.* 521. *Pine and poplar chest, one of many versions of the unicorn motif with horsemen, typical of Berks County, Pa.*

522. *Boxes with sliding lids were used to store candles. This example, made around 1800, was ornamented with a stylized vine and grape clusters.*

523. *This pine candlebox was painted in 1777 with the classical folk pattern of vivid tulips and the geometric star seen on Pennsylvania German barns.*

Right, top to bottom. 524. *Pennsylvania German craftsmen rarely signed their work, but this pine and poplar chest bears the name of its decorator, Christian Selzer, 1749–1831, Jonestown, Lebanon County, Pa., who scratched his signature on the painted vases. Selzer decorated many such chests.*

525. *Chests decorated with birds, as this one dated 1782 with doves and peacocks on the panels, were particularly popular in Lancaster County, Pa.*

526. *Freshly mixed dough was set to rise in wooden troughs. The dough trough shown here is poplar; its decorations are attributed to Selzer.*

Im Jahr

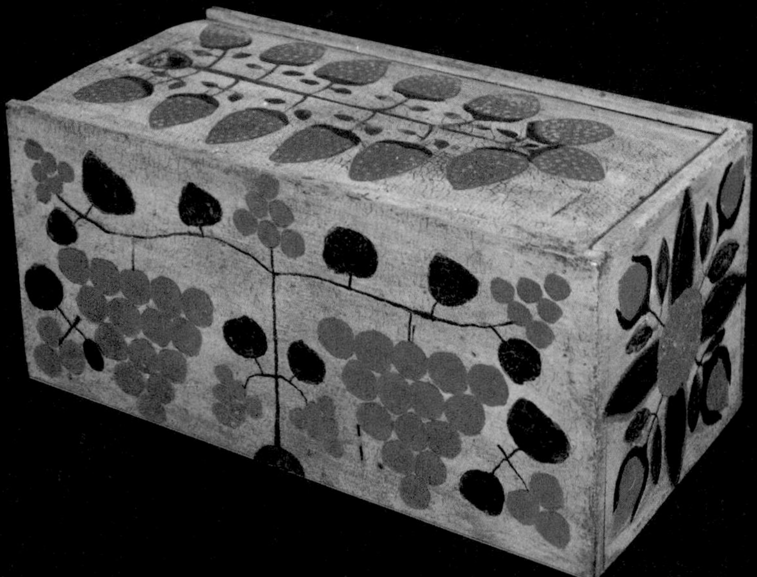

IA COB
RICKERT
AN NO

527. *Above: detail of a quotation from the 34th Psalm illuminated in* fraktur, *1802*

528. *Below:* fraktur *illustration of the Old World folk tale of the "Seven Swabians"*

529. *Above:* fraktur *of "Georg General Waschingdon" and his "Ledy"*

530. *Below: women's faces, an unusual motif, decorate a pine chest.*

Wares of Tin

Very little tinware was made in America before the Revolution. England, with her rich tin mines in Cornwall, shipped finished articles rather than the raw materials in accordance with her restrictive trade policies designed to discourage independent colonial industry. But in the years following the Revolution tinware became an important American product, and whitesmiths, as workers in tin were called, busily manufactured a remarkable assortment of objects, from everyday household utensils to trinket boxes, speaking trumpets, toys, and trunks. Tinkers, or tin peddlers, ranged throughout the country, carrying their pack of wares on foot, or on horseback, or traveling in wagons laden with "as many tin vessels as the horse can conveniently draw." Although the colonial years had passed, Pennsylvania German whitesmiths clung to the folk patterns they had always loved, and their tinware carried the familiar motifs of birds, tulips, hearts, stars, and clusters of fruit. The metal used was not entirely of tin, but a thin sheet of iron dipped in molten tin, which protected the iron from rust and was easy to solder at the joints. The brightly painted pieces are generally called toleware, an adaptation of the japanned tin originally made in the Far East, and many early examples, such as this (534), may have been imported from England. Unpainted tin, if not left plain, was engraved, pierced, or punched.

531. Top: a cooky cutter. 532. Above: an engraved coffeepot

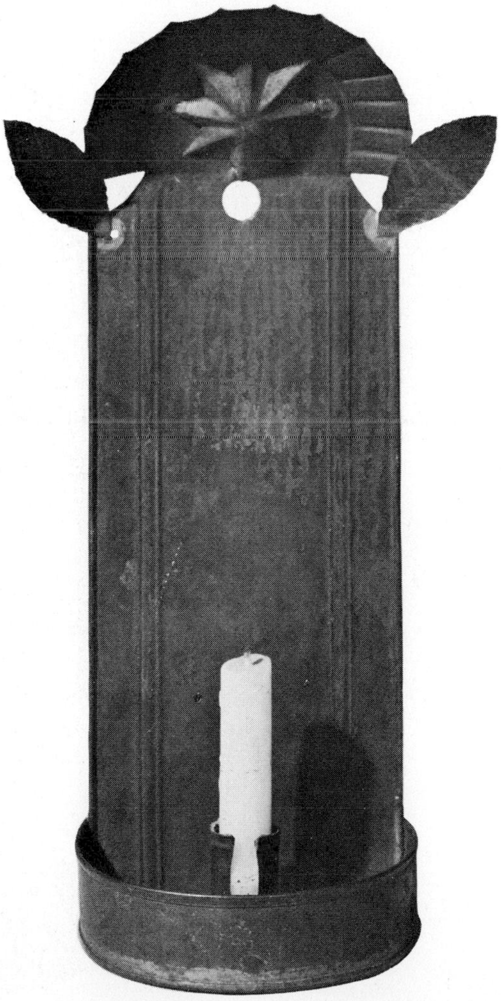

533. Top: a chandelier made with curving tin supports

534. Above: a toleware coffeepot with bright designs

535. Right: candleholder with crimped trim and a star; the tall, narrow back designed to serve as a reflector

Designs in Pottery

In their pottery the Pennsylvania German artisans displayed the traditional deftness and imaginative sense of decoration that so clearly distinguishes all handicrafts of these resourceful people. Again, the familiar Old World motifs were used. The tulip design was shaped, for example, into the base of the handle on the pottery mug (541), which is inscribed: "I say what is true and drink what is clear." Birds abound, in toy figurines (536), in the water whistle (547), or *wasserpfeife*, on a jar (545), and on the plate made for Cadarina Raeder (543), which in this instance is decorated with the double-headed eagle, a familiar German insignia presumably introduced into Europe during the Crusades from Turkoman emblems. A pie plate (537) pictures a horseman dressed as a soldier or a cavalier. His antecedents reach back into European folk stories telling of ghostly riders on ghostly horses leading "armies which were in heaven," a direct reference to one of the four horsemen of the apocalypse described in *The Revelation*: "And I saw heaven opened, and behold a white horse; and he that sat upon him was called Faithful and True."

Humorous sayings were also popular. A plate (538) bears the sly message that, "God hath created all the beautiful maidens. They are for the potter, but not for the priests." And on the shaving basin (548), appropriately patterned with a cake of soap, scissors, razor, and comb, the words are fair warning to the "poor beard" that it will be lathered and separated from its "hide."

536. Opposite: toy pottery figures of a hen and rooster done in a yellow glaze with brown tail feathers, combs, and wings
537. Above: a schimmelreiter, *the bold rider on a white horse, was a traditional figure in German folklore and decoration.*

538. *A courtship scene, dated "October, Anno 1793"*

539. *Left: a slip ware dish, made about 1769.* 540. *Right: sgraffito decorations with an eight-pointed star as the central motif*

541. *Mug with inscription and peasant designs*

542. *A plate with fish, an early Christian symbol*

543. *Left: a dish made for Cadarina Raeder, dated 1786.* 544. *Right: an earthenware plate with sgraffito floral decorations*

545. *Jar patterned in polka-dot birds and tulips*

546. Above: Pennsylvania German cupboard, the open shelves arrayed with earthenware

547. Opposite: a bird-shaped water whistle. 548. Far right: a slip ware shaving basin

The application of patterns onto pottery fell into two basic techniques, slip decoration and sgraffito. Both these methods are among the most ancient of the ceramic arts, and as used by the Pennsylvania Germans, both were colorful additions to the already colorful local clay, which turned to a deep reddish-brown when baked in a kiln.

Slip decorations were drawn with goose quills filled with a light-colored liquid clay, or "slip," which was imported from New Jersey. The designs, applied before the final firing of the pottery, were often nothing more than initials or a name or a random squiggle across the face of a plate, but line drawings of such motifs as birds and flowers were frequently made, and slip ware was also done in highly elaborate patterns, as it was on the dish (539) with two rows of inscriptions encircling a bouquet.

Sgraffito, a word derived from the Italian verb *sgraffiare*, to scratch, was a technique extensively used by Pennsylvania German potters. The design was, indeed, achieved by "scratching"; the piece to be decorated was coated with New Jersey slip, into which the pattern was incised with a sharp stick, thus revealing the red clay base underneath. This method was used on the mug (541) and brightly decorated plates illustrated on the preceding pages (537, 538, 542, 543, and 544).

A pottery noted for its fine wares was also thriving in the Moravian town of Bethabara, North Carolina. So proficient were these German artisans, not only in ceramics but in all their crafts, that when a competition among local industries was planned by the provincial congress at Hillsboro in 1775, a request was submitted "to debar the Moravians, for they would win all the premiums."

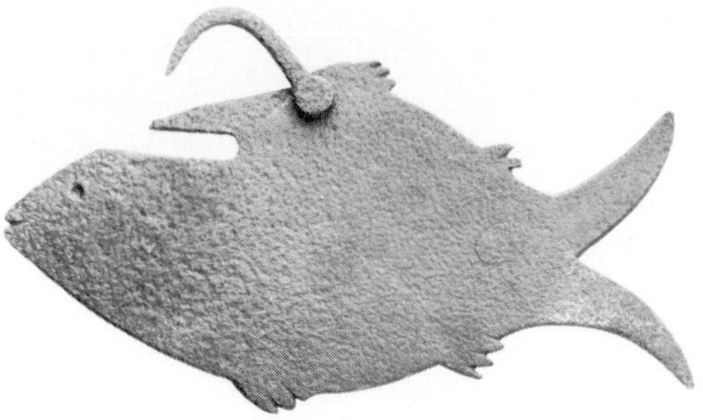

Hammer & Anvil

Michel Jean de Crèvecoeur, the French consul to the United States from 1783 to 1790, declared that the unrivaled prosperity of Pennsylvania owed much to the mechanical knowledge of its German-born artisans. Among the thousands upon thousands of Palatinate emigrants arriving during the 1700's were appreciable numbers of trained ironworkers and blacksmiths. These men found a ready market for their skills in Pennsylvania, which was well on its way to becoming the center of American iron manufacture. The colony was rich in the natural resources necessary for production—limestone for flux, timber for charcoal, and the ore, as many early travelers remarked, often lay just below the surface of the ground and could be mined with no more complicated equipment than a crowbar and pickaxe and similar rudimentary tools.

By 1776 eighty-one ironworks of one type or another had been set up in Pennsylvania—blast furnaces, forges, plating mills, slitting mills, steel furnaces, and bloomeries. The extent and variety of production is remarkable in view of the Iron Act of 1750, in which the opening paragraph firmly stated that the bill had been drawn up by Parliament "to prevent the Erection of any Mill or other Engine for Slitting or Rolling of Iron; or any Plateing Forge to work with a Tilt Hammer; or any Furnace for making Steel in any of the said Colonies." The law, however, had been flouted, and with the outbreak of the Revolution Pennsylvania's iron industry was largely responsible for the vitally needed manufacture of cannon, mortars, shells, and shot. In Northampton County, gunsmiths—often of Swiss or German background—were excused from combat.

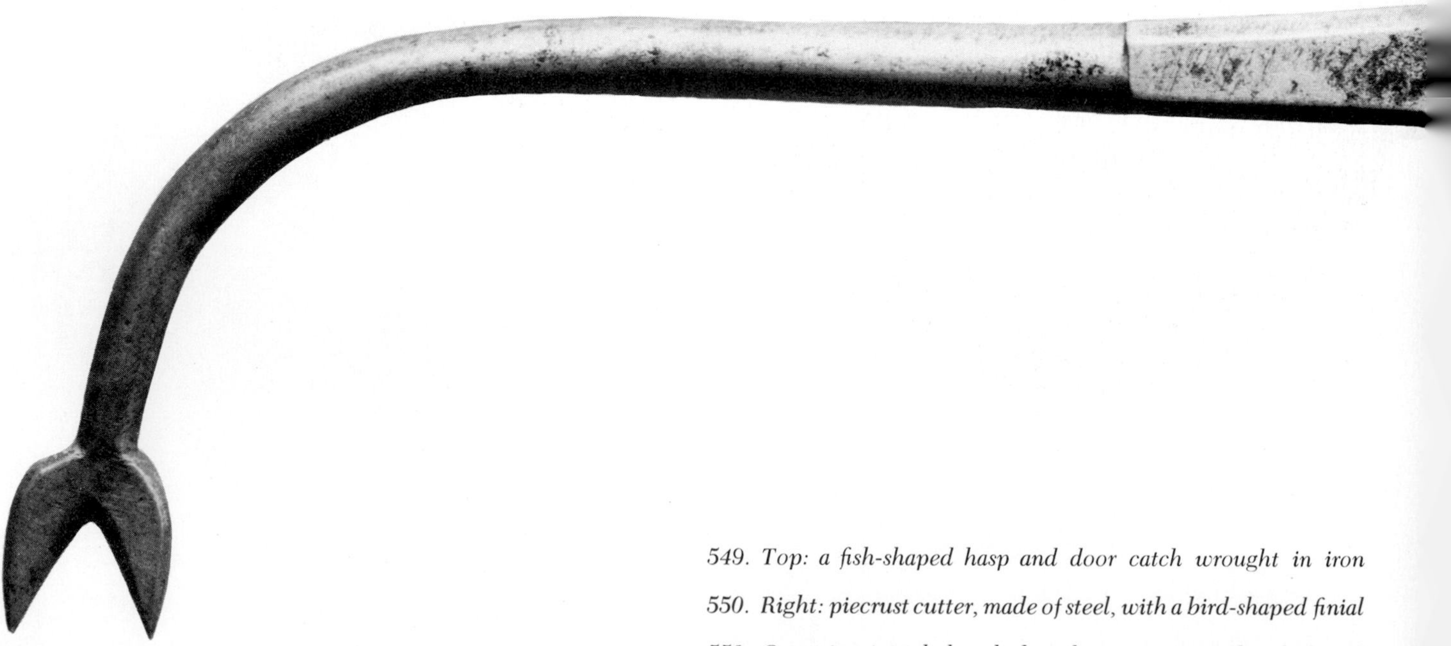

549. Top: a fish-shaped hasp and door catch wrought in iron

550. Right: piecrust cutter, made of steel, with a bird-shaped finial

551. Opposite: initialed and chased scraper for a dough board

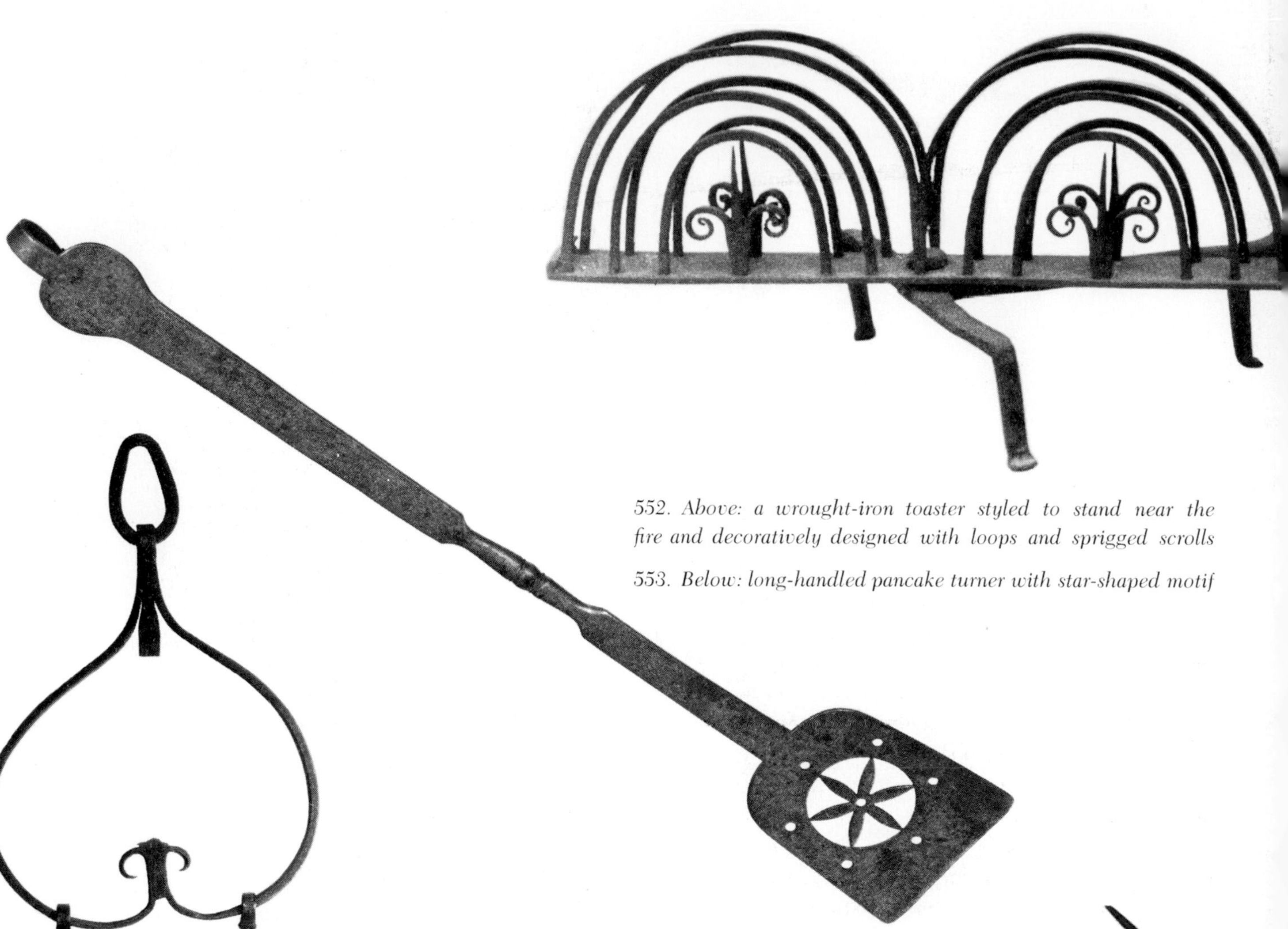

552. *Above: a wrought-iron toaster styled to stand near the fire and decoratively designed with loops and sprigged scrolls*

553. *Below: long-handled pancake turner with star-shaped motif*

554. *Left: double trammel for hanging pots over an open fire*

555. *Right: 18th-century Pennsylvania German meat fork with the heart pattern worked into the design of the three tines*

556. *Opposite: door latch in the skillful and elaborate style typical of ironwork wrought by the Pennsylvania German smiths*

The importance of the blacksmith in early America is best shown by the number at work, as compared with the number of men in other metal trades. In Bucks County, Pennsylvania, for example, between 1750 and 1800 there were one hundred and four blacksmiths, but only one tinsmith, one edge-tool maker, one brass founder, and so forth. In the town of Lancaster, alone, thirteen blacksmiths were listed in the 1770's. Pennsylvania German smiths at their forges and anvils, working the bar iron bought from Pennsylvania's furnaces, fashioned the household and farm implements needed by their neighbors, and with their inbred tradition of European folk designs they left few objects in iron undecorated. Hasps and hinges of Conestoga wagon toolboxes were forged in flowering patterns, waffle irons in heart designs, cranes and ladles with ornamental motifs. As can be seen by the objects on these pages, all of which are Pennsylvania German, theirs was probably the most accomplished and intricate of early American wrought iron.

"Baron Stiegel ist der Mann"

Although it is somewhat less euphonious, the name Henry William Stiegel is as celebrated among early American glassmakers as the name Benvenuto Cellini is among Renaissance goldsmiths. It would stretch the point to carry the analogy much further. However, there does seem to have been something in Stiegel's temperament and personality—at least in so far as can be gathered from legend and the rather scanty surviving documentation—more akin to the picaresque Cellini than to the sober, conservative folk who emigrated from the Rhine Valley.

Like most settlers of the Pennsylvania German country, Stiegel was industrious and religious. Unlike most of them, however, he was a slaveholder (if only on a small scale), and an inordinately vain fellow much given to ostentation—ruinously so, in fact—and altogether lacking in the prudence that enabled lesser men to succeed commercially where he failed. A self-styled "baron" (apparently he used the assumed title sparingly), Stiegel lived in baronial splendor, maintaining a mansion, two fantastical castles, a private fort, and—at least according to persistent legend—a coach and eight complete with liveried outriders, blaring trumpets, and pack of hounds in full cry. Upon the "baron's" arrival at or departure from one or another of his residences or factories (so the legend continues), a cannon salute would be fired from the towers erected for that purpose. A part-time orchestra made up of his glass-works employees would break into music when he returned from a journey.

Heinrich Wilhelm Stiegel was born near Cologne in 1729 and emigrated to Philadelphia, along with his widowed mother and a younger brother, in 1750, at about the peak of the German immigration to Pennsylvania. Almost nothing is known of Stiegel's early life in the Rhineland or of the year or so he spent in Philadelphia. He is next heard of in Lancaster County working for an iron founder whose daughter, Elizabeth Huber, he married in 1752.

By 1756 Stiegel was a partner in the ironworks, which was by then being run on a co-operative basis and which he named Elizabeth Furnace. Four years later Stiegel became a "natural born" subject of Great Britain, and officially Anglicized his name to Henry William Stiegel. He was by then a community leader—an enthusiastic supporter of education and a lay delegate to the Lutheran Ministerium of Pennsylvania.

At this point in his career, Stiegel's future seemed assured. Elizabeth Furnace had been modernized, a small company town had been built around it, and the whole operation had expanded enormously under Stiegel's energetic direction. The factory's most lucrative products were stoves, heating devices, and "IRON CASTINGS, Of all dimensions and sizes, such as kettles or boilers for pot-ash works, soap boilers pans, pots, from a barrel to 300 gallons, ship cabooses, kachels, and sugar-house stoves, with cast funnels of any height for refining sugars, weights of all sizes, grate-bars, and other castings for sugar-works in the West-Indies, &c...all done by HENRY WILLIAM STIEGEL, iron-master."

Even though Stiegel held only a part interest in the concern, he was never one

to hide his light. Stove plates were cast with a German verse inscribed upon them, unequivocally informing colonial America that when it came to making a fine stove, "*Baron Stiegel ist der Mann*"—one place where he did use his self-bestowed title. Various kinds of stoves were apparently produced, one a version of Franklin's earlier "Pennsylvanian Fire-place," others in German designs, including a tall, cylindrical "cannon stove" adorned with tulips cast in the upper drums.

By the 1760's he seemed well on his way to becoming one of the most successful businessmen in America. Elizabeth Furnace was prospering apace and Stiegel acquired a second ironworks, Charming Forge, near Womelsdorf, along with considerable acreage at the future site of Manheim township. His wife had died in the meantime (and had been buried beneath a lugubrious and long-winded inscription that began: "Here rests Elizabeth lifeless given over to worms..."), but eight months later Stiegel had found himself another Elizabeth—Elizabeth Hölz, a native Philadelphian of German extraction—and married her. During this period little took place to indicate that Stiegel's story would end tragically—or that he would eventually win lasting fame in an entirely different field.

Stiegel's first glassware was produced at Elizabeth Furnace in 1763, a venture that was primarily of an experimental nature. Where the ten craftsmen he recruited for this operation got their experience is not known. In any case, the wares, which were produced under the supervision of his brother, Anthony, were restricted for the most part to window glass and green bottles in various sizes. The Elizabeth Furnace output was sold in and around Lancaster, Reading, and York, and the effect on Stiegel of the initial results of his fledgling enterprise added to his enthusiasm. Three days after he had fired up his glass oven for the first time, Stiegel made the first of a series of money withdrawals for a trip to England, where he apparently intended to acquaint himself with advanced glassmaking techniques, and where he hoped to find a new complement of well-trained European artisans.

On Stiegel's return to America, he and his partners lost little time in setting up a glassworks on their holdings some ten miles north of Lancaster. The place was called Manheim, it was to be self-sustaining, and its chief source of sustenance was to be the glassworks. "This day the glass ovens being finished the fire was put in," reads an account book entry for October 29, 1765. And a week later, "paid 16/ for 4 gallons of rum treating the workmen. Charged to building account." On November 11, 1765, Stiegel's ambitious enterprise went into

operation. By mid-April, 1766, the Manheim glassworks ended its first season, "the workmen being worn out." (Glassblowing was arduous work and injurious to the health; the men usually worked only part of a year.) The first two seasons were fairly prosperous, but business subsequently went downhill, until 1769 when Stiegel built a larger and better-equipped glassworks staffed with upward of one hundred and thirty hands, including Venetian, German, Irish, and English workers, all engaged in producing "American FLINT GLASS [as well as other kinds]...equal in quality with any imported from *Europe*." Distribution agencies were set up in York, Carlisle, Lancaster, Reading, Hanover, Lebanon, Heidelberg, and other Pennsylvania German communities, and later, farther afield, in Philadelphia, Boston, New York, and Baltimore.

With Manheim prospering and Stiegel glass selling well, the "baron's" inclination toward conspicuous consumption became a headlong slide. He allegedly imported such luxuries as bricks from England and tapestries and musical instruments from Europe, maintained several lavishly appointed establishments, and treated himself to a degree of pomp that might have given pause to the holder of an authentic baronetcy. Stiegel might have survived the financial havoc wrought by his self-indulgent way of life had good times continued. Unfortunately they did not; money became increasingly tight in the colonies, taxes became more and more oppressive, and far more prudent men than Stiegel began to feel the pinch. Stiegel himself, however, instead of pulling in his horns, gave free reign to ever more grandiose schemes. He had mortgaged his two ironworks and his real-estate holdings to build the second glass factory. For a while he managed somehow to stay afloat even while more cautiously run enterprises foundered, but by the end of 1772 the bubble burst. Creditors were hounding Stiegel on all sides, and in a desperate effort to stave off complete financial collapse, he embarked on an elaborate lottery scheme that failed resoundingly. Mortgages were foreclosed, unpaid employees were discharged, and, in 1774, Stiegel went into debtor's prison. On Christmas Eve of that year he was freed but relieved of virtually all his earthly belongings. In 1776 he

was offered employment by the new proprietor of his old foundry, Elizabeth Furnace, which was then turning out cannon balls for the Continental Army. When the battle front shifted from southeastern Pennsylvania, cannon ball production at the forge was discontinued and Stiegel was out of a job.

Stiegel spent the next few years eking out a meager living as a schoolteacher. He died in poverty at Charming Forge on January 10, 1785.

It is difficult to isolate the truth in Stiegel's life story. The glass associated with his name includes the finest, most colorful examples from the colonial period. Yet there is hardly a piece than can with any assurance be finally attributed to his glasshouses. But the legend of the man persists. Each June the town of Manheim holds its Rose Festival, during which the Lutheran church pays a a nominal annual rent of one red rose for the land the "baron" gave them nearly two centuries ago.

German Glassmakers

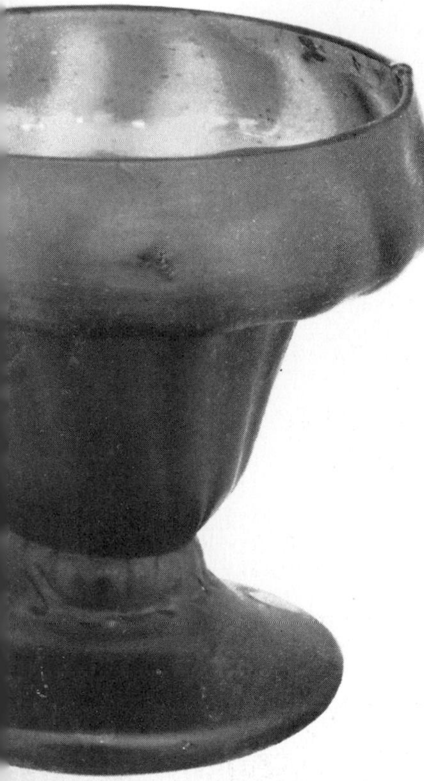

557. A pattern-molded saltcellar

558. A Stiegel-type tea caddy engraved with floral decoration

559. A bottle that may have been blown at Wistar's glasshouse for Wm. Savery, Philadelphia cabinetmaker; dated 1752 on the seal

"Be sure to furnish yourselves with...glasse for windows," wrote the Reverend Francis Higginson to prospective colonists shortly after the settlement of the Massachusetts Bay colony. By then, two short-lived glassmaking experiments at Jamestown had already failed. The need for window glass and bottles was persistent, imported glass was expensive, but for more than a century to come no colonial glasshouse enjoyed more than a brief and partial success. The first successful producers of glass in America were German immigrants: Caspar Wistar, Henry William Stiegel, and John Frederick Amelung. They all employed skilled European craftsmen. Wistar opened his glasshouse in Salem County, New Jersey, in 1739. It was the first enduring operation of the kind in the colonies, continuing after Caspar's death, in 1752, under the direction of his son, Richard, until 1780. Stiegel operated three separate glasshouses in Pennsylvania (see pages 338–39) from 1763 to 1774 and acquired a lasting reputation in the process. Both men manufactured window glass and bottles along with a variety of other forms. Stiegel, particularly, advertised for sale more types of glassware than can today be identified. In 1771 the American Philosophical Society judged his products "equal in beauty and quality" to English imports.

560. Cream pitcher of expanded, pattern-molded design, possibly made by Stiegel

561. Two Stiegel-type flasks with enameled decorations and inscriptions in German

Virtually no surviving glassware can with certainty be attributed to the Wistar or Stiegel factories. However, the examples shown here are types that have been associated with their output. The bottle (559) and covered bowl (566) may have been made at Wistar's works. The enamelers and glass cutters listed in Stiegel's account books no doubt produced canisters (558), flasks (561), and flip glasses (562) with naïvely colored and engraved decorations, similar to the commodity glass of southern Germany and central Europe. Other workmen, following English precedent, produced salts (557), cream pitchers (560), bottles (563), bowls (565), and other forms enriched with graduated designs formed by the expansion of patterns impressed on a small gathering of glass before it was expanded.

562. Upper left: Stiegel-type enameled flip glass similar to those that were made in Germany and elsewhere on the Continent

563. Left: toilet-water bottle, with an expanded-mold design in a daisy-in-a-diamond pattern, associated with Stiegel's work

564. Above: a glass hunting horn expanded and shaped after the original gathering of glass had been dipped in a pattern mold

565. Opposite, top: a covered, pattern-molded sugar bowl with spiral finial of a type believed to have been made by Stiegel

566. Opposite, bottom: a two-handled, covered sugar bowl probably made in southern New Jersey in the late 18th century

On February 13, 1789, George Washington wrote to Thomas Jefferson, "A desire of encouraging whatever is useful and economical seems now generally to prevail. Several capitol [sic!] artists, in different branches, have lately arrived in this Country. A factory of Glass is established, upon a large scale on Monocasy, near Frederick-Town in Maryld." The last sentence referred to the New Bremen Glassmanufactory established by Amelung some years earlier. (One month after Washington wrote this letter, Amelung presented the President with two large goblets engraved with the Washington arms.) Amelung had arrived in America from Bremen, Germany, in 1784 armed with letters of recommendation from John Adams and Benjamin Franklin, both of whom were then in Europe, and funds provided by backers in Bremen. He was accompanied by sixty-eight experienced workmen.

In all subsequent advertisements he offered to supply the public with "all kinds of flint glass such as decanters with glasses; tumblers, all sizes; every other sort of table glass," which he would embellish with "cut devices, syphers; Coats of Arms or any other Fancy figures." The illustrations on these two pages, all plausibly identified as examples of his output, indicate the high level of his performance along these lines. One of his earliest products was a presentation goblet (569), or *pokal*, engraved with the arms of the city of Bremen and inscribed in part, "Old Bremen Success and the New Progress." Here and in the other pieces illustrated the engraving is skillfully varied in the depth of cutting and precise in the indication of detail, in contrast to the roughly ground motifs on Stiegel-type examples. The venture collapsed in 1795 and Amelung's craftsmen went on to other factories elsewhere.

567. An engraved sugar bowl, probably made at New Bremen for Miss Catherine Geeting

568. *A presentation piece for Amelung's wife*

569. A pokal *sent to Amelung's backers in Bremen*

570. *Drinking glass with Masonic emblems*

571. *Right: engraved detail from a flip glass by Amelung for George and Metha Repold*

Colonial Glassmaking

In the Middle Ages crafts and guilds were referred to as "mysteries," suggesting that secret skills were involved in their occupations. No craft practiced in colonial America better deserved the term than glassmaking. To transform opaque and inert solid materials into a glowing liquid mass that could then be worked into infinitely varied, transparent, and even lustrous shapes required skills and knowledge that to most people bordered on wizardry. Most early American glassmakers were lured from European factories; they followed formulas and methods that had been handed down with little change from century to century. The operations of the colonial craftsman, in fact, differed little from those familiar to the artisans of Sidon, Alexandria, and other glassmaking centers of the ancient Roman Empire.

The essential ingredients of colonial glass were silica, usually in the form of sand, and such alkalies as potash, carbonate of soda or lime, plus certain accessory materials depending on the type and color of glass desired. Much colonial glass was colored, either fortuitously or by intent. Common bottle and window glass, made of relatively unrefined ingredients, was green in color because of certain metallic oxides present as impurities in the raw materials. Other oxides were used to produce artificial colors. However, a clear glass was also produced by the use of black oxide of manganese, called glass soap.

By substituting an oxide of red lead for soda or lime a softer, more lustrous glass—called "lead" or "flint" glass—was achieved. In its clear state this was also called crystal glass, although the word "crystal" had been used for centuries to denote glass of any composition that approached the clarity and purity of rock crystal. (There are as many recipes for glassmaking as there are for making a cake.) These materials, called the "batch," were "cooked" in clay crucibles that were constructed for the purpose with the same painstaking care that went into the production of the finest porcelain and that were allowed to age for at least a year before they were put to use. Even so the crucibles lasted only a limited time—a matter of months. Before the glassmaking actually began, the crucibles, or melting pots, were fired to white heat in the furnace; only then were they ready for the batch, to which bits of cleansed and broken glass, called "cullet," had been added to help the fusion of the various ingredients. Under a heat of about 2500 degrees F. these were reduced in a day or two to a molten state. When vitrification was complete the furnace temperature was somewhat lowered to cool the fluid mass to a plastic state in which it could be manipulated.

From that point three basic tools were used to fashion the end product, a blowpipe, a pontil or punty rod, and some sort of shaping tool, although others were used for various special purposes and other factory equipment was required to facilitate the use of those tools. To start, a workman secured from the melting pot a gather of the red-hot glass on a blowpipe and rolled this on the polished surface of a marver to give the material its first shape and an even surface. This blob was then inflated by blowing on the pipe until it reached a workable size and form. The pipe was then handed to the master craftsman, or "gaffer," who sat at a specially designed chair. Resting the

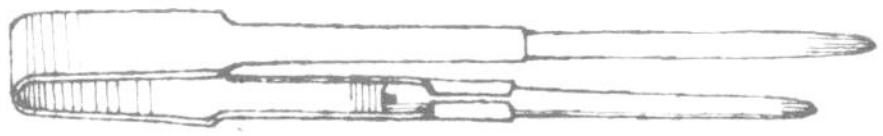

pipe on the slanting arms of his chair, the gaffer rolled the pipe with his left hand to keep the blob of glass in constant rotation to prevent it from becoming lopsided. Meanwhile, he manipulated it with his right hand to shape the piece, using a pair of iron tongs (pucellas), and a wooden paddle (battledore) to flatten the bottom. From time to time as the glass cooled it had to be reheated in the furnace before work could continue; to know just when to do this called for experienced judgment. In the hands of a skilled gaffer the glass could be worked into any conceivable shape. While the glass was still hot other elements could be added to the body of a piece, such as the stems and bases of glasses, the handles of pitchers, and thin threads or heavier overlays for decorative effects.

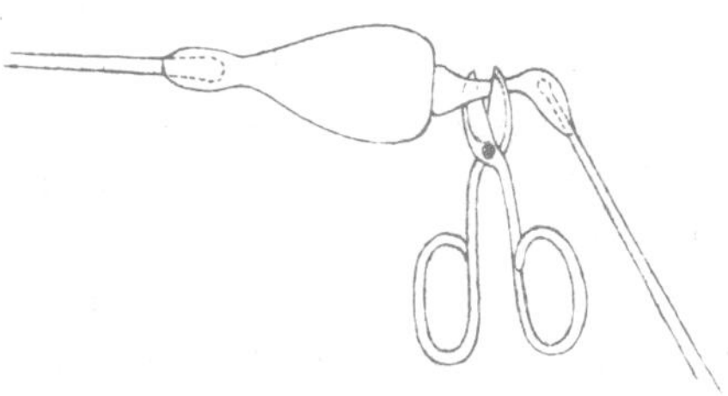

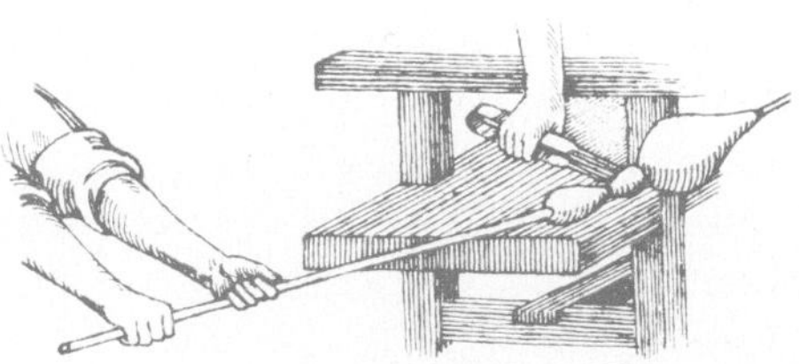

To complete the blowpipe end of a form, the punty was fixed to the opposite, or base end by means of a small glob of molten glass; the blowpipe was then detached by touching the wet ends of the pucellas to the hot glass, causing a fracture, and tapping the pipe free. With shears and shaping tools the open end was worked to its final size and outline, such as the rim of a drinking vessel or the curved lip of a pitcher. When the punty was ultimately knocked off the finished piece, it left the rough punty mark on the base, a characteristic of old glass made by such methods.

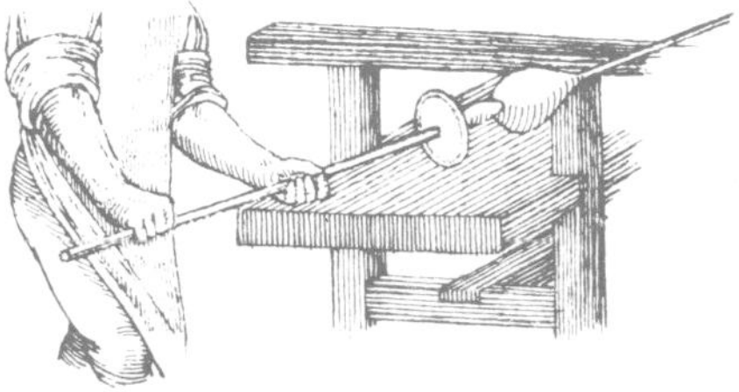

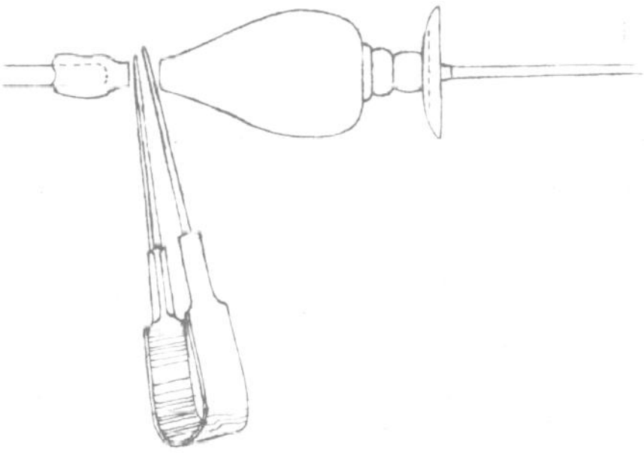

There were other ways of varying the shape and pattern of glass objects. In the case of many examples that are attributed to Stiegel, for instance, the first gathering of molten glass from the furnace was inflated directly into a small, open-top mold, about one third, or less, the size of the finished article and with intaglio patterns cut into the interior surface of the mold. When the decorative pattern had been impressed on the sufficiently inflated gather, the latter was contracted enough to be withdrawn from the mold and then blown and otherwise fashioned to its final size and shape. As the piece was blown larger the impressed pattern expanded, much like the printed design on a child's balloon, more here, less there, in subtle gradations according to the degree of expansion of the form.

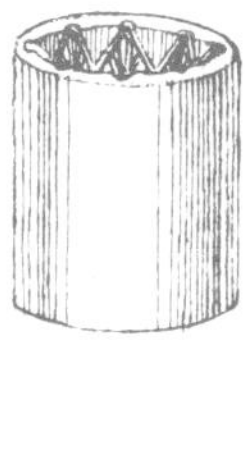

Much of the window glass used in colonial America was of "crown" glass, made by blowing a large gathering into a bulbous mass, attaching the punty to the opposite end, and breaking off the blowpipe. The opened "bubble" was then spun vigorously, constantly reheated to keep it workable, until by centrifugal force it reached the form of a relatively flat disc. After it was cooled the disc was cut into diamond- or square-shaped panes of glass. The center of the disc, when the punty was knocked off, was an irregularly conical protuberance called a "bull's-eye."

No piece of glass was ready for service until it had been first reheated and then very gradually cooled in an annealing oven. Glass that is cooled too quickly will break into fragments. From beginning to end the process of completing a piece of glass required time for preparation, more time for finishing, and in between quick judgments, co-operative skills, and business organization greater than that of any of the other crafts.

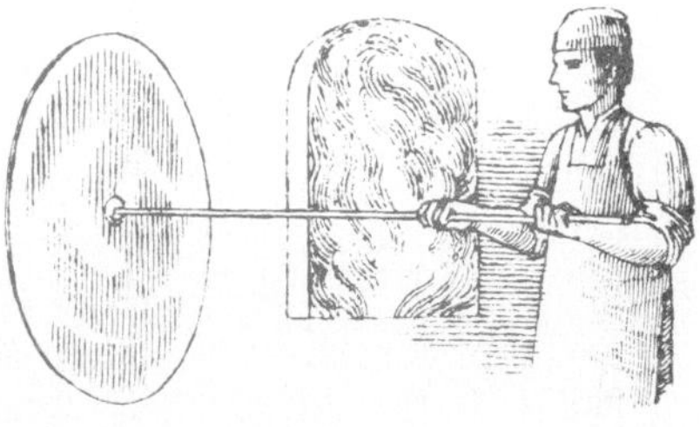

Riflemen & Wagoners

The American frontiersman faced problems that were new and strange to immigrants from the Old World, and indeed to those who lived in snug communities along the eastern seaboard. He traveled on foot, often for weeks at a time, through a wilderness that offered him no convenience or sustenance beyond what he could carry with him or provide by his own resources. Most urgently he needed a shooting weapon that was accurate at long range, that could easily be handled in the forests, and that required no more powder and ball than he could carry on his extended and solitary treks. From these requirements evolved the Kentucky rifle, so called because it proved so effective in the "dark and bloody ground" during the years following the Revolutionary War.

Actually, this superb weapon was developed by German and Swiss (and Scotch-Irish) gunsmiths in Pennsylvania over a long period of years. Rifling, that is cutting the barrel in spiral grooves, gave a spin to the ball and assured greater accuracy and range, and was a practice well known to immigrant German gunsmiths. However, the European rifles with which early settlers were familiar were heavy and short, with a large bore that demanded relatively large balls and great quantities of powder for firing. Starting about the 1720's in Lancaster and later in Reading, that cumbersome firearm was adapted and refined to meet the needs and conditions of frontier life. The caliber of the rifle was greatly reduced to accommodate smaller and lighter balls, and these slender barrels were lengthened (572) to allow for complete consumption of the slow-burning powder charge, to improve accuracy, and to increase the velocity of the ball. In charging the weapon, the ball was wrapped in a patch of greased cloth, kept in a handsomely designed brass patchbox in the stock of the rifle, and easily and quickly pushed home with a hickory rod. The patch made a snug fit and thereby increased the impetus of the shot. It also tended to keep the barrel clean.

In the hands of a sharpshooter, this weapon—"a peculiar kind of musket, called a rifle," as John Adams described it from Philadelphia just before the Revolution—could find a small target at an unusually long range. The ordinary musket was rarely effective at more than one hundred yards. At Bemis Heights in 1777, far beyond reach of the fire from enemy muskets, one of Daniel Morgan's riflemen picked off the British general, Simon Fraser, at three hundred yards. The feats of such marksmen became legendary. Recalling his experiences in the Revolutionary War, British Major General John Money wrote of "the unequal contest between high-dressed corps and corps of skillful marksmen. Seldom were the Americans' Riflemen seen—the reports of their guns you heard, but their bullets were felt." And his blood ran cold with the remembrance.

The most elaborate and handsome examples of these rifles were made in the years following the Revolution. In the details of its design each Kentucky rifle was a unique product. One example (573, a, b) was inlaid with thirty-three designs in silver and brass. The brass patchbox was pierced and engraved in Chippendale motifs and the opposite face of the stock—the cheekpiece—was carved in scrolled tendrils. The stock itself was fashioned of "tiger-stripe" maple, as were many other fine rifles of the period.

572. *Above: Kentucky rifle, made by J. Kuntz of Philadelphia, late 18th century. The hickory ramrod is clasped beneath the barrel.*

573. *Below: engraved silver inlay of a Kentucky rifle by P. Smith*

573a. *Bottom: flintlock and engraved silver and brass inlays on the opposite side of the same rifle. Smith worked in Franklin Co., Pa.*

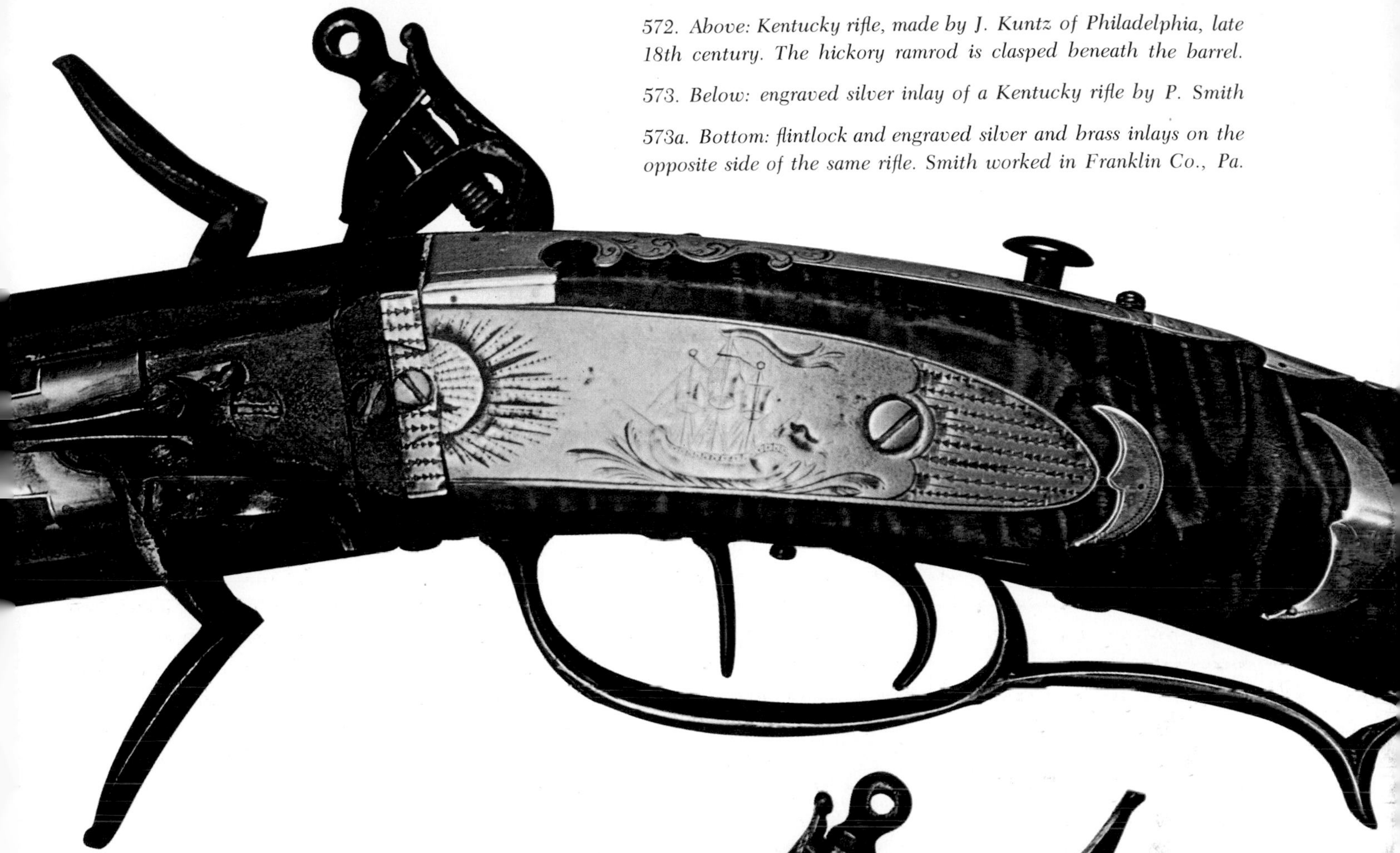

The common accompaniment of the rifle was a container for powder (575), made of the horn of an ox or cow. Light and durable, with a curved shape that conformed to the human figure, it facilitated pouring the powder into the rifle barrel and it was easily filled with a funnel. Most of such horns were engraved with decorative motifs and inscriptions that were meaningful to their owners.

It was also among the Germans in Pennsylvania that, in the 1720's, the Conestoga wagon developed into a unique and majestic vehicle (579). The long, deep-bedded bodies of these "inland ships" were curved, rising at both ends, to keep the cargo from shifting in rough terrain; the white homespun top was similarly shaped. Also, the bodies were painted blue; the wheels with their heavy iron tires were painted vermilion. Wrought-iron work reinforced the structure and, especially on the toolbox (576, 577, 578), added to the handsome appearance of the wagon. Large examples, with six well-matched horses hauling a load of six or eight tons, stretched sixty feet along the road. An arch of bells was attached to the harness of each horse. The driver sat astride the left wheel horse and, it is said, by pulling to the right inaugurated the "keep to the right" traffic we still observe. Other vehicles, attracted to the ruts left by the Conestoga's broad wheels, followed the precedent.

573b. Below: inlaid curly maple stock of the rifle by P. Smith

574. Opposite, top: a Pennsylvania German pottery dish, by David Spinner, about 1800–1810, with figures of militiamen

575. Opposite, bottom: powder horn engraved with riding figures

576, 577, 578. Above: decoratively shaped 18th-century wrought-iron hasps designed for toolboxes used on Conestoga wagons

579. Left: wagon made in the Conestoga Valley of Pennsylvania

OVERLEAF: *580. An 18th-century wrought-iron weather vane, Pa.*

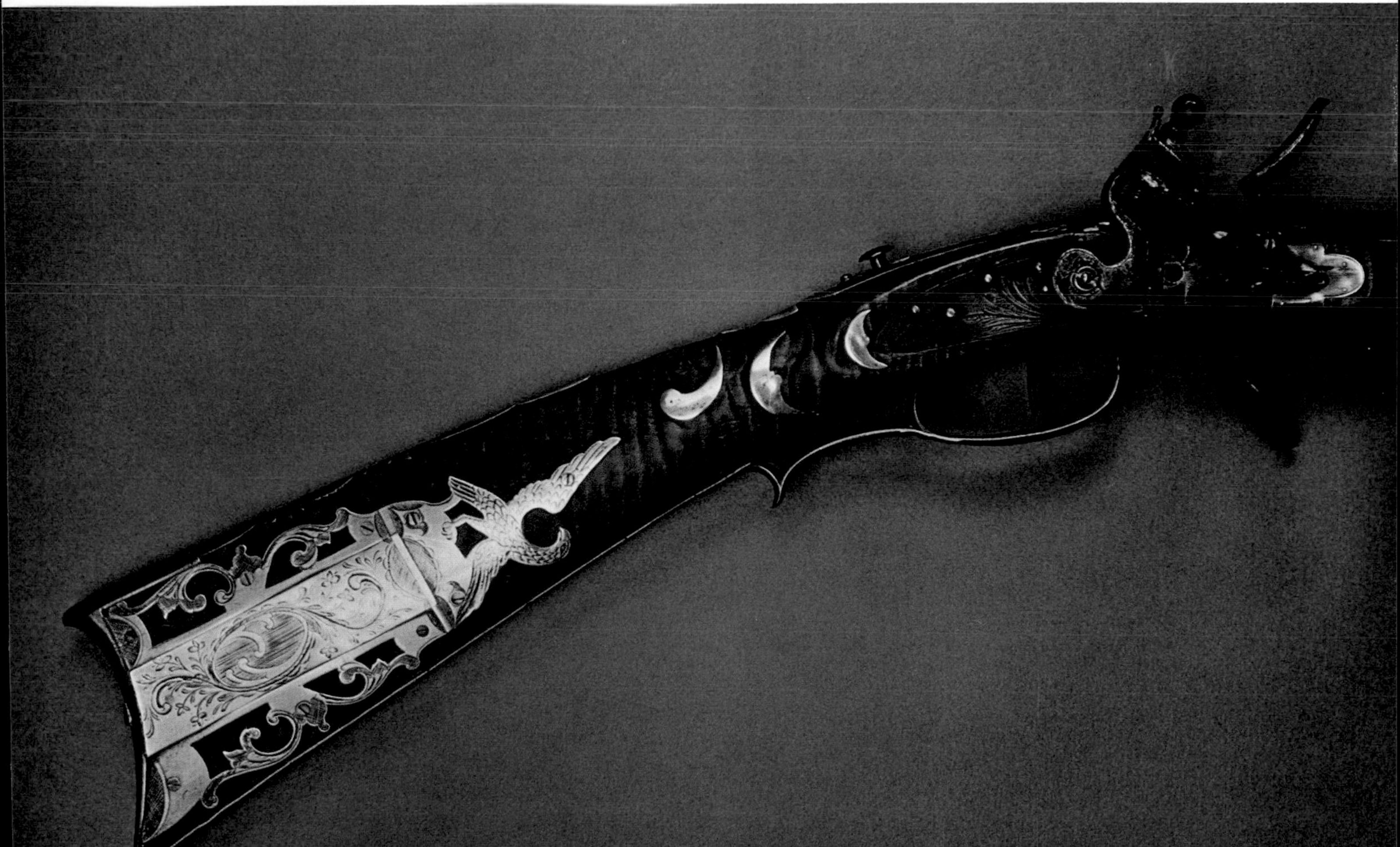

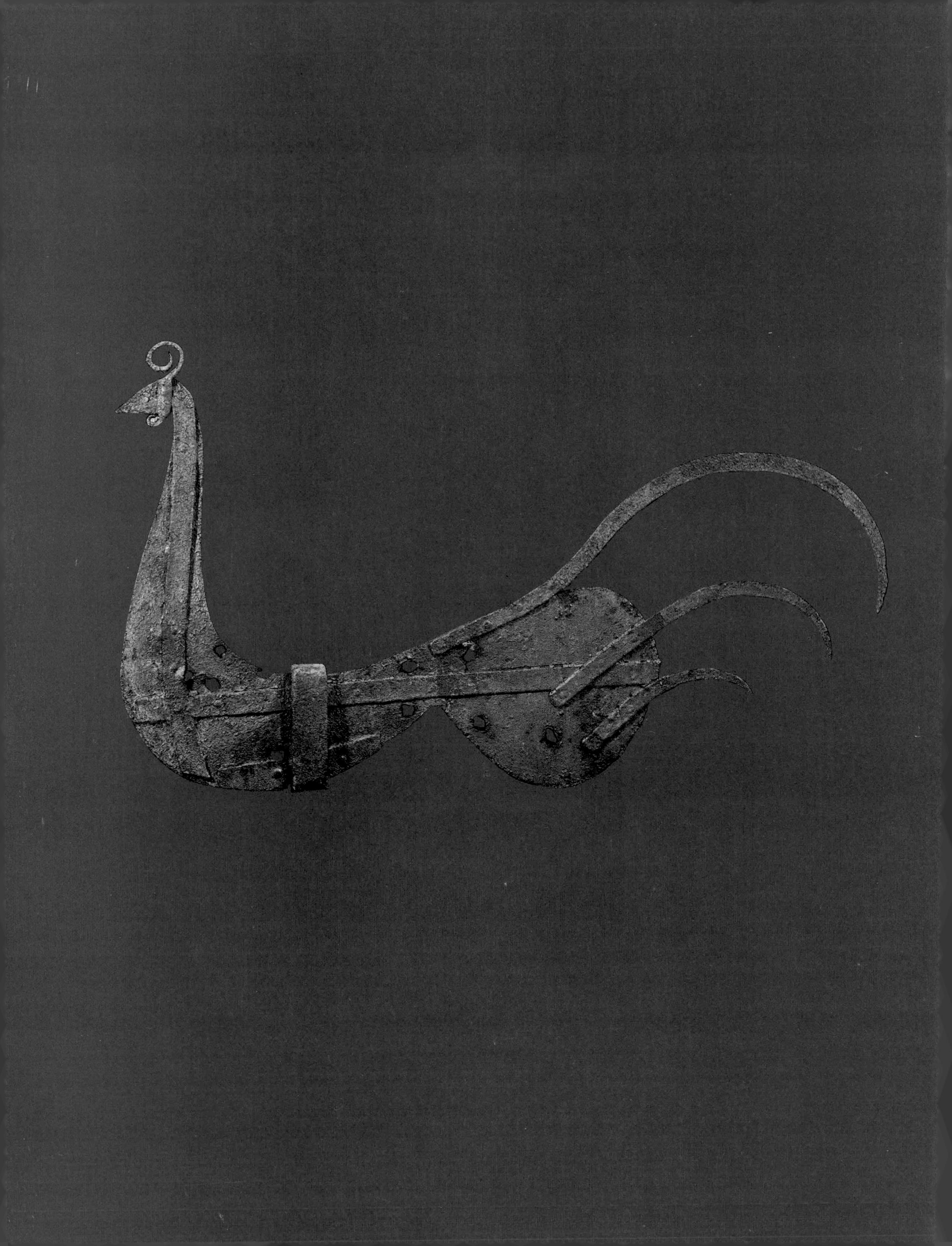

Glossary of Terms

Acanthus

ACANTHUS A carved ornamentation patterned after acanthus leaves, used decoratively on furniture, (291); used in architecture principally on Corinthian and Composite capitals

ACORN A finial or pendant drop resembling an acorn, often used as decoration on William and Mary furniture (70)

ANNEALING In silvermaking, the reheating of the metal to keep it malleable while it is being shaped; in glassmaking, the gradual cooling of hot glass to render it less brittle

APPLIQUE Any applied ornament

APRON The horizontal piece of wood below a table top, chair seat, looking glass, or underframing of a case piece, frequently carved, pierced, or scalloped; also called a skirt (17)

ARABESQUE A painted, inlaid, or carved design in interlacing patterns of floral, geometric, or figural forms

ARCHITRAVE In architecture, the lowest division of the entablature resting directly on a column; also, the molded frame above and at the sides of a door or window. See CLASSICAL ORDER for illustration

ASSAY The test made to determine the quality of metals, such as silver and gold

ASTRAGAL A small, semicircular, convex bead molding resembling a string of beads. See MOLDINGS for illustration

BACK STOOL An early term for a chair without arms (57)

BAIL A curving drawer pull, usually brass, hanging from bolts and backed by a decorative plate. See HARDWARE for illustration

BALL-AND-RING An early turning composed of alternating balls and narrow indentations (rings). See TURNINGS for illustration

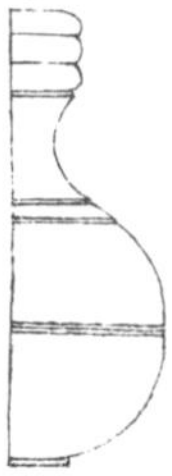

Ball foot

BALL FOOT A round, turned foot used chiefly on furniture of the 17th and early 18th centuries

BALUSTER An upright support, usually turned and vase shaped, topped by a rail; also called a banister. See TURNINGS for illustration

BANISTER-BACK CHAIR A chair with a back made of vertically placed slats or split balusters (138)

BARGELLO WORK A needlework pattern of zigzag stripes; also called flamestitch or Hungarian stitch (95)

BAROQUE A style of art and architecture developed in the late 16th and 17th centuries in Europe, featuring dynamic curved elements and extravagantly and dramatically contorted classical forms

BEAD-AND-REEL A round, convex molding or turning of alternating oval beads with disks. See MOLDINGS for illustration

BELLARMINE A salt-glazed, stoneware jug from the Rhineland with a bearded mask molded on the front. It is said to have been named in the late 16th century for its resemblance to Cardinal Bellarmine (54)

BETTY LAMP An early device for illumination, usually iron or tin, consisting of a shallow holder for grease, a wick, and a handle for hanging (420)

BIBLE BOX An early, carved wooden box to hold books or writing materials, with a hinged, often sloping, lid (10)

BIRD-CAGE A device with four short balusters and central pivot, fitted between the top and the shaft of a tripod table, designed to allow the top to be rotated and tilted (frontispiece, p. 182)

BLOCK FOOT An enlarged square block of wood terminating a plain, straight leg

BLOCK-FRONT A popular colonial form of the Chippendale period distinguished

The numbers in parentheses refer back to illustrations in the text.

by block-like projections across the front of a case piece, the center one concave, and the sides convex (313a)

BLOWN-MOLDED GLASS Glass blown into a small mold to impress a pattern or establish a shape, then withdrawn and expanded, by further blowing and manipulating, into final form (563)

BOBECHE A plain or ornamental disk, often of glass, set on the candle socket of a candlestick, chandelier, or sconce, to catch the drippings (443)

BOLECTION A prominent molding with a bold projecting roll used to frame or divide panel sections and the openings of fireplaces

BOMBE A term applied to furniture with rounded, convex or bulging front and sides; also called a kettle base (304)

BONNET TOP A broken-scroll pediment forming a hood from front to back atop tall case furniture (319)

BOSS A knoblike, projecting ornament used as decoration, usually on chests in Jacobean furniture (64)

BOW-BACK See WINDSOR CHAIRS

BRACE-BACK See WINDSOR CHAIRS

BRACKET A shaped, often pierced decorative support bracing the leg to a chair seat, table top, or body of a case piece (281); also, a small decorative shelf (261), or simply the brace upon which the shelf rests

BRACKET FOOT A foot shaped like a bracket with mitered corners, often scrolled on the free sides, and found on case furniture

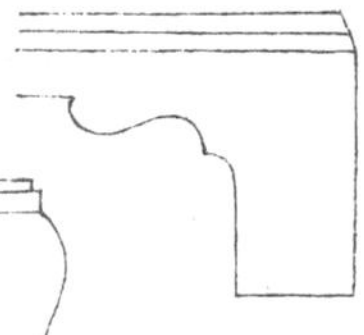
Bracket foot

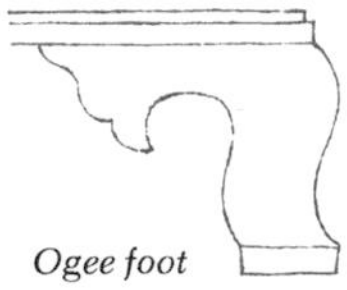
Ogee foot

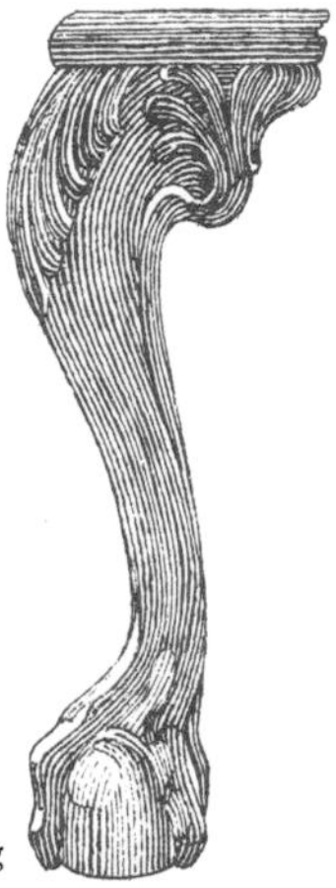
Cabriole leg

BRAZIER A pierced receptacle, usually with a wooden handle, to hold burning coal or charcoal for warming a plate or vessel placed upon it; also called a chafing dish (136)

BREAK FRONT A case piece with a projecting center section, usually surmounted by a pediment

BREWSTER CHAIR A Pilgrim chair with boldly turned posts and decorative spindles applied both to the back of the chair and below the seat and arms (1)

BROKEN PEDIMENT A triangular or curved pediment interrupted at the apex. See PEDIMENT for illustration

BULL'S-EYE See CROWN GLASS

BUN FOOT A slightly flattened, round foot extending from a small turned shaft

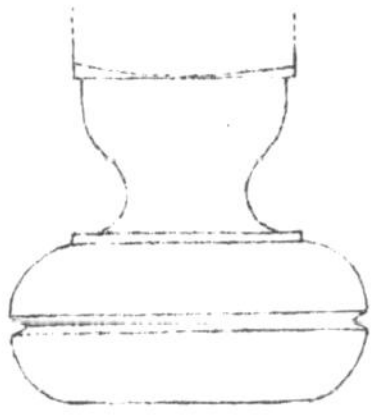
Bun foot

BURIN See GRAVER

BURL A protruding, irregularly grained growth on a tree; used in sections as a thin veneer, or hollowed into bowls (100)

BURNISHER A small, hard, smooth hand tool for polishing gold, silver, and other materials

BUTTERFLY HINGE A butterfly-shaped hinge with the pivot at the narrow part; also called dovetail hinge

Butterfly hinge

BUTTERFLY TABLE A drop-leaf table with solid wing- or rudder-shaped brackets supporting the leaves (148)

CABRIOLE A reverse-curved leg ending in a shaped foot that was extremely popular during the Queen Anne and Chippendale periods

CALICO Cotton fabric imported from Calcutta in the 17th and 18th centuries; called chintz when painted or printed (85)

CANE Split rattan used to weave chair backs and seats (69)

CANN An early term for a lidless, one-handled silver drinking vessel (236)

Cartouche

CAPITAL The ornamental upper section of a column or pilaster on which the entablature rests. See CLASSICAL ORDER for illustration

CARTOUCHE A decorative motif in the form of a shield or partially unrolled scroll with curled edges

CARVER CHAIR A Pilgrim chair usually with a rush seat, similar in turnings to the Brewster chair, but with spindles only on the back

CAUDLE CUP A two-handled, deep bowl, often gourd-shaped, used to serve beverage, specifically the warm gruel of flavored wine called "caudle" (40)

CAVETTO A concave molding, usually one-quarter round in section. See MOLDINGS for illustration

CHAFING DISH See BRAZIER

CHAMFER The flat surface made by smoothing off or planing an angle or an edge (300)

CHASING A decoration on metal surfaces produced by a relatively blunt instrument that does not cut into the surface (84)

CHINOISERIE A style of decoration in imitation of Chinese decoration; in the Chinese taste (87)

CHINTZ See CALICO

CLASSICAL ORDER The formal arrangement of columns or pilasters, including their base moldings and capitals and their entablatures, as developed in ancient Greece and Rome and revived during the Renaissance. The elements and proportions represented in the classical order were widely copied and adapted in architecture and furniture throughout the Georgian period.

CLAW-AND-BALL A carved foot resembling a bird's claw holding a ball, commonly used as the termination of a cabriole leg in the Chippendale period

Claw-and-ball foot

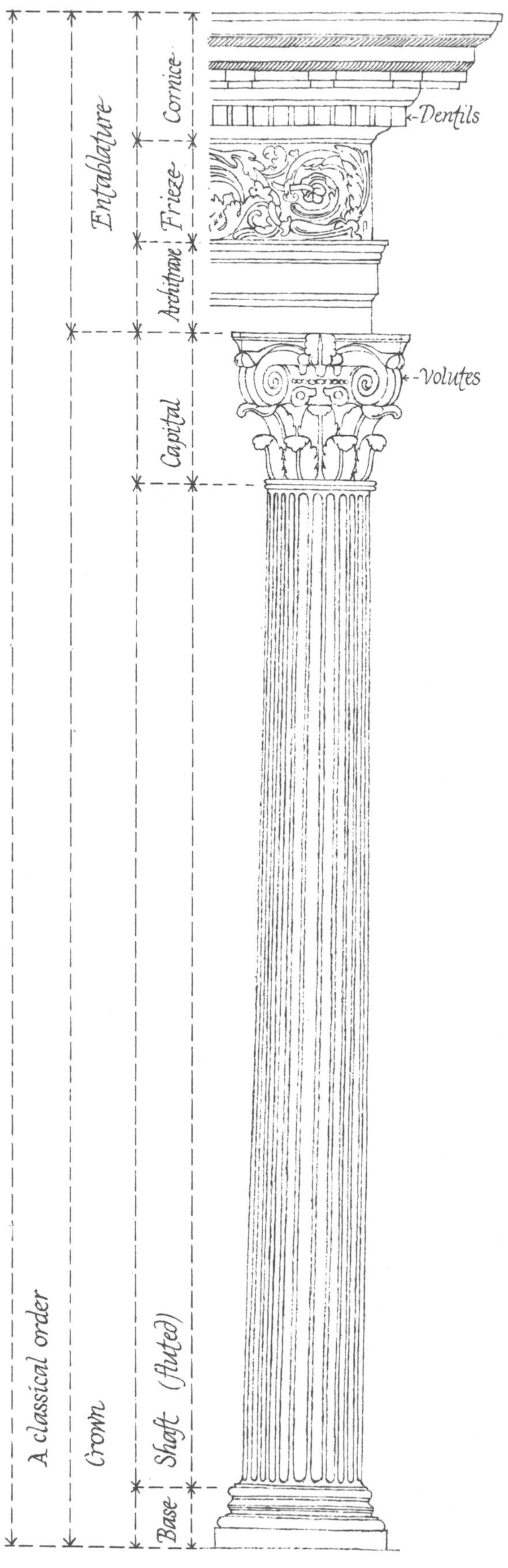

COCK'S-HEAD HINGE A type of hinge whose terminations are shaped in the form of a cock's head

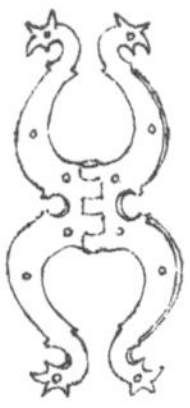

Cock's-head hinge

COMB-BACK See WINDSOR CHAIRS

CONVOLUTE A coiled or scrolled form

CORBEL In architecture, a wall projection of stone or timber serving as a support; in cabinetmaking, a term sometimes used for a bracket

CORNER CHAIR See ROUNDABOUT CHAIR

CORNICE In architecture, the uppermost division of an entablature; also the projecting molding at the top of a window or large case piece. See CLASSICAL ORDER for illustration

COURT CUPBOARD A rectangular cupboard of the Jacobean period either with an enclosed, recessed cabinet above and an open bottom shelf, or two tiers of open shelves (16)

COVE A large, concave molding generally applied to cornices. See MOLDINGS for illustration

CRANE A swinging iron bracket used to hang cooking utensils in a fireplace

CREAMWARE A lead-glazed, ivory-colored earthenware perfected by Josiah Wedgwood; first called by him, then commonly known as "Queen's Ware," in homage to Queen Charlotte (384)

CREST RAIL The top rail of a chair, settee, or any other seating form (140)

CREWELWORK A type of needlework using embroidery of worsted yarn on linen or cotton (214)

CRIMPER A tool used for decorating a rim of glass, metal, or other materials with a wavy, undulating line

CROSS-STRETCHER A horizontal brace in the form of an X connecting the legs of chairs, tables, and case pieces (70)

CROWN GLASS A type of blown glass spun rapidly, at the end of a punty rod, into the form of a disc. A scar or knob of glass, called a bull's-eye, remains in the center, caused when the punty rod is disengaged from the disc.

CRYSTAL A term used for clear, brilliant glass of excellent quality commonly containing lead oxide; also called flint or lead glass

C-SCROLL A scroll carved in the form of the letter C

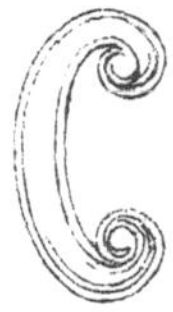

C-scroll

CULLET In glassmaking, cleansed and broken glass remelted with each new batch to promote fusion

CUPID'S BOW A shaped top rail resembling a bow, commonly used on Chippendale chairs (333)

CUP TURNING A turning resembling an inverted bowl or cup common on William and Mary furniture. See TURNINGS for illustration

CUTCARD A flat decoration cut from thin silver sheets and applied to the surface of a piece of silver

CYMA A double curve (216); a cyma recta is concave above and convex below, a cyma reversa, convex above and concave below; also called an ogee. See MOLDINGS for illustration

CIPHER Interweaving of initials in a monogram, often surrounded by a decorative scroll (186)

DELFTWARE A tin-glazed earthenware of a type made in Holland, England, and elsewhere, often decorated to resemble Chinese porcelain (88)

DENTILS Decorative series of rectangular, equally spaced blocks, usually projecting below a cornice. See CLASSICAL ORDER for illustration

DESK BOX See BIBLE BOX

DIAPER PATTERN Decorative effect achieved by a repeating design of lozenges, squares, diamonds, and related shapes in a diagonal pattern

DISHED-CORNER A table top with slight, dishlike depressions at the corners (298)

DOVETAIL A right-angled joint formed by interlacing tenons which resemble in shape the tail of a dove

DOWEL The wooden pin or peg used to fasten two pieces of wood

DRAKE FOOT See TRIFID FOOT

DRESSING TABLE See LOWBOY

DROP An ornamental, turned pendant, either applied or free-hanging; in silver, the reinforcement joining the back of the bowl of a spoon and the stem

EGG-AND-DART A convex molding with an alternating design resembling an egg and a dart. See MOLDINGS for illustration

EMBOSS To raise decorations in relief from a surface

ENGRAVE To produce a pattern on a hard surface by incising with a graver

ENTABLATURE The uppermost horizontal section of a columnar system consisting of the cornice, frieze, and architrave. See CLASSICAL ORDER for illustration

ESCUTCHEON Shaped surface on which armorial bearings are displayed; also a decorative plate about a keyhole

FAN-BACK See WINDSOR CHAIRS

FIDDLE-BACK The violin-shaped solid splat of a chair, a characteristic of the Queen Anne style

FILIGREE Delicate and intricate ornamental work. See also QUILLWORK

FINIAL A device used as a terminal ornament (320)

FLAMESTITCH See BARGELLO WORK

FLEMISH SCROLL A reversed C- or florid S-Scroll, commonly used on stretchers and chair legs of the William and Mary period

Flemish scroll

Fluting

FLINT GLASS Glass of a heavy, brilliant quality containing lead; also called lead glass or crystal

FLUTING A series of half-round, parallel furrows or channels carved into the surface of a piece of wood

FORM An early term for a long bench or stool (12)

FRAKTUR Term used for Pennsylvania German hand-lettered illustrated manuscripts and drawings (527)

FREE-BLOWN GLASS Glass blown without molds, given form by the use of hand tools

FRETWORK An ornamental design resembling latticework, either applied, free standing, or cut in low relief; popular in the Chippendale period (311, 318)

FRIESIAN CARVING Traditional Dutch carving of simple geometric patterns named for Friesland, a province of the Netherlands (11)

FRIEZE In architecture, the flat central division between the cornice and architrave of an entablature; also, a decorative band extending horizontally around the wall of a room. See CLASSICAL ORDER for illustration

GADROON Ornamentation used on silver and furniture formed by fluting or reeding or both, often in a spiral design (283)

GALLERY Open fretwork or small balustrade forming a railing around the top of a piece of furniture (322)

GATE-LEG TABLE An early type of dropleaf table in which the legs, connected by stretchers, form a swinging gate to support the leaves (47)

GATHER In glassmaking, a globular mass of molten glass affixed to a blowpipe, ready to be blown

GEORGIAN A term broadly used to refer to the styles developed during the reigns of Georges I–IV

GESSO Plaster of Paris applied to the surface of a piece to provide a smooth base for painting or gilding

GIRANDOLE A wall mirror having candle branches as part of its structure

GOUGE CARVING Early simple carving formed by repeating chisel cuts

GRANDFATHER CLOCK See TALL CASE CLOCK

GRANDMOTHER CLOCK A modern term for a miniature tall case clock

GRAVER An engraver's tool; a burin

GRISAILLE A form of decorative painting in shades of gray

GUILLOCHE An ornamental motif consisting of a series of loosely interlacing, circular forms (13)

Guilloche

HADLEY CHEST An early chest with a hinged top and usually with one or two drawers, made in and around Hadley, Massachusetts, and decorated with overall, abstract floral carving and often with the owner's initials (66)

HAIRY-PAW FOOT A foot of a chair or any other seating form resembling the hairy paw of an animal

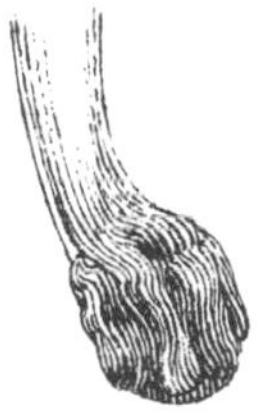

Hairy-paw foot

HALLMARKS The marks stamped on English gold and silver to indicate its maker, date, origin, and quality

HANDKERCHIEF TABLE A triangular drop-leaf table with a triangular single leaf. When opened, it makes a square; closed, it fits into a corner (200)

HARDWARE: DRAWER PULLS AND ESCUTCHEONS

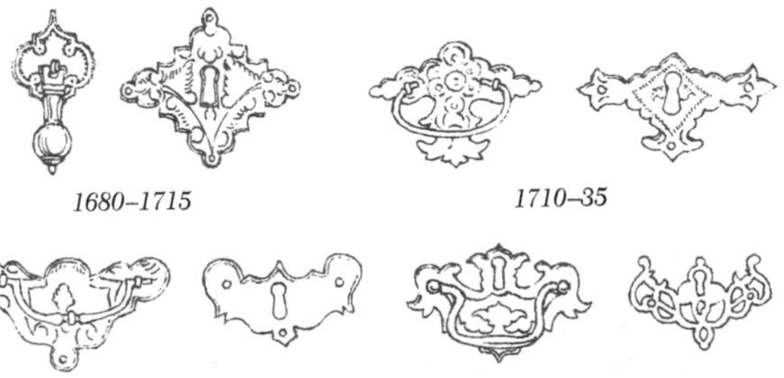

1680–1715 *1710–35* *1720–50* *1740–85*

HERRINGBONE Decorative inlay composed of veneer cut obliquely and fitted together in a herringbone pattern

H-HINGE A metal hinge with long, vertical leaves held in the center by a short horizontal bar, so that the hinge, when opened, resembles the letter H

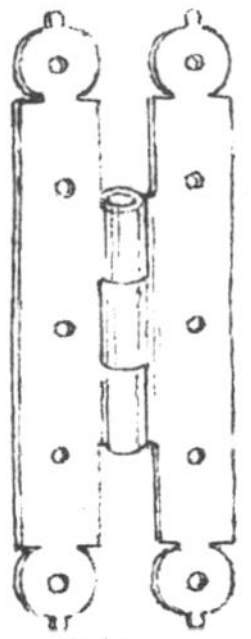

H-hinge

HIGHBOY A modern term for a high chest of drawers comprised of two sections: an upper case, with drawers of varied depth and length, set upon a lower case, also with drawers, supported by legs (77)

HORSESHOE SEAT A chair seat curved in a horseshoe or bell shape, often used in Queen Anne chairs (159)

HUTCH A storage cupboard

IMARI WARE A type of Japanese porcelain exported from the port of Imari in the 17th and early 18th centuries (86)

INLAY Decoration formed by contrasting materials set into the surface of a piece (105)

INTAGLIO Designs depressed below the surface, opposite of relief

JAPANNING The process of simulating Oriental lacquer by the use of varnish or paint with decoration in low relief, usually in *chinoiserie* designs (193)

JEWELWORK Carved ornamentation resembling cut gems (4)

JOINT STOOL A small, backless seat with turned legs strengthened by stretchers (14)

KAS A large cupboard in the Dutch style, usually with heavy overhanging cornice; often painted in *grisaille* (63)

KETTLE BASE See BOMBE

KNEEHOLE The open space in the center front of a desk or chest of drawers, flanked by two rows of drawers (313a)

KNOTTY PINE Pine wood with knots, usually avoided by colonial craftsmen

KNUCKLE A carved pattern resembling knuckles often used as terminals on the arms of Chippendale and Windsor chairs (355)

KNURL FOOT See WHORL FOOT

LACQUER Spirit varnish applied in many layers on wood to build up a hard, highly polished surface

LADDER-BACK CHAIR A type of chair, with horizontal back slats resembling the rungs of a ladder, found on early simple country furniture; sometimes called a slat-back chair (7). In the Chippendale period the rungs were cut in curved lines (336).

LANTERN CLOCK A small, weight-driven wall or bracket clock, usually brass and resembling a lantern, surmounted by a bell to sound the hours (73)

LATTICE Cutout, crisscross design found in highboy pediments, chair backs, and other furniture forms (265)

LEAD GLASS See FLINT GLASS

LONG CASE CLOCK See TALL CASE CLOCK

LOW-BACK See WINDSOR CHAIRS

LOWBOY The modern term for a form of dressing table with small drawers, mounted on legs, often matching a highboy (274)

MARBLEIZE To paint wood or other material in imitation of marble (46)

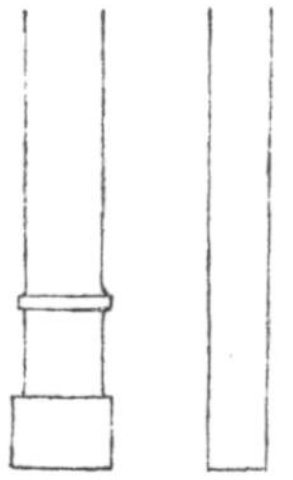

Marlborough leg

MARLBOROUGH LEG A leg of square section, often with a block foot, used for Chippendale chairs, tables, and other forms (283)

MARQUETRY Decorative inlay in which a pattern is formed of various woods or other materials before being glued to a groundwork (74)

MARVER The metal slab on which viscous glass is rolled and flattened

MATTING An ornamental effect, particularly on silver, achieved by punching tiny dots close together in an area usually contrasted with an adjoining smooth area

MODILLION The ornamented bracket or block under a cornice

MOLDINGS

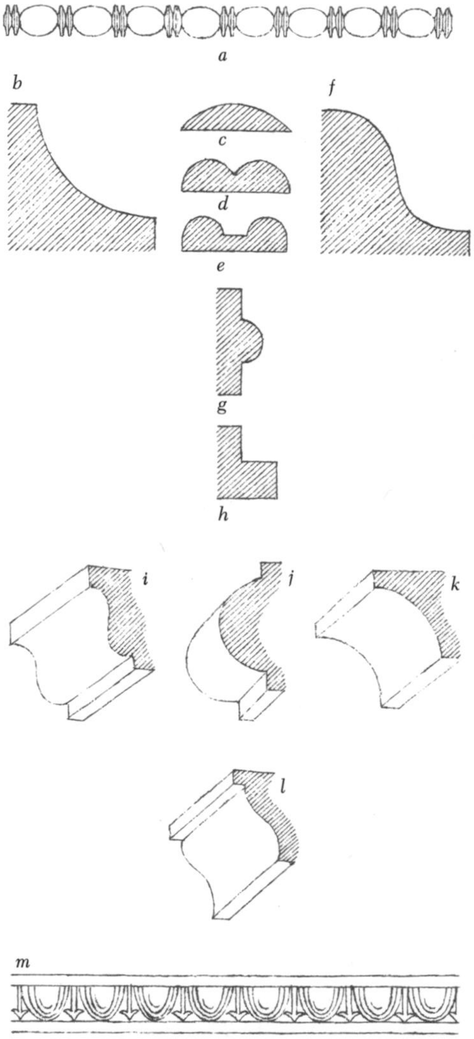

(a) Bead-and-reel. (b) Cove. (c) Single arch. (d) Double arch. (e) Canal. (f) Cyma. (g) Astragal. (h) Fillet. (i) Cyma recta. (j) Torus. (k) Cavetto. (l) Cyma reversa. (m) Egg-and-dart

MONTEITH A large bowl with a notched rim for chilling drinking glasses (107)

MORTISE AND TENON The method of joining two pieces of wood by inserting a tenon, or extension of one piece, into the mortise, or socket, of another; usually further secured by a pin piercing both pieces

OGEE See CYMA

OXBOW FRONT A reverse-curved front —concave in the center, convex at the ends—often found on Chippendale case pieces

PAD FOOT An oval-shaped foot used on cabriole legs; called a cushioned pad foot when it has a disc-shaped support or cushion underneath

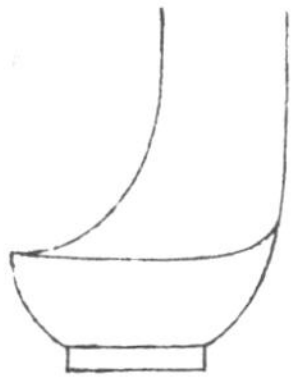

Pad foot

PALAMPORE An India painted cotton, or chintz wall hanging, or bed cover (85). See also CALICO

PATINA The color or finish achieved by the mellowing of the surface of woods and metals from age or use

PEAR-DROP HANDLE An example of furniture hardware, typical of the William and Mary period, distinguished by a patterned brass backplate and a pull shaped like a teardrop or pear. See HARDWARE for illustration

PEDIMENT In architecture, a triangular or arched section above the entablature; in cabinetmaking, a similar top, either straight, or curving, for case pieces

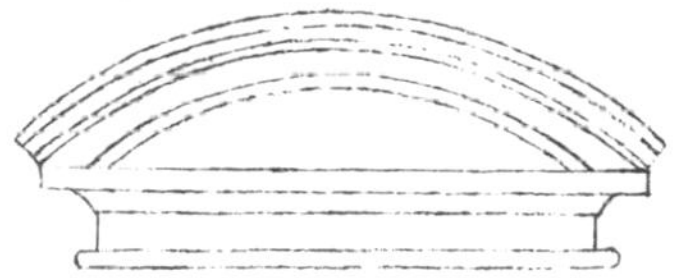

Arched pediment

Triangular pediment

Broken-scroll pediment

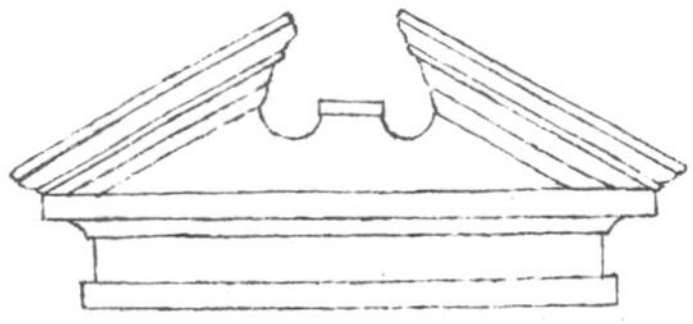

Broken pediment

PEMBROKE TABLE A rectangular drop-leaf table usually having straight slender legs

PIECRUST TABLE A tripod table whose circular top has a scalloped, molded rim resembling a crimped piecrust (269)

PILASTER A flat attached pier treated architecturally as a column (213)

PLANISHING Light hammering of metal to produce a smooth surface

POLE SCREEN An adjustable fire screen attached to an upright rod or pole supported by a base (468)

PONTIL An iron or steel rod which holds hot glass for finishing after it has been blown; also called a punty

PONTIL MARK The mark on a piece of blown glass where it was attached to the pontil; also called punty mark

PORCELAIN A fine ware, distinguished by its hardness, translucency, and superior whiteness, made of clay (kaolin) and stone (pentuntze), fired at extremely high temperatures (180)

POTTERY Earthenware made from clay and fired at low temperatures (536)

PRESS CUPBOARD Similar to the court cupboard, but with both the lower and upper sections containing drawers or storage space with doors

QUATREFOIL A stylized decoration with four lobes or leaves

QUEEN'S WARE See CREAMWARE

QUILLWORK Designs made by scrolled paper filigree, usually with gilt edges and incorporating other ornamental materials (68)

RAISING A process of making hollow ware by hammering a flat metal sheet on a series of anvils

RAT-TAIL An ornamental reinforcement, resembling a tail, on the underside of the bowl of a spoon (119)

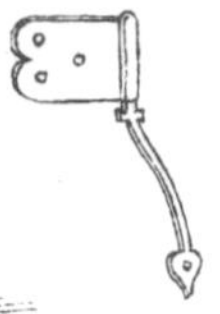

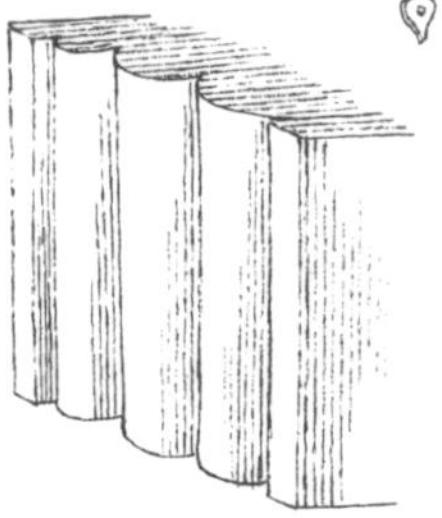

Top: rat-tail hinge
Above: reeding

RAT-TAIL HINGE A type of hinge with a tapered, curved extension running downward, usually with a cutout decoration at the end

REEDING Parallel, semicircular molding which protrudes from the surface

RELIEF Decoration that is raised above the surface

REPOUSSE Designs in metal raised on the surface by hammering from the back

RIBBAND BACK A type of chair back of the Chippendale period characterized by a series of horizontal, interlaced elements connecting the stiles (252)

ROCOCO A style of art and decoration developed in the 18th century in France, characterized by designs curvilinear in form and imitative of shellwork, scrolls, and foliage asymmetrically arranged

ROUNDABOUT CHAIR An armchair of diamond shape with one leg at the front, another at the back, and two at each side; the back and arms encompass the back half of the chair. Also called a corner chair (97)

RUSTICATION Ornamentally roughened surfaces and recessed joints in stonework

SADDLE SEAT A wooden chair seat shaped like a saddle, common to Windsor chairs (351)

SALT GLAZE A hard, rough, transparent glaze produced by introducing rock salt to the kiln during the firing of earthenware or stoneware

SCONCE A wall bracket fitted with one or more candlesticks (68)

SCROLL A spiral or rolled decoration

SCROLL PEDIMENT A pediment formed by interrupting confronting cyma curves; also called a broken-scroll. See PEDIMENT for illustration

SGRAFFITO The design on pottery made by cutting through the outer glaze to expose the color of the base clay (537)

SKIRT See APRON

SLAT-BACK CHAIR See LADDER-BACK CHAIR

SLIPPER CHAIR A high-back chair with short legs, usually upholstered, and without arms (217)

Slipper foot

SLIPPER FOOT A slim, elongated, pointed foot

SLIP WARE Red earthenware decorated by the application of colored slip (diluted clay) to the glazed surface (548)

Snake foot

SNAKE FOOT A foot shaped like the head of a snake

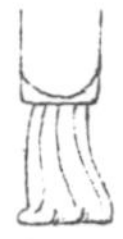

Spanish foot

SPANISH FOOT A scroll foot with vertical ribs following the curve of the scroll, usually found on furniture in the William and Mary period

SPINDLE A slender turning used primarily in a chair back for support. See TURNINGS for illustration

SPLAT The upright, center support in a chair back (158)

SPOON-BACK Chair back curved to accommodate the contours of a human back (154)

SQUAB A removable cushion for a seat

S-SCROLL A scroll in the form of the letter S. Also called a Flemish scroll (69)

STERLING The standard established by English law affixing the exact amount of pure silver required for articles fashioned from the metal

STICK CHAIR See WINDSOR CHAIRS

STILES The upright side supports of a chair back (158)

STONEWARE A form of hard, nonporous pottery made of clay fired at high temperatures; often salt glazed (54)

STOPPED FLUTING Fluting in which the lower parts of the furrows or channels are fitted with reeding

STRAP HINGE A simple hinge with long leaves resembling straps

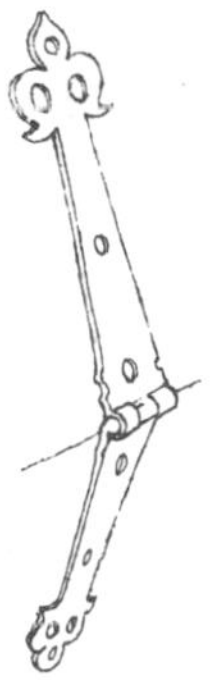
Strap hinge

STRAPWORK Decorative, flat interlaced bands applied or carved on a surface (4)

STRETCHER A horizontal support bracing the legs of chairs, tables, stools, or case pieces (15)

STUMP LEG A plain, square rear leg with a slight backward curve

SUNFLOWER Floral motif found on early chests carved in Connecticut (64)

TALL CASE CLOCK A clock incorporated within a tall, standing case to protect the works and accommodate the pendulum. Also called long case clock and grandfather clock (208)

TAVERN TABLE A rectangular low table, used in public meeting houses, with a sturdy framework and turned legs and stretchers (frontispiece, page 8)

TENON See MORTISE AND TENON

TESTER The canopy of a high-post bed, made of wood or fabric (214)

TOLE Painted tinware

TORUS A bold, semicircular, convex molding. See MOLDINGS for illustration

TOUCHSTONE A stone used to test the purity of gold and silver by the mark left on it when rubbed by the metal

TRAMMEL A pothook, adjusted by ratchets, to be hung from a crane in a fireplace; also a similar device for raising and lowering lamps (421)

TREEN Small domestic objects made of wood (482)

TREFOIL A stylized decoration with three lobes or leaves

TRIFID FOOT A three-toed foot; sometimes known as a drake foot

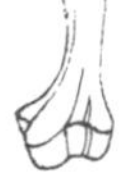
Trifid foot

TRUMPET TURNING A turned leg with the profile of an upturned trumpet. See TURNINGS for illustration

TRUNDLE BED A low, rolling bed, usually for a child, designed to fit under a large bed; also called a truckle bed

TURKEY WORK A type of needlework imitative of the pile carpets imported from the East in the 17th century (57)

TURNINGS

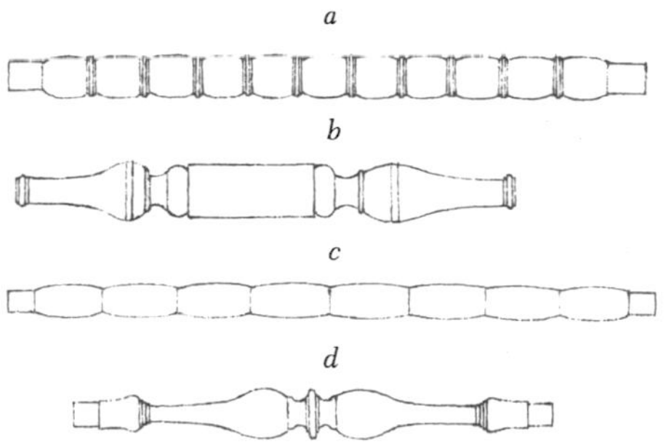

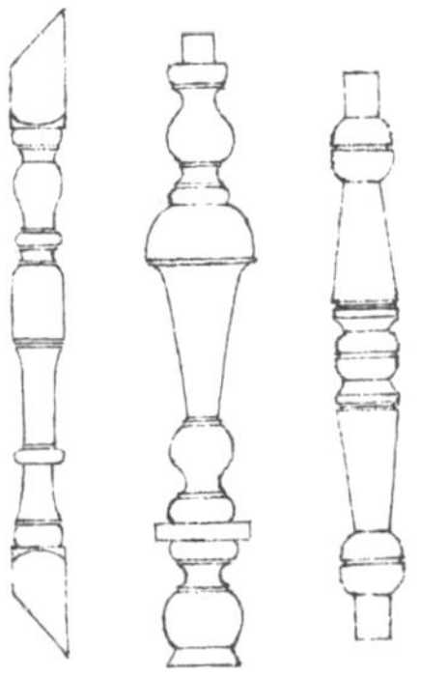
e *f* *g*

(a) Ball-and-ring. (b) Block-and-vase. (c) Sausage. (d) Vase-and-ring. (e) Baluster. (f) Cup. (g) Spindle. (h) Trumpet. (i) Spiral

h

i

VALANCE The drapery hanging across the top of a window or at the edges of a bed or table (473)

VASE TURNING A turning resembling a vase with a taper above a bulbous base. See TURNINGS (b, d) for illustration

VENEER Thin layers of wood or other materials glued to a solid ground

VOLUTE A scroll-like conformation used in classical capitals, especially of the Ionic order. See CLASSICAL ORDER

WAG ON THE WALL An early wall clock in which a short pendulum hung freely without a covering (73)

WHORL FOOT A foot consisting of an upturned scroll; also called a knurl foot

Whorl foot

WINDSOR CHAIRS Chairs constructed with a solid wooden seat and turned, splayed legs. The variously shaped backs of Windsors are made of spindles joined to the back rail. The most commonly used names for five types of Windsors are: bow-back, also called a hoop-back (351); fan-back (358); comb-back (352); low-back (353); brace-back (354).

Style Chart of Chairs & Seating

1650-1700 *1700-1725*

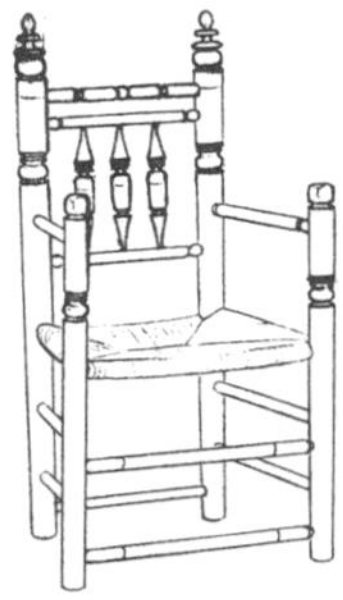

Carver chair

Tall-back caned chair

Banister-back chair

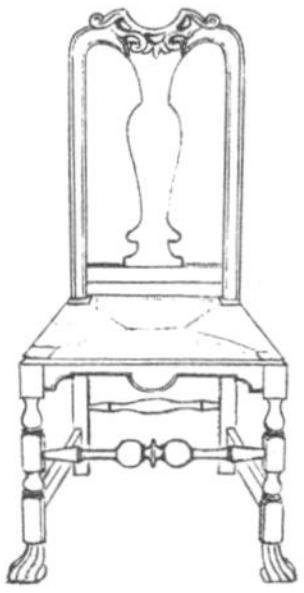

Transitional chair

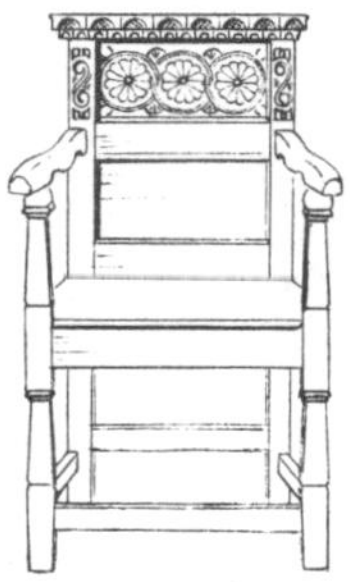

Wainscot chair

Joint stool

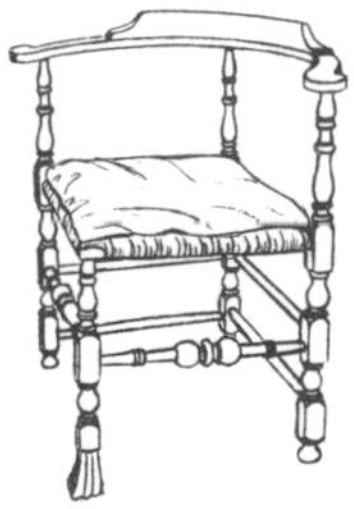

Corner chair

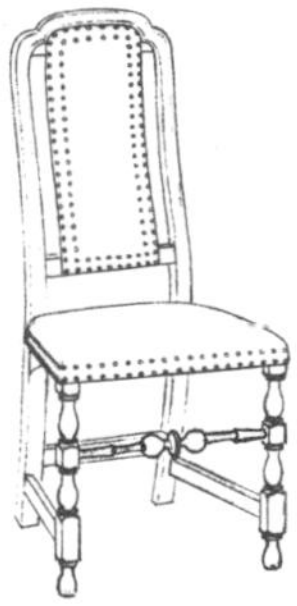

Boston chair

Flemish-scroll day bed

Slat-back chair

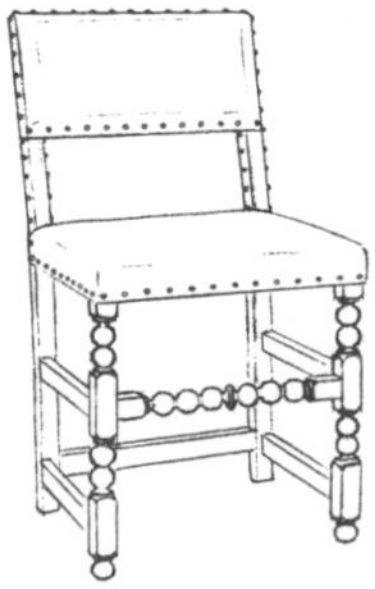

Cromwell chair

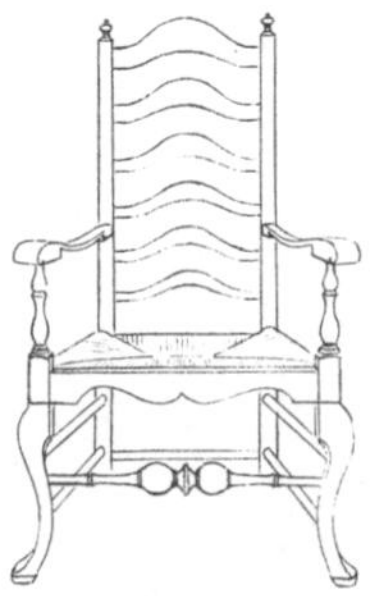

Ladder-back chair

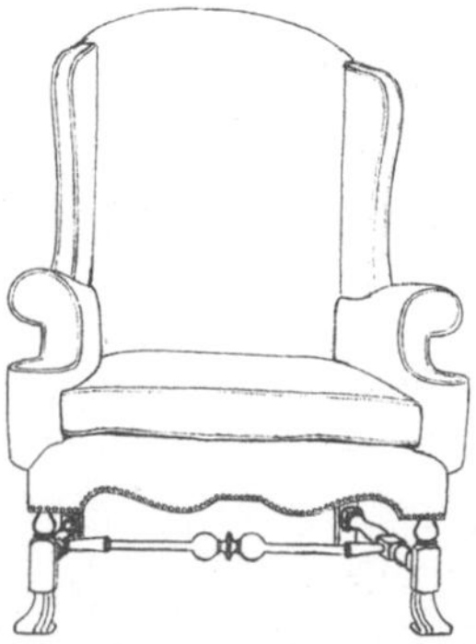

Easy chair

Furniture

1725-1750

1750-1785

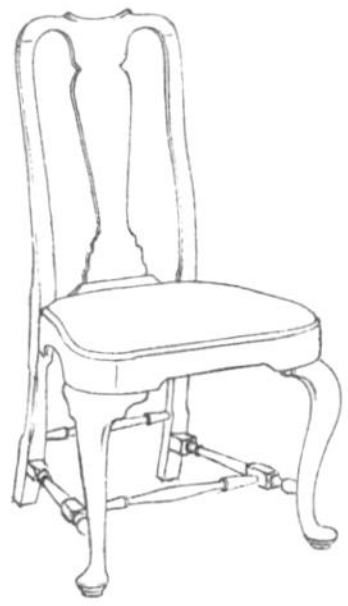
Splat-back chair

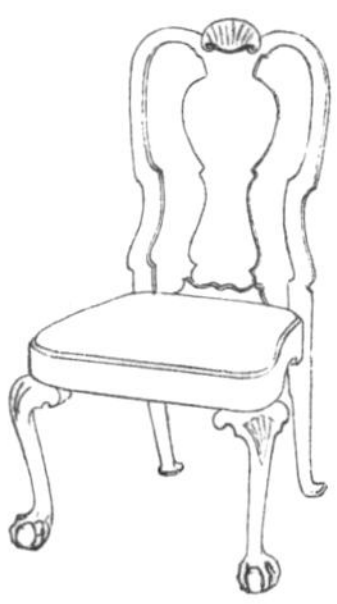
Fiddle-back chair

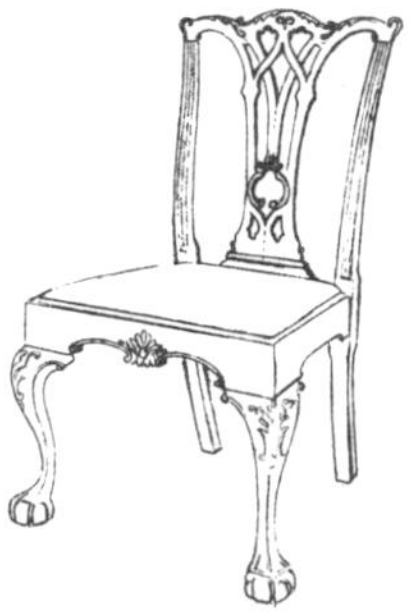
Pierced-splat chair

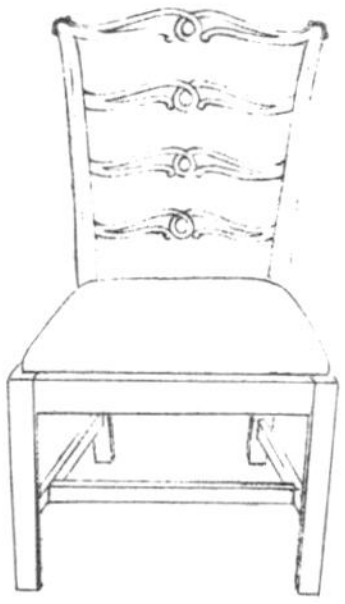
Ladder-back chair

Corner chair

Upholstered stool

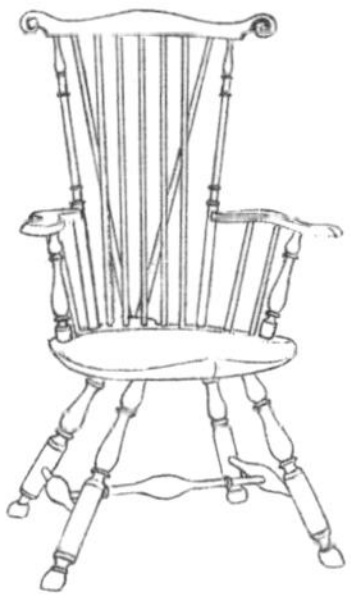
Brace-back Windsor chair

Bow-back Windsor chair

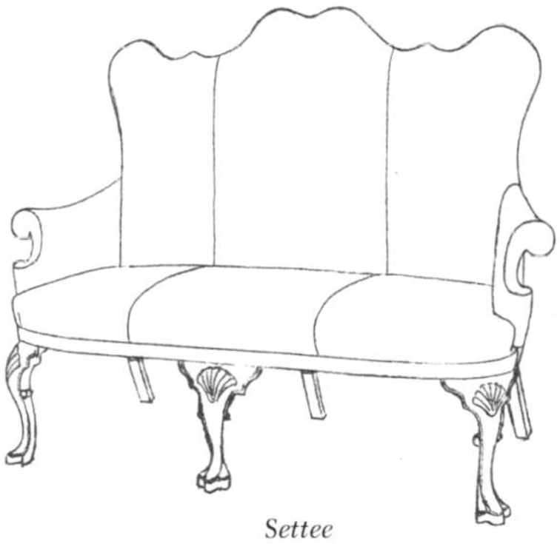
Settee

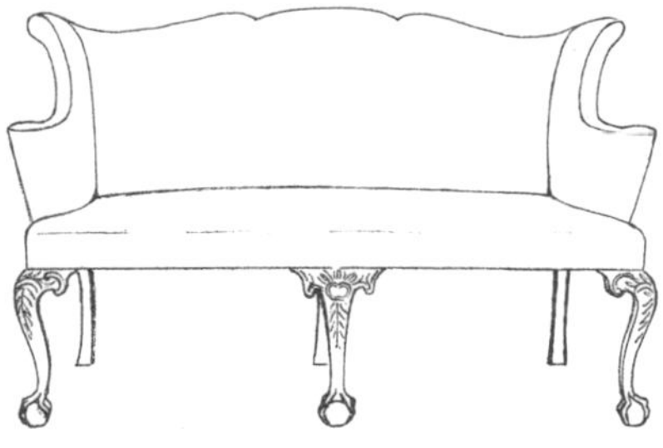
Settee

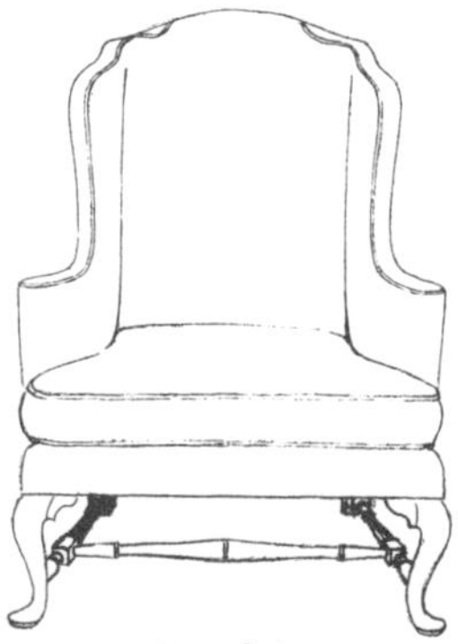
Easy chair

Easy chair

Upholstered armchair

Style Chart of Tables

1650-1700

1700-1725

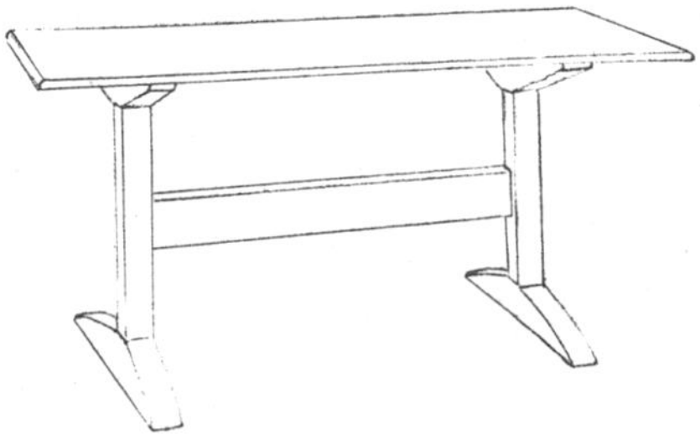

Trestle table

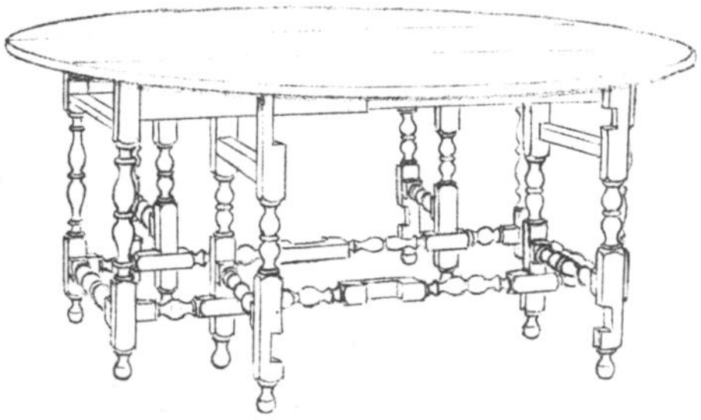

Gate-leg table

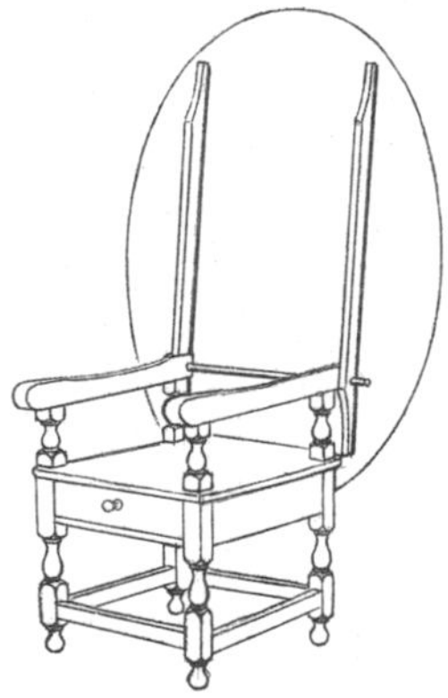

Chair-table

Butterfly table

Splay-leg table

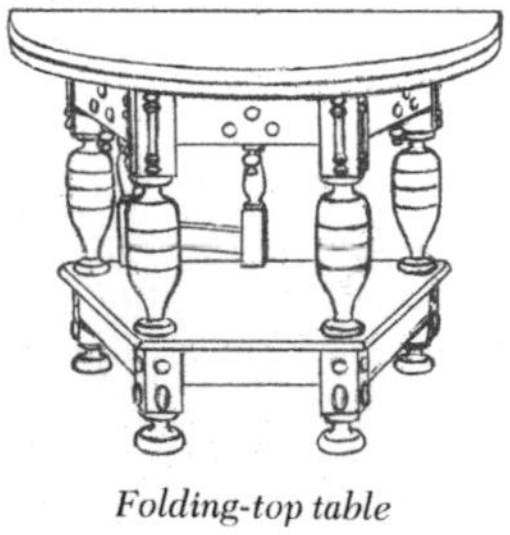

Folding-top table

Mixing table

Stretcher-base table

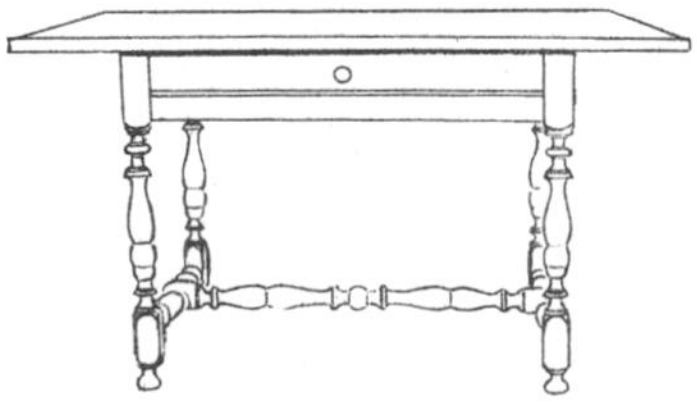

Tavern table

1725-1750

Drop-leaf dining table

Breakfast table

Tea table

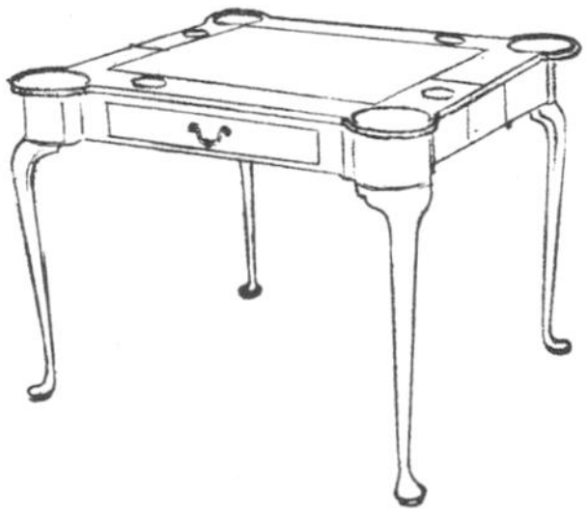

Gaming table

1750-1785

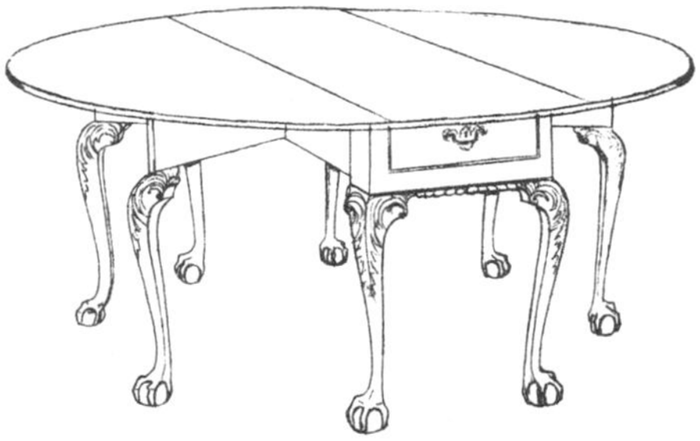

Drop-leaf dining table

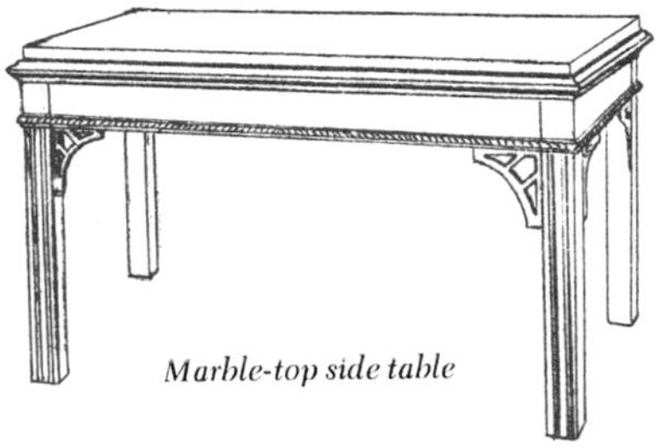

Marble-top side table

Tilt-top table

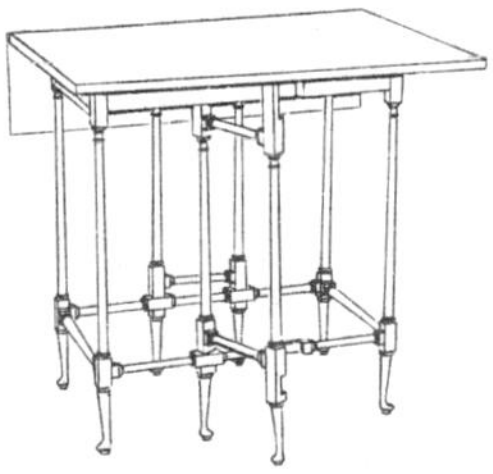

Spider-leg table

Tea table

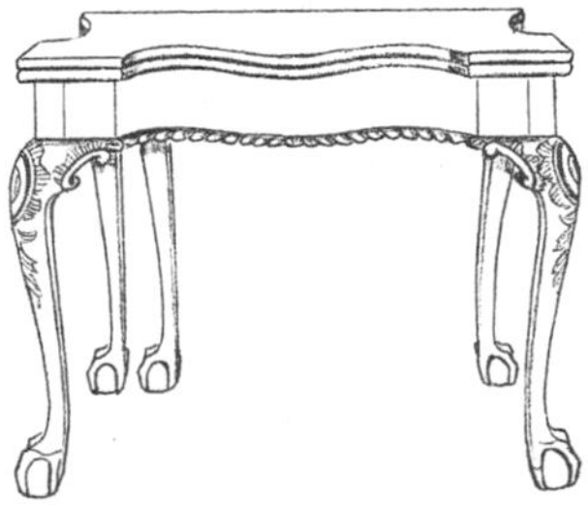

Card table

Style Chart of Case Pieces

1650-1700

Bible box

Desk-on-frame

Paneled chest

Connecticut Valley chest

Court cupboard

Kas

1700-1725

Fall-front desk

Secretary

Chest-on-frame

Highboy

Chest of drawers

Lowboy

1725-1750

Fall-front desk

Secretary

Highboy

Lowboy

1750-1785

Bombé secretary

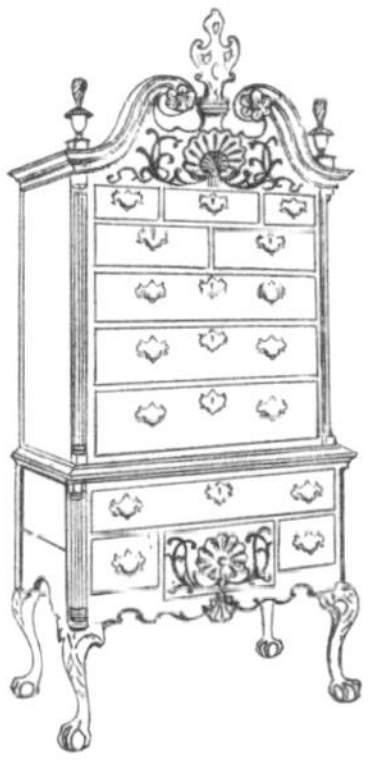

Highboy

Chest-on-chest

Lowboy

Style Chart of Typical Forms

1650-1700 | *1700-1725*

TEAPOTS

TEAKETTLES

COFFEEPOTS

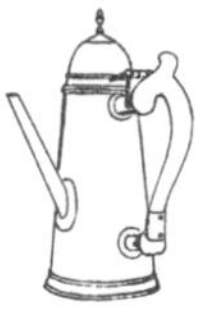

CANDLESTICKS

SUGAR BOWLS

CREAM PITCHERS

SALTS

CASTERS

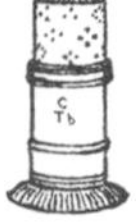

in Silver

1725-1750 *1750-1785*

Acknowledgments

The editors wish to express their deep gratitude to the institutions and individuals mentioned below for their generous help in providing pictorial material from the collections in their custody and for supplying information and advice.

Antiques Magazine
Ruth B. Davidson

Colonial Williamsburg
Marguerite Gignilliat

Connecticut Historical Society
Thompson R. Harlow

Corning Museum of Glass
Paul N. Perrot
Kenneth M. Wilson
Jane S. Shadel

Ginsburg & Levy Inc.
Benjamin Ginsburg

Henry Ford Museum and Greenfield Village
Dr. Donald A. Shelley
Katharine Hagler
George O. Bird
Charles Miller

Heritage Foundation, Deerfield
Henry N. Flynt
J. P. Spang III

Metropolitan Museum of Art
James Biddle
Janet S. Byrne
Margaret Nolan
Ellen B. Franklin
Mary C. Glaze

Museum of the City of New York
Ralph Miller
Margaret Stearns
Henriette Beal

Museum of Fine Arts, Boston
Caroline P. Wistar
Wendy O. Goodell

New York Public Library
Donald Anderle
Anthony Cardillo
Mrs. Maud D. Cole
Mrs. Philomena C. Houlihan
Elizabeth Roth

New-York Historical Society
James J. Heslin
Caroline Scoon

Old Sturbridge Village
Henry J. Harlow
Etta Falkner
Robert Chase

Philadelphia Museum of Art
Calvin Hathaway
Elvira L. Honoré
Alfred J. Wyatt

Shelburne Museum
Bradley Smith

Smithsonian Institution
C. Malcolm Watkins

Society for the Preservation
of New England Antiquities
Abbott Lowell Cummings

Wadsworth Atheneum
Henry P. Maynard
Elva B. McCormick

Henry Francis du Pont Winterthur Museum
Ian M. G. Quimby
Helen M. Schlatter
Gilbert Ask

Yale University Art Gallery
Caroline Rollins
John T. Kirk
Graham Hood

Historical Society of York County
Robert P. Turner

Grateful acknowledgment is made for permission to quote from the following publications:

William Threipland Baxter, *The House of Hancock: Business in Boston, 1724–1775*, copyright 1945 by Harvard University Press, reprinted 1965 by Russell & Russell, New York

Gentleman's Progress: The Itinerarium of Dr. Alexander Hamilton, 1744, ed. Carl Bridenbaugh, copyright 1948 by The University of North Carolina Press, Chapel Hill

Lyman H. Butterfield, *The Diary and Autobiography of John Adams*, Vols. I and II, The Belknap Press of Harvard University Press, Cambridge, Mass., copyright 1961 by The Massachusetts Historical Society

Marquis de Chastellux, *Travels in North America in the Years 1780, 1781, and 1782*, Vol. II, trans. Howard C. Rice, Jr., copyright © 1963 by The University of North Carolina Press, Chapel Hill

The Journal and Letters of Philip Vickers Fithian, ed. Hunter Dickinson Farish, copyright 1957 by Colonial Williamsburg, Incorporated, Williamsburg, Virginia

Esther Forbes, *Paul Revere and the World He Lived In*, copyright 1942 by Esther Forbes, Houghton Mifflin Company, The Riverside Press, Cambridge, Massachusetts

Peter Kalm, *Peter Kalm's Travels in North America*, Vol. I, ed. Adolph B. Benson, copyright 1964 by Dover Publications, Inc., New York

The Papers of Benjamin Franklin, Vol. VII, ed. Leonard W. Labaree, Yale University Press, copyright 1963 by Yale University, New Haven

Jules David Prown, *John Singleton Copley in England, 1774–1815*, Vol. II, © copyright 1966 by Harvard University, Harvard University Press, Cambridge, Massachusetts

Edward M. Riley, "Franklin's Home," *Historic Philadelphia*, Vol. XLIII, Part I, 1953, Transactions, American Philosophical Society, Philadelphia

Carl Van Doren, *Benjamin Franklin*, copyright 1938 by Carl Van Doren, © 1966 by Anne Van Doren Ross, Margaret Van Doren Bevans, and Barbara Van Doren Klaw, The Viking Press, New York

The Secret Diary of William Byrd of Westover 1709–1712, ed. Louis B. Wright and Marion Tinling, copyright 1941 by Louis B. Wright and Marion Tinling, The Dietz Press, Richmond, Virginia

Picture Credits

Frontispieces

The color plates for the frontispieces of the separate chapters were made from photographs taken especially for this book by Ben Somoroff. The objects shown in the illustrations on pages 8, 60, 120, 182, and 260 were, with the exceptions noted, very generously lent for the purpose by Ginsburg & Levy Inc., New York. Those shown in the illustration on page 298 were made available through the generosity of John Gordon and Robert Bishop.

Page 8: early tavern table and carved oak Bible box, American, 17th century; brass candlesticks, pewter plates, and beadwork looking glass, English, 16th and 17th centuries; apothecary jar, Dutch Delftware, about 1720

Page 60: walnut-veneered desk, American, early 18th century; Flemish scroll cane-back chair, late 17th century; silver caudle cup, English, dated 1661; brass chandelier, Delftware, and other accessories, William and Mary period

Page 120: side chair and stool, Philadelphia; dressing table, Newport, R.I., possibly by John Goddard, I; portrait of an unidentified British colonial officer, by John Wollaston (around 1750) [The Knoedler Galleries, N.Y.]; these and the English Jacobite wine glasses and other objects all of the Queen Anne period

Page 182: pole screen and easy chair, Philadelphia; dished top tripod table, with birdcage, and looking glass, American; silver cann by John Clark, Boston; these and the other objects, English, all in the Chippendale style

Page 260: furniture and various other household accessories dating from the 17th, 18th, and early 19th centuries; tin candlestick and horse weather vane [John Gordon]; rug, rushlight and candleholder, mortar and pestle, stool, and masher [Robert Bishop]

Page 298: painted furniture, slip ware, *fraktur*, and other accessories, Pennsylvania German, 18th and 19th centuries. Toy horse and coverlet [Robert Bishop], all other items [John Gordon]

The location of each of the other objects illustrated in this volume is listed below. Special photographic credits appear in parentheses; the other photographs were supplied by the institutions and individuals mentioned. Unnumbered illustrations are described after the page number; numbered illustrations follow the figure number. Both page and figure numbers are in boldface type. Where two or more illustrations appear on one page, the references are separated by dashes. To simplify the listings the following abbreviations are used:

AAS: American Antiquarian Society

AIC: Art Institute of Chicago

AIHA: Albany Institute of History and Art

BM: Brooklyn Museum

CHS: Connecticut Historical Society

CMB: Chase Manhattan Bank, Museum of Moneys of the World

CMG: Corning Museum of Glass

CW: Colonial Williamsburg

duP: Henry Francis du Pont Winterthur Museum

EI: Essex Institute

FAH: Museum of Fine Arts, Houston

HFM: Henry Ford Museum and Greenfield Village

IAD: Index of American Design, National Gallery of Art

LC: Library of Congress

MCNY: Museum of the City of New York

MFA: Museum of Fine Arts, Boston

MMA: Metropolitan Museum of Art

NHHS: New Hampshire Historical Society

NYHS: New-York Historical Society

NYPL: New York Public Library

R. B. Div.: Rare Book Division

P. Div.: Print Division

A. & A. Div.: Art & Architecture Division

NYSH: New York State Historical Association, Cooperstown

OSV: Old Sturbridge Village

PM: Philadelphia Museum of Art

PS: Pilgrim Society, Pilgrim Hall, Plymouth, Massachusetts

Rijk: Rijksmuseum, Amsterdam

SHR: Sleepy Hollow Restorations, Inc.

SI: Smithsonian Institution

SM: Shelburne Museum

WA: Wadsworth Atheneum

YHS: Historical Society of York County

YU: Yale University Art Gallery

The drawings on pages 40–41, 108–9, 154, 346–47, and 354–63 were executed by Chas. B. Slackman; those on pages 364–71 by Helen Disbrow.

Front matter—Jacket: Stiegel-type glass bottle, figure 563. (MMA)—Chippendale chair, figure 282. (MMA)—Silver teakettle by Cornelius Kierstede, figure 125. (MMA) These photographs were taken by Lee Boltin. Also by Boltin, figures: 69, 116, 170, 269, 282, 332, 563, 565. All other special photography at MMA by Geoffrey Clements. Back jacket: Puzzle jug, figure 49. (MMA)—Finial of Philadelphia Chippendale highboy, figure 267. PM—Sgraffito Pennsylvania German plate, figure 537. (MMA)

Endsheets: Engraving, "Prospective View of part of the Commons," after a water color by Christian Remick, 1768. NYPL, Stokes Collection. Title page and preface: Details from silver tankard by Edward Winslow. (MFA) Collection of Mr. and Mrs. Mark Bortman. Table of contents page: Silver dram cup by John Hull and Robert Sanderson, figure 39. YU

Our Medieval Heritage
The Puritan Century (1607–1685)

UNNUMBERED ILLUSTRATIONS LISTED BY PAGE:

9 English delft platter. duP **10** Pewter platter and iron cauldron. PS—Candleholder. MMA, Gift of Mrs. Russell Sage, 1909 **11** Detail from frontispiece of *A New Touch Stone for Gold and Silver Wares* by William Badcock, 1679. NYPL—Fireback. MCNY **12** Halberd. PS—Frontispiece from *The Whole Psalms in Foure Partes* by John Day, 1563. Folger Shakespeare Library **13** Portrait of John Smith from his *A Description of New England*, 1616. NYPL, R. B. Div.—Drawing of the second Plymouth meetinghouse, 1683. PS **14** St. Luke's Church, Virginia. LC—Old Ship meetinghouse. (Dorothy Abbe) **15** Gravestone rubbings from *Graven Images* by Allan Ludwig, 1966—Woodcut of Richard Mather. Original, Massachusetts Historical Society **16** Portrait of Thomas Savage. Collection of Henry L. Shattuck **16–17** View of London. By Permission of the Trustees of the British Museum **17** *The Morning Toilet* by Pieter de Hooch. Rijk—Coins. CMB **19** Detail of sunflower carving from Connecticut chest. MMA, Gift of Mrs. Russell Sage, 1909 **32** Pine-tree shilling. duP—Detail of sailboat from view of New York City, 1716–18, by William Burgis. NYPL, P. Div.—Silver mark of John Hull and Robert Sanderson. MFA **33** Detail of carriage from engraving after William Burgis drawing. MMA **35** Detail from silver plate by John Coney. MFA **40** Detail from porringer cover. MMA, Gift of Sylvester Dering, 1915 **42–43** London silversmith workshop from *The Plate of the Worshipful Company of Goldsmiths* by John Carrington and George Hughes, 1926. NYPL, A. & A. Div. **54**, **56** Details of Hudson and Connecticut rivers from 1675 map by John Sellers. The John Carter Brown Library, Brown University

FIGURE NUMBERS:

1 (MMA) Gift of Mrs. J. Insley Blair, 1951 **2** duP **3** MFA, Gift of J. Templeman Coolidge **4** MFA, Gift of Maurice Geeraerts in Memory of Mr. and Mrs. William R. Robeson **5** EI **6** duP **7** MMA, Gift of Mrs. Russell Sage, 1909 **8** PS **9** HFM **10** duP **11** Long Island Historical Society **12** duP **13** MFA, Samuel Putnam Avery Fund **14** WA **15** SI, Gift of Dr. and Mrs. Arthur M. Greenwood **16**, **17** WA **18** duP **19** Rijk **20** MMA, Gift of Mrs. J. Insley Blair, 1949 **21** (MMA) on loan from Mr. James de Peyster, Jr. **22** SM **23** (MMA) on loan from Mr. James de Peyster, Jr. **24** (National Gallery, London) **25** Ginsburg & Levy Inc. **26** NYPL, Spencer Collection **27** PS **28** SHR **29** AIC **30** MCNY **31** MFA, Spalding Collection **32** YU, Mabel Brady Garvan Collection **33** BM **34** MFA **35**, **36** duP **37** MFA, Gift of John S. Ames and Mary Ames Frothingham **38** YU, Mabel Brady Garvan Collection **39** YU **40** duP **41a–e** YU, Mabel Brady Garvan Collection **42a**, **b** MMA, Gift of Mrs. Russell Sage, 1909 **43** Israel Sack, Inc. **44** SI **45** MMA, Gift of Mrs. Russell Sage, 1909 **46** MMA, Gift of Mrs. J. Insley Blair, 1951 **47a**, **b** HFM **48** duP **49** (MMA) Gift of Mrs. Russell S. Carter, 1945 **50**, **51** duP **52** MCNY, on loan from Dr. and Mrs. Roger Gerry **53** MMA, Gift of W. R. Valentiner, 1908 **54** From the Collections of the University of Pennsylvania Museum **55** (MMA) Rogers Fund, 1930 **56** (HFM) **57** (MMA) Gift of Mrs. J. Insley Blair, 1952 **58** duP **59** EI **60** MMA, Gift of Mrs. Russell Sage, 1909 **61** MMA, Rogers Fund, 1909 **62** AIHA **63** MMA, Rogers Fund, 1909 **64** duP **65** (MMA) Gift of Mrs. J. Insley Blair, 1945 **66** MFA (Eliot Elisofon) **67** (MMA) Gift of Mrs. J. Insley Blair, 1945

Fashions from Abroad
The William and Mary Style (1685–1720)

UNNUMBERED ILLUSTRATIONS LISTED BY PAGE:

61 Detail from tankard by Cornelius Kierstede. duP **62** Chinese lacquer chest. Victoria and Albert Museum **63** Lambeth delft cup. duP—English print, *The Tea-Table.* The British Museum **64** Lambeth delft jug. NYHS—Detail of Indian warfare from 1675 map by John Sellers. The John Carter Brown Library **64–65** Fire of London. London Museum **65** Sir Christopher Wren attributed to J. B. Closterman. Royal Society, London—Engraving of church from *The Parochial Churches of Sir Christopher Wren 1666–1718*, 1932. NYPL **66** Engraving of College of William and Mary. CW—Drawing of New York City Hall from *The Iconography of Manhattan Island* by I. N. Phelps Stokes, 1915–28. NYHS—Painting of Clark-Frankland house. The Bostonian Society **67** Portrait of Elisha Cooke, Sr. Peabody Museum of Salem—Detail of tankard lid by Gerrit Onckelbag. MMA, Bequest of A. T. Clearwater, 1933 **68** Portrait of Blackbeard from *A General History of the Pirates* by Charles Johnson, 1724. NYPL, R. B. Div. **69** Portrait of William Byrd II by Sir Godfrey Kneller. By Courtesy of the Owner **71** Detail from table top, figure 74. MMA **80** Drawer from highboy, figure 83. (MMA)—Near East India embroidery. Ginsburg & Levy Inc.—Detail from *A Treatise of Japaning and Varnishing* by John Stalker and George Parker, 1688. NYPL, A. & A. Div. **94** Detail from thirty-six shilling note engraved by Paul Revere. NYPL, R. B. Div.—Detail from advertisement of Benjamin Harbeson. duP **95** Tavern sign. CHS—Detail from table of silver weights and measures engraved by Nathaniel Hurd. AAS **96** Detail from silver tankard by Cornelius Kierstede. duP **99** Jeremiah Dummer's mark. duP **118** SVVR initials from Boston chair. AIHA

FIGURE NUMBERS:

68 (MMA) Gift of Mrs. Screven Lorillard, 1952 **69** (MMA) Bequest of Herbert Lee Pratt, 1945 **70, 71, 71a** HFM **72** Ginsburg & Levy Inc. **73** MMA, Gift of Mrs. J. Insley Blair, 1942 **74** MMA, Gift of George Coe Graves, The Sylmaris Collection, 1930 **75** HFM **76** WA **77, 78, 78a** HFM **79** MFA **80, 81** The Warner House Association, Portsmouth, N.H. **82** City of Albany, Office of the Mayor **83** (MMA), Purchase from Joseph Pulitzer Bequest, 1940 **84** MMA, Gift of Robert L. Cammann, 1957 **85** MMA, Rogers Fund, 1930 **86** PM **87** MMA, Gift of Mrs. George F. Baker, 1953 **88** Collection of Phelps Warren **89** Victoria and Albert Museum **90, 91** Collection of Phelps Warren **92** duP **93** NYHS **94** (IAD) **95** NHHS, Prentis Collection **96** MMA, Gift of Mrs. Russell Sage, 1909 **97** NHHS, Prentis Collection **98** Columbia University Libraries **99** MMA, Bequest of Charles Allen Munn, 1924 **100** MMA, Gift of Mrs. Russell Sage, 1909 **101** MMA, Bequest of Charles A. Munn, 1924 **102** MMA, Rogers Fund, 1944 **103** The Library Company of Philadelphia **104** duP **105** MCNY **106–108** YU, Mabel Brady Garvan Collection **109** From *Jeremiah Dummer, Colonial Craftsman and Merchant, 1645–1718* by Hermann F. Clarke, 1935. NYPL, A. & A. Div. **110** YU **111, 111a** MMA, Bequest of A. T. Clearwater, 1933 **112** Courtesy of the Owner **113, 114** MFA **115, 115a** duP **116** (MMA) Rogers Fund, 1941 **117** MFA **118** MMA, Bequest of A. T. Clearwater, 1933 **119** MFA, Pickman Collection **120** MMA, Gift of Sylvester Dering, 1915 **121, 122** Harvard University **123** By Permission of the Trustees of the British Museum **124** YU, Mabel Brady Garvan Collection **125** MMA, Bequest of James Stevenson Van Cortlandt, 1917 **126** MMA, Gift of Mrs. Lloyd K. Garrison, 1961 **127** Tankard. YU, Mabel Brady Garvan Collection—Mark of Jacobus Vanderspiegel. duP **128** YU, Mabel Brady Garvan Collection **129** duP **130** MMA, Bequest of A. T. Clearwater, 1933 **131** MMA, Given in Memory of William Bayard Van Rensselaer, 1937 **132** MMA, Samuel D. Lee Fund, 1938 **133** duP **134** PM **135** duP **136** PM **137** duP **138, 138a** (MMA) Bequest of Charles Allen Munn, 1924 **139, 140** HFM **141** duP **142, 143** HFM **144** MMA, Gift of Mrs. Screven Lorillard, 1952 **145** AIHA **146** duP **147** WA **148** HFM **149** AIC **150** HFM **151** Ginsburg & Levy Inc. **152** Israel Sack, Inc. **153** HFM **154** MMA, Gift of Mrs. Russell Sage, 1909 **155** HFM **156** duP **157** The Library Company of Philadelphia

The Triumph of the Curve
The Queen Anne Style (1720–1750)

UNNUMBERED ILLUSTRATIONS LISTED BY PAGE:

121 Pewter porringer handle by Francis Bassett. YU, Mabel Brady Garvan Collection **122–123** Six porcelain plates. HFM **123** English armchair. AIC **124** Top of highboy. duP—Title page from architecture book. NYPL, A. & A. Div. **125** Classical orders. NYPL, A. & A. Div. **126** Plan of Pennsylvania State House. Historical Society of Pennsylvania—Hancock house. Courtesy of the Owner **127** Engraving of Boston. LC **128–129** Engraving of Philadelphia. NYPL, Stokes Collection **128** Painting of girl. duP **130** Woodcut from Germantown almanac by Christopher Sower, 1748. Princeton University Library, Sinclair Hamilton Collection **131** Armchair. (MMA) Gift of Mary Stillman Harkness, 1950 **132** Details of shell and acanthus carvings from crests of two Queen Anne chairs. HFM **147** 18th-century shop sign. SI **148** Detail from japanned lowboy, figure 193. MMA **154** Detail from Thomas Hancock trade card. Massachusetts Historical Society **156** Detail from Connecticut secretary, figure 209. HFM **177** Leg detail from saltcellar, figure 239. MMA

FIGURE NUMBERS:

158, 159 HFM **160** Ginsburg & Levy Inc. **161** OSV **162** duP **163** YU, Mabel Brady Garvan Collection **164** duP **165** YU, Bequest of Olive Louise Dann **166** HFM **167** MFA, Gift of Miss Dorothy Buhler **168** duP **169** (MMA) Gift of Mrs. J. Insley Blair, 1950 **170** (MMA) Gift of Mrs. J. Insley Blair, 1946 **171** AIHA **172, 173** duP **174** CW **175** MFA, Gift of William S. Eaton **176** duP **177** MMA, Gift of Edward Robinson, 1923 **178** MMA, Rogers Fund, 1955 **179** Courtesy of the Owner **180** MCNY, Collection of Waldron Phoenix Belknap, Jr. **181** MMA, Winfield Foundation Gift, 1961 **182** YU, Mabel Brady Garvan Collection **183** MMA, Gift of Mrs. J. Insley Blair, 1945 **184** duP **185** YU, Mabel Brady Garvan Collection **186** MCNY **187a, b, 188** duP **189** HFM **190** From the collection of Colonel Edgar William and Bernice Chrysler Garbisch **191** SI **192** MCNY **193** MMA, Joseph Pulitzer Bequest, 1940 **194** MMA, Purchase from Joseph Pulitzer Bequest, 1940 (Courtesy Shell Oil Company) **195** FAH, Bayou Bend Collection **196** BM **197** (Ginsburg & Levy Inc.) **198** Collection of Joseph V. McMullan **199** Harvard University **200** John Walton, Inc. **201** duP **202** HFM **203** MFA **204** MMA, Rogers Fund, 1916 **205** MMA, Rogers Fund, 1925 **206** CW **207** (MMA) Rogers Fund, 1925 **208, 209** HFM **210** MFA, Karolik Collection **211** MMA, Purchase from Joseph Pulitzer Bequest, 1933 **212** HFM **213** (MMA) Rogers Fund, 1916 **214–217** duP **218** FAH, Bayou Bend Collection **219** MMA, Rogers Fund, 1925 **220** HFM **221** MMA **222–225** CW **226** AAS **227, 228** CW **229** MFA, William E. Nickerson Fund **230** CW **231** Collection of Mr. and Mrs. Samuel Schwartz **232** NYSH **233** MMA, Gift of Mrs. Lewis Morris, 1950 **234** Maryland Historical Society **235** Johns Hopkins University Library **236** PM **237** MCNY **238** MMA, Bequest of A. T. Clearwater, 1933 **239** MMA, Dodge Fund, 1935 **240** duP **241** MCNY **242–45** duP **246** MMA, Bequest of Charles Allen Munn, 1924 **247** duP **248** MMA, Gift of Mrs. Abraham Lansing, 1901 **249** AIC **250** MFA, Gift of Dr. J. H. Means **251** Rhode Island School of Design

Patterns of Elegance
The Chippendale Period (1750–1785)

UNNUMBERED ILLUSTRATIONS LISTED BY PAGE:

183 Cartouche from highboy. MFA, M. & M. Karolik Collection **184–185** Detail of plan of Louisbourg, 1758. LC **186** Portrait of Sir William Pepperrell. EI **186–187** Benjamin Franklin's cartoon. AAS **187** Portrait of George Washington. Washington and Lee University **188** "Line of beauty" from William Hogarth's essay, 1753. NYPL, A. & A. Div.—Hogarth engraving, 1742. NYPL, P. Div. **189** Corset, chair legs, faces from Hogarth's essay, 1753. NYPL, A. & A. Div. **190** Architectural detail. MMA—Design for girandole. NYPL, A. & A. Div. **191** Portrait of Nicholas Boylston. Fogg Art Museum, Harvard University—Portrait of William Buckland. YU, Mabel Brady Garvan Collection **192** Doorway. Hammond-Harwood House Association (Francis Engle) **193** Portrait of Marinus Willett. MMA, Bequest of George Willett Van Nest, 1917—Benjamin Frothingham label (Courtesy *Antiques Magazine*) **200** Clock designs originally from *Designs for Furniture* by Thomas Johnson, 1758 and 1768. NYPL, A. & A. Div.—Card table designs from *Genteel Household Furniture in the Present Taste by a Society of Upholsterers* . . . 1760. NYPL, A. & A. Div.—Secretary-bookcase design from *The Gentleman and Cabinet-Maker's Director* by Thomas Chippendale, 1762. NYPL, A. & A. Div. **201** Trade card. The Library Company of Philadelphia **232** Engraving from *Bowles, Moral Pictures,* 1795. PM—Woodcut from *Poor Richard Improved*, 1749. Princeton University Library, Sinclair Hamilton Collection **233** Franklin's drawing of bifocals. Franklin Institute—Engraving of Franklin by François Denis Née. PM **235** Detail from pewter dish by Francis Bassett. SI, on loan from Dr. Joseph Kler, 1961 **236** Touch mark, left. YU, Mabel Brady Garvan Collection—Touch mark, center. PM—Touch mark, right. YU **237** Communion tokens, left and right. duP—Touch mark, top center. MMA, Gift of Joseph France, 1943 **246** Snuff box. duP **254** Advertisement. MMA, from *The Homes of Our Ancestors* by R. T. H. Halsey and Elizabeth Tower, 1937

FIGURE NUMBERS:

252–254 NYPL, A. & A. Div. **255** MMA, Rogers Fund, Library, 1918 **256** MMA, Gift of Mrs. Paul Moore, 1939 **257** MFA, M. & M. Karolik Collection **258** Ginsburg & Levy Inc. **259** NYPL, A. & A. Div. **260, 261** duP **262** (Samuel Chamberlain) **263** MMA **264** NYPL, Stokes Collection **265, 265a** PM **266** Free Library of Philadelphia **267** PM **268** duP **269** (MMA) Rogers Fund, 1925 **270** (MMA) Funds from various donors, 1959 **271** (MMA) Rogers Fund, 1935 **272** MMA, Rogers Fund, 1925 **273, 274** (MMA) on loan from John Cadwalader **275** MMA, Morris K. Jesup Fund, 1932 **276** MMA, Kennedy Fund, 1918 **277** MFA, M. & M. Karolik Collection **278, 279** PM **280** YU, Mabel Brady Garvan Collection **281** HFM **282** (MMA) Gift of George Coe Graves, The Sylmaris Collection, 1932 **283** MMA, Gift of George Coe Graves, The Sylmaris Collection, 1932 **284–286** HFM **287** duP **288** MFA, M. & M. Karolik Collection **289** (MMA) **290** MMA, Victor Wibour Fund, 1955 **291** MCNY **292** MMA, Purchased with funds from Ella E. Russell Bequest, in Memory of Salem Towne Russell, 1933 **293** NYHS **294, 295** duP **296** MMA, Rogers Fund, 1937 **297**

HFM **298** Israel Sack, Inc. **299** duP **300** Ginsburg & Levy Inc. **301** AIHA **302** MFA, M. & M. Karolik Collection **303** MFA **304** Ginsburg & Levy Inc. **305** duP **306, 306a** MFA, M. & M. Karolik Collection **307** HFM **308** MMA, Gift of George Coe Graves, The Sylmaris Collection, 1930 **309** Ginsburg & Levy Inc. **310** MFA, M. & M. Karolik Collection **311** HFM **312** YU, Mabel Brady Garvan Collection **313, 313a** MFA, M. & M. Karolik Collection **314** John Brown House, Rhode Island Historical Society **315** MMA, Rogers Fund, 1927 **316** duP **317** Ginsburg & Levy Inc. **318** Israel Sack, Inc. **319** MMA, Rogers Fund, 1915 **320** duP **321** Ginsburg & Levy Inc. **322** duP **323** WA **324** MMA, Kennedy Fund, 1918 **325** YU, Mabel Brady Garvan Collection **326** Israel Sack, Inc. **327** duP **328** The Charleston Museum **329** OSV **330** duP **331** Courtesy of John Devereux Kernan, Jr. **332** MMA, Gift of Mrs. J. Insley Blair, 1943 **333** duP **334** CHS **335** BM **336** HFM **337** SI **338** MMA, Gift of Mrs. J. Insley Blair, 1940 **339** duP **340** MMA, Gift of Mrs. J. Insley Blair, 1940 **341** MMA, Gift of Mrs. J. Insley Blair, 1940 **342** MMA, Gift of Mrs. J. Insley Blair, 1946 **343** MMA, Rogers Fund, 1945 **344** MMA, Gift of Mrs. J. Insley Blair, 1940 **345** duP **346** MMA, Gift of Joseph France, 1943 **347** duP **348** PM **349** YU **350** Los Angeles County Museum **351** James Monroe Memorial Library **352** PM **353** Ginsburg & Levy Inc. **354** AIC **355, 356** duP **357** LC **358, 359** duP **360** Ginsburg & Levy Inc. **361** duP **362** Ginsburg & Levy Inc. **363** MCNY **364** YU, Mabel Brady Garvan Collection **365** Heritage Foundation, Deerfield **366** MFA, Pauline Revere Thayer Collection **367, 367a** MFA, Gift of Revere Family **368, 369** MMA, Bequest of A. T. Clearwater, 1933 **370** MFA, Gift of Mrs. Henry B. Chapin and Edward H. R. Revere **371** MMA, Bequest of A. T. Clearwater, 1933 **372** MFA, Pauline Revere Thayer Collection **373** MFA, Purchased by Public Subscription and Francis Bartlett Fund **374** Free Library of Philadelphia **375** MFA, Sleeper Collection **376** MFA, Gift of Mrs. Nathaniel Thayer **377, 377a** MFA, Sleeper Collection **378** HFM **379** NYHS **380** CW **381** MMA, Morris K. Jesup Fund, 1954 **382** duP **383** Independence National Historical Park **384** HFM **385** AIC **386** Heritage Foundation, Deerfield **387** CW **388** MFA **389** duP **390** LC **391** Historical Society of Pennsylvania **392** MMA, Gift of the Winfield Foundation, 1951 **393** duP **394** Courtesy of Mrs. H. Edward Dreier, Mrs. George B. B. Lamb and Mrs. Thomas Louden

The Colonial House at Work
Functioning Forms in the Home

UNNUMBERED ILLUSTRATIONS LISTED BY PAGE:

261 Flax comber. MMA, Gift of Mrs. Robert W. de Forest, 1933 **262** Drawing of frame house. OSV—Detail from painting of house raising by William P. Chappel. MCNY **263** Doorway and hall of Ashley house. (Heritage Foundation, Deerfield, Arnold Newman) **281** Trade card of William Parker. MMA, Gift of Mrs. Morris Hawkes, 1927

FIGURE NUMBERS:

395 (Eliot Elisofon) **396** PM **397** (Eliot Elisofon, Courtesy of *Life* magazine) **398** MMA, Gift of Mrs. J. Insley Blair, 1947 **399** PM **400, 401** duP **402** Ginsburg & Levy Inc. **403** MMA, Gift of Mrs. Russell Sage, 1909 **404** IAD **405** PM **406–408** duP **409** MMA, Gift of Mrs. Russell Sage, 1909 **410** (MMA) Gift of George Coe Graves, The Sylmaris Collection, 1930 **411** MMA, Rogers Fund, 1938 **412** (MMA) **413** MMA, Rogers Fund, 1922 **414** From *The Works of Benjamin Franklin* by Jared Sparks, 1882. MMA **415** HFM **416** NYPL **417** Old Salem Restorations, Winston-Salem, N.C. **418** Woodcut from *Flickering Flames* by Leroy Thwing, 1965 **419, 420** MMA, Gift of Mrs. Russell Sage, 1909 **421** PM **422** Heritage Foundation, Deerfield **423** MMA **424, 425** duP **426** IAD **427, 428** duP **429** OSV **430, 431** duP **432** MMA, Rogers Fund, 1943 **433–436** duP **437** MMA: candlesticks, Gift of Mrs. Clermont L. Barnwell, 1964; snuffer, Gift of Mr. and Mrs. William A. Moore, 1923 **438** MMA, Rogers Fund, 1922 **439** Heritage Foundation, Deerfield **440** MMA, Purchase, 1937, Gift of George Coe Graves, The Sylmaris Collection **441** The Mount Vernon Ladies Association **442** St. Michael's Church, Marblehead, Mass. (Richard Merrill) **443** HFM **444** duP **445** Massachusetts Historical Society **446** The First Church in Albany **447, 448** duP **449** (Taylor and Dull) **450** duP **451** Collection of Col. Edgar William and Bernice Chrysler Garbisch **452, 453** OSV **454** YHS **455** (Heritage Foundation, Deerfield, Samuel Chamberlain) **456** HFM **457** (EI, Richard Merrill) **458** AIC **459** (WA, Eliot Elisofon, Courtesy *Life*) **460** Collection of Mrs. Thomas G. Hazard, Jr. (The Preservation Society of Newport County) **461** From *L'Encyclopédie, ou Dictionnaire Raisonne des Sciences, des Arts et des Metiers* by Denis Diderot, 1763 **462, 463** duP **464** CHS **465, 466** duP **467** (MMA) Pulitzer Fund, 1939 **468** (MMA) Gift of Mrs. Russell Sage, 1909 **469** IAD **470** (CHS) **471** CHS **472** Toledo Museum of Art **473** Massachusetts Historical Society **474** *L'art du Menuisier* by Andre J. Roubo, 1769. NYPL, A.&A. Div. **475** The Old Print Shop **476** duP **477** OSV **478, 479** duP **480** NYPL, Arents Collection **481, 482** OSV **483** WA **484** HFM **485** OSV

From the Rhine to the Susquehanna
The Pennsylvania Germans

UNNUMBERED ILLUSTRATIONS LISTED BY PAGE:

299 Detail from *fraktur*, figure 515. MMA **300** Playing card. Worcester College, England **301** Tract from *Der Neue americanische Landwirthschafts-Calendar*, 1819. NYPL, R. B. Div.—Engraving from *Der Gantz Neue Verbesserte Nord-Americanische Calendar*, 1779. NYPL, R. B. Div. **302** Water color drawing of Bethlehem, Pa., 1742. Kennedy & Co. **303** Engraving of soldier of Continental Army. MMA **338** Stove plate. The Mercer Museum, Doylestown, Pa.—Cannon stove. SI **339** Illustrations of glassmaking. MMA **346** "Bull's-eye" from crown glass. Society for the Preservation of New England Antiquities

FIGURE NUMBERS:

486 duP **487** MMA, Anonymous Gift, 1948 **488, 489** PM **490** NYSH **491–494** PM **495** David Stockwell, Inc. **496** PM **497** duP **498** PM **499** Single Brothers house, Old Salem, Winston-Salem, N.C. **500** HFM **501** PM **502, 503** duP **504–513** YHS **514** (MMA) Rogers Fund, 1944 **515** (MMA) Gift of Mrs. Robert W. de Forest, 1933 **516, 517** PM **518** HFM **519** duP **520** Museum of New Mexico Collections, Santa Fe **521** (MMA) Rogers Fund, 1923 **522** (MMA) Gift of Mrs. Robert W. de Forest, 1933 **523** IAD **524** (MMA) Gift of Mrs. Robert W. de Forest, 1933 **525** IAD **526** (MMA) Gift of Mrs. Robert W. de Forest, 1933 **527** PM **528** (MMA) Rogers Fund, 1948 **529** CW, The Abby Aldrich Rockefeller Folk Art Collection **530–533** PM **534** IAD **535, 536** PM **537** (MMA) Gift of Mrs. Robert W. de Forest, 1933 **538, 539** PM **540** HFM **541** PM **542** duP **543** IAD **544** (MMA) Gift of Mrs. Robert W. de Forest, 1933 **545** PM **546** duP **547, 548** PM **549** Pennsylvania Historical and Museum Commission **550** MMA, Gift of George Coe Graves, The Sylmaris Collection, 1930 **551** MMA, Gift of Mrs. J. Insley Blair, 1937 **552** MMA, Gift of Mrs. Robert W. de Forest, 1933 **553–555** PM **556** Collection of John Gordon **557** MMA, Gift of F. W. Hunter, 1914 **558** CMG **559** PM **560** (MMA) Gift of F. W. Hunter, 1913 **561** CMG **562** IAD **563** (MMA) Gift of F. W. Hunter, 1914 **564** CMG **565** (MMA) Gift of F. W. Hunter, 1913 **566** CMG **567** duP **568** CMG **569** MMA, Rogers Fund, 1928 **570, 571** CMG **572** MMA, Gift of Wilfred Wood, 1956 **573a, b** From *100 Great Guns* by Merrill K. Lindsay, 1967 (Bruce Pendleton) **574** PM **575** duP **576–578** PM **579** IAD **580** Collection of Herbert W. Hemphill (Courtesy of Museum of American Folk Art)

Index

The figures in parentheses refer to the numbered illustrations and in each case precede the number of the page on which the reference is made. Matter appearing in the glossary and style charts is not indexed.

A

ACANTHUS LEAVES, (illus.) 132, 133, 151, (291) 214
ACORN FINIAL. See Finials
ADAM AND EVE, as sampler motif, (459) 288, 289; as wood carving motif, (490) 305
ADAM BROTHERS, Robert and James, 193, 258; Robert, 195
ADAMS, ABIGAIL, 186, 232
ADAMS, JOHN, on amusements, 170; on Benjamin Franklin, 232; on English influences, 185–86; favorite Windsor of, 242; on John Amelung, 344; on John Cadwalader, 207; on Kentucky rifle, 348; on New York, 215; on Nicholas Boylston, 189; on Philadelphia, 191–92
ADAMS, JOHN QUINCY, 28
AESOP'S FABLES, 198; as motifs, (265, 265a, 266) 199, (275) 206, (276, 277) 207
AFFLECK, THOMAS, 209; possible attributions to, (267) 202, 203, (281) 209
AGATEWARE, (pottery) 255
ALBANY, N.Y., 72, 118, 140, 147, 282
ALBANY CONGRESS, 184
ALCOHOLIC BEVERAGES, 16–17, 104, 162, 238, 263
ALDEN, JOHN, 17, 33
ALDEN, JOHN, JR., 33
ALEXANDRIA, EGYPT, 346
ALEXANDRIA, VA., 270, 271
AMELUNG, JOHN FREDERICK, 341, 344; examples of glass by, (567–71) 344–45
AMERICAN PHILOSOPHICAL SOCIETY, 341
AMISH, 301, 316
AMUSEMENTS, 168–75. See also Cards, Games, and specific sports
ANALYSIS OF BEAUTY, THE. See Hogarth, William
ANCIENT AND HONORABLE ARTILLERY COMPANY, 33
ANDIRONS, brass, (410) 270; with spit hooks, 268, (408) 269
ANDROS, EDMUND, 66
ANGLICAN CHURCH, 186
ANNAPOLIS, MD., 190, 198
ANNAPOLIS ROYAL, N.S., 183
ANNE, QUEEN OF GREAT BRITAIN AND IRELAND, 69, 72, 74, 79, 121, 122, 123, 127, 300
ANTIMONY, 238
APPALACHIAN MOUNTAINS, 188
APTHORP FAMILY, chairs of, (160) 134
ARCHITECTS, 190
ARCHITECTURE, AMERICAN, church, 11–12, 65; domestic, 12–13, 15, 44, 65–66, 69, 78–79, 126–27, 154–55, 156, 162–63, 190, 261–63; Georgian style in, 65–66, 78–79, 125, 212; Gothic influences in, 10–12; Renaissance influences in, 64, 66, 79, 156, 157
ARCHITECTURE, CLASSICAL, orders in, 124–25, (illus.) 125, 148, 159, 195
ARCHITECTURE, ENGLISH, 11, 12; classical orders in, 124; effect of London fire on, 66; of Wren, 64–65
ARCHITECTURAL MANUALS, 154, 156, 159, 190, 191, 195
ARCHITECTURAL WOODWORK, 156–62, (213) 161, 162, top (illus.) 190, 309
ARGAND, AIME, 280
ARNOLD, BENEDICT, 242
ARROW-STRETCHERS, (215) 164–65
ARTICLES OF ASSOCIATION, 242
ARTISTS, as portraitists, 95
ASH, (wood) 24, 241
ASH, GILBERT, 215
ASHLEY HOUSE, Old Deerfield, (illus.) 263
ASHLEY RIVER, 125
AUST, GOTTFRIED, stove by, (417) 273
AUSTRIAN SUCCESSION, WAR OF THE, 183
AVERY, MARY, bed rug by, 286, (457) 287

B

BACK RAIL, 88, (97) 89, (272) 205
BACK STOOL, 53. See also Chairs, Side and French chairs
BALTIMORE, MD., 339
BAMBOO DESIGN, (362) 245
BANCKER, ADRIAN, silver casters by, (237) 176, 177; handle of silver porringer by, (240) 178
BANISTER-BACK CHAIRS, (138) 110, (139) 111
BAPTISMAL CERTIFICATE, (451) 284, 316, (515) 317
BARGELLO WORK. See Flamestitch
BARNS, designs on Pennsylvania German, 320
BAROQUE STYLE, 71, 76, 86
BARWELL, BARTHOLOMEW, clockworks by, (196) 150, 151
BASSETT, FRANCIS, 238; engraving by, (illus.) 235; pewter dish by, (337) 234
BASSETT, FREDERICK, pewterer's mark of, top center (illus.) 237
BATHROOMS, 263
BAYEUX TAPESTRY, 286
BAYONET CLASP, (237) 176, 177
BEACON HILL, Boston, 126, 127, 154, 221; endpapers
BEAKERS, 14; silver, (41a–e) 38–39, 252, (382) 253
BED HANGINGS, (214) 164, (455) 286
BED RUGS, 286, (457, 458) 287
BEDROOMS, 262, 286
BEDS, 11, 164; folding, (43) 45; four-post, (214) 164; trussing, 44. See also Day Beds
BEECH, (wood) 53, 241
BELCHER, JONATHAN, inkstand of, (99) 90
BELLARMINE, (stoneware) 48, (54) 50
BELLINGHAM, RICHARD, 17
BELLOMONT, EARL OF, 67, 102
BELLOWS, FIREPLACE, (409) 270
BEMIS HEIGHTS, BATTLE OF, 348
BENCHES, 11, (12) 22–23, 53; Dutch, (62) 54–55
BENTLEY, THOMAS, 255
BENTLEY, WILLIAM, 262
BERKELEY, GEORGE, 128
BERKS COUNTY, PA., 300, 302, 303, 320
BERRIEN, JOHN, gaming tables of, (298) 217
BESLEY, THAUVET, handle of silver porringer by, (241) 178; silver tea caddy by, (186) 145
BETHABARA, N.C., 333
BETHLEHEM, PA., 263, 301, (illus.) 302, 303
BIBLES, 301; title page of Bradford's, (8) 22
BIBLE BOXES, (illus.) 8, 23; (19) 22; Pennsylvania German, (500) 310
BILLIARD TABLE, (224) 170
BILSTED, (wood) 218
BIRDCAGE. See Tables, tilt-top
BISMUTH, 238
BLACK TULIP, THE, 302
BLACKBEARD. See Teach, Edward
BLACKSMITHS, 334, 337
BLANCK, JURIAN, silver cup by, 106, (135) 107
BLANKET CHEST, (64) 56, (67) 59, 318, (518) 319
BLENHEIM, BATTLE OF, 121
BLIN, PETER, 56
BLINDS. See Window Hangings
BLOCK-FRONT, clock, (315) 225; desk, (324) 229; desk drawers, 222, (310) 223; regional differences in, 192, 217, 222, 227; with shell carvings, (315) 225, (319) 226, (313a) 227
BLOWPIPE, 346, 347
BOARD OF TRADE AND PLANTATIONS, 118
BOELEN, JACOB, silverwork by—spoon, (36) 35; teapot, 102, (126) 103
BOMBE, 217; secretary, (304) 220, 221
BONNET (ROOFED) TOP, 124, (319) 226, (320) 227
BONNIE PRINCE CHARLIE. See Stuart, Charles Edward
BORLAND, FRANCIS, 222; tea table of, 222, (309) 223
BOSTON, MASS., 74, 125, 152, 198, 303, 339; architecture of, 12, 64, 126, 154; characteristics of furniture, 118–19, 130–31, 133, 221, 222; Common, endpapers; engraving of, 127; as japanning center, 148, 151; metal crafts in, 32–33, 35, 68, 235; social and economic life of, 13, 17, 66, 129, 162, 191–92, 238, 262
BOSTON CHAIRS, 118, (154–56) 119
BOSTON GAZETTE, THE, 177
BOSTON-GAZETTE AND COUNTRY JOURNAL, THE, 222, 251
BOSTON NEWS-LETTER, THE, 291
BOSTON TEA PARTY, 192
BOSTON WEEKLY NEWS-LETTER, THE, 155
BOTTLES, Dutch Delft, 48, (90) 85; English delft, 48, (51) 50; glass, 48, 339, (559) 340, 341, (563) 342; leather, 10
BOW-BACK CHAIRS. See Windsor Chairs
BOWLS, maple burl, (483) 296, (484) 297, (485) 297; pewter, (340) 235; porcelain, (Chinese) (385) 254, (Japanese) (86) 82, 83; silver, 104, (132) 105, 248, (373) 250
BOWLER, METCALF, 162; paneled wall from home of, 162, (213) 163
BOXES, (9-11) 22-23, (497) 309. See also Bible Boxes and specific forms
BOYLE, JOHN, 192
BOYLSTON, NICHOLAS, 189; portrait of, 191
BRACE-BACK CHAIRS. See Windsor Chairs
BRACKET FEET, (285) 211; (319) 226, (313a) 227
BRACKETS, 222, (309) 223; on wall, (260, 261) 197, 217

BRADDOCK, EDWARD, 184
BRADFORD, WILLIAM, 9; Bible of, (8) 22, 23
BRANDY WARMER, (250) 180, 181
BRAZIERS, silver, 106, (136) 107, (249) 180, 181; silverplated brass, (402) 266
BREMEN, GERMANY, coat of arms of, 344, (569) 345
BREWSTER, WILLIAM, 11, 17, 19
BREWSTER-TYPE CHAIRS, (1) 18, 19, 21, (29) 31, 72
BRICE HOUSE, Annapolis, 198
BRIDE'S BOX, 320, (520) 321
BRIGHT, GEORGE, 221
BRINCKERHOFF FAMILY, secretary of, 92, (105) 93
BRITISH ARCHITECT, THE. See Swan, Abraham
BROADSIDES, 198, (390) 257
BROCATELLE, (215) 164–65
BROOKLYN, N.Y., 265
BROWN, GAWEN, 222; clock by, 222, (311) 223
BROWN, JOHN, roundabout chair of, 224, (314) 225
BROWN, MOSES, 224
BROWN UNIVERSITY, 127
BUCKLAND, WILLIAM, 190; house designed by, (illus.) 192; portrait of, 191
BUCKS COUNTY, PA., 337
BULFINCH, THOMAS, 262
BULL'S-EYE GLASS, 347
BUN FEET, (17) 25
BUREAU, 76
BURLING, THOMAS, 215
BURLINGTON, EARL OF, 124
BURNET, WILLIAM, 152, 169, 177
BURNHAM, BENJAMIN, 228; desk by, 228, (324) 229
BURT, JOHN, 181; silver brazier by, (249) 180, 181
BUTLER, JAMES, silver tea strainer by, (191) 147
BUTTON FEET, 118, (155) 119
BYRD, WILLIAM, II, 12, 68–69, 92, 116, 144, 189; builds Westover, 125; library of, 92, 125, 130; portrait of, 69
BYRD, WILLIAM, III, 174

C

CABINET AND CHAIR-MAKER'S REAL FRIEND & COMPANION, THE. See Manwaring, Robert
CABINETMAKERS AND CABINETMAKING, 71, 74, 92, 159, 195. See also Woodworking
CABRIOLE LEGS, 86, 123, 133, 210, 241, (257) 196; on four-post bed, (214) 164; on seating forms, (217, 218) 166, (219) 167, (256, 257) 196, 197, (278) 208–9, (291) 214; on silver teapot, 246, (364) 247; on tea table, (305) 221. See also Queen Anne and Chippendale periods
CADWALADER, JOHN, AND FAMILY, 207; card table owned by, (274) 206; portrait of, (273) 206
CAKE BASKET, silver, 252, (381) 253
CALICO, 63, (85) 82, 83, 86, 155
CALLIGRAPHY, 90, (98) 90
CAMBRIDGE, MASS., 92
CAMPBELL, COLIN, 130
CANDELABRA, 217
CANDLE-DIPPING STAND, (432) 277
CANDLE LIGHTER, (434) 278
CANDLE MOLD, tin, (426) 276
CANDLE SNUFFERS, brass, (433, 435) 278; silver stand, (437) 279
CANDLEBOX, 320, (523) 322
CANDLEHOLDERS, (illus.) 10, 92, (104) 93, 274, (422) 275, (424) 276, (433) 278, (535) 327
CANDLES, 276, 278, 280, 286
CANDLESTANDS, 114, (146) 115, (149) 116, (425) 276, (429, 431) 277
CANDLESTICKS, brass, (illus.) 8, (20) 27, (423, 428) 276, (434) 278; delft, (427) 276; silver, (38) 36, (84) 82, 83, (238) 177, (437) 279; tin, (illus.) 260
CANDLEWOOD HOLDER. See Rushlight
CANE, 62, 67, 71, 72, 88, (96) 88–89, 112; chairs, (illus.) 60, (69) 70, (137) 110, 111
CANNS, silver, (illus.) 182. See also Mugs
CANTON, CHINA, 258, 259
CAPE COD, MASS., 33, 264
CAPTAIN'S CHAIR. See Windsor Chairs
CARDS, PLAYING, (228) 172, (illus.) 300
CARLISLE, PA., 339
CAROLINAS, 124, 300
CARPENTERS AND CARPENTRY, 12, 19, 71, 108–9, 126–27
CARPENTERS' COMPANY OF THE CITY AND COUNTY OF PHILADELPHIA, 126–27, 233
CARPETS, floorcloths, 152; Turkish, 152; Wilton, 155
CARROLL, CHARLES, in engraving, (357) 242–43
CARTER, ROBERT, AND FAMILY, 170, 276, 289, 291
CARTOUCHE, 178, (247) 179, 212, 228, (323) 229
CARVER, JOHN, 19
CARVER CHAIRS, 19, 21
CARVING, 19, 22, 23, 25, 54, 56, 71, 123, 133, 156, 210-11. See also Wood Carving Motifs
CASE PIECES. See specific forms
CASTERS, 104; silver, (128) 105, (237) 176, 177, 246, (365) 247
CASTING, in silver, 177, (239) 178, 246, (365) 247
CATESBY, MARK, 195
CATHERINE OF ARAGON, 44
CATHERINE OF BRAGANZA, 61, 62, 63, 80, 86, 96
CATS, JACOBUS, (FATHER CATS), 38
CAUDLE CUP, silver, 36, (40) 37, (illus.) 60; as motif, 112
CAULIFLOWER POTTERY, (illus.) 254, 255
CEDAR, (wood) 24
CEILINGS, 160, 212
CELLINI, BENVENUTO, 338
CHAFING DISHES. See Braziers
CHAIRS, development and characteristics of, 11, 21, 23, 53, 62, 71, 72, 110–11, 118, 123, 133, 197. See also Cane, chairs and specific forms
CHAIRS, ARMCHAIRS, Chippendale—New England, (306) 221; New York, (287) 212, (293) 215; Philadelphia, (270) 203, (272) 205. Queen Anne, (illus.) 123, (illus.) 131, (159) 134, (168) 136; William and Mary, 72, (71) 73, (138) 110, (139) 111, (143) 113, (156) 119
CHAIRS, SIDE, Chippendale—New England, (312) 223, (317) 226; New York, (288) 212, (291) 214, 215; Philadelphia, (256) 196, (282) 210. Queen Anne, (illus.) 120, (158) 133, (160, 161) 134, (163) 135, (165–67) 136, (170) 138, (171, 172) 139, (195) 150; William and Mary, (69) 70, (154, 155) 119
CHAIR-TABLES, (42) 44, (44) 46
CHAMFERED CORNERS, 218, (303) 219
CHANDELIERS, 280; brass, (illus.) 60, (442) 281; tin, (440) 280, (533) 327
CHAPIN, ELIPHALET, 228; highboy by, 228, (323) 229
CHARLES II, KING OF ENGLAND, 25, 61, 62, 63, 66, 67, 80, 86, 122; portrait on delft cup, 63
CHARLES TOWN, S.C., See Charleston
CHARLESTON, S.C., 64, 125, 128, 130, 189–90, 230, 232, 294
CHARLESTOWN, MASS., 193
CHARLOTTE, QUEEN CONSORT, 255
CHARMING FORGE, Pa., 339
CHASTELLUX, MARQUIS DE, 221, 230, 265
CHELSEA, ENGLAND, 258
CHESAPEAKE BAY, 15
CHESTS, 9, 24. See also Connecticut Valley Chests
CHESTS OF DRAWERS, (2) 18–19, 21; Chippendale, (280) 209, 215, (307) 222, (325) 229; Pennsylvania German, (516) 318; William and Mary, (65) 58, 76. See also Highboys
CHESTS-ON-CHESTS, 215, 218, (303) 219, (326) 229
CHEST-ON-FRAME, (20) 26, 27
CHESTER COUNTY, PA., 304, 310
CHILDREN, discipline and care, 30; furniture for, (25) 29, (26–28) 30, (29, 30) 31, (359) 244, (362) 245; toys of, (21, 22) 28, (23, 24) 29, 30, (222, 223) 169, (illus.) 298
CHIMNEY PIECES, (262, 263) 198, 270, (412) 271
CHIMNEYS, GLASS, 280
CHINA, 62, 80, 140, 258–59; influences of, 83, 133, 195; lacquer of, (illus.) 62, (195) 150, 151; pottery of, 48, 85, (illus.) 123, 143, 258. See also Oriental Influences and Motifs
CHINOISERIES, 82–83; frescoes, 162; decorations, 222, (311) 223
CHINTZ. See Calico
CHIPPENDALE, THOMAS, 186, 187, 193, 195, 197, 198, 202. See also *Gentlemen and Cabinet-Maker's Director, The*
CHIPPENDALE PERIOD, 127, 182–253; country chairs, 230–31; designs and details, 133, 194–201, 230, 306, 348; New England style, 220–29; New York style, 212–18; Philadelphia style, 199–211, 228; silver of, 246–53
CHOCOLATE POTS, copper, (401) 266; silver, (111) 98, 99, (111a) 101
CHRISTENING BASIN, silver, (117) 100
CHRISTMAS TREE, (504) 312
CHURCHES. See Architecture, American and by specific name
CIDER, 36, 162
CITY AND COUNTRY BUILDER'S AND WORKMAN'S TREASURY OF DESIGNS, quotation from, 159
CLAESZ, PIETER, still-life painting by, (19) 26
CLAGGETT, WILLIAM, clock by, (208) 160
CLARKE, JONATHAN, 178; handle of silver porringer by, (245) 179
CLARKE FAMILY, silver coffeepot of, 178, (247) 179
CLARKE, WILLIAM, house of, (illus.) 66
CLASSICAL MOTIFS, 66, 133, 148, (194) 149, 159, 161, 162, (213) 163, (304) 220, (388) 256–57, 306, (494) 307
CLAW-AND-BALL FEET, on andiron, (410) 270; Chippendale, illustrations of, (257) 196, 197, (272) 205, (282) 210; on grate, (411) 270; Queen Anne with dragon talon, (158) 133; square cut, (291, 292) 214, (293, 294) 215; talon pattern of Massachusetts Chippendale, (304) 220, (305, 306) 221; undercut, 227, (320) 227
CLAY, 333. See also Glass, Slip Ware, and Pottery
CLINTON, SIR HENRY, 155
CLOCKS, 74, 210, 283; on bracket, (297) 217; lantern, (73) 74; tall case (grandfather), (72) 74, 76, (196) 150, 151, (208) 160, 161, (284) 210, 222, (311) 223, (315) 225, (502) 311, (517) 318
CLOSESTOOL, 263, (456) 286
CLOSETS, 262
COACHMAKING, 125
COAL, 273
COCKFIGHTING, 170
CODDINGTON, JOHN, silver tankard by, (251) 181
COFFEE, 11, 62, 68, 102, 129
COFFEEHOUSES, 66, 102; illustration of London, (123) 103
COFFEEPOTS, 11, 102; porcelain, (392) 259; silver, (124) 103, 177, 178, (247) 179, 248, (376) 251; tin, (532) 326, (534) 327
COFFEY, MARY, 263
COGSWELL, JOHN, 221
COINS, 14, (illus.) 17
COLCHESTER, CONN., 228
COLLAPSIBLE FURNITURE, 44–47
COLLEGE OF NEW JERSEY, (PRINCETON), 127
COLMAN, JOHN, silver monteith of, 96, (107) 97
COMMERCE, 13–15, 33, 61–62, 64, 80, 118, 121, 125, 155, 162, 188–89
COMMITTEE OF CORRESPONDENCE, Boston, 192
COMMUNICATIONS, 14–15
COMMUNION TOKENS, pewter, (illus.) 237
CONESTOGA VALLEY, PA., 351
CONESTOGA WAGON, 303, 337, 350, (570) 351, ironwork on, (576–78) 351
CONEY, JOHN, 33, 96, 99; silver mark of, (118) 101; silverwork by—christening basin, (117) 100; fork and spoon, (119) 101; inkstand, (99) 90; monteith, 96, (107) 97; tankard, (112) 98, 99
CONGRESS VOTING INDEPENDENCE, engraving of, (357) 242–43, (475) 293
CONNECTICUT, 10, 15, 183; Chippendale furniture characteristic of, 222, 228, (323, 324, 326) 229, (327) 230, (334) 231; currency of, (109) 98, 99; Queen Anne furniture characteristic of, (168) 136, (170) 138, (172) 139, (209) 160, 161, 164, (216) 165; weaving in, 285. See also Connecticut River and Valley and Connecticut Valley Chests
CONNECTICUT COURANT, THE, 296
CONNECTICUT RIVER AND VALLEY, 15; regional style of, 56, 154, 156, (204) 157
CONNECTICUT VALLEY CHESTS, (64) 56, (65a) 57, (65) 58, (67) 59
CONSTITUTION OF THE UNITED STATES, 242, 252
CONSTITUTIONAL SOCIETY, 193
CONTINENTAL ARMY, 339
CONTINENTAL CONGRESS, First, 185, 192; Second, 174, 242, 252
COOKE, ELISHA, SR., portrait of, 67
COOKY BOARD, (490) 305
COOKY CUTTER, (531) 326

COPLEY, JOHN SINGLETON, 94, 95, 181, 248, 257; on American empire, 257; on Philadelphia, 202; portraits by—Boylston, 191; Izard, (388) 256–57; Revere and detail, (367) 248, (367a) 249; self-portrait, 256, (389) 257; Winslow, 218, (302) 219
COPPERPLATING, 255
CORINTHIAN CAPITALS, 154
CORINTHIAN COLUMNS, 148, (194) 149
CORINTHIAN PILASTERS, (80) 78, 79, 156
CORNELYS, THERESA, 195
CORNER CHAIRS. See Roundabout Chairs
CORNICE, classical, 306, (494) 307
CORNWALL, ENGLAND, 235, 326
COSTUMES, 17, 128, 129
COUCHES, Chippendale design for, (253, 254) 194
COUNTRY CHAIRS, 230; arm, (330) 230; side, (327–29) 230, (331–36) 231
COURT CUPBOARDS, (16) 25, 47, 76
COVERLET, (illus.) 298
COWELL, WILLIAM, SR., silver porringer by, (116) 100, 101
COX, JOSEPH, 215; settee by, (289) 212–13
CRADLES, Dutch-type, (28) 30; wicker, (26, 27) 30; Windsor, (362) 245
CRAFTS AND CRAFTSMEN, 10, 14–16, 19, 25, 35, 62, 68, 69, 111, 112, 114, 122, 130–31, 133, 159, 186–87, 190, 191, 300; European, 16, 61–62; excellence of, 74, 95, 190–92, 334; training of, 94–95. See also specific crafts
CRAGGS, JAMES, porcelain bowl from tea service of, (181) 143
CREAMWARE. See Queen's Ware
CRESTINGS, 133; illustrated, (68, 69) 70, 71, 72, (71a) 72, 90, (100) 91, (140) 111, (160) 134. See also specific forms
CREVECŒUR, MICHEL JEAN DE, 334
CREWELWORK, 286, 288–89; bed hangings, (455) 286; bedspread and wall hangings, (214) 164; chair seat, (170) 138; peacock, (464) 290, 291; picture, (466) 291; purse, (469) 291; sampler, (459) 288, 289
CROMWELL, OLIVER, 14, 61, 72
CROMWELL STYLE, settee, (59) 52–53; side chair, (57) 52
CROSS-STITCHING, (468) 291. See also Needlework
CRUET STAND, silver, 246, (365) 247
CRUGER, ELIZABETH BLAIR, silver bowl from tea service of, (182) 143
CUPBOARDS, corner, (205) 158, 159, (501) 310–11; shell-topped, (207) 159, (384) 254, 255
CUPIDS, (193) 148
CUPS, communion, (32) 34, 35; delft, (illus.) 63; two-handled silver, 106, (135) 107. See also Beakers, Standing Cups, and Teacups
CURRENCY, 32, (109) 98, 99, 122
CURVES, in Chippendale style, 195; in Queen Anne style, 123–24, 127, 133
CYMA CURVE, 133, (161) 134, 164, (216) 165

D

DAISY-IN-A-DIAMOND PATTERN, in glass, (563) 342
DARTMOUTH HALL, 127
DAUPHIN COUNTY, PA., 300, 318
DAWES, WILLIAM, 95
DAY BEDS, 62, 88, (96) 88–89, (142) 112, (218) 166
DAYLIGHT-SAVING TIME, 274
DECKER, PHILIP, 313
DECLARATION OF INDEPENDENCE, 155, 190, 200, 242; inkstand used by signers, 252, (383) 253; as motif, (393) 259
DEERFIELD, MASS. See Old Deerfield
DEFOE, DANIEL, 62
DELAWARE, 358
DELAWARE RIVER AND VALLEY, 12; ladder-back chair refined in, 112, (143) 113
DELFT, NETHERLANDS, 48
DELFTWARE, Dutch, (illus.) 8, 48, (53) 50, (55) 51, (illus.) 60, (88, 89) 84, 85, (90–91) 85, 155, 162, (189) 146, 147, (213) 163; English, (18) 26, (20) 27, (48) 48, (49) 49, (51) 50, (56) 51, (illus.) 63, (illus.) 64, (92) 85, (386) 254, (427) 276
DENNIS, THOMAS, 21; press cupboard in style of, (4) 20; spice chest attributed to, (6) 21
DENTIL MOLDING, (493) 307
DE PEYSTER, JACQUES, portrait of, (21) 28; whistle of, (23) 29
DERBY, ENGLAND, 258
DERBY, SARAH, embroidery by, (465) 290, 291
DE RIEMER, PIETER, silver tea set by, (363) 246
DESIGNS FOR FURNITURE. See Johnson, Thomas
DESIGNS IN ARCHITECTURE, 191
DESIGNS OF INIGO JONES, THE, title page from, (illus.) 124
DESKS, 76, 116; desk-bookcase, 224; fall-front, (illus.) 60, 90, (100) 91, (295) 216, 217, 222, (310) 223, (324) 229; kneehole, (313) 224, (313a) 227. See also Secretaries
DESKS-ON-FRAME, (102) 92, 116, (152) 117
DEVONSHIRE, ENGLAND, 48, 50
DINING ROOMS, 262
DIRECTIONS TO SERVANTS, 278
DIRECTOR. See *Gentleman and Cabinet-Maker's Director, The*
DISH CROSS, silver, (380) 252
DOLLS, 30; English wax doll, (22) 28
DOLPHINS, as garlands and feet motif, (239) 178
DOOR LATCH, Pennsylvania German, (549) 334, (556) 337
DOORWAYS, 154, 156, (204) 157, (209) 160, 161
DORCHESTER HEIGHTS, MASS., 155
DORIC COLUMNS, 161; on clockcase, (208) 160
DOUBLE-SCROLL SKIRT, on highboy, (322) 228
DOUGH TROUGH, 320, (526) 323
DOVETAIL JOINT, 109
DOWER CHESTS, 56, (66) 59; Pennsylvania German, 302, (496) 308, 320, (521) 322, (525) 322–23, (524) 323, (530) 325
DRAM CUP, silver, (illus.) 5, 36, (39) 37
DRAMSHOPS, 104
DRAPERIES. See Window Hangings
DRAWERS, 26, (77) 77, four-tier, 166, (220) 167, 306, (491) 307
DRAYTON, JOHN, 125
DRAYTON HALL, S.C., 125
DRESSING CHEST, (258) 197; design for, (259) 197
DRESSING TABLES. See Lowboys
DRINKING HORNS, 10, 38
DROWNE, SHEM, 283; weather vane by, (445) 282
DUDLEY, THOMAS, 13
DUMAS, ALEXANDRE, (*père*), 302
DUMMER, JEREMIAH, 32, 95, 96, 99; engraving by, (109) 98; silver mark of, (113) 99; silverwork by—candlesticks, (38) 36; communion cup, (113) 99; punch bowl, (108) 97
DUNKARDS, 301
DUNKERLY, JOSEPH, portrait of Rachel Revere by, (366) 248
DUNLAP FAMILY, 228; chair attributed to, 230, (332) 231; chest by, (325) 229; highboy by, (322) 228
DUTCH CARVING, (11) 22
DUTCH LITTLE MASTERS, 15
DUTCH REFORMED CHURCH. See Reformed Protestant Dutch Church
DUYCKINCK, GERARDUS, JR., 151; clockcase japanning attributed to, (196) 150, 151
DUYCKINCK, GERARDUS, SR., 151; possible attribution to, (197) 151
DYER, sketch of a, (454) 285
DYES, 286

E

EARL, RALPH, portraits by—Sherman, (349) 240, 242; Willett, 193
EAST INDIA COMPANY, Dutch, 83; English, 62, 80
EAST INDIES, 80
EAST WINDSOR, CONN., 228
EASTHAM, MASS., 99
EASTON'S POINT, Newport, 224
EASY CHAIRS, 86; Chippendale, (illus.) 182, (279) 208, 209, (294) 215; Pennsylvania German, 310, (503) 311; Queen Anne, (169) 137; William and Mary, (94) 87
EATON, MARY, crewel purse by, (469) 291
ECONOMY, COLONIAL, 129–30
EDENTON, N.C., 257
EDGELL, SIMON, pewter tankard by, (347) 239
EDUCATION, COLONIAL, 30, 95, 186, 283
EGYPT, 123
ELIOT, JOHN, 301
ELIZABETH I, QUEEN OF ENGLAND AND IRELAND, 25, 94, 296
ELIZABETH FURNACE, Pa., 338–39
ELIZABETHAN FORMS, 21; in folding-top table, (46) 47; in standing salt, (114) 99
ELLIOTT, JOHN, 205
EMBROIDERY. See Needlework and specific forms
EMPIRE STYLE, 224
EMPRESS OF CHINA, (ship) 258; as motif, (391) 258
ENDECOTT, JOHN, 17
ENFIELD, CONN., 59
ENGLAND, 9, 11, 12, 13, 15, 23, 40, 63–64, 68, 122–23, 127, 156, 189, 265, 296; and American Revolution, 192–93, 257, 258; becomes Great Britain, 121–22; chocolate, tea, and punch in, 62, 96, 99, 140, (174) 141, 143; coffeehouses in, (123) 103; colonial competition with, 118, 190; colonial defiance of laws of, 14, 190; colonists returning to, 186, 256; earthenware made in, 48–51, 85; Great Migration from, 10, 32; Huguenot craftsmen in, 177; imports from, 15, 68–69, 74, 125, 131, 154, 155, (212) 162, 205, 212, 235, 255, 293, 326, 339; influence and prestige of, 66, 69, 121, 131, 159, 184–85, 186–87, 190–91, 192; invasion of by "Bonnie Prince Charlie," 252; and the Orient, 80, 83, 148; origin of Windsor chairs in, 241; quillwork in, 71; restoration of monarchy in, 61–62; rococo style in, 187–88, 198; and Seven Years' War, 184, 185; and South Sea Company, 121; and Stamp Act, 190, 255; tobacco trade with, 15; trade with, 33, 156, 195, 326; trade guilds in, 94, 235; Treaty of Utrecht signed by, 121; and War of the Austrian Succession,. 183. See also Architecture, English; Furniture, English; and Great Britain
ENGRAVING, by Dummer, (109) 98; by Hurd, 181, (illus.) 193; by Revere, (374) 250, 251; on silver, (119) 101, (127) 104, (128, 129, 130) 105, (372) 249, (373) 250, (375, 376) 251, (379) 252, (382) 253. See also Glass and Pewter
EUROPE, 11, 16, 21, 48, 99, 121, 162; influences in colonies, 14–15, 61, 111, 133
EVELYN, JOHN, 62, 80, 170
EYEGLASSES, (illus.) 233

F

FAN, (391) 258
FAN-BACK CHAIRS. See Windsor Chairs
FANEUIL, PETER, 152, 177
FANEUIL HALL, Boston, 126, 177, 283
FARM IMPLEMENTS, 337
FEET. See specific forms
FEKE, ROBERT, portrait of Royall family by, (199) 152
FIELDING, GEORGE, silver sugar tongs by, (192) 146–47
FINIALS, (76) 75; acorn, (237) 176, 177; bird, (550) 334–35; flame, (319) 226, (320) 227, 270, (411) 271; spiral, (410) 270, (565) 343
FIRE SCOOP, (406) 268
FIRE SCREEN, (illus.) 182, 200, (468) 291
FIREBACKS, (illus.) 11, (398) 265
FIREHOUSE CHAIR. See Windsor Chairs, low-back
FIREPLACE TILES, Delft, 48, (53) 50, 162
FIREPLACES, 126, 162, (213) 163, (395, 397) 264, (399) 265, 270, (412) 271; equipment for, (404–8) 268–69
FIRST CHURCH, Boston, 23
FIRST PARISH CHURCH, Hingham. See Old Ship Meetinghouse
FITHIAN, PHILIP VICKERS, 291; on cockfighting, 170; on embroidery, 289; on lighting, 276
FITZHUGH, WILLIAM, 14, 15
FLAMESTITCH, on armchair—front view, (169) 137; on stool, (95) 88, (164) 135
FLATBUSH, N.Y., 174
FLAX, 285
FLEESON, PLUNKET, 118, 205, 207
FLEMISH DESIGNS, 21, 62, (69) 70, 71
FLEMISH SCROLLS. See Scrolls
FLETCHER, BENJAMIN, 38
FLIP GLASS. See Glass
FLOORCLOTHS. See Carpets
FLOORS, 11, 152
FLUTING, on chamfered corners, 218, (303) 219; on legs, 230, (332, 333) 231;

on pilasters, (205) 158, 159; stopped, 162, (213) 163, (317, 318) 226
FOOT WARMER, 268, (407) 269
FORKS, 11, 101; iron, (555) 336–37; silver, (34) 35, (119) 101
FORM. See Benches
FORT GOOD HOPE, CONN., 56
FORT NECESSITY, PA., 184
FORT STANWIX, N.Y., 193
FOX HUNTING, 174; motif in overmantel, (231) 174
FRAKTUR, (illus.) 298, 316, (514) 316, (515) 317, (519) 320, (527, 528) 324, (529) 325
FRANCE, 121, 183, 187; influences of in England and America, 62, 71, 133, 187
FRANKLIN, BENJAMIN, 95, 130, 255; and Argand lamps, 280; on bifocals, (illus.) 233; book on logic owned by (103) 93; biography of, 232–33; and Cotton Mather's house, 13, 160; on England, 186; in engraving (357) 242–43; on French and Indian raids, 183; on house heating, 12; on interior decoration, 233; on John Amelung, 344; "Join or Die" slogan, 184, (illus.) 187–88; on lighting, 274; on Moravian music, 303; and musical glasses, 170; on open hearth, 265; Pennsylvanian Fire-Place of, (414) 272, (416) 273, 338; on Pennsylvania Germans, 300; on population growth, 188; portrait of, 233; publishes German-language newspaper, 301; and Ralph Izard, 256; stove named for, (413) 272; tea table of, 203; and Windsor chairs, 243
FRANKLIN COUNTY, PA., 349
FRASER, SIMON, 348
FREDERICK, MD., 344
FREDERICK II, KING OF PRUSSIA, 232
FREDERICKSBURG, VA., 242
FRENCH AND INDIAN WARS, 155, 159, 183–85
FRENCH CHAIRS, 202, (270) 203
FRENCH SCROLL FEET, 222, (309, 312) 222, (316) 225
FRESCOES, *CHINOISERIE*, 162
FRETWORK, (307) 222, (311) 223, (318) 226, (322) 228
FRIENDSHIP, (ship) 33
FRIEZES, 156, 306, (494) 307
FRONTIERSMEN, 170, 303, 348; (illus.) 303
FROTHINGHAM, BENJAMIN, 193, 221; label of, (illus.) 193
FUDDLING CUP, 48, (56) 51
FUETER, DANIEL CHRISTIAN, 252; silverwork by—beaker, 252, (382) 253; cruet stand, 246, (365) 247
FUETER, LEWIS, silver salver by, (379) 252
FURNITURE, AMERICAN, Chippendale style, 186–87, 191–231; Dutch, 54–56, 92, 215; Jacobean style, 16–27, 44–47, 52–53, 56–59; Pennsylvania German, 302, 304–11, 318–23; Queen Anne style, 130–31, 133–39, 148–53, 158–67; William and Mary style, 69–77, 86–93, 110–19; Windsors, 240–45. See also Children, furniture for
FURNITURE, ENGLISH, Chippendale style, 186, 187, 195, 197, 198, 200, 205, 217, 218, 227; Jacobean style, 11, 21, 24, 25, 26, 44, 46, 47, 53; Queen Anne style, 123, 124, 131, 148, 159; William and Mary style, 61, 62, 63, 69, 71, 72, 74, 75, 86, 88, 90; Windsors, 241, 243
FURNITURE MAKING, 19, 25, 26, 95, 108–9, 111, 195

G

GADROONING, (283) 210, (291) 214, 215, (293) 215
GADSBY'S TAVERN, Alexandria, 270; fireplace from, 270, (412) 271
GAFFERS, 346–47
GAGE, THOMAS, 155
GAINES, JOHN, armchair by, (illus.) 130
GAMES, backgammon, bowls, cribbage (225) 170; dicing, draughts, shuffleboard, skittles, 170; golf, 168, (221) 169; goose, 172, (230) 173; parchesi, 172. See also Billiard Table and Cards
GARDENS, 154, 162
GARDINERS ISLAND, N.Y., 263
GARRAWAY, RICHARD, 32
GAVET, JONATHAN, tilt-top stand by, 152, (203) 153
GAY, JOHN, 63
GEDDES, CHARLES, 217; brass clock dial by, (297) 217
GEETING, CATHERINE, glass sugar bowl of, (567) 344
GEIGER FARM, sketch of, (508) 314
GEISTWEIT, GEORGE, 313
GENTLEMAN AND CABINET-MAKER'S DIRECTOR, THE, 186, 187, 202, 218; designs and patterns from, 188, (illus.) 190, (252–54) 194, 195, (259) 197, (illus., secretary) 200, 210, 217; influence of, 186–87, 191, 198, 200; (illus., on Randolph trade card) 201, 202, (270) 203, (275) 206, (276) 207, (290, 291) 214, 215
GERMANS. See Pennsylvania Germans
GERMAN LANGUAGE, 300–301, 313
GERMAN REFORMED CHURCH, 302
GERMANTOWN, PA., 125, 166, 301; settlement of, 299, 302, 303
GERMANY, 300, 301, 302, 306, 342, 344
GESSO, 80, 148, 162
GEORGE I, KING OF GREAT BRITAIN AND IRELAND, 121, 122, 131; George II, 131, 227; George III, 155, 188, 255
GEORGIA, 300
GEORGIAN STYLE, 131; in woodwork, 162, (213) 163. See also Architecture, American
GHISELIN, CESAR, 68, 106; silver folding spoon by, (134) 107
GINSENG, 258
GLASS, 9, 11, 13, 338–47; makers of—Amelung, 341, 344; Stiegel, 338–39, 341; Wistar, 341; objects of—bottles, 48, (559) 340, (563) 342; cream pitcher, (560) 341, 342; drinking glass, (570) 345; engraving on, (558) 340, 342, (567) 344, (568–71) 345; flasks, (561) 341, 342; flip glasses, (562) 342, presentation piece, (568) 345; (detail), (571) 345; goblet (*pokal*), 344, (569) 345; hunting horn, (564) 342–43; saltcellar, (557) 340, 342; sugar bowls, 342, (565, 566) 343, (567) 344; tea caddy, (558) 340, 342; techniques of making, (illus.) 346–47; types of—bottle, 339, 346; crown, 346; crystal, 346; flint, 339, 344, 346; window, 339, 346; wine glasses, (illus.) 120
GLASS SOAP (MANGANESE OXIDE), 346
GLEN, JAMES, 128
GLORIOUS REVOLUTION, 62
GODDARD, JOHN, I, 224, 227; lowboy in style of, (321) 227; possible attributions to—roundabout chair, 224, (314) 225; secretary, (319) 226, 227
GODDARD, JOHN, II, 224
GOERING, JACOB, 314
GOLD AND GOLDSMITHING, (illus.) 11, 14, 32–33, 35, 38, 40–41, 67–68
GOLF, (221) 168, 169
GOOSE QUILLS, 333
GOSTELOWE, JONATHAN, 209; possible attribution to, (280) 209
GOTHIC STYLE, 72; in architecture, 11–12, 65; designs of, (5) 21, 24–25, (38) 36, 195
GRANDFATHER'S CHAIR, 32
"GRANDFATHER'S CLOCK," 76
GRATE, COAL-BURNING, (411) 270
GRAVESTONES, 12, rubbings, (illus.) 15
GREAT BRITAIN, 121, 122, 124, 140, 183, 186, 187, 255. See also Architecture, English, and Furniture, English
GREAT MIGRATION, 10, 32
GREEN, JOHN RICHARD, 185
GRENVILLE, GEORGE, 255
GRISAILLE, 54, (63) 55
GROTESQUES, 21
GUILDS, 19, 94; in America, 94, 126–27; in England, 94, 235. See also Crafts and Craftsmen
GUILFORD, CONN., 56; chest from, (67) 59; imitation inlay in furniture of, 112
GUILLOCHE CARVING, (13) 23
GUNS. See Rifles
GUNSMITHS, 334, 348
GUNSTON HALL, Va., 190
GWYN, NELL, 96

H

HADLEY, MASS., chest made in, (66) 59
HAIR-CURLING IRON, (462) 289
HAIRY-PAW FEET, (274) 206, 207, 222, (310) 223
HALBERD, (illus.) 12
HALF-MOON CARVING. See Lunette Carving
HALLS, as principal room, 13; 44, 262
HAMILTON, DR. ALEXANDER, on amusements, 169; on Boston ladies, 129; on colonists, 130; on Indian dress, 128, 129; on Malbone house, 126; on Philadelphia, 130; possible attributions of sketches to, (234, 235) 175
HAMILTON, GAWEN, painting by, 141
HAMMOND, JOHN, 15
HAMMOND-HARWOOD HOUSE, Annapolis, 190, 191; door, (illus.) 192
HANCOCK, JOHN, 28; bedspread owned by, (214) 164; and Hancock house, 155
HANCOCK, LYDIA HENCHMAN, 155
HANCOCK, THOMAS, bedspread owned by, (214) 164; biography of, 155; on his gardens, 154; wealth of, 155, 189. See also Hancock House
HANCOCK HOUSE, Boston, 154–55, 156; (illus.) 126, 127; drawing of, 154
HANGING BETTY. See Lamps
HANOVER, PA., 339
HAREWOOD HOUSE, England, 195
HARRINGTON, SIR JOHN, 53
HARRIS, WILLIAM, 13
HARTFORD, CONN., 10, 56
HARVARD COLLEGE, 11, 17, 102; loving cup of, (122) 102; in Stoughton portrait, (121) 102
HARVEST JUG, 48, (50) 50
HASPS, 337; fish-shaped, (549) 334; wrought-iron (576–78) 351
HAUSMAN, MRS., sketch of (505) 312
HAWTHORNE, NATHANIEL, 16, 32; on highboys, 207
HAY, SARAH, 291
HAYDN, FRANZ JOSEPH, 303
HEATING, 12–13, 266–73
HEILBRONN, GERMANY, 299
HEIDELBERG, PA., 339
HEMP, 285
HENCHMAN, DANIEL, 130, 155
HENRY VIII, KING OF ENGLAND, 53, 88
HEYNE, JOHANN CHRISTOPHER, pewter standing cup by, (346) 239
HIBBINS, ANNE, 83
HICKORY, (wood) 241
HIGGINSON, FRANCIS, on abundance of firewood, 265; on lighting, 274; on what to bring to New World, 9–10; 341
HIGH CHAIRS, 30, (29) 31, 241, (359) 244
HIGHBOYS, 26, 27, 192, 202, 207; Chippendale, 198, (265, detail 265a) 199, (267) 202, (276) 207, (300) 218, (320) 227, (322) 228, (323) 229; Queen Anne, (illus.) 124, 148, (194) 149; William and Mary, 76, (78a) 76, (77, 78) 77, (83) 81, (141) 112
HIGHWAYS, 130
HILLSBORO, N.C., 333
HINGES, 337. See also Hasps
HINGHAM, MASS., 12
HISTORY OF THE ENGLISH PEOPLE, quotation from, 185
HOCKESSEN, ELIZABETH, blanket chest of, 318, (518) 319
HOGARTH, WILLIAM, on Chippendale designs, 187–88, 205; essay on beauty by, (illus.) 188–89
HOLLAND. See Netherlands
HOLLINGSWORTH FAMILY, highboy of, (267) 202, 203
HOLYOKE, EDWARD, chairs of, (163) 135
HÖLZ, ELIZABETH (MRS. STIEGEL), 339
HOMES, WILLIAM, silver milk pitcher by, (177) 142, 143
HOOKED RUGS, 286; as bed rugs, (457, 458) 287
HOPKINS, STEPHEN, 224
HORSE BREEDING, 33
HORSE RACING, 174; motif in overmantel, (232) 174–75
HORSEMAN, as motif, 328, (537) 329
HORSESHOE-SHAPED SEAT, 133, (272) 205
HOURGLASS, (448) 283
HOUSE OF BURGESSES, Va., Speaker's Chair of, (206) 158, 159
HOUSE OF THE SEVEN GABLES, Salem, 13
HOUSEHOLD FURNITURE IN THE PRESENT TASTE . . . BY A SOCIETY OF UPHOLSTERERS, card tables (illus.) 200; influence of on Randolph trade card 200, (illus.) 201
HOUSERAISING, 169, (illus.) 262, 263
HOUSES, COLONIAL, 9, 10, 261–81; construction of, 126–27, (illus.) 262, 263. See also specific houses
HOUSEWRIGHTS, 126–27, 156, 190
HOWE, SIR WILLIAM, 155
HUBER, ELIZABETH (MRS. STIEGEL), 338, 339
HUDSON RIVER AND VALLEY, 15, 300; development of regional style in, 54–55; painted chair in style of, (171) 139
HUGUENOTS, 62, 68, 177
HULL, EDWARD, 33
HULL, HANNAH, 32
HULL, JOHN, 95, 96; biography of, 32–33; made mintmaster, 14; silverwork made with Sanderson by—coins, (illus.) 17; dram cup, (illus.) 5, 36, (39) 37; porringer, (31) 34; spoon, (35) 35; standing cup, (32) 34

HUMPHREYS, RICHARD, silver dish cross by, (380) 252
HUNGARIAN WORK. See *Bargèllo* Work
HURD, JACOB, silverwork by—candlestick (238) 177; coffeepot, 178, (247) 179; milk pitcher, (178) 142; saucepan, (250) 180, 181; teakettle, (179) 142, 143; teapot, 140, (175) 141
HURD, NATHANIEL, 181; label engraved by, (illus.) 193
HUTCHINSON, ELIAKIM, 83

I

INCE, WILLIAM, 218
INDENTURED SERVANTS, 300
INDEPENDENCE HALL, Philadelphia, 126 (illus.), 127, 209, (396) 264
INDIA, 62, 96, 184; textiles from, 63, 83, 86
INDIA STYLE. See Cane
INDIANS, 10, 112, 128, 166, 188; (illus.) 64, (81) 78–79
INDIGO PLANT, 286
INKSTANDS, on needlework, (471) 292; silver, (99) 90, 252, (383) 253
INLAY, 19, 56, 71, 76, 92, (105) 93, (210) 161; imitation of, (141) 112; Pennsylvania German, 306, (494) 307, (495, 496) 308, (500, 502) 310, 311
INNER TEMPLE, 294
INNS OF COURT, 186
INTERIOR DECORATION, 261–62, 293
INTAGLIO PATTERN, in glass, 347
IRELAND, 164
IRISH FURNITURE MOTIF, 134, 164
IRON AND IRONWORK, 334–37, 338
IRON ACT OF1750, ENGLISH, 334
IRON AND TRIVET, (463) 289
IRON POT, (illus.) 10
IROQUOIS INDIANS, portraits of sachems, (81) 78–79
ISLE OF WIGHT COUNTY, VA., 11
ITALY, influences of, 11, 65–66, 88
IZARD, MR. AND MRS. RALPH, 256; portrait of, (388) 256–57

J

JACOBEAN STYLE, 17, 19, 24, 25, 71; in case pieces, (4) 20, 21, (16) 25, 26, (20) 27, 76; designs of, 56, (64) 56; in trestle table, 46, (45) 47
JACOBITES, 252; anti-Jacobite engraving, 252, (382) 253
JAMAICA, 33
JAMBS, 265
JAMES I, KING OF ENGLAND, 17; on tobacco, 294
JAMES II, KING OF ENGLAND, 62, 121, 122
JAMES RIVER, 125
JAMESTOWN, VA., 9, 10, 15, 65, 341
JAPAN, 83, 148
JAPANNING, 80, 112, 148–51; of coffeepot, 326, (534) 327; of clockcases, (196) 150, 151, 222, (311) 223; of highboys, 80, (83) 81, 148, (194) 149; of looking-glass frame, (197) 151; of lowboy, (193) 148
JAR, apothecary, (illus.) 8; Pennsylvania German pottery, 328, (545) 331
JARRATT, DEVEREUX, 129
JEFFERSON, THOMAS, as cellist, 170; and Argand lamps, 280; desk of, 200, (illus.) 201; and drapery designs, (473) 293; and letter from Washington, 344; and Venetian blinds, 293; and Windsor chairs, 242, 243
JEFFRIES, DAVID AND ELIZABETH, silver candlesticks of, (38) 36
JEWELWORK, 21, 24
JOHN OF GAUNT, 44
JOHNSON, EDWARD, 12, 19
JOHNSON, HANNAH, bed rug by, 286, (458) 287
JOHNSON, SAMUEL, 123
JOHNSON, THOMAS, 200; designs by—tall clocks, (illus.) 200; wall bracket, (260) 197; influence of designs on Randolph trade card, 200, (illus.) 201
JOHNSTON, THOMAS, 148; japanned lowboy by, (193) 148
JOINERS, 12, 19. See also Carpenters
JOINT STOOL, (14) 24
JONES, HUGH, 68
JONES, INIGO, 124
JONES, JOHN PAUL, 232–33
JONESTOWN, PA., 320
JONSON, BEN, 11
JOURNAL. See Winthrop, John
JUG, delft, (illus.) 64

K

KALM, PETER, on coal use in New York, 273; on colonial prosperity, 189; on color in homes, 261; on Philadelphia, 130; on popularity of tea, 140; on use of sugar in Albany, 147
KAS (Kast), 54, (63) 55, 306
KEITH, SIR WILLIAM, 300
KENMORE, house in Md., 198
KENT, WILLIAM, 124, 131; title page from design book by, (illus.) 124
KETTLE BASE. See *Bombé*
KETTLE, brass, (400) 266. See also Teakettles
KEYHOLE PATTERN, 178, (245) 179
KIDD, CAPTAIN WILLIAM, 53, 67, 69
KIERSTEDE, CORNELIUS, silverwork by—bowl, 104, (132) 105; candlesticks and snuffer stand, (437) 279, detail from candlestick, (84) 82, 83; tankard, (129) 105; teakettle, 102, (125) 103
KING, WILLIAM, 222; chest of drawers by, (307) 222
KING GEORGE'S WAR, 183
KING PHILIP, Wampanoag chief, 33, 63
KING PHILIP'S WAR, 33, 63
KIRBY, PETER, pewter porringer by, (344) 238
KIRBY, WILLIAM, pewter teapot by, (342) 237
KITCHENS, 13, 262, 270
KITTERY POINT, ME., 183
KLEINFELTER, SHERIFF, 314
KNELLER, SIR GODFREY, Byrd portrait by, 69
KNIGHT, MADAM SARAH, 116, 262
KNITTING, 289
KNUCKLE CARVINGS, (355) 242–43
KUNTZ, J., rifle by, (572) 348–49

L

LACQUER, 63, 80, 151; Chinese cabinet, (illus.) 62. See also Japanning
LADDER-BACK CHAIRS, Chippendale, (334, 336) 231; Delaware Valley, 112, (143) 113. See also Slat-back Chairs
LAFAYETTE, MARQUIS DE, 162
LAMPS, Argand, (441) 280, (444) 281; Betty, 274, (420) 275; open, 274, (421) 275, (438) 280; spirit, (179) 142, 143, (364) 247, (380) 252
LANCASTER, PA., 239, 301, 303, 337, 339; Kentucky rifle developed in, 348
LANCASTER COUNTY, PA., 300; bird decorations popular in, 320, (525) 322–23; riflemen from, 303; Stiegel glassworks in, 338–39
LANGLEY, BATTY, 159
LANTERLOO, counters for, (327) 171. See also Games
LANTERN, tin, (439) 280
LATHES, 19, 108
LAW, JOHN, 121, 123
LEAD, 238
LEATHER, bottles, 10; as upholstery material, (60) 53, 72, (71) 73, (154, 155) 119, (217) 166, (503) 311
LEBANON, PA., 339
LEBANON COUNTY, PA., 300, 320
LEDDELL, JOSEPH, JR., 238; possible attribution of pewter bowl to, (340) 235
LEDDELL, JOSEPH, SR., pewter tankard by, (339) 255
LEE, JEREMIAH, 198; chimney piece in house of, (262) 198
LEE, ROBERT E., 125
LEE, THOMAS, 125
LEEDS, N.Y., 174
LEHIGH COUNTY, PA., 300
LEHMAN, CHRISTIAN, 313
LEIBNITZ, BARON VON, 232
LEPAUTRE, JEAN, embroidered scene after engraving by, (465) 291
LE ROUX, BARTHOLOMEW, 178; silver caster by, (128) 105
LE ROUX, CHARLES, 95, 178; silverwork by—coffeepot, 102, (124) 103; saltcellar, (239) 178
LIBRARIES, 92, 125, 130, 262
LIBRARY COMPANY OF PHILADELPHIA, 92, 233
LIGHTING, AND EQUIPMENT FOR, 274–81
LINEN, 285; use in crewelwork, 164; use in floorcloths, 152
LINEN PRESS, (30) 31
LIVINGSTON, PHILIP, 212
LIVINGSTON, ROBERT, silver beaker commissioned by, (41) 38, (41a-e) 39
LOG CABINS, 12, 305
LONG ISLAND, N.Y., 174
LOGAN, JAMES, 130; chair of, (217) 166; coat of arms of, 178, (246) 179; settee of, 166, (219) 167. See also Stenton
LOGAN, SARAH, silver sauceboat of, 178, (246) 179
LONDON, ENGLAND, 66, 190, 195, 198, 200, 235; fire of, (illus.) 64–65, 66; view of, (illus.) 16–17
LONGFELLOW, HENRY WADSWORTH, 95, 248
LOO. See Lanterloo
LOOKING GLASSES, 74, 151, 162; advertisement for, 205; beadwork, (illus.) 8; chimney, (436) 278–79; Chippendale, (illus.) 182, (271) 204, 205, (280) 209, 306, (493) 307; Queen Anne, (197) 151, (211) 161, (212) 162, (220) 167, (436) 278–79; William and Mary, (75) 75, 90, (100) 91. See also Shaving Stand
LORDS OF TRADE, 13. See also Board of Trade and Plantations
LOTTERIES, 144, 169, 339
LOUIS XV STYLE, 187, 195, 221
LOUISBOURG, CAPE BRETON I., 183–84; plan of in 1758, 184–85
LOUISIANA, 123
LOVELACE, FRANCIS, 67
LOVING CUP, silver, presented to Harvard by Stoughton, (122) 102
LOWBOYS, Chippendale, 192, (275) 206, 207, detail (277) 207, (321) 227; Queen Anne, (illus.) 120, (193) 148, 164, (216) 165; William and Mary, (70) 71, 74, (76) 75
LOWELL, JAMES RUSSELL, 142; silver teakettle of, (179) 142
LUNETTE CARVING, (9) 22, (15) 24
LUTHERAN MINISTERIUM OF PENNSYLVANIA, 338
LUTHERANS, 301, 302, 316

M

MACPHEADRIS, ARCHIBALD, 79
MACPHEADRIS-WARNER HOUSE, Portsmouth, (80) 78, 79; murals of (81) 78–79
MADAGASCAR, 67, 80, 102, 104
MADEIRA, 33, 224
MAHOGANY, (wood) block-front panels cut from, 227; carving on, 210–211; popularity of, 123, 152, 156. See also Furniture, Chippendale
MAIL SERVICE, 130
MALBONE, GODFREY, home of, 126
MANHATTAN ISLAND, N.Y., 54
MANHEIM, PA., 339
MANIGAULT, PETER, 294; in sketch, (476) 294
MANTLING, 140, (175) 141
MANWARING, ROBERT, 197; chair design by, (255) 196, 197
MAPLE, (wood) 24, 108, 148, 164; tiger-stripe, (322) 228, 348; close-grained, 241; in wooden tableware, 296
MAROT, DANIEL, 62
MARBLE, simulation of, 47, 152, 261, (417) 273; table top of, (201) 153
MARBLEHEAD, MASS., 198, 281
MARE, JOHN, 215; painting by, (290) 214
MARLBOROUGH, DUKE OF, 121
MARLBOROUGH LEGS, (283) 210
MARQUETRY, 19, 74, (74) 75; imitation of, (2) 19, (141) 112
MARRIAGE, as sampler motif, (226) 171; (460) 289
MARROW SCOOP, (343) 238
MARY II, QUEEN OF ENGLAND, 62, 63. See also William and Mary Period
MARYLAND, 190, 339, 344
MASON, ARTHUR AND JOHANNA, silver porringer of, (31) 34
MASON, GEORGE, 190
MASONIC EMBLEM, on drinking glass, (570) 345
MASSACHUSETTS, 155, 183, 235, 341; Chippendale furniture characteristic of, (256) 196 (304–9, 311) 220–223; currency of, (illus.) 17, 32, 99; early furniture made in, (4) 20, (6) 21, 23, 26, (20) 27, (46) 47; Queen Anne furniture characteristic of, (163) 135, (195) 150, (197) 151, 152, (201, 203) 153; spinning in, 285; William and Mary furniture characteristic of, (83) 81, (96) 88, (100) 91, (144) 114. See also Connecticut River and Valley
MASSACHUSETTS, GENERAL COURT OF, 14
MASSACHUSETTS BAY COLONY, 9, 10, 12, 13–14, 63

MASSACHUSETTS GAZETTE, AND BOSTON NEWS-LETTER, THE, 197
MASSACHUSETTS SPY, THE, 187
MATHER, COTTON, on alehouses, 17; house of, 160; on house heating, 13; portrait of, (101) 92
MATHER, INCREASE, 66
MATHER, RICHARD, woodcut of, 15
MAYHEW, JOHN, 218
MAYFLOWER, 9, 12, 17, 30
MELVILLE, DAVID, detail of pewter porringer by, (338) 234
MELVILLE, ROBERT, 224
MENNONITES, 301, 316
METALWORK, 15, 40, 282–83
MEXICO, 99
MIDDLE AGES, 10, 11, 12, 21, 26, 35, 44
MIDDLETOWN, CONN., 154
MILLER, LEWIS, 312–15; self-portrait, (506) 313; water-color sketches of Pennsylvania German life, (454) 285, (504, 505) 312, (507–9) 314, (510–13) 315
MING WARE, (porcelain) 48
MINT, MASSACHUSETTS, 14
MIRRORS, 151. See also Looking Glasses
MISSISSIPPI BUBBLE PLATES, (Chinese export porcelain) 122–123
MISSISSIPPI RIVER AND VALLEY, 121
MOLDINGS, 24, 66, (77) 77, 161; classical, 65, (205) 158, 159; double-arch, (70) 71. See also Architectural Woodwork
MONEY, JOHN, 348
MONROE, JAMES, Windsor chair of, (351) 240, 241, 242
MONTCALM, MARQUIS DE, 184
MONTEITH, silver, 96, (107) 97
MONTEZUMA, II, Aztec Emperor, 99
MONTICELLO, Va., design for curtains in, (473) 293; Windsor chairs ordered for, 243
MOORE, SIR HENRY, 285
MORAVIANS, 301, 303, 333; side chair of, (499) 310
MOREAU DE SAINT-MERY, MEDERIC, 243
MORGAN, DANIEL, 348
MORRIS, ANTHONY, 106; silver brazier of, 106, (136) 107
MORRIS, GOUVERNEUR, 263
MORRIS, JOHN, 314
MORRIS, LEWIS, JR., silver trophy of, 174, (233) 175
MORRIS, ROBERT, 205
MORRIS, SAMUEL, 190, 191
MORTAR AND PESTLE, (illus.) 260
MORTISE AND TENON, 12, 19, 109, 263
MOUNT VERNON, Va., 190; Argand lamp in, (441) 280; overmantel of, 198; renovation of, 191; Swan's designs used in, 198; Windsor chairs bought for, 242
MUGS, Pennsylvania German pottery, 328, (541) 330, 333; silver, (236) 176, 177
MUSIC AND MUSICAL INSTRUMENTS, 170, 303
MYERS, MYER, 252; silver cake basket by, 252, (381) 253

N

NANTES, EDICT OF, revocation of, 33, 62
NAPKINS, 11
NARRAGANSET INDIANS, 33
NARRAGANSETT BAY, 15
NASSAU, (ship). (illus.) 67, 104
NASSAU HALL (PRINCETON), 127
NAVAL STORES, 300
NAVIGATION, ACTS OF TRADE AND, 155
NEEDLE-POINT, (460) 289
NEEDLEWORK, 261, 286–92; gaming table top, (229) 172; pictures, (467) 291, (470) 292, 293; silk embroidery, (465) 290, (468) 291; samplers, (226) 171, (459) 288. See also specific stitches
NEOCLASSIC STYLE, 193, 195
NETHERLANDS, 15, 28, 29, 30, 56, 62, 74, 85; influences in colonial architecture, 65; influences in furniture, (58) 52, 53, 54, 56, 306; influences in silver, 35, 38–39, 68, 104
NEW AMSTERDAM, 16, 22, 31, 125, 306
NEW BREMEN GLASSMANUFACTORY, Md. 344
NEW BRITAIN, CONN., 228
NEW BRUNSWICK, N.J., 130
NEW ENGLAND, 12, 23, 63, 66, 68, 124, 170, 189–90, 265; architecture of, 11–13, 15, 79, 126, 154, 156; Chippendale furniture characteristic of, 220–29; commerce of, 33, 118; crafts in, 10, 12, 25, 224, 238; settlement of, 10, 11, 16–17
NEW-ENGLAND COURANT, THE, 95
NEW-ENGLAND PRIMER, THE, quotation from, 30
NEW-ENGLAND WEEKLY JOURNAL, THE, 129
NEW HAMPSHIRE, 33, 88, 183; Chippendale furniture characteristic of, 228, (322) 228, (325) 229, 230, (332, 333, 336) 231
NEW HAVEN, CONN., 74
NEW JERSEY, 183, 300; glassmaking in, 333, 341, 342, 343; spiral-turned chair made in, (58) 52, 53
NEW NETHERLAND, 9, 15–16. See also Netherlands, influences in colonial architecture, furniture, silver and New Amsterdam
NEW ORLEANS, LA., 121
NEW ORLEANS, BATTLE OF, 303
NEW YORK COLONY, 16, 174, 178, 183, 215
NEW YORK CITY, N.Y., 126, 130, 192, 193, 198, 200, 258, 300, 339; aspects of life in, 102, 104, 169, 170, 174, 280; Chippendale style characteristic of (290–301, 303) 213–19; as commercial center, 66–67, 125, 192, 212, 221; interior decoration in homes of, 67, 152, 215, 261; Queen Anne chairs, characteristic of, 131 (illus.) 132, 133, (160) 134; pewter made in, 234–237; as silvermaking center, 35, 38, 68, 82, 84, 102, 103–7, 144, 145, 178, 181, 246; William and Mary style characteristic of, (69) 70, 71, (71) 73, (102) 92, (105) 93. See also New Amsterdam and Hudson River and Valley
NEW YORK CITY HALL, First, 65; Second, (illus.) 66
NEW-YORK GAZETTE, THE, 254
NEW-YORK WEEKLY JOURNAL, THE, 151
NEW YORK'S FEDERAL PROCESSION, (1788), 245
NEWBURGH, N.Y., 265
NEWPORT, R.I., 126, 128, 162, 192, 263; as commercial and craft center, 162, 224; Chippendale style characteristic of, (313–21) 224–27; Queen Anne silver characteristic of, 178, (242) 178, (243) 179, (251) 181; Queen Anne style furniture characteristic of, 131, 133, (164) 135, 152, (202) 153, (208) 160
NEWPORT MERCURY, THE, 224
NEWTON, SIR ISAAC, 232
NIDDY NODDY, (452) 284, 285
NIPPERS, for sugar loaf, (173) 140, 147
NORD-AMERICANISCHE CALENDAR, illustration from, 301
NORTH BRITON, THE, 255
NORTH CAROLINA, 272, 311
NORTHAMPTON COUNTY, PA., 303, 334
NOSTELL PRIORY, house in England, 195
NYS, JOHANNIS, 68; silverwork by—brazier, (136) 107; handle of porringer, 178, (244) 179

O

OAK, (wood) 24, 156, 263. See also Furniture, American and English Jacobean
OAK-TREE SHILLING, 14
OGEE. See Cyma Curve
OHIO VALLEY, 184
OIL, for lamps, 274
OLD DEERFIELD, MASS., 263
OLD DOMINION. See Virginia
OLD SHIP MEETINGHOUSE, Hingham, 12, (illus.) 14
OLD SOUTH CHURCH (MEETINGHOUSE), Boston, 33, 222
ONCKELBAG, GERRIT, 106; silver tankard by, 104, (130) 105
ORDERS OF CLASSICAL ARCHITECTURE. See Architecture, Classical
ORIENTAL INFLUENCES AND MOTIFS, 63, 67, 71, 80, 82–83, 85, 133, 140, 143, 148, 151, 286–87
OVERMANTELS, (231) 174, (232) 174–75

P

PACIFIC ISLANDS, 121
PAD FEET, (161) 134, (214) 164, (330) 230, (491) 306
PADDY, SAMUEL, 32
PAINTING, of furniture, 19, 20, 54–59 (illus.) 298; of interiors, 261. See also Pennsylvania Germans, painted forms
PALAMPORE, (85) 82, 83
PALATINES, 299–300
PALLADIO, ANDREA, 124
PALLADIO LONDINENSIS, classical orders from, (illus.) 125
PANCAKE TURNER, (553) 336
PANELED FURNITURE, chest, (3) 19; chest of drawers, (516) 318; cradle, (28) 30; shutters, (476) 294
PANELING, 66, 126, 162, (213) 163
PARIS, FRANCE, 293
PARKER, GEORGE, 80, 148
PARLORS, 13, 262
PARTRIDGE, NEHEMIAH, 80
PASTORIUS, FRANCIS DANIEL, 302
PATCHBOX, brass, 348
PATTERN BOOKS, furniture, 186–87, 191, 192, 193, 195, 197, 198, (illus.) 200; needlework, 291
PEALE, CHARLES WILLSON, 193; portraits by—Buckland, 191; Cadwalader family, (273) 206, 207; Washington, 187
PEASE, JOHN, possible attribution to, (66) 59
PEASE, MARY, Hadley chest of, (66) 59
PEDIMENTS, 124, 227; broken-arch, 79; broken-scroll, 154, 156, (204) 157, (209) 160, 161, (210) 161, 228, (323) 229, 270, (412) 271; carved, (267) 202, 203, (276) 207, (285) 211
PENDULUMS, 74, 217
PENMAN'S PARADISE, calligraphy from, (98) 90
PENN, JOHN, 210
PENN, WILLIAM, 64, 68, 125; attracts Germans to Pennsylvania, 299, 302, 305
PENNSYLVANIA, 112, 140, 166, 183, 285, 301, 302, 303, 304, 311, 318. See also Pennsylvania Germans and Philadelphia
PENNSYLVANIA, ASSEMBLY OF, silver inkstand of, 252, (383) 253
PENNSYLVANIA COMPANY, THE, 300
PENNSYLVANIA GAZETTE, THE, 118, 130, 241
PENNSYLVANIA GERMAN MOTIFS, 302, 316; angels, (516) 318, (519) 320; Biblical themes, 268, 328; birds, (516, 517) 318, (519) 320, (525) 322–23, 326, (536) 328, (543, 545) 331, (547) 333, (550) 334–35; fish, (542) 331; flowers, (518) 319, (519) 320, 333, 337; fruit, 320, (522) 322, 326; hearts, (486, 488) 304, (493) 307, (501) 310–11, (519) 320, 326, (555) 336–37; hen and rooster, (536) 328; leaves, (517) 318; stag, (486) 304; stars, 326, (540) 330, (553) 336; swastika, (493) 307; tulips, (493) 307, (502) 311, 320, (523) 322, 326, 328, (545) 331, 338; unicorn, 320, (521) 322; urn, (517) 318; vines, (517) 318
PENNSYLVANIA GERMANS, 298–352; glassmaking and glass of, 338–47; Kentucky rifles made by, 348–51; Lewis Miller sketches of life of, 312–15; metalware of, 334–37; painted forms and *fraktur* of, 316–25; pottery of, 328–33; tinware of, 326–27; walnut furniture of, 304–11
PENNSYLVANIA STATE HOUSE. See Independence Hall
PENNSYLVANIAN FIRE-PLACES, (414) 272, (416) 273, 338
PEPPERRELL, SIR WILLIAM, 183; Smibert portrait of, 186
PEPYS, SAMUEL, on Charles II, 62, on chintz, 83; on chocolate drinking, 99; on wooden tableware, 296
PERIWIGS, 66, 67, 86, 129
PETTAQUAMSCUTT PURCHASE, R.I., 33
PEWTER, 10, 11. 234–39, 296; engraving on bed-warming pan, (348) 239; dish, (337) 234; fish detail, (illus.) top 235, 238; tankards, (341) 236, (347) 239; pewter-making, 235, 236, 238; pewterer's marks, (illus.) top, 236–37. See also individual forms
PHILADELPHIA, PA., 67, 74, 126, 185, 186, 192, 198, 207, 221, 232, 233, 277, 289, 300, 301, 305, 338, 339; as center of trade and culture, 64, 130, 170, 191–92, 202; Chippendale furniture characteristic of, 191, 192, (257) 196, (258) 197, 198, (265, 265a) 199, 202–11 (267–86); as craft center, 68, 118, 126–27, 191–92, 205, 235, 302; painting of, (157) 118–19; engraving of, 128–29; Queen Anne furniture characteristic of, 131, 133, (159) 134, (165, 166) 136, (215) 164, (218) 166, (219) 167; Queen Anne silver characteristic of, (236) 176, 177, 178, (244) 179; Windsor chairs of, 241, (354) 242
PHILADELPHISCHE ZEITUNG, 301
PHILIPPINES, 184

PHILIPSE, FREDERICK, 102, 125; silver teapot of, 102, (126) 103
PHILIPSE MANOR HALL, Yonkers, 125
PIECRUST CUTTER, (550) 334–35
PIECRUST PATTERN, 202, (269) 203
PIERCINGS, on silver braziers, (249) 180, 181; on porringer handles, (240–42) 178, (243–45) 179
PIKE POLES, 263
PILASTERS, Corinthian, 79, 154, 156; carved leafage on, (209) 160, 161; fluted, (205) 158, 159
PINE, (wood) 24, 148, 156, 241
PINE-TREE SHILLINGS, 14, 32, 63
PIPE BOX, (477) 295
PIPE SMOKING, 294
PIPE TONGS, (478, 479) 295
PIRATES, 67, 69, 80
PITCHERS, for cream and milk, 129, 143; glass, (560) 341, 342; silver, (177, 178) 142, 143, (363) 246
PITT, WILLIAM, on American resistance to the Stamp Act, 255
PLAINS OF ABRAHAM, BATTLE OF, 184–85
PLANK CHAIR, (486) 304, 305
PLATES, Delft, (55) 51; (illus.) Mississippi Bubble, 122–23; Pennsylvania German, 328, (537) 329, (538–40) 330, (542–44) 331, 333, (574) 350, 351; pewter (illus.) 8, (337) 234; porcelain (Chinese) 48, (52) 50
PLATTER, pewter, (illus.) 10
PLUMBING, 263
PLYMOUTH COLONY, 9, 10, 11, 13
PLYMOUTH MEETINGHOUSE, SECOND, (illus.) 13
POISON IVY, 286
POKAL. See Glass, goblet
POKEBERRY, 286
"POMPADOUR" HIGHBOY, (276) 207
PONTIL (PUNTY ROD), 346, 347
POOR RICHARD, 232–33, 276
POPE, ALEXANDER, 124
PORRINGERS, 14; pewter, (338) 234, (344) 238; silver, (31) 34, 35, (116) 100, 101, (240–42) 178, (243–45) 179
PORT ROYAL. See Annapolis Royal
PORTSMOUTH, N.H., 79
PORTSMOUTH, R.I., 162
PORTUGAL, 61, 62, 80; influence of, 96
POTASH, 346
POTOMAC RIVER, 125
PORCELAIN, 85, 258, 346; Far Eastern, 83, 85, 143, 258. See also individual forms and specific types
POTTERY, 258; English, 48, (384) 254, 255; Pennsylvania German, 303, 328–33, (546) 332. See also individual forms and specific types
POUNCE SHAKER, silver, (99) 90
POWDER HORN, 350, (575) 351
POWEL, SAMUEL, 190, 191, 256; detail from house of, (illus.) 190, 198
PRESIDENT'S HOUSE (WHITE HOUSE), Washington, D.C., 293
PRESS CUPBOARDS, (4) 20, 21, 76
PRINCE, SAMUEL, 215, 218
PRINCETON, BATTLE OF, 193
PRINCETON UNIVERSITY. See College of New Jersey
PRINTING PRESS, 92, 233
PRIOR, MATTHEW, 143
PRIVATEERING, 33, 126
PROCLAMATION OF 1763, 188
PROVINCE HOUSE, Boston, 283
PROVIDENCE, R.I., 127
PUBLIC HOUSES, 104. See also Taverns
PUCELLAS (IRON TONGS), 347
PUNCH BOWLS, porcelain, (394) 259; silver, 96, (108) 97
PUNCH LADLE, silver, detail (106) 96
PUNDERSON, PRUDENCE, 293; needlework picture by, (470) 292, 293
PURITANS, in America, 9, 12, 16–17, 23; in England, 61
PUZZLE JUG, delft, (20) 27, 48, (49) 49

Q

QUAKERS, 68, 224, 302
QUEBEC, NEW FRANCE, 184–85
QUEBEC ACT, (1774), 188
QUEEN ANNE PERIOD, 69, 120–81; architecture of, 154–55; architectural woodwork of, 156–61; chairs of, 132–39; comfortable accommodations of, 162–63; japanned furniture of, 148–51; silver of, 176–81; tables of, 152–53; tea services of, 140–47
QUEEN ANNE STYLE, 86, 187, 205, 230
QUEEN ANNE'S WAR, 124–25, 183
QUEEN'S WARE, 255. See also Wedgwood, Josiah
QUILLWORK, (68) 70, 71
QUINCY, JOSIAH, JR., 189–90
QUINTARD, PETER, engraving from silver tankard by, (248) 180, 181

R

RAEDER, CADARINA, plate of, 328, (543) 331
RAISING, (of metal) 40
RAMILLIES, BATTLE OF, 121
RANDOLPH, BENJAMIN, 200; card table possible attribution to, (274) 206, 207; Chippendale designs and trade card of, 191, 200, (illus.) 201; easy chair by, (279) 208, 209
RAT-TAIL SPOON, 101
RATTAN. See Cane
RATTLES, (toys) 30
READING, PA., 301, 339, 348
REFORMED PROTESTANT DUTCH CHURCH, 215
RENAISSANCE, influences of, 10–11, 21, 35, 64, 66, 79, 133, 156, 157, 162
RENSSELAERSWYCK MANOR, N.Y., 212
REPOLD, GEORGE AND METHA, flip glass of, (571) 345
RESTORATION MOTIFS, 111
REVELATION, THE, 328
REVERE, PAUL, 95, 192–93, 248–51; brass andirons by, (410) 270; detail of engraving by, (374) 250, 251; gold thimble by, (370) 248; portrait of, (367) 248, (367a) 249; silverwork by—coffeepot, (376) 251; Sons of Liberty bowl, 248, (373) 250; spoons, (368, 369) 248; spurs, (371) 248; tankard, (377, 377a) 251; teapot, 248 (372) 249; tray, (375) 251
REVERE, PAUL, SR., 33
REVERE, RACHEL (MRS. PAUL REVERE), portrait of, (366) 248
REVOIRE, APOLLOS DE. See Revere, Paul, Sr.
REVOLUTIONARY WAR, 140, 155, 186, 303, 334, 348; effect on American crafts, 190–93, 258
RHINE VALLEY, 299–300. See also Rhineland and Pennsylvania Germans
RHINELAND, emigration from, 299; stoneware from, 48, (54) 50
RHOADES, SAMUEL, 233
RHODE ISLAND, 10, 33, 162, 183, 224; Chippendale furniture characteristic of, 192, 222, 224–27, 244; Queen Anne furniture characteristic of, (162) 135, (167) 136, (202) 153, (214) 164, (220) 167. See also Newport
"RIBBAND BACK" CHAIR, design of, (252) 194
RICHARDSON, FRANCIS, JR., silver mug by, (236) 176, 177
RICHARDSON, JOSEPH, 95; silverwork by—sauceboat, 178, (246) 179; teapot, 246, (364) 247
RIFLES, KENTUCKY, 303, (572) 348–49, (573, 573a) 349, 350, (573b) 351
RITZ, ANTHONY, 313
RIVERS AND WATERWAYS, 14–15, 54, 56
RIVOIRE, APOLLOS DE. See Revere, Paul, Sr.
ROADS, 130
ROBERTS, AARON, 228; possible attribution to, (326) 229
ROBIN, ABBE, 221
ROBINSON, JOHN, 159
ROCAILLE. See Rococo Style
ROCHAMBEAU, COMTE DE, 162
ROCKING CHAIR, (child's) 30, (30) 31
ROCOCO STYLE, 133; examples of elements, 178, (247) 179, 198, (289) 212–13, (304) 220, (318) 226, 248, (372) 249; influence in Chippendale period, 187–88, (illus.) 190, 195, 198, 228
ROMAN EMPIRE, 346. See also Classical Motifs
ROMEO AND JULIET, 46
ROOMS, specialization of in colonial home, 13, 65, 155, 238, 261, 262, 263
ROSSITER, MRS. TIMOTHY. See Punderson, Prudence
ROUNDABOUT CHAIRS, Chippendale, (314) 225; Queen Anne, (162) 135; William and Mary, 88, (97) 89
ROUSE, WILLIAM, 16; silver sucket forks by, (34) 35
ROYALL, ISAAC, portrait of family of, (199) 152
"ROYAL BED AND STAR IN WALL-STREET," (shop) 215
ROYAL SOCIETY, THE, 69
ROYALIST CLUB, satiric sketches of, (234, 235) 175
RUGS. See Carpets and Bed Rugs
RUM, 238
RUPP, JACOB, 313
RUSH, for chair seats, 112, (329) 230
RUSHLIGHT, 112, (419) 274, (illus.) 260, (422) 275
RUTGERS, CATHARINA DE PEYSTER, porcelain tea set of, (180) 143

S

ST. JAMES'S PALACE, London, 241
ST. LUKE'S CHURCH, Smithfield, 11–12, (illus.) 14
ST. MARY-LE-BOW, London, 64, (illus.) 65
ST. MICHAEL'S CHURCH, Marblehead, 281
ST. PETERSBURG, RUSSIA, 232
SAINT GEORGE, (115a) 100
SALEM, MASS., 9, 152, 170, 283, 291; Chippendale furniture of, (306) 221, (307) 222
SALEM COUNTY, N.J., 341
SALMON, WILLIAM, 125
SALTS, 26, 105; delft, (18) 26; glass, (557) 340, 343; silver, (33) 34, 35, (114) 99, 104, (131) 105, (239) 178
SALVERS, 106; silver, (133) 106, (379) 252
SAMPLERS, (226) 171, (459) 288, 289
SANDERSEN, ROBBERT, 38; silver beaker of, (41) 38, (41 a-e) 39
SANDERSON, ROBERT, 32, 33, 96; silverwork by—caudle cup, 36, (40) 37; tankard, (37) 36; silverwork made with Hull by—coins, (illus.) 17; dram cup, 36, (39) 37; porringer, (31) 34, 35; slip-end spoon, (35) 35; standing cup, (32) 34, 35
SANTO DOMINGO, 152
SAUCEBOAT, silver, 178, (246) 179
SAVAGE, EDWARD, engraving by, "Congress Voting Independence," (357) 242–43, detail of same, (475) 293
SAVAGE, THOMAS, portrait of, 16
SAVERY, WILLIAM, glass bottle of, (559) 340
SAXON WHEEL, (for flax), (450) 284, 285
SAYBROOK, CONN., 112
SCALES, (378) 252
SCHENCK HOUSE, Brooklyn, fireplace from, (399) 265
SCHILEY, MRS., 313
SCHIMMELREITER, as Pennsylvania German pottery motif, 328, (537) 329, 333
SCHOLAR'S BOX, 23, 90
SCHRANK, 306, (494) 307
SCHUYLER, JOHANNES AND MRS., portrait of, (93) 86
SCHUYLER, PETER, 72, 79; chair possibly owned by, 72, (71) 73; portrait of, (82) 79
SCHWENKFELDERS, 301
SCONCES, on chimney looking glass, (436) 278–79; crested, (68) 70, 71; glass, (443) 281
SCOTLAND, 121
SCRAPER, (for dough board) iron, (551) 335
SCREEN, Chinese porcelain, (393) 259
SCROLLS, 205; broken, 122; C-scrolls, (71) 73; Flemish 62, (96) 88–89; rococo, 198; S-scrolls, (69) 70, 71; sprigged, (552) 336–37
SCRUTORES. See Secretaries
S-CURVE, 187, (illus.) 188, (illus.) 189
SECRETARIES, 76, 92; Chippendale, (285) 211, (304) 220, (319) 226, 227; Queen Anne, (209) 160, 161, (210) 161; William and Mary, 92, (105) 93
SEIFFERT, CATHARINA, birth and baptismal certificate of, 316, (515) 317
SELZER, CHRISTIAN, dough trough attributed to, 320, (526) 323; dower chest by, 320, (524) 323
SERPENTINE FRONT, 217; card table, (281) 209
SETTEES, 164; Chippendale, (308) 222; Cromwellian style, (59) 52–53; Queen Anne, 166, (219) 167; Windsor, (355) 242–43
SETTLES, high-back, (403) 267; Pennsylvania German, (492) 306, 307
"SEVEN SWABIANS," 316, (528) 324
SEVEN YEARS' WAR, 184–85
SEWALL, HANNAH (MRS. SAMUEL SEWALL), 32, 262
SEWALL, SAMUEL, 92; and chocolate, 99; dowry of wife, Hannah, 32; English influences on, 66; entertaining in wife's chamber, 262; on presenting Stoughton cup to Harvard, 102; on unheated colonial churches, 268; wedding in chamber of, 13; and William

and Mary suite of furniture, 127
SEWING CASE, needle-point, (460) 289
SGRAFFITO DECORATIONS, 48, (537) 329, (538, 540, 541) 330, (542–44) 331, 333
SHADES. See Window Hangings
SHAFTESBURY, LORD, 123
SHAKERS, 273
SHAPING TOOL, 346
SHAVING BASIN, slip ware, 328, (548) 333
SHAVING BOWL, delft, (48) 48
SHAVING STAND, 166, (220) 167
SHELL MOTIF, 192; on looking glass, (212) 162; on silver, 246, (364) 247; woodcarved, top (illus.) 132, (158) 133, (193) 148, (194) 149, (207) 159, (218) 166, (219) 167, (282) 210, (313) 224, (315) 225, (319) 226, (313a, 320, 321) 227, (324) 229, (384) 254
SHELLEY, GILES, 67; silver tankard of, 104, (130) 105
SHEPHERD, THOMAS AND ANN, silver caudle cup of, (40) 37
SHERALD, JOSIAH, 241
SHERMAN, ROGER, 242; portrait of, (349) 240
SHILLINGS, 14, (109) 98
SHIPBUILDING, 12, 156
SHIRLEY, WILLIAM, 183
SHUTTERS. See Window Hangings
SIDEBOARDS, 25. See also Court Cupboards
SIDON, 346
SILICA, 346
SILVER, 10, 14, 15, 26, 34–39, 67–68, 83, 101, 235; Chippendale, 198, (363–83) 246–53; Puritan century, (31–41) 34–39; Queen Anne, 122–23, (236–51) 176–81; William and Mary, (106–8, 111–20, 122, 124–36) 96–107. See also specific forms
SILVERING, (on glass) 151
SILVERSMITHS AND SILVERSMITHING, (illus.) 11, 14, 26, 32–33, 35, 68, 95, 96, 99, 102, 104, 106, 192; art of, 40–41, (illus.) 42–43. See also Goldsmiths and Goldsmithing
SIMPKINS, WILLIAM, silver teaspoon by, (187a, b) 146
SIXPENCE, 14
SLAT-BACK CHAIRS, (7) 21. See also Ladder-back Chairs
SLAVE TRADE, 33, 301, 302
SLIP COVERS, 292, 293
SLIP DECORATIONS, on pottery, 333
SLIP WARE, (illus.) 298, (539) 330, (548) 333
SLIPPER CHAIR, (217) 166
SMIBERT, JOHN, portraits by—Pepperrell, 186; Winslow, (110) 98
SMITH, JOHN, 10; portrait of, 13
SMITH, P., Kentucky rifle made by, (573, 573 a) 349, (573 b) 351
SMITH, ROBERT, 127
SMITHFIELD, VA., 14
SMOKING. See Tobacco
SMUGGLING, 155
SOAP AND SOAPMAKING, 10, 286
SOCKS, (as furniture motif) (159) 134, (215) 164–65
SOFAS, 164; Chippendale, (278) 208–9; Queen Anne, (215) 164–65
SOLDIER, 33, 183–85, (illus.) 303, 348. See also Frontiersmen
SONS OF LIBERTY, 248; names on Revere silver bowl, (373) 250
SOUMAIN, SIMEON, 144; silver bowl by, (182) 143
SOUTH AMERICA, 118, 121
SOUTH CAROLINA, 25. See also Carolinas
SOUTH SEA COMPANY, 121
SOWER, CHRISTOPHER, 301
SOWERS, THOMAS, silver salver of, (379) 252
SPAIN, 184
SPANISH FEET, 86, (95) 88, (97) 89, (138) 110, (139) 111, (144) 114, (154) 119, (329) 230
SPANISH SUCCESSION, WAR OF THE, 121, 124, 299
SPERMACETI, for candles, 276, 278
SPICE CABINET, Pennsylvania German, (495) 308
SPICE CHEST, (6) 21
SPIDER-LEG, 218, (301) 219
SPINDLES, 24, 111; on Brewster-type chairs, (1) 18, (29) 31; on Carver chairs, 19; split, 19, (64) 56; on Windsor chairs, 243
SPINNER, DAVID, pottery dish by, 350, (574) 351
SPINNING AND WEAVING, 284–85
SPINNING WHEELS, (450, 451) 284, 285
SPIRAL EARS, (as furniture motif), (354) 242
SPLATS, double scrolled, (218) 166; pierced, 205, (282) 210, (293) 215, 222, (312) 223, (327, 328) 230, (331) 231, 241; rounded, 133; scrolled, (159) 134; solid, 123, (158) 133; vase-shaped, 230, (330) 230
SPLAYED LEGS, (12) 22–23, 114, (144) 114, on Windsor chairs, 243
SPOON-BACK CHAIRS, 118, (154, 155) 119
SPOONS, 11, 14, 101; pewter, (343, 345) 238; silver, (35, 36) 35, (119) 101, 106, (134) 107, (188) 146, 147, (369) 248. See also Teaspoons
SPIRIT LAMP. See Lamps
SPOTSWOOD, MRS. ALEXANDER, 144
SPRUCE, (wood) 156
SPURS, silver, (371) 248
S-SCROLLS. See Scrolls
STAFFORDSHIRE, ENGLAND, 255
STALKER, JOHN, 80, 148
STAMP ACT, 190, 254, 255; on teapot, (387) 254
STANDING CUPS, pewter, (346) 239; silver, (32) 34, 35, (113) 99
STANDISH. See Inkstands
STANDISH, MILES, 296; pewter platter and iron pot of, (illus.) 10
STATUTE OF ARTIFICERS, 94
STEENWYCK, CORNELIS, 262
STENTON, Logan home, Pa., 125, 178; chair from, (217) 166; settee from, (219) 167
STERLING. See Silver
STICK CHAIRS. See Windsor Chairs
STIEGEL, ANTHONY, 338, 339
STIEGEL, HENRY WILLIAM, biography of, 338–39; easy chair possibly owned by, 310, (503) 311; nature of glass made by, 339, 341, 347; type of glass made by, (558) 340, (560, 561) 341, (562, 563) 342, (565) 343
STONEWARE BOTTLE. See Bellarmine
STOOLS, 11, 23, (14) 24, 88; Queen Anne, (164) 135; William and Mary, (95) 88. See also Back Stool and French Chairs
STOUGHTON, WILLIAM, 99; as benefactor of Harvard, 102; portrait of, (121) 102; silver cup given Harvard by, (122) 102
STOUGHTON HALL (HARVARD), 102
STOVE PLATES, (405) 268, 338
STOVES, 264, 265, 272–73, 305, 338; "cannon," (illus.) 338; cast-iron "box," (415) 272, 273; Franklin, (413) 272, 273; marbleized tile, 272, (417) 273. See also Pennsylvanian Fire-Places
STRAIGHT LEGS, (299) 218, 222, (309) 223
STRAPWORK, 21, (41) 38
STRATFORD, Lee home, Va., 125
STRETCHERS, 53; arrow-shaped, (215) 164; curved, 76, (77, 78) 77, 222 (309) 223; pierced, (318) 226, 227; serpentine, 133; turned, (151) 117; X-shaped, (70) 71, (76) 75. See also Tables, stretcher-base
STUART, CHARLES EDWARD, 252, (382) 253
STUARTS, 61, 252, 253
STUCCO CEILING DECORATIONS, 191
STUYVESANT, PETER, 15
SUGAR, use of, 101, 147
SUGAR BOWLS, glass, 342, (565, 566) 343, (567) 344; maple burl, (482) 296, 297; porcelain, (181) 143; silver, (182) 143, (363) 246
SUGAR BOX, silver, (115, 115a) 100, 101
"SUMMER," (poem) 122
"SUMMONS TO NEW ENGLAND," (ballad) 10
SUNDIAL, (449) 283
SWAN, ABRAHAM, 191, 198; adaptation of design of, (262) 198; chimney-piece from design book by, (263) 198
SWEDES, 12, 305
SWEETGUM. See Bilsted
SWEETMEAT BOX. See Sugar Box
SWIFT, JONATHAN, 278
SWITZERLAND, 252
SYNG, PHILIP, JR., scales used by, (378) 252; silver inkstand by, 252, (383) 253

T

TABLE COVERS, 152
TABLES, 9, 11, 24, 62, 114, 116, 123, 152, (491) 306, 307; butterfly, (illus.) 109, 116, (148) 116, (150, 151) 117; card, 121, 123, (274) 206, 207, (281) 209; dressing. See Lowboys; drop-leaf, 114, 152, (202) 153, 202, (268) 203, (292) 214, 215; folding-top, (46) 47, 114; gaming, 61, (296) 216, (316) 225, (229) 172; gate-leg, (47) 47, (145) 114–15, (147) 115, 116; handkerchief, 152, (200) 153; marble-top, 152, (201) 153; mixing, (74) 75, (189) 146, 147; sawbuck, 304, (489) 305; spider-leg, 218, (301, 302) 219; splay-leg, (144) 114, (498) 309; stretcher-base, (15) 24, (17) 25, 116, (153) 117, (488) 304; tavern, (illus.) 8, 114; tea, 61, 114, 123, 140, (174) 141, 147, 202, 203, (305) 221, 222, (309) 223, (318) 226, 227; tilt-top, (183) 144, 152, (203) 153, 200, (illus.) 201, 202, (269) 203, with bird-cage, (illus.) 182; toilet, 200, (illus.) 201; trestle, 46, (45) 46–47. See also Chair-tables
TACONIC (TACHKANICK) PURCHASE, N.Y., 38
TAMPER, for pipe, (479) 295
TANKARDS, 14, 104, 177; pewter, (339) 235, (341) 236, (347) 239; silver, (37) 36, (112) 98, 99, (detail, 120) 101, (127) 104, (129, 130) 105, (detail, 248) 180, 181, (251) 181, 248, (377, 377a) 251
TAPE LOOM, (453) 285
TAPER JACK, English brass, (430) 277
TAPESTRY, 82, (87) 83. See also Bayeux Tapestry
TAUFSCHEIN. See Baptismal Certificate
TAVERNS, 170, 230, 315; sketches about, (234, 235) 175, (512) 315
TAZZA. See Salvers
TEA CADDIES, 144; glass, (558) 340; silver, (186) 145
TEA DRINKING, (illus.) 63; popularity of and development of service and ceremony for, 62, 68, 102, 123, 128–29, 140–47; tax on, 257
TEA SERVICES, porcelain, (180) 143; silver, (363) 246
TEA STRAINER, silver, (191) 147
TEA TABLES. See Tables
TEACH, EDWARD, 69; portrait of, 68
TEACUPS, Oriental style, (180) 143
TEAKETTLES, 11; silver, 102, (125) 103, (179) 142, 143, 246, (364) 247; stand for, (184) 144
TEAPOTS, pewter, (342) 237; pottery, 254, (387) 255; silver, 102, (126) 103, 140, (175) 141, 144, (185) 145, (363) 246, 248, (367a, 372) 249
TEARDROP DRAWER PULLS, 90, (100) 91
TEASPOONS, silver, (187a, b) 146, 147, (368) 248
TEETHERS, 28
TEN EYCK, JACOB, 95; silver trencher salt by, 104, (131) 105
TENON. See Mortise and Tenon
TEXTILES, 21, 25, 33, 53, 63, 72, 83, 285
THIMBLE, gold, (370) 248
THIRTY YEARS' WAR, 299
THOMSON, JAMES, 122
THOROUGHGOOD, ADAM, 30
TIGER-STRIPE. See Maple
TILES, Delft, 48, (53) 50, (189) 146, 147, (illus.) 161, 162
TIMOTHEE, LOUIS, 301
TINDER BOX, 268; brass, (424) 276
TINWARE, English, 235; Pennsylvania German (531–35) 326–27. See also Toleware
TITCOMB, MARY SARAH, sampler by, (459) 289
TOASTER, wrought-iron, (552) 336–37
TOBACCO, 15, 33, 66; equipment for use of, (477–79) 295; King James I protest against, 294; trade card advertising, (480) 295
TOILET MIRROR. See Shaving Stand
TOLEWARE, 326, (534) 327
TORTOISE-SHELL POTTERY, 255
TOWNSEND, EDMUND, chest of drawers by, (313) 224, (313a) 227
TOWNSEND, JOB, JR., 224
TOWNSEND, JOB, SR., 224; clockcase by, (315) 225
TOWNSEND, JOHN, side chair by, (317) 226; tea table by, (318) 226, 227
TOWNSEND FAMILY, 224, 227; bracket foot with scroll used by, (319) 226, (313a) 227; urn finials with corkscrew flames used by, (319) 226, 227
TOWNSHEND ACTS, 248
TOYS. See Children, toys of
TRADE. See Commerce and Trade
TRADE CARDS, 198, 200, (illus.) 201, (480) 295
TRAMMELS, (421) 275, (554) 336
TRANSYLVANIA RUG, (198) 152
TRAYS, silver, 248, (375) 251
TREATISE OF JAPANING, A, 148
TREEN OR TREENWARE. See Wooden Tableware

TRENCHERS, 296, (481) 296, 297. See also Salts
TRENTON, BATTLE OF, 193
TRINITY CHURCH, Newport, 126
TRIVETS, for iron, (463) 289; for kettle, (176) 141
TROPHY, silver, of Lewis Morris, Jr., 174, (233) 175
TRUAX, SUSANNA, portrait of, (190) 146, 147
TUCK-AWAY TABLE. See Tables, gate-leg
TUDOR PERIOD, 44, 47, 123; motifs of, (16) 25, 56, 59
TURKEY CARPETS, 152, (199) 152
TURKEY WORK, (57) 52, 53
TURNINGS, 19, 24, (61) 54; ball, (57) 52, 53, (59) 53; ball-and-ring, 112, (143) 113; bulbous, 21, (17) 24; cup, (78a) 76, (78) 77; Dutch, 62; spiral, (58) 52, 53; trumpet, 76, (77) 77
TURPIN, E., 170

U

UNDERHILL, JOHN, 23
UNITED COMPANY OF SPERMACETI CANDLERS, 276
UNIVERSAL SPECTATOR AND WEEKLY JOURNAL, THE, 148
UNIVERSAL SYSTEM OF HOUSEHOLD FURNITURE, 218
UNIVERSITY HALL (BROWN), 127
UPHOLSTERED FURNITURE, 52–53, 72, 86, 88. See also specific types
UTRECHT, TREATY OF, 121

V

VADE MECUM FOR AMERICA: OR A COMPANION FOR TRADERS AND TRAVELLERS, THE, 130
VAN BERGEN, MARTIN, overmantel painting from farmhouse of, (232) 174–75
VAN DYCK, PETER, 144; silver teapot by, 144, (185) 145
VAN KEUREN, ISAAC, looking glass of, (197) 151
VAN RENSSELAER, KILLIAEN, 95
VAN RENSSELAER, SOLOMON VAN VECHTEN, initials of (illus.) 118
VAN RENSSELAER, STEPHEN, II, 212; central hall from home of, (289) 212–13
VAN RENSSELAER FAMILY, chairs owned by, 118, (287, 288) 212; tea service of, (363) 246
VAN RENSSELAER MANOR HOUSE, Albany, 215; center hall from, (289) 212–13
VAN VARICK, MARGHARITA, 67; *kas* of, 54
VANDERBANK, JOHN, tapestry by, 82, (87) 83
VANDERBURGH, CORNELIUS, 38; silver beaker by, (41) 38, (41 a–e) 39
VANDERSPIEGEL, JACOBUS, 35; silverwork by—salt, (33) 34, 35; salver (133) 106; tankard, (127) 104
VASSALL, HENRY, 262
VENEERS, 62, 71, 76, 112
VENNE, ADRIAEN VAN DER, influence of designs by, (41) 38, (41 a-e) 39
VERNON, SAMUEL, silverwork by—detail of tankard, (120) 101; handles of porringers, (242) 178, (243) 179
VERNON HOUSE, Newport, 162
VIRGINIA, 10, 11–12, 14, 15, 25, 30, 33, 65, 66, 68–69, 114, 125, 129, 130, 170, 294, 295
VIRGINIA COMPANY OF LONDON, 15, 235
VITRUVIUS BRITANNICUS, 130
VOLTAIRE, 184, 232
VOYAGE AUX ETATS-UNIS DE L AMERIQUE, 243

W

WACHSEINLEGEN. See Wax Inlay
"WAG ON THE WALL." See Clocks, lantern
WAINSCOT CHAIRS, (5) 21, (13) 23, (487) 304, 305
WALKER, children's, (24, 25) 29
WALLPAPER, 155, 205; Chinese, (271) 204; in Van Rensselaer house, (289) 212–13
WALNUT, (wood) 24, 53, 71, 76, 123, 156; Pennsylvania German furniture of, 304–11, 487–91, 493–97, 499, 500, 502, 503
WALPOLE, HORACE, 124, 255
WALPOLE, ROBERT, 121–22
WAMPLER, JOSEPH. 312
WAMPANOAG INDIANS, 63
WARE, ISAAC, 195
WAR OF 1812, 303
WARMING PAN, brass, (404) 268; pewter, (348) 239
WARNER, JONATHAN, 79; portrait of, (79) 78. See also Macpheadris-Warner House
WASHINGTON, GEORGE, 76, 108, 159, 162, 184, 186, 190, 191, 193, 258, 265, 303; Amelung goblets of, 344; Argand lamp of, (441) 280; and candles, 276, 278; and cards and billiards, 170; and Gadsby's Tavern, 270; as "Father of his Country," 193, (illus.) 301; and floorcloths, 152; and fox hunting, 174; *fraktur* representing, (529) 325; gaming tables of, (298) 217; Gouverneur Morris letter to, 263; on John Cadwalader, 207; letter to Jefferson, 344; overmantel of, 198; portrait of, 187; and slip covers, 293; sofa of, 209; and Venetian blinds, 293; and Windsor chairs, 242. See also Mount Vernon
WASHINGTON, MARTHA, 28; *fraktur* representing, (529) 325
WASHINGTON, MARY BALL, 76; highboy possibly owned by, (78) 77
WATCH BOX, (497) 309
WATER LENS, (418) 274
WATSON, JOHN, 86; portrait of Schuylers attributed to, (93) 86
WAX INLAY, 306, (494) 307
WEATHER VANES, (445) 282, 283, (447) 283, 351, (580) 352
WEATHERCOCK, (446) 282
WEAVING. See Spinning and Weaving
WEAVING HOUSE, 285
WEDGWOOD, JOSIAH, 241, 255
WELLS, 263
WENDELL, JACOB, 262
WERTMÜLLER, GEORGE, 300
WEST, BENJAMIN, 186
WEST INDIES TRADE, 33, 124, 126, 156, 162, 224, 245
WESTFIELD, MASS., 156
WESTOVER, Byrd home, Va., 69, 125, 189
WETHERSFIELD, CONN., 56
WHISTLES, 28; De Peyster, (21) 28, (23) 29; (24) 29; water, 328, (547) 333
WHITE HOUSE. See President's House
WHITE, PEREGRINE, cradle of, (27) 30
WHITEWOOD, 241
WHITESMITHS, 326. See also Tinware
WHITING, 148
WHORL FEET. See French Scroll Feet
WICKER CRADLE, 30
WIG-STAND, Delft, (89) 84
WILKES, JOHN, 255, 256; delft dish celebrates, 254, (386) 255
WILMINGTON, DEL., 244
WILL, HENRY, pewterer's mark of, top, left (illus.) 236
WILL, JOHN, pewterer's mark of, top, right (illus.) 236; pewter tankard by, (341) 236
WILL, WILLIAM, pewterwork by—bed-warming pan, (348) 239; spoon, (345) 238; pewterer's mark of, top, center (illus.) 236
WILLET, THOMAS, 35; silver standing cup commissioned by, (32) 34
WILLETT, MARINUS, 193; portrait of, 193
WILLIAM III AND MARY II, KING AND QUEEN OF ENGLAND, 62, 63–64, 65, 66; portraits of on delft jug, 64
WILLIAM AND MARY COLLEGE, 65; main building of, (illus.) 66
WILLIAM AND MARY PERIOD, 60–119, 122, 177; Boston chairs of, 118–19; comforts and conveniences of, 86–93; craftsmen of, 94–95; native strain in furniture of, 110–17, 127, 230; new elegance of, 70–79; Oriental influences in, 80–85; silver of, 96–107
WILLIAMSBURG, VA., 65, 159, 169
WILLOW-TREE SHILLING, 14
WILSON, BENJAMIN, painting by, (472) 292
WILT, MRS., 315
WINDOW HANGINGS, curtains, (470) 292, 293, (473) 293; shutters, (476) 294; Venetian blinds, (474, 475) 293
WINDOWS, 11, 12–13, 65, 79. See also Glass
WINDSOR, ENGLAND, 241
WINDSOR CHAIRS, 192, 240–45; bow-back, (351) 241, (356) 243; brace-back, (350) 240, 241; comb-back, (352) 241; fan-back, (354) 242, (358) 244; high chair, 241, (359) 244; low-back (captain's chair), (353) 241, 245; writing chair, (360) 244
WINDSORS, other forms, cradle, (362) 245; settee, (355) 242–43; table, (361) 245
WING CHAIR. See Easy Chairs
WINSLOW, EDWARD, 99, 274; portrait of, (110) 98; silverwork by—chocolate pot, (111) 98, 99, (111a) 101; punch ladle, (106) 96; salt, (114) 99; sugar box, (115, 115a) 100, 101
WINSLOW, MR. AND MRS. ISAAC, portrait of, 218, (302) 219
WINTHROP, JOHN, JR., 26
WINTHROP, JOHN, SR., 9, 10, 11, 23; from *Journal* on severity of New England winter, 265
WINTHROP, MRS. JOHN, 10
WINTHROP FAMILY, lacquered chairs of, (195) 150, 151
WISTAR, CASPAR, 341, 343; examples of glass possibly made by, (559) 340, 342, (566) 343
WISTAR, RICHARD, 341
WOLFE, JAMES, 184
WOLSEY, CARDINAL THOMAS, 44
WOMEN, COLONIAL, 286
WOOD, in early homes, 12, 65, 156, 273. See also specific kinds.
WOOD, JOHN, SR., clockcase by, (72) 74
WOOD, WILLIAM, 10, 108
WOOD CARVING MOTIFS, bird-head, (306a) 221; fan, (491) 306; heart, (486, 488) 304, (493) 307, (501) 310–11; pin-wheel, 228, (326) 229; ram's-horn, (138, 138a) 110, 111; rope-twist, 228, (326) 229; rosettes, (13) 23, (16) 25; Scotch thistle, 56; seaweed, 90, (100) 91; sunburst, (322) 228; sunflower, or aster, (64) 56; tulip, (10) 22, (16) 25, (64) 56, (493) 307; vine, leaf, and flower, 56, (66) 59, 156, (204) 157, (209) 160, 161. See also Aesop's Fables, Scrolls, Shell Motif, Dutch Carving, Guilloche Carving, and Lunette Carving
WOODEN TABLEWARE, (481–85) 296–97
WOODRUFF, MARY A., dressing table of, 164, (216) 165
WOODWORKING, 108–09. See also Architectural Woodwork
WOOL REEL. See Niddy Noddy
WORCESTER, ENGLAND, 258
WORSHIPFUL COMPANY OF CARPENTERS OF LONDON, 126
WORSHIPFUL COMPANY OF JOINERS, 140
WORSHIPFUL COMPANY OF PEWTERERS, 235
WOVEN SPLINT, (499) 310
WREN, SIR CHRISTOPHER, 64–65; engraving of church designed by, 64, (illus.) 65; portrait of, 65
WRITING CHAIR. See Windsor Chairs
WROUGHT-IRON, 334–37; used in Conestoga wagons, 350, (576–78) 351. See also specific items

Y

YARN FRAME, (461) 289
YONKERS, N.Y., 125
YORK, PA., 313, 339; Lewis Miller sketches of life in, (510–13) 315
YORK COUNTY, PA., 300, 303

Z

ZERCHEER, FREDERICK, 312